THE CHARACTER OF AMERICANS

A Book of Readings

The CHARACTER of AMERICANS

A Book of Readings

Edited by MICHAEL McGIFFERT
Associate Professor of History
University of Denver

1964

THE DORSEY PRESS • HOMEWOOD, ILLINOIS

First Printing, September, 1964

Library of Congress Catalog Card No. 64–24703

PRINTED IN THE UNITED STATES OF AMERICA

Foreword

"What, then, is the American, this new man?" The study of American national character began with that question, posed by a French immigrant on the morn of American independence in 1782. The fascination of Crèvecoeur's query has not been diminished by reiteration; for nearly two centuries Americans have been trying to explain themselves to themselves, and they are still actively engaged in the undertaking. This collection of readings offers a sampling of observations, conjectures, and interpretations, drawn from several fields of scholarship and different periods of history. Essays by American authors are supplemented by the writings of visitors from overseas to whom Americans have turned an interested, if often irritable, ear. The perspectives of the past, by which continuities and changes in the American character can be appraised, are presented by several historians. Some of the selections—and all of them to some extent—are impressionistic and intuitive: they carry the mark and merit, as well as the liabilities, of highly individualized perception and reflection. Others represent the work of anthropologists, sociologists, and psychologists who have held up a mirror to America and, over the last two decades, have developed a formal theory for the analysis of national character as an enterprise of the behavioral sciences. Among these documents the reader will find materials from which to fashion or refashion an understanding of what it has meant, and what it means, to be an American.

Crèvecoeur's *Letters from an American Farmer,* from which a selection is given below, are noteworthy as the pioneer examination of American character. They command abiding interest also for what they reveal respecting the problems of dealing with so complex a subject—problems which continue to challenge Crèvecoeur's successors. When the French observer remarked "The difficulty consists in the manner of viewing so extensive a scene," he was referring not merely to the formidable spaciousness of a country that stretched from the rocky bays of Maine to the pine barrens of Georgia and extended indefinitely westward beyond the Appalachian ridges, nor was he speaking only, if at all, of the inconveniences of travel by horse and stage over a land which was only partially redeemed from the primeval forest. The real "difficulty" was more fundamental: it was essentially a problem of procedure and perspective, and it arose less from the spread of the land than from the social and cultural heterogeneity of its inhabitants.

No special acuity was needed to perceive that America consisted of a patchwork of peoples who were not yet accustomed to thinking of themselves, either collectively or individually, as Americans. For scarcely more than one generation the term "American" had been occasionally used to distinguish the British colonists in North America from their countrymen across the sea, and less than twenty years had passed, when Crèvecoeur wrote, since Christopher Gadsden's memorable declaration at the Stamp Act Congress, "There ought to be no New England man, no New Yorker, known on the Continent, but all of us Americans." Though a political union had been contrived, and national independence proclaimed, the former subjects of George III were far from possessing a sense of common nationality. The viability of the Confederation was likewise doubtful. Many observers, both American and foreign, concurred with Alexander Hamilton in 1783 that "the centrifugal is much stronger than the centripetal force in these states—the seeds of disunion much more numerous than those of union."[1]

If it was venturesome to believe that a durable nation could be created out of the thirteen disparate and disputatious states, it was still more audacious to posit, as Crèvecoeur did, the existence of a normative American character, definable in national terms. What congruities could be located among persons so diverse as the hardy Nantucket fishermen, the aristocratic planters of the Chesapeake, the plain Yankee farmers, and the rough backwoodsmen who occupied the far expanding fringes of settlement? Though the ready availability of land, the prevalence of opportunities for social and economic advancement, and the selective factors of immigration reduced the disparities of class status among white Americans, so that, as Crèvecoeur noted, "the rich and poor are not so far removed from each other as they are in Europe," yet there were diversities enough to baffle the search for a pattern in the patchwork of population.

Crèvecoeur was keenly sensitive to the heterogeneity of the people. Americans, he wrote, were "not only Americans in general, but either Pennsylvanians, Virginians, or provincials under some other name," and he predicted that the "strong differences" which they exhibited would grow increasingly evident in time. Yet back of all distinctions he perceived a common type, forged from a common experience—the type of the "American in general"—and he detected the leading characteristics of that type in the figure of the industrious, self-sufficient, prosperous farmer whose sturdy republican virtues Thomas Jefferson also celebrated. This was *homo Americanus* in his most representative role and guise. The United States of Crèvecoeur's acquaintance was in fact a nation of farmers, and Crèvecoeur's *Letters* are the *locus classicus* of the stereotype of the agrarian hero in whom were concentrated those personal and civil qualities which, to Crèvecoeur's eye, were most characteristically American.

Like his successors, Crèvecoeur was interested not only in the *product,* labeled standard American, but in the *process* whereby transplanted Europeans were transformed into "a new race of men" by the action upon them of the

[1]Harold C. Syrett and Jacob E. Cooke, eds., *The Papers of Alexander Hamilton* (New York: Columbia University Press, 1962), III, 304.

natural and cultural environment. A thorough-going environmental determinist, he employed a horticultural metaphor to describe the making of Americans. "Every thing has tended to regenerate them; new laws, a new mode of living, a new social system; here they are become men: in Europe they were as so many useless plants, wanting vegetative mould, and refreshing showers; they withered, and were mowed down by want, hunger, and war; but now by the power of transplantation, like all other plants they have taken root and flourished!" The outcome was a radically "new man," the archetypical man of the West, shaped by the experience of emancipation from the rigid constraints of Old World society and by the opportunities which the New World proffered with an open hand. "*He* is an American, who, leaving behind him all his ancient prejudices and manners, receives new ones from the new mode of life he has embraced, the new government he obeys, and the new rank he holds. He becomes an American by being received in the broad lap of our great *Alma Mater*." Crèvecoeur thus boldly espoused a doctrine of American exceptionalism. The "new man" sprang fresh and virile from the New World soil; his ways of thinking and doing were distinctively different from those of his European forebears.

Crèvecoeur's observations and major propositions have been substantially modified by later writers. His vivid portrait of the happy husbandman has been disputed on the ground that it expressed more the bucolic romanticism of the European pastoral mystique than the actual character of the enterprising, restless, acquisitive American farmer to whom the land was something less to hold than to have, less to cherish over the passage of generations than to exploit for profit. Few scholars, moreover, have shared Crèvecoeur's belief that the dominant traits of American character are epitomized by a single representative figure, although fruitful studies have been made of the changing conventions of the hero in America—the fortunate farmer, the frontiersman, the self-made man and others, not excluding the contemporary antiheroic types of the gray-flannel "organization man" and the "other-directed" personality—in quest of clues to the structure of values which such popular images body forth. Crèvecoeur's comparatively unsophisticated theses of environmentalism and exceptionalism, later cast in the form of an influential explanation of American character by the historian Frederick Jackson Turner, have also been appreciably qualified and refined. These modifications having been noted, however, the major themes which Crèvecoeur explored continue to control the analysis of American character, and the objectives remain essentially the same: to trace whatever characterological patterns may exist (with a watchful eye to variations as well as to norms), to examine the ways in which Americans differ, whether markedly or marginally, from the people of other nations in point of values, behavior, and traits of personality, and to inquire into the factors and forces which have conditioned the experience by which the national character has been formed and may be altered.

The principal problems also persist, among them the problem of generalization. Unlike the artist who is concerned with the idiosyncratic and intensely personal experience of individuals or the historian who, eschewing the quest for general laws, modestly prefers to chronicle the sequences of unique and unrepeatable events,[2] the student of national character is a generalizer by necessity. In this respect his enterprise is related to the social or behavioral sciences, yet it also partakes of art insofar as he engages to depict a composite character by selecting and ordering the complex data which the modern nation presents to the inquiring eye. The "portrait" that results is necessarily a synthetic abstraction, derived from extensive observation disciplined by sagacity. It has the look of what the German sociologist Max Weber called an "ideal-type," that is, not an exact empirical description but a construction designed for conceptual clarity and analytical utility.[3] It also has the appearance of myth: "I speak," said the philosopher George Santayana, "of the American in the singular, as if there were not millions of them, north and south, east and west, of both sexes, of all ages, and of various races, professions, and religions. Of course the one American I speak of is mythical; but to speak in parables is inevitable in such a subject, and it is perhaps as well to do so frankly."[4] In its treatment of dominant and recessive features, the portrait is thus rather a caricature than a photographic likeness of, say, the passport type, but what it sacrifices in literal exactitude it may recoup by revelation of essentials. Blurring detail and risking distortion for the sake of expressive emphasis and manageable simplicity, the student of national character works in broad strokes on an immense canvas to delineate the distinctive qualities of a nation's people.

These observations on the identification of a normative national character lead to some remarks on the problem of exceptionalism, with particular reference to the American case. To what extent can it be justly stated that the American has been, through his historical career, a "new man" or at least a distinctively different man, as Crèvecoeur thought him to be? Popular sentiment endorses belief in the exceptionality of the inhabitants of the United States. Since the landing of the Puritans in the 1630s, Americans have regarded themselves as a "peculiar people," specially favored by God or nature, exempt from many of the ordinary tribulations of mankind, commissioned to enact a singularly significant role in human history. This presumption of a distinctive national status and destiny was reinforced by long years of political and military isolation from the Old World, by the achievements of democracy and economic enterprise, by the heady experience of conquering a continent, and by the commentaries of visitors from abroad who expatiated, curiously or critically, on the peculiarities of Americans. Such writers as Crèvecoeur, Tocque-

[2]Cf. Fred A. Shannon's review of David M. Potter's *People of Plenty* in *The Mississippi Valley Historical Review,* XLI (March, 1955), p. 733: "I can envision 162,000,000 different American characters, perhaps divisible into 327 categories with wide divergencies in each, but I still cannot see an American national character."

[3]Cf., for example, David Riesman, "Some Observations on the Study of American Character," *Psychiatry,* XV (August, 1952), p. 333.

[4]Santayana, *Character and Opinion in the United States* (New York: George Braziller, 1955), pp. 94–95.

ville, and Turner, as the selections given in this volume show, worked within the convention of American exceptionalism, either assuming or attempting to demonstrate its validity.

Because an understanding of the ways in which Americans see and have seen themselves is essential to an understanding of American character, the conviction of peculiarity constitutes a significant subject for inquiry; it is one of the data with which the student of American character is concerned.[5] The issue of its validity, however, poses another sort of problem, one which requires circumspect treatment. No doubt the concept of exceptionality contains an important truth: the *total constellation* of American characteristics is evidently unique. At the same time, the concept stands in need of qualification by the recognition that, taken singly and out of context, most, if not all, of those characteristics are exemplified elsewhere. As David Riesman aptly remarks, "It is often said that a burger of Lyons is closer in type to a burger of Bremen or Buffalo than any of them is to a factory worker in his own country."[6] To say that Americans are different—which collectively they are, though the implications need not be invidious—is not to say that they are radically different—which is not necessarily so. The task of investigation is to check the proposition of exceptionalism by examining the nature and extent of supposed characterological differences.

Critics of the concept of national character sometimes object that excessive attention to the peculiarities of nations is pernicious because it impedes the realization of an international or supranational community of mankind. It is contended that "men are more alike" and that the differences which divide the nations ought to be de-emphasized in the interest of world order and concord.[7] Such remonstrances, however well intended, appear to be misdirected: national differences will not be wished away by refusal to examine them, let alone by denying that they exist. On the contrary, quite aside from national strategies of survival, the general interests of humanity are better served by candid assessment of differences to the end that erroneous stereotypes may be corrected and avenues of international communication may be improved. Furthermore, the investigation of national character is not restricted to the elements of contrast; correctly conceived, although the inquiry may sometimes be warped to the purposes of chauvinism and propaganda, it is concerned as much with the transnational congruities of character as with culturally conditioned differences.[8] This fact furnishes an additional argument for comparative studies of national character.

---

[5]See, among other writings, Ralph Henry Gabriel, *The Course of American Democratic Thought* (2nd ed.; New York: Ronald Press Co., 1956), and Edward McNall Burns, *The American Idea of Mission: Concepts of National Purpose and Destiny* (New Brunswick, N. J.: Rutgers University Press, 1957).

[6]"Psychological Types and National Character: An Informal Commentary," *American Quarterly*, V (Winter, 1953), p. 328.

[7]See, for example, Boyd Shafer, *Nationalism: Myth and Reality* (New York: Harcourt, Brace & World, 1955), ch. 12.

[8]For a caustic indictment of the misuse of the idea of national character see Hamilton Fyfe, *The Illusion of National Character* (London, 1940).

The acknowledgment of these and other difficulties by contemporary scholars may be taken to mark the coming of age of national character study as a collaborative project of the social sciences. Fortunately, the value of the undertaking does not entirely depend on the solution of such problems. Useful results may be obtained from less than perfect methods, provided the investigator is cognizant of the hazards that he runs, and only the most rigorous theoretician would insist that all analysis be suspended until the apparatus be made scientifically impeccable. At the very least, recognition of obstacles to be overcome imposes a discipline of modesty which was often lacking among the impressionistic writers who dominated the field until about the time of World War II. At its best, fortified by wisdom and experience, impressionism could produce such masterwork as Alexis de Tocqueville's *Democracy in America,* from which a selection appears in this volume. At its worst, it exhibited the shoddy defects of prejudice, superficiality, stereotypical opinion, and fragmentary observation. When these deficiencies were compounded with a malignant ethnocentrism, as in the Aryan dogma of Nazi Germany, the idea of national character itself was discredited among sober scholars.

During the last twenty-odd years national character has been restored to respectability as a legitimate subject for inquiry by the allied forces of the behavioral sciences. From the disciplines of social psychology, psychoanalysis, and cultural anthropology, linked in the study of "culture and personality," national character has acquired formulas which, though not altogether free of imperfection, have greatly reduced the liabilities under which the concept formerly labored. The result has been a large and growing literature whose worth, in reference to the analysis of American character, is exemplified in this collection by the writings of Lee Coleman, Cora Du Bois, John Gillin, Francis L. K. Hsu, Max Lerner, S. M. Lipset, Margaret Mead, David Riesman, Robin M. Williams, Jr., and, representing the historians, George W. Pierson, David M. Potter, and Arthur M. Schlesinger.[9] When the findings of the behavioral scientists are illuminated by a knowledge of history it becomes evident that never before has there been better hope and more adequate intellectual equipment for discovering what the American is, has been, and may become.

DENVER, COLORADO
July, 1964

MICHAEL MCGIFFERT

[9]See the Bibliography for a checklist of recent writings on culture and personality, national character, and American character in particular.

Table of Contents

PAGE

I. INTRODUCTION

Introduction I 2
The Dispraising of America by JOHN A. KOUWENHOVEN 4
The Idea of American Civilization by MAX LERNER 10
What Is American? by LEE COLEMAN 21

II. AS OTHERS HAVE SEEN US

Introduction II 32
What Is an American? by J. HECTOR ST. JOHN DE CRÈVECOEUR 35
Democracy in America by ALEXIS DE TOCQUEVILLE 41
The American Character in the 1880s by JAMES BRYCE 66

III. PERSPECTIVES, PAST AND PRESENT

Introduction III 84
The Shaping of National Character by HENRY ADAMS 89
The Frontier Experience by FREDERICK JACKSON TURNER 96
What Then Is the American, This New Man?
by ARTHUR M. SCHLESINGER 102
The M-Factor in American History by GEORGE W. PIERSON 118
We Are All Third Generation by MARGARET MEAD 131

IV. AS THE TWIG IS BENT

Introduction IV 144
Economic Abundance and the Formation of American Character
by DAVID M. POTTER 146
Americans and Chinese: The Beginnings of Contrast
by FRANCIS L. K. HSU 156

PAGE

V. AMERICAN VALUES

Introduction V 170
Values and Beliefs in American Society by ROBIN M. WILLIAMS, JR. 173
National and Regional Values by JOHN GILLIN 217
The Dominant Value Profile of American Culture by CORA DU BOIS 224
Individuality and Conformity by DAVID M. POTTER 232

VI. CHANGE AND CONTINUITY

Introduction VI 246
From Morality to Morale by DAVID RIESMAN 250
The Found Generation by DAVID RIESMAN 265
Groupthink by WILLIAM H. WHYTE, JR. 277
The Outgoing Life by WILLIAM H. WHYTE, JR. 288
A Changing American Character? by SEYMOUR MARTIN LIPSET 302
The Orgamerican Phantasy by HAROLD ROSENBERG 331
The Saving Remnant by DAVID RIESMAN 340
Adieu to America by SIMONE DE BEAUVOIR 354

Selected Writings on American National Character 361

INTRODUCTION

I

INTRODUCTION I

Each of the three following selections is concerned with the quest for an American identity; collectively they introduce most of the major themes of the volume. Contending that it is characteristically American to be intensely inquisitive about the American character, John A. Kouwenhoven locates the sources of our national self-consciousness in the discontinuities of the American experience and the mixture of cultural traditions to which Americans lay claim. A people of many and varied pasts whose national character is a matter more of achievement than of birthright, Americans derive a common identity from their experience of "estrangement" from the past. "Americans have never been sure what it was to be Americans," and their search for a national character has been perennially spurred by that nagging uncertainty. Kouwenhoven's essay, subtitled "Some Un-American Advice to Non-Americans," grew out of a talk to a group of foreign students in 1959.

Max Lerner's discussion of "The Idea of American Civilization" is taken from his *America as a Civilization* (1957), an encyclopedic examination of contemporary life and thought in the United States. Dealing circumspectly with the problems of defining the character of Americans, Lerner argues that the American is at once "the archetypal modern man" and the exemplar of a pattern of culture which is unique. To solve the riddle that is posed by these apparently contradictory propositions, he advances a qualified doctrine of exceptionalism: "The idea of American exceptionalism and the idea of American integration into the broader Western pattern are not mutually exclusive. . . ." With respect to American character Lerner discovers no simple formula, no single organizing principle, no all-encompassing explanation but rather a diversity of traits, values, and impulses so great that American civilization must be viewed as "a highly polarized field of meaning."

Lerner's observations on the inner tensions and conflicts of American culture rest on the evidence furnished by scholars like Lee Coleman whose article, "What is American?" (1941), summarized the traits which earlier writers had alleged to be characteristically American. Though certain ascriptions were found by "lexicographic analysis" to have been fairly constant over the course of American history, Coleman stressed "the amazing diversity" of American character. The article has historical importance as a pioneering effort by an anthropologist to direct his colleagues to the study of national character in the United States. The primitive condition of that undertaking is shown by the indiscriminate lumping of such disparate "traits" as a high valuation of equality (a character trait), restlessness (a trait of temperament), "monotony" (a cultural condition), and the protective tariff (a public policy). A more careful discrimination of terms, coupled with a ranking of traits in order of significance, might have qualified the author's suggestion that diversity itself might be regarded as "the most fundamental of all American characteristics."

JOHN A. KOUWENHOVEN

The Dispraising of America

I imagine that one of the most curious, one of the oddest, things that non–Americans notice in America is what might be called the American's self-consciousness about his American-ness. We have been like that for many years —from the very beginning, in fact.

The first published answer to the question "What is an American?" appeared in 1782—just one year after the battle of Yorktown victoriously ended six years of fighting for American independence. The question forms the title of a much-quoted chapter in *Letters from an American Farmer; Describing Certain Provincial Situations, Manners, and Customs, Not Generally Known.*

This book, which first posed the self-conscious "American" question, was written in the English language, for an English audience, by a man born and educated in France, who lived while writing it in New York, but who referred to himself as a Pennsylvanian, and who stopped off in London, to arrange for the book's publication there, while he was on his way back to his native France —whence he would soon return to America as French consul in New York where (as he told his friend Benjamin Franklin) he enjoyed "The Privileges of double citizenship."

I have deliberately emphasized the mix-up of tradition in Hector St. John de Crèvecoeur's background because I want to suggest that, in a sense, the American self-consciousness about his American-ness is still—as it was in 1782 —in great part the result of a feeling or sense of "double citizenship." We Americans are all, in one way or another, aware of a double or bifurcated heritage. The eleventh-generation descendant of immigrants from Holland and the second-generation descendant of immigrants from China are no different in this respect from the eleventh-generation descendant of Negro slaves imported from the Congo. Each of us is conscious of a heritage as an American, and each of us is conscious of another heritage—or, more commonly, of a complex mixture of heritages—from cultures whose values are, in varying degrees, unlike those we have acquired as Americans.

Reproduced by permission of the author from John A. Kouwenhoven, *The Beer Can by the Highway: Essays on What's "American" about America* (Garden City, N.Y.: Doubleday & Co., Inc., 1961).

In some sense this is no doubt true of other peoples as well as Americans. One thinks of the Canadians and Australians, for example, or the Liberians or the Israelis. Canada, with its bilingual culture, presents a special problem. It lives with a clear-cut, external duality between English-speaking Canadians and French Canadians, a cleavage which is marked by geographical as well as linguistic boundaries. But in so far as the French Canadian has been cut off from his French heritage, he was cut off from it by the Englishmen who have become his fellow Canadians, not by an act of his own will. Neither the English-speaking nor the French Canadians, nor the Australians, have voluntarily shattered the continuity of their non–Canadian or non–Australian heritage by an appeal to revolutionary violence, with its inevitable aftermath of resentment and passionate self-assertion.

As for the Liberians and Israelis, however diverse their national origins may be, their motive in immigrating to the countries in which they now live was to re-establish their ties to a heritage even older and more deeply rooted in them than that of the nation from which they came. The immigrant to the United States, however, has always been required (or has deliberately sought) to attach himself to a heritage-in-the-making—a heritage which is not in any sense one to which he is entitled by his ancestry, but one to whose shaping he, as much as (but no more than) anyone else, has the right and duty to contribute.

What James Baldwin, the American novelist, once said of the American Negro can be said with some justice of the white American as well: he arrives at his identity "by virtue of the absoluteness of his estrangement from his past." We Americans do, of course, nourish illusions of recovering the European or African or Asian or American–Indian half of our dual heritage. Some of us even maintain an illusory sort of psychologically dual citizenship. Such illusions may, indeed, be necessary as long as men are uncertain about the legitimacy of their status, and the American—white or non-white—has never been quite sure what his status is. For we are all, as it were, the younger sons, the disinherited, the bastard offspring of the past. The American estate to which we lay claim is not, and cannot be, ours by right of primogeniture. It is ours only by squatters' right, or by virtue of conquest or piracy or love.

For all these reasons it is true, I think, that the citizens of no other major world power share the special sense of "double citizenship" which from Crèvecoeur's time to ours has made the Americans so self-consciously inquisitive about "What is an American?" A century after Crèvecoeur, Henry James, one of the greatest American novelists, devoted his major energies to the imaginative exploration of the implications of that question, and entitled one of his major novels *The American.* I do not know of (and cannot imagine) any important French author writing a novel called *The Frenchman,* or any Russian writing one called *The Russian.* Our libraries are full of disputatious writings by Americans with titles like *The American Spirit in Art* and *The American Style in Politics.* There *is,* of course, a book called *The Englishness of English Art*—but it was not written by an Englishman, I assure you. Until recently, at least, the English have confidently known what was English about England and therefore have not had to be self-conscious about it. But the Americans have never been sure what it was to be Americans—which is why, from the beginning, they have asserted so loudly and so inconclusively that they *were* sure. I have a shelfful of books purporting to define the American spirit or the American character and they offer as many different definitions as there are books—all mistaken definitions, too, except one (the one I wrote), and even that one strikes me as slightly tinted by its author's myopia.

Now, the reasons for dwelling at some length on this characteristic in remarks which are addressed to non-Americans is that if you are a visitor or temporary resident in the United States, you probably have some reason to want to understand what the "American spirit" is, or what the "American character's" characteristics are. If you are curious about such things, we will be delighted; and if, when you return to your homes, you write a book about us, telling your countrymen the truth about America, be sure to get the book published in this country, too. It will almost certainly be a best seller—especially if it is very critical and says disagreeable things about the "Snow Queen" frigidity of American women; the low, materialistic interests of American men (and their humble subservience to their womenfolk); the disparity between our professions of democratic equality and our economic and educational segregation of Negroes; our addiction to comic books and bottled pop; and the rest.

If you write a book giving the lowdown on America from a foreign observer's point of view, you will be in good company. Some very intelligent foreigners have written some very interesting books about us—ranging from the Frenchman De Tocqueville's great work on *Democracy in America,* down through Lord Bryce's study of the *American Commonwealth,* to the Swedish Gunnar Myrdal's *The American Dilemma.* Each of these was and is popular with American readers. But you don't have to be as judicious and encyclopedic as De Tocqueville, Bryce, and Myrdal to be a hit with us. You can be as intemperate as Mrs. Trollope, who flatly told her English countrymen in 1832 that she had discovered the Americans to be horrid: "I do not like their principles," she wrote, "I do not like their manners, I do not like their opinions." And for her courtesy we have rewarded her by buying up unnumbered editions of her book—which is still—after a hundred and twenty years—in print.

The Derogatory Stance

This appetite of ours for comment about us, abusive or judicious, may seem an endearing quality, especially if you are looking forward to getting substantial royalty checks from an American publisher, but you should be warned that from other points of view it might prove to be a trap.

Put it this way, to start with. Our appetite for criticism and analysis of America by foreigners is an aspect of our self-conscious interest in discovering what "an American" is, and this in turn is a symptom of our not knowing.

Since we don't know, and wish very much that we did (our philanthropic foundations spend hundreds of thousands of dollars a year subsidizing studies of precisely this question), we love to listen to anyone who talks as if he knew. If he bases what he says on statistical studies and the paraphernalia of sociological research, so much the better. But if he spins it all out of his head, we don't mind that either.

Being an essentially modest people—or shall I say a people who by education and admonition have been taught that the architecture of Greece, and the Roman code of law, and the painting of Flanders and France, and the ethical wisdom of the Orient, and the poetry and drama of England are unsurpassed and unsurpassable, and that even in technology and science the basic work is all European and we have merely applied the principles ingeniously—being whatever you want to call this, a modest or fundamentally unself-assured people—we find it easier to believe the derogatory things about ourselves than the approving ones. We also find it easier to say the derogatory things—in fiction, drama, and the expressive arts in general.

Of course there was a time when we could (and did) say the self-approving things. But nobody but an ass could have taken us very seriously in our moods of slapping ourselves on the back, and—as a matter of fact—few people did take it seriously. It was too obviously a kind of whistling in the dark. Not even the writers who "made the eagle scream," as the saying was in the nineteenth century, took themselves seriously; often they were being intentionally funny and fooled nobody except humorless English travelers and some uncommonly stuffy politicians. (I am, of course, oversimplifying here—but it is generally true, I think, that whenever an American says anything very flattering about American civilization, he hastens to counteract it with something unflattering, in order to avoid what he feels would be an air of "I'm better than you," in order to "take himself down a peg.")

The result is that in serious writing about the nature and quality of the American experience, both fiction and non-fiction, whether written by foreigners or by Americans, you are likely to find more that is derogatory than that is approving. And most of what is approving can easily be discounted as ignorant, or superficial, or mere high spirits.

Furthermore—and this is the root of the difficulty, if one is really intent upon learning what America means—it is very easy to mistake the significance of the literature which criticizes or rejects American culture for its bourgeois values, its materialism, its complacency, and so on. We are all quite likely to take such criticism at its face value, and thereby miss the point. We are likely either to praise it for its success in embodying values "superior" to America's standardized middle-class mediocrity, or, if we are in a chauvinistic or jingoistic mood, to damn it out of hand for its wrongheadedness.

The significance of a novel like Sinclair Lewis's *Babbitt* is, I believe, missed if you conclude from it either that Lewis was "un-American" because he disapproved of businessmen like Babbitt or that his book represents a set of values "superior" to (and therefore not characteristic of) the values of the civilization men like Babbitt had created in America. For Lewis was not writing as one who has descended from a "higher" plane to observe our civilization. He writes as one of us, who has seen—from a perspective which he assumes his fellow Americans can share—the inadequacies, the forlorn limitations of certain aspects of American life—aspects which his readers will reject just as he does. And of course he was right. His novel was a great popular success. His readers, most of whom were in business or commerce, saw in Babbitt some of the very things that they saw in themselves, and toward which they felt, like Lewis, an odd mixture of sardonic amusement and of loyalty.

What I am trying to suggest is that, if a foreign reader concluded, from the quality of photographic, tape-recorded reality which Lewis's technique imparts to his novel, that Babbitt was the typical American businessman of the 1920's—and if he further concluded that, since American civilization is a business civilization, he could draw from the novel some conclusions about the inadequacies and forlorn limitations of the civilization itself, he would have run a serious risk. Hitler and his cohorts took such a risk, gambling that a nation of Babbitts would not rise to the challenge of Nazi domination of Europe. The leaders of other nations may make a similar mistake if they get the impression from our current non-fiction that we are a nation of juvenile delinquents or if they conclude from our young poets and novelists that our young people are beatniks. For Jack Kerouac and Ginsberg, like Lewis and Mencken in the twenties, do not quite signify what they appear to be saying. Their significance, I think, is that they are witnesses to the basic and never-ceasing drive within our culture to lift itself, to be dissatisfied with its limitations, to try—at whatever cost in self-distrust or self-reproach—to discover what, indeed, is an American.

Citizens of a New World

I am afraid I am beginning to sound apocalyptic, as if, like the cheap politician whom the nineteenth-century humorists burlesqued, I were about to make the American eagle scream. I hope that is not what I am about to do.

For what interests me about American civilization is that it is not—even in name—the civilization of the United States. As that name "American" suggests, it is something whose relevance is not confined in political boundaries. I know that we use it that way some of the time. I know that our neighbors in Latin America sometimes are hurt by what they assume to be our arrogance in speaking of ourselves as Americans; for geographically, they are as much Americans as we who live in the United States. But I like to think that at least some of the time we know this as well as they do, and that when we call ourselves Americans we are not implying that they are *not* Americans, but are—on the contrary—thinking of ourselves not merely as citizens of the United States but as people living in a New World. For in a very real sense we, like all people whose lives have felt the impact of the twin energies of democracy and technology, *are* living in a New World—not merely the hemispheric New World of the geographers, but the New World which the great seventeenth-century English physician, Sir Thomas Browne, called "the America and untravelled parts of truth." Everyone who lives in *this* America, in *this* new and untraveled world, is as much concerned as are those of us who live in the United States to discover "What is an American?"

I am sure that I forget from time to time, as most of my fellow citizens forget, that this New World is not coextensive with my nation, or—more provincial still—with my precinct. I know that United States foreign policy is often not synonymous with a policy which would be genuinely American in the sense of that word I have tried to suggest. But our tendency to behave, much of the time, as citizens of the United States is as human and natural as it is for people in other lands to behave as citizens of Ghana or India or France. We cannot ignore, nor should non–Americans who wish to understand us ignore, the national heritage of the United States and the privileges and obligations of its citizens. But if I am not mistaken what we all really want to know is what Crèvecoeur wanted to know a century and three quarters ago: what is an American? And that question can be answered, I think, only when we discover that non-geographical "America" which is, in fact, the community in whose citizenship all our bifurcated heritages, our dual citizenships, are ultimately involved. We shall know "what is an American," I suspect, only when we know who is fit to be a citizen of the New World to whose dynamics and energies the United States has made large contributions, but which is being shaped by people in all lands where the influence of modern technology, and of a democratic faith in man's unexplored potentialities, have been felt. For America, in this sense, is still in the making—is still the New World to which mankind has for so many centuries been adventuring.

MAX LERNER

The Idea of American Civilization

Archetypal Man of the West

Commentators on American traits delight in quoting De Crèvecoeur's classic remark that "the American is a new man who acts on new principles." One should add that while the American was a *novus homo* when De Crèvecoeur wrote his *Letters from an American Farmer* toward the end of the eighteenth century, he is no longer so in the mid-twentieth. He is no longer an experiment: he has been proved a success, by every standard of wealth, glitter, prestige, freedom, and power. Wherever history pours fresh molten metal, in industrial achievement, living standards, and political freedom, inevitably it makes him at least in part the mold. The American has become the "New World man"—the archetypal man of the West.

For an American to write thus may seem too boastful, yet I try to write it as if I were not American but a detached observer noting a new phenomenon. Americans are not loved in the world today, although they deeply desire affection. In the countries of color there is a good deal of suspicion of them, and even some hatred. In the older civilizations of Europe there is a kind of patronizing contempt which passes for anti–Americanism. Throughout the world there is a fear of the current American stress on arms and money. Yet it remains true that the principal imperialism the American exercises is the imperialism of attraction. If he is not admired, he is envied; and even his enemies and rivals pay him the homage of imitation. People throughout the world turn almost as by a tropism to the American image. To be American is no longer to be only a nationality. It has become, along with Communism and in rivalry with it, a key pattern of action and values.

So summary a conquest of the world's imagination, never before achieved without arms and colonization, is proof of an inner harmony between America and the modern spirit. It is because of this harmony that America has acted

Reproduced by permission of the author from Max Lerner, *America as a Civilization: Life and Thought in the United States Today* (New York: Simon and Schuster, 1957). Footnotes omitted.

as a suction force, drawing from everywhere people attuned to its basic modes of life. The migration to America, from the start, of capital and of human labor and talent, was followed by the migration from America of capital, talent, economic and military strength. Both migrations, to and from America, have multiplied its influence. Having absorbed the world's strength to form its own, America has been fusing its own strength with the world's.

There has been from the start a marriage of true minds between the American and the type-man of the modern era, the New World man. To the question, wonderfully put in 1782 by De Crèvecoeur in his *American Farmer,* "What then is the American, this new man?" De Tocqueville sought an answer on his visit in the 1830s. The greatness of his book lay at least partly in its portrayal of a young civilization in which incipient European forces could reach their climactic form. In America the main trends of tendency that were dammed up in Europe itself were to find expression. As Robert Payne has put it, "America is Europe with all the walls down." Although I have insisted that America is a definable civilization in itself, it first emerged as an offshoot from the larger entity of the West which was seeking a New World form. The American is thus the concentrated embodiment of Western man, more sharply delineated, developed under more urgent conditions, but with most of the essential traits present.

Consider some of these traits. I am trying here to describe, not the American alone, but a type which has cropped up all over Europe as well since the Reformation and the rise of science.

He is mobile, restless. He has largely broken with status and moves more freely than Old World man moved up and down the ladder of wealth and class rank, as he moved over large areas, conquering space. He rifles the sciences as he opens up the continents, quenchless in his thirst for experience. He is this-worldly and not otherworldly, with a sharp sense of time and its uses: the objects of his ambition are secular rather than sacred. Accustomed to thinking in terms of the attainable, he is optimistic, with a belief in progress and a respect for technical skills and material success. He is *homo faber,* stamping his imprint on products and on machines that make products and on machines that run machines, and increasingly in the same spirit on art and ideas. He believes in whatever can be touched, grasped, measured. He is a technical man, whose absorption is not with *to what good* but with *how.* He is non-ascetic, with a taste for comfort and a belief that the means, if not the goal, of life are found in a higher living standard.

He is *l'homme moyen sensuel,* not too finicky in his sexual life about caste or class lines or about rigid standards of virtue. Hungering for a sense of personal worth, he is torn between the materialisms he can achieve and the feeling of wholeness which eludes him. He has a disquieting sense that the old gods too have eluded him and wonders when the new ones will arrive. Yet, unlike men of previous ages, it is not salvation he is after, nor virtue, nor saintliness, nor beauty, nor status. He is an amoral man of energy, mastery, and power. Above all else, he is a man for whom the walls have been broken down. He is the double figure in Marlowe, of Tamerlane and Dr. Faustus, the one sweeping like a footloose barbarian across the plains to overleap the barriers of earlier civilizations, the other breaking the taboos against knowledge and experience, even at the cost of his soul.

For this modern man the world has not yet become one world, and as the contemporary tensions attest, some time will elapse before it does. Yet what is likely to count in this direction is less the outlook of the diplomats than of the new geographers who complete the work of the cartographers of the Renaissance. Being technical men, they turn the globe around every possible way, but basically theirs is the airman's view for whom political boundaries are minor, and the heavens arch over them to be pierced and the earth stretches out to be engirded by flight. For the airman, racial boundaries do not exist either: what he sees from the air is not the color of men but how well the fields are laid out and irrigated and cultivated, what has been done in uncovering and using Nature's resources, what chimneys and spires are the witnesses of industry and culture, what clusters of community life there are in villages, cities, metropolitan areas. This was the glimpse that Wendell Willkie had—that despite divergences of economic systems, of race and color and language and social structure, the world is compassable, interdependent, organic.

Thus the great themes of the Renaissance and Reformation are fulfilled in the American as the archetypal modern man—the discovery of new areas, the charting of the skies, the lure of power, the realization of self in works, the magic of science, the consciousness of the individual, the sense of the unity of history. These are the themes that have left their mark on modern man. Perceiving this, Wyndham Lewis said of America that "the logic of the geographical position and history of the U. S. leads . . . to the ultimate formation of a society that will not be as other societies, but an epitome of all societies." He had in mind specifically the ethnic pluralism and democratic inclusiveness of America which hold the world in microcosm. It is this trans-national character of American society which, despite the surviving American tribalisms, makes it congruous with the strivings of other peoples. The same applies to the structure of the American personality, which is mobile, ethnically diverse, energy-charged, amoral, optimistic, genial, technic-minded, power-oriented. The question is not whether these traits are admirable or lovable but whether they polarized the energies of much of the world—as they do.

American Exceptionalism

The portrait of American—and New World—man I have just drawn is not meant to be an idealized one. It has shadows as well as lights. And it poses a riddle of both logic and history: logically, how we can speak of the American as the "archetypal" man of the modern world and at the same time assert that American civilization is a pattern within itself, whole and unique; historically, how America has developed out of the common conditions of the modern world, yet developed with such an acceleration of energy and power; and whether the future arc of its development is likely to recapitulate the course of experience of European and Asiatic civilizations.

I do not underestimate the difficulties of this riddle. That is why I am little inclined to see America within any of the rather grandiose schemes of historical determinism, whose real value is to suggest lines of study and not to close them. The seduction of historical parallels should not lure us away from studying America as a civilization pattern in itself—its tensions, its lines of development, its weaknesses and strengths. The learning of Vico and Hegel, of Marx, of Spengler and Toynbee, of Sorokin, would still leave unexplained the unlikely genesis of America, its rapid rise to power, the contrast of its outer image and its inner qualities, its materialism and idealism, its isolationism and leadership role. Whether such a civilization will survive or is doomed will depend less on grand historical "laws" than upon how Americans grapple with their problems and use their characteristic resources and energies.

If I do not subscribe to the cry of "America is doomed," neither am I pleading for the distorted version of "American exceptionalism" which has been the pious theme of spread-eagle theorists seeking to depict America as immune from the forces of history and the laws of life. This version of exceptionalism is easily used as an idea weapon in the anti-democratic struggle, as Schlesinger shows in citing the attack on the efforts to organize trade-unions in the Jacksonian period. Even since then the cry that "America is different" has been an unfailing answer to any challenge that might disturb the structure of existing power, and the carriers of the challenge have been regarded as "un-American," "alien," and therefore "subversive."

But these distortions should not blind us to the valid elements in the theory of exceptionalism. The fact is that while American civilization is not immune to the surging beat of world forces, it has developed its own characteristic institutions, traits, and social conditions within the larger frame. America represents, as I have stressed above, the naked embodiment of the most dynamic elements of modern Western history. What this implies is that exceptionalism *includes* an acceptance of the European ties and does not reject them. The idea of American exceptionalism and the idea of American integration into the broader Western pattern are not mutually exclusive but are polar facets of the same field of energy. When you speak of American uniqueness, you must speak also in the same framework about the European diversity. It is in this sense of what is *characteristically American* that I use the idea of exceptionalism.

A rapid listing of some of the outstanding books on America will show that almost every commentator has fixed on some unique elements in it. De Tocqueville saw the whole of American life as a new form of society which he called *democracy*. Charles Dickens had never seen anything to equal American money-mad materialism. Bryce was impressed with the uniqueness of the Federal system and the party system. Whitman, castigating American corruption, nevertheless glimpsed democratic vistas beyond them more stirring than ever before in history. Henry and Brooks Adams saw the degradation of the democratic dogma stretched further in America than anywhere else in the democratic world. Thorstein Veblen, who felt that American capitalism had been carried to a unique degree of power, concentration, and finesse, did a series of studies in absentee ownership showing how business enterprise in modern times had taken characteristic forms in the case of America—developing such home-grown products as the country town, the independent farmer, the captain of industry, the technology of physics and chemistry.

Herbert Croly found a peculiar "promise" in American life he found nowhere else. Waldo Frank, in his "rediscovery" of America, found equally a characteristically excessive power and excessive childishness in the American mind. D. H. Lawrence found in "classical" American literature a mixture of the primitive and the bourgeois, in the clash of which he located the characteristic split in the American soul. H. L. Mencken, studying the one feature of American life which might have been expected to follow the pattern of its English parent—its speech—found elements of originality in it so marked as to make it a separate American language. André Siegfried, explaining America in the 1920s and again in the 1950s, saw its peculiar problems in the clash between the "Anglo-Saxon tradition" and the later immigrant strains; but he also asserted that America was a new civilization that had left the European far behind. Robert and Helen Lynd, in their two *Middletown* studies, wryly found the distillation of American thinking in the "Middletown spirit"—a body of folk-belief that set Americans off from any other culture. Margaret Mead saw the core of the American character in the distinctive effects of the authority-and-freedom pattern on the interaction of the sexes and the growing-up process within the family. D. W. Brogan saw an interrelation between the paradoxes within the American political system and within the national character. Geoffrey Gorer, arguing that the child in America is conditioned to seek love and success above all else, deduced from it a different but still characteristic American personality pattern. Wyndham Lewis saw in the ethnic mixtures of the American stock, and their ways of living together, the seeds of "cosmic man."

David Riesman explored the American character in terms of its increasing submission to the tyranny of opinion and the failure of the individual to heal his loneliness in the crowd. David M. Potter saw the Americans as a "people of plenty" and the crucial traits of the American character as arising from situations of abundance and opportunity. Daniel Boorstin saw the genius of American politics in the American's habit of taking his own premises and values for granted as "givens," not to be thought about. Louis Hartz saw the specific character of an institution as shaped by the fact that Americans never had an old feudal order to destroy by revolutionary overturn, as the Europeans did.

I do not mean to imply that each of these writers was an adherent of the theory of American exceptionalism. I do say that these important studies of the whole or some segment of American life use, as a practical matter, the working hypothesis of an American character and culture which are set off distinctively from others in history and in the contemporary world.

National Character and the Civilization Pattern

The convenient way to deal with the problem of national character is to list a people's traits, presenting them as "American traits," the "American mind," or the "American spirit." Some of the commentators enumerate the traits mechanically, as if it were a question of a grocery list or a warehouse inventory of odds-and-ends items. One trouble with this method of delineating character by enumeration is that the lists tend to cancel each other out. Lee Coleman, culling the lists of American traits from the available commentaries on America, found he could spot the exact opposite in some other list. Thus Americans are generous and niggardly, sympathetic and unfeeling, idealistic and cynical, visionary and practical—which leaves us with the conclusion, true but not novel, that Americans are bewilderingly human. Another difficulty is that the traits change over the generations. Compare the Garden of Eden picture of American traits in De Crèvecoeur at the end of the eighteenth century with De Tocqueville's for the late 1830s and 1840s, Bryce's contemporary picture for the 1880s and 1890s, or (retrospectively) Commager's *The American Mind* for the same period.

There are, however, certain salient traits which commentators attribute to the American in every period: Coleman finds that these are the tendency to club together or "join" in associations, the belief in democracy, the belief in equality, individual freedom, "direct action" in disregard of law, stress on local government, practicality, prosperity and material well-being, Puritanism, the influence of religion, uniformity and conformity.

It is hard to define the American national character by listing traits or even "value clusters," mainly because there are difficulties inherent in the idea of national character itself. Many writers are wary of it because it has been used cynically in war and power struggles to blacken the enemy symbol or sustain the conceit of a God-given or history-given national superiority. Caught between the Fascist theorists who have used it to bolster their doctrine of racist purity and pollution, and the Marxist theorists who reject it for placing too little stress on class interest and class militancy, the idea of national character has become a thorny and controversial one.

While it is risky to attribute a national character to any people, as if its qualities and destiny could be ripped out of the living body of history, it is also true that nations are realities, that their cultures develop along different paths, and that the world inside the heads of their people is a characteristic world. Much of the chauvinist and racist treachery of the term can be avoided if it is remembered that national character is a doctrine not of blood but of culture. It consists of a body of values, social habits, attitudes, traits held in common by most members of the culture. Thus the psychological field of action, thought, and emotion into which an American is born differs not only from the Russian or Chinese but even from that of an Englishman.

Traditionally, national character has been used as a semi-literary rule-of-thumb to differentiate one nationality type from another or give impressionistic force to generalization about a whole people. One of the classics here is Emerson's *English Traits,* which is witness that literary insight may be worth more than all the paraphernalia of recent social science. Yet the new anthropological and psychiatric techniques did mark a turning point in the approach to national character. First they were applied to the study of primitive personality structure, and then to psychological warfare in World War II. The psychiatrists knew from their experience that diagnosis and therapy vary with individuals of differing character types, and that these character types apply not only to neurotics and psychotics but to presumably normal persons. At the same time the anthropologists, studying contemporary primitive groups, found that each culture has its own pattern, within which there are also several different variants of character and personality. In World War II, before the military strategists could lay their plans for an assault on the enemy mind, they had to know what the enemy mind was like—hence the American studies of the Germans and Japanese, in which the theory of national character was tested in the crucible of life-and-death action. Thus the war studies converged with the work of the psychiatrists and anthropologists to form a new strain, one whose by-product has been an effort to apply the same techniques to contemporary America.

This strain of inquiry now makes possible a new way of getting at what has usually been called the "American character" or the "American spirit." It is not a disembodied presence in the sky or some mystical force inherent in race or history. Neither is it the body of folk-belief that Americans derive from their mass media and their whole cultural environment. It is best sought at the point where cultural norms in America shape personality and character, and where in turn the human material and the energies of Americans leave their impact on the fabric of the culture.

I may cite as an example of this process the way children are brought up in America, how their personalities are shaped by the emotional atmosphere of the family and the structure of authority and freedom within it, how the whole tone of growing up is set by the inordinate concentration on the child, the pervasive influence of the new big-audience media, the seeping in of the cultural values of success, prestige, and security, and the clash between permissive and restrictive codes as it is reflected in the child's mind. One can find similar examples in what is happening to the American character and spirit today as a result of suburban living, or the conditions of work and incentive within the new corporate structures, or the wave of "do-it-yourself" amateurism which has come as a recoil from the trend toward complete mechanization, or the sense of encirclement that leads to a stress on "loyalty" and "security," or the virtual ending of immigration, or the emergence of new elites and a complex, far-reaching middle class. These are only a few instances of how the energies of the individual American are channeled by characteristic cultural conditions of training and living, shaping certain common character traits for whole groups of individuals and weaving them into the fabric of the civilization.

This does not mean that, by some necromantic determinism, every little American who is born alive comes out stamped with exactly the same traits or propensities. There are in-groups, out-groups, and marginal groups; there are regional, class, and ethnic variations; there is a bewildering variety of individual personality patterns and traits. Yet the central stream of tendency remains, and with it the shaping interrelations of American personality and culture.

What are some of the ways of uncovering this interrelation? One way is a study of mental disorders, asking, as the psychiatrists do, what are the characteristic sources of personality breakdown—what it is that makes Americans crack up when and as they do? To answer this means to get some insight into the strains under which men live in America, the expectations the culture sets up in them as against the satisfactions it places within their reach, the norms of conduct and thought it seeks to enforce, the fault lines and frustrations that develop within them. Another way is to ask what personality types can be most clearly discerned among Americans, and what modes of life and striving within the culture account for the impulse toward those personality types. A third is to ask what life goals the Americans set up for themselves and what they make a cult of and are obsessed with, making sure to distinguish between the conscious and irrational levels of their striving.

One can dig deeper, perhaps, and seek some hidden dimension of the American character which symbolizes the basic American life view. Thus F. S. C. Northrop (*The Meeting of East and West*) takes the deepest thing about any civilization to be its metaphysic—its assumptions and beliefs about the constitution of the unseen universe, and he suggests that it was the reception by America of the atomistic metaphysics of Locke and Hume which has influenced the individualism and fragmentation of American life. Thus also Charles W. Morris (*Six Ways of Life*) attempts an approach through symbolic value systems. He lists the crucial systems in history as the Dionysian (surrender to the instinctual life), the Buddhist (annihilation of self for serenity), the Christian (purifying of self for spiritual values), the Mohammedan (merging of self in a holy war against the enemies of the true way), the Apollonian (conserving of traditional values), and the Promethean (conquest and organization of the environment by science and technology). He sees American civilization as primarily Promethean, but with elements of the Christian and the Apollonian, pointing out that the Promethean strain puts the emphasis on the instrumental, that the Apollonian has hardened into a Toryism of the spirit which could mean a static civilization, and that the Christian strain has had to be subordinated when it has conflicted with the more dominant elements of the civilization. I cite this suggestive scheme to illustrate how the study of the great world myths can shed light on what Americans are like and what they live by.

Since most of this is speculative, American observers have tried to approach their own civilization by the very different and more modest road of community surveys and cross-section area studies—of "Middletown," "Jonesville," "Yankeetown," "Elmtown," "Southern Town," "Plainville." What these studies offer is a degree of verification for certain theoretical leads, or of doubt cast upon others; they can show the extent to which the members of the American culture verbalize the articles in the American creed, and how they see themselves (and others) in the class system and the success-and-rating system of their time. But the community studies can never be broader or deeper than the issues they pose, nor more imaginative than the questions they raise.

Discussions of national character sometimes remind you of one of Cagliostro's magical spells or the incantatory hokum of a side-show barker telling the virtues of some nostrum. There is no talismanic quality in any of the newer approaches to national character. The hard work of giving contour to the mass of known material on American civilization cannot be dispensed with. The insights of the psychiatrists and anthropologists are all to the good, if they do not overstress some single symbolic key to the national character. The method of Gorer, for example, as used in the Gorer–Rickman study, *The People of Great Russia,* has been sharply satirized as the "swaddling theory" because it takes the infantile experience of the Russian peasant child, who was closely swaddled in the early months of his life, as a pre-verbal emotional conditioning to the rage, guilt, and violent alternations of emotion in the Russian as an adult. In *The American People,* Gorer put stress on the cult of the mother, the rejection of the father, the child's craving for affection, and the fear of loneliness, and again saw them as clue—if not cause—to the national character. A good deal depends on how hard the thesis is pushed. If we take it not as a verified truth but as impressionistic lead for further research and analysis, it is all to the good. The course of wisdom is to recognize the limits of any study of personality traits and to see the whole of the national character as one phase of the total civilization pattern.

Single Key—or Polar Pattern?

The question then arises whether there is some single organizing principle in this civilization pattern, some key that unlocks all the doors. For generations Western thinkers have been haunted by the dream of finding the single factor that shapes all else in its image. It might be Hegel or Spencer, Marx or Sorel,

Spengler, Freud or Jung, Veblen, Henry George, Brooks Adams or Henry Adams, but it was always a form of cabala. I can offer the reader no single talisman to the secret of American civilization.

The temptation is great to seek it. Following the lead of Marx or Veblen, one might stress the march of technology and the system of business power, and build all the rest on that. After Laski's *American Democracy,* which applied that method unsparingly to the analysis of contemporary America, such an approach would yield sharply decreasing returns. While Laski's theme is democracy, as with De Tocqueville and Bryce, it is the subject of the book only as a corpse is the subject of a murder mystery. The real theme is the system of capitalist power and its business civilization: between these and democracy Laski depicts a bitter feud. Democracy in Laski's study is a little like the hero of Clifford Odet's early play, *Waiting for Lefty:* the stage is set for the hero, everyone measures his life and aspirations by him, but he never shows up because he has fallen victim to the forces of greed and reaction. Obviously economic power and class structure are important themes in the American civilization pattern, and I shall dwell a good deal on them. But an analysis which makes them the sole key distorts a good deal and misses many of the most dramatic recent changes in American life.

Laski's approach, like Veblen's, marked a recoil from the school of political idealism, which seemed to make political institutions and ideas the end and beginning and everything in the middle. In one sense De Tocqueville belonged to that tradition, since he started with the idea of democracy and traced its ramifications through phase after phase of American life. But De Tocqueville set an example of breadth of view which could not be matched by the later students of America, even someone with the insight of Bryce, whose approach was more narrowly through the political institutions of *The American Commonwealth,* while De Tocqueville's traced out imaginatively the political and moral ramifications of the democratic idea. Bryce, moreover, had lost much of the sense of wonder and excitement one finds in De Tocqueville about the revolutionary implications of democracy and was more interested in how the political actuality had worked out. In both cases, however, the organizing principle is political.

Another approach lays the key stress on psychological and moral values. It gives primacy to beliefs and attitudes, and the creative force of religion and ideas, and derives the technology and economic achievement of America from them rather than the other way round. The unacknowledged assumption is that the way to understand America is to start with the human psyche in its American form and with its whole intellectual and moral world. One finds this approach, with mystical overtones, in Waldo Frank's *Rediscovery of America;* one finds it, with religious overtones in Toynbee and Niebuhr; one finds it, in its more direct psychological form, in the writing of the young American scholars today who are exploring the relation of culture and personality.

My own view is that both economic man and psychological man—the materialist emphasis and the individualist emphasis—are each stripped of meaning without the other. The problem of social analysis is only partially illumined by the search for causes. In much of our thinking, causation is giving way to relation and interaction. "America is this," says one observer of American life. "America is that," says another. It is likely that America is both, because America is a highly polarized field of meaning, but that neither can be fully understood except in relation to the other and to the whole intricate civilization pattern. The study of American civilization becomes thus the study of the polar pattern itself, not a search for some single key that will unlock causation. It is largely a question of what you focus upon, and against what background. The problem of American interpretation is best seen in a figure-ground perspective: but what will be figure and what will be ground will vary with the purpose at hand.

Thus my concern will be neither with the material world alone nor with the moral-psychological world alone, but with the interplay between them. If there is a figure-ground relation in American civilization it must be sought in the relation between power and ideas, science and conscience, the revolutionary machine and the conservative crust of tradition, mass production and social creativeness, individualist values and collective action, capitalist economics and democratic freedom, class structure and the image of prestige and success in the American mind, elite power and the popular arts, the growth of military power and the persistence of civilian control, the fact of an American imperium and the image of an open constitutional world.

One may see in these polar impulses the proof that American life is deeply split. One may prefer to see them as contradictory parts of a bewildering puzzle. Or one may see them as signs of an effort, on a grander scale than ever in history, to resolve the conflicting impulses that are to be found in every civilization but each of which occurs here with a strength and tenacity scarcely witnessed elsewhere.

LEE COLEMAN

What Is American?

Few people in America today can escape an awareness of the terms "Americanism" and the "American Way." "American" and "un-American" are on the tongues of all, but few can define what they mean by the terms. It is certain, however, that they are being used to blanket widely divergent concepts.

This paper summarizes some of the data and conclusions of a study intended as a first step toward a more adequate definition of the term "American." The study, made under the auspices of the Institute for Research in Social Science at the University of North Carolina, is described as a "lexicographic analysis" of alleged American characteristics, ideals, and principles. It represents but one approach to a large problem and a vast literature, and it was not anticipated that the product would be a definitive answer to the question "What is American?"

The data were obtained by collecting, from a large number of books dealing with "Americanism" or "the American Way," and from incidental discussions in other books and periodicals, all statements that some characteristic or principle is distinctively American, together with the author's evidence for such an assertion. Statements collected were limited to those alleging some trait to be American in the sense that it is characteristic of the country as a whole. The books and authors included in the survey were chosen at random and represent a wide variety of viewpoints. Both contemporary and earlier commentators are included.

When the traits were grouped according to subject matter it was immediately apparent that there is far from complete agreement as to what is or is not American. In the case of practically every trait which one or more authors allege to be characteristically American, an opposing trait is by other authors asserted to be ditinctively American, or evidence is advanced in contradiction of the alleged trait. The extent of this contrast and contradiction in the use of "American" is indicated by the illustrations which follow.

Reproduced by permission of The University of North Carolina Press from Lee Coleman, "What is American? A Study of Alleged American Traits," *Social Forces,* XIX (May, 1941), pp. 492–99.

A large number of the authors, as might be expected, assert that democracy is an American institution and a characteristically American way of life. In addition to democracy as such, the alleged American traits centering around this idea range from "a republican form of government" to specific types of democracy—Jeffersonianism, economic democracy, political democracy—and special manifestations of democracy, such as lack of class, lack of aloofness on the part of the wealthy, absence of a servile manner on the part of servants, hatred of social distinctions, universal suffrage, sovereignty of the people, freedom of women, equality of all, and representation on the basis of numbers.

By no means all of the observers, however, are willing unqualifiedly to list "democracy" as an American trait. It is asserted, for example, that the Founding Fathers were almost unanimously followers of the aristocratic ideal, that the American people have always been fascinated by aristocracy, that our business and economic life is one of complete autocracy, that we are exclusive as a people, that we have, if not class, an occupational stratification by nationality group—and finally that democracy itself is "un-American."

This contrast in opinion is well summed up in the words of Dr. George S. Counts, "The authenticity of American democracy cannot be successfully challenged. Whatever may have been its defects and limitations . . . it was and is one of the realities of history,"[1] as against those of Mr. Gerald Johnson, "Heretical as it may sound, I do not believe that either democracy or liberty is a fundamental part of Americanism, much less that 'equality of opportunity' which is supplanting universal suffrage as the theoretical expression of liberty."[2]

In the matter of obedience to law, a striking contrast of opinion appears. While one group of observers assert that Americans have a feeling of personal interest in the law and a consequent disposition to obey it, another group point out a strong tradition of "direct action," mob violence, and complete disregard of the law when it gets in one's way. The one group picture America as "a government of laws and not of men," whose citizens accomplish needed reforms by use of the ballot and are characterized by deference to law as final authority. The other group assert that our laws are poor, that they are unstable, and that we are extremely lax in enforcing them. One author combines the two points of view in his statement that we have "an outward respect for law and order combined with a secret itch for violence and direct action."

The observers find much in American life to justify the widespread conception of America as a land of education. They profess to see an almost blind worship of schooling, a belief that knowledge is power, and an intense desire to gain that power on a national scale. In the words of Nicholas Murray Butler, we have

> a never-failing faith in the power of education to promote both individual and national happiness, efficiency, and virtue. . . . The American people are almost Socratic

[1] *The Prospects of American Democracy*, p. 12.

[2] "The American Way: The Two Fundamentals," *Harper's Magazine* (April, 1938), p. 493.

> in their acceptance of the principle that knowledge will lead to right and useful action and conduct. . . . The American people have an almost fanatical belief in education because of the practical results which they feel certain will flow from it.[3]

Even as early as 1835 we find de Tocqueville asserting that

> . . . it is by the attention it [the law] pays to Public Education that the original character of American civilization is at once placed in the clearest light.[4]

But some of the observers see another side of the picture. These charge that we believe the principal value of schooling is a money value, and that we go to school only for financial gain. Others assert that we do not know why we go to school, and that we have more respect for the correspondence school than for the university. A number mention the strong frontier tradition which scorns "book learning," "culture," and the expert. It is charged further that we still have a low regard for intellectual achievement, that our standards of scholarship are low and our teachers poorly-trained, that we lack respect for teachers, that our thinking is external, that we seek information instead of knowledge, that our glorified "education for the masses" is superficial, that our business world looks with disdain on academic theory.

Both native and foreign critics, though more particularly the latter, devote page after page to discussions of our "worship of money," our "dedication to profit," our commercialism and materialism. There are those who see desire for economic advancement as the central, almost exclusive, motivation in American society, and some go so far as to assert that we have elevated money-making to the status of virtue and patriotic duty. Our highly commercialized crime and our professionalized and commercialized sport are pointed out as examples of the all-pervasiveness of this motivation.

But there are others, and they are not confined to the native critics, who present strong evidence in refutation, or partial refutation of these alleged traits. Especially emphasized is a strong current of idealism which many observers believe runs through our history down to the present time. Another group of authors stress, as further evidence against the purely materialistic concept of the American, the things that Americans do with their money. They assert that philanthropy has reached its highest development in America and that our schools and churches are the world's best supported. Still other elements in American life which are seen by some observers as modifying or raising some doubts about our materialism include the doctrine of "service" which pervades the business world, the attitude that money-making is a "game," the widespread distribution of wealth, the relatively high standards of business honor, and the efforts through governmental action to curb the undue amassing of wealth and the growth of monopolies.

Most of the critics who see America as dominated by the profit motive see a consequent neglect of the "spiritual" side of life, including religion, literature, and the arts. It is claimed by some that our religion, however conspicuous it

---

[3]*The American as He Is,* p. 68.
[4]*Democracy in America,* I, 40.

may be in national life, is chiefly a "Sunday religion," which can be conveniently forgotten during the business week. Other alleged American characteristics which are purported to illustrate the relative unimportance of religion in American life are the separation of the church and state and the distinctness of the sphere of religion, the emphasis on commercial buildings instead of cathedrals, secularized education, the individualistic religion, the belief that one religion is as good as another, and the belief that religion should not be discussed in public.

Against these alleged traits stands the evidence presented by other observers to show the great influence of religion in our national life—especially the intermingling of religious issues in political and economic life, the importance of church membership in individual success, the large element of religious motivation in our history, our evangelism, and the fervor and vividness of our religious emotion.

Here the contrast in opinion can be summed up in the question whether, with Alexis de Tocqueville, we can still say that "there is no country in the whole world in which the Christian religion retains a greater influence over the souls of men than in America,"[5] and with James Bryce that the Americans are "on the whole, a religious people," and that in America "Christianity influences conduct, not indeed half as much as in theory it ought, but probably more than it does in any other modern country,"[6] or whether we must conclude that these comments are no longer applicable, and agree with a more modern observer that

> We will let all Christian and even non-Christian religions—provided they are 'moral' —strictly alone . . . with the understanding that religions let us strictly alone, too, in our everyday secular and political life. That is, with us Americans religion—as far as we have any—is a strictly Sunday or festival . . . affair. And even on the Sabbath it must not any longer deprive us (and no longer does it, in the majority of States) of Sunday 'movies' or baseball and football games, of Sunday automobile rides, or even of a Sunday glass of beer.[7]

There is a sharp division of opinion among the authors concerning the American citizen's participation in governmental affairs. While some see as characteristic of Americans an aptitude for politics, a passion for politics and political debates, widespread interest in and knowledge of politics, incessant political activity, and a universal indulgence in "playing politics," the same or other authors point out an indifference to political life on the part of the educated and wealthy, the absence of the most able men from politics, the poor quality of our politicians as contrasted with the high quality of the people in general, the general distrust of politicians, lack of interest in the business of the state, a remoteness and abstractness of government for the average citizen, the poor government of our cities, and the evils of the spoils system and the political boss.

[5] *Democracy in America,* I, 308.
[6] *The American Commonwealth,* I, 290.
[7] Harold E. Stearns, *America: A Re-Appraisal,* p. 48.

Even the much-vaunted "American freedom" does not escape the doubters. There is of course strong support for liberty as an American trait, both as ideal and as fact, and many observers stress the specific liberties of speech, the press, religion, and association for political purposes. Others assert that we possess a large measure of personal freedom, that we not only believe in liberty but in equal liberty, and that we have faith in free inquiry and discussion for the solution of our problems. But there are also those who find in America a continual interference with personal liberty, a complete lack of independence in politics, a considerable degree of religious intolerance, and a lack of real freedom of discussion and independence of spirit. In support of their position these observers point to our censorship of books and movies, our straight-party voting, our high regard for convention and conformity, and the great power of the partisan press.

Contrast, then, the point of view of Alexander Meiklejohn:

> America has an ideal. It is Liberty. That is, I am sure, our deepest commitment. No one who reads our national literature, who listens to our daily speech, who mingles in the common course of our living, can fail to hear the note rising above all the others in which we express ourselves. The man who fails to find in us a deep, consuming passion for freedom does not know what we are.[8]

with that of Alexis de Tocqueville, who, although he wrote more than a hundred years ago, best expresses what many of the observers are still saying today:

> I know no country where there obtains, in general, less independence of spirit and true freedom of discussion than in America. The majority sets a formidable wall around thought. Within these limits, the writer is free, but unfortunate is he if he dares to go outside them . . . he is the butt of all kinds of aversions and persecutions every day. A political career is closed to him; he has offended the only power that has the capacity for opening it. He is refused everything, even glory.[9]

Some of the commentators have another way of looking at "American freedom." They see in it a strong tendency toward anarchy. They claim that we are so jealous of our liberties that we will accept only the most limited conception of the function of government, and that we place all kinds of limitations on the agents of government. They assert that we are quick to protect the "rights of men against government," and that we are ashamed to accept governmental employment. They point to our constant criticism of government and our humor at its expense. Their summaries of our supposed point of view range from "belief that regulation is the limit of governmental function" to "negative conception of government."

But here again the critics are by no means unanimous. Others are just as emphatic that ours is the positive conception of government. They find support for this position in the Declaration of Independence itself, pointing out that in

[8] *What Does America Mean?* p. 71.

[9] Quoted in James Bryce, *The American Commonwealth,* II, 343. (Translation by present author.)

this document we go so far as to accept as a responsibility of government the happiness of the citizen. They point to a long tradition of "reform by use of the ballot," and many acts of government, throughout our history, which they believe demonstrate that we long ago accepted the protection and security of the economic rights of the people as a governmental function.

Illustrations of contrast and contradicting opinion among the authors included in the study might be continued indefinitely. In some cases an alleged characteristic is directly contradicted by another alleged trait, both traits being supported by reputable writers who present evidence from observable fact or established sources. More often, however, the "opposing trait" does not represent a complete contradiction of the other trait, but rather the interpretation of the same set of facts from a different point of view, or the emphasizing of another set of facts. For example, our "government of checks and balances" to one observer may mean a carefully-worked-out "division of responsibility," while to another it may mean "lack of unity in government" and undue limitation on the agents of government. To one critic our idealism may be the predominant and significant fact, while to another our "flagrant disregard and defilement of our ideals" may be the important fact.

The illustrations given above will suffice to show the wide divergence of opinion as to what is "American." It is not meant, however, to convey the impression that the evidence was found to be equal on both sides of each disputed trait or group of traits. Despite opposing evidence and diverging opinion, it was possible to make up a list of traits which were so often mentioned and so little contradicted that they may safely be assumed to constitute at least a preliminary list of important American characteristics.

List of American Traits upon Which There Is Relative Agreement among the Authors Used in the Study

Sovereignty of the people, characteristically exercised through *public opinion* (a manifestation of democracy that receives such emphasis as to necessitate separate mention).

Equality of all, a fundamental belief and in large degree a fact.

Individualism, rugged or otherwise, in all realms of life, but especially in the economic.

Worship of schooling, and universal public education—this whether the motivation be materialistic or idealistic, and despite superficiality of the schooling and a distrust of academic theory in practical life.

Distrust of strong government, especially as expressed in an over-emphasis on division of responsibility and "checks and balances."

Love of size and bigness, based on an actual fact of bigness everywhere.

Adaptability and freedom from the past; openness to change, and fact of constant change and revolution.

Associational activity, an aptitude for organization that makes Americans the world's greatest organizers and joiners, and the doing by means of such voluntary organizations of many things that elsewhere would be done by governmental action or not at all.

Optimism, especially as expressed in a belief in progress and a faith in the perfectability of man.

Opportunity, especially the belief in equal opportunity for all and the fact of much greater opportunity than in most other countries.
Constitutional government and the great power of the judiciary—limitation on the immediate will of the majority and the presence of a power higher than the legislature, plus the position of the judges as arbiters of the validity of laws.
"Localism"—local government, local patriotism, local initiative and responsibility.
"Missionary Spirit"—reforming others, interfering with their lives, making over the world.
Humanitarianism and philanthropy, sympathy for the "under-dog"—this more than in any other country in the world.
Spirit of the pioneer and tradition of the frontier—the strong influence of the "great open spaces" and the pioneer way.
National self-consciousness and conceit, incessant bragging and boasting, sensitiveness to criticism.
Mobility, migration, restlessness—the world's most mobile people.
Liberty, freedom, independence—all-important ideals and to a large extent actualities, except for some notable exceptions.
Emphasis on money-making, and belief that it is duty and virtue—but not money-making to the exclusion of idealism, philanthropy, and "service."
Desire for peace and disbelief in war, especially as expressed in pacifism, and a belief in arbitration and the rights of neutrals.
Political isolationism, "freedom from entangling alliances."
Practicality, absence of theories and philosophizing, and disbelief in them.
Dominance of women, their freedom and high status.
Party government and party loyalty, straight-party voting.
Widespread popular knowledge and education—this despite credulousness and a "passion for humbug."
Glorification of the "common man" at the expense of the "expert" and the intellectual.
Ingenuity and invention, high level of initiative and research.

It is difficult to set lines of demarcation between degrees of importance or the degrees to which the various traits are "proved" or "disproved." The following traits, however, seem to be mentioned less often or to attract less unanimity of support, though among the authors studied there is nevertheless considerably more support for them than dissent from them.

Idealism, despite widespread and flagrant disregard and defilement of ideals.
Prosperity and high standard of living, widespread distribution of wealth.
Energy, alertness, incessant activity, love of action, craving for excitement.
Dominance of the machine and of applied and mechanistic science.
Trial and error experimentation, belief in evolutionary progress.
Emphasis on youth, special interest in the welfare of children.
Gambling, speculation, chance-taking.
"Mass" activity—mass production, mass education, mass entertainment.
Protestantism, Puritanism, Calvinism.
"Property-ism"—excessive emphasis on the accumulation and protection of property.
Glorification of labor and belief that work is a virtue.
Emphasis on efficiency, and fact of very high degree of efficiency.
Freedom of relationships, candor, openness, casualness.

The preceding list of "largely-agreed-upon" American traits does not take into consideration whether the support for a given trait came from authors who were merely describing contemporary characteristics or whether a part of it came from authors writing in each of the various periods of our history. Since some definitions of "American" exclude all traits but those which can be shown to have been consistently predominant throughout our history as a people, a separate analysis of the traits by dates of allegation was made. American history was divided somewhat arbitrarily into four periods, Pre-Civil War (to 1865), Civil War to World War (1866–1917), World War to Depression (1918–1929), and Depression to present (1930–1940). The decreasing length of the periods was determined partly by the fact that the great majority of the authors used in the study were relatively modern, but it is believed that the events and dates selected as dividing lines between periods do represent significant turning points in American history.

For each of these periods a list was made of all the traits alleged by one or more persons writing or speaking during that period. From these lists, another list which includes all the traits mentioned in each of the four periods or in as many as three of them was made. This list differs from the preceding list of "largely-agreed-upon" American traits in that the present list utilizes the original headings under which the quotations were grouped, whereas the former list was made up of generalized statements covering a number of similar traits. It will be observed, however, that the content of the two lists is almost identical. Furthermore, when the lists for each of the four time periods were compared, no important difference between the traits mentioned by modern observers and those writing in the earlier periods of American history was discovered.

TRAITS MENTIONED IN ALL FOUR PERIODS:

Associational activity
"Democracy," and belief and faith in it
Belief in the equality of all as a fact and as a right
Freedom of the individual: an ideal and a fact
Disregard of law—"direct action"
Local government
Practicality
Prosperity and general material well-being
Puritanism
Emphasis on religion, and its great influence in national life
Uniformity and conformity

TRAITS MENTIONED IN THREE OF THE FOUR PERIODS

Ceaseless activity and agitation
Bragging and boasting
Precedence of business over politics and religion
Openness to change and love of it
Changeability
Separation of church and state—distinctness of the sphere of religion
Absence of class and class-consciousness
Commercialism
Faith in the common man—"the people"
Domination of economic motivation
Public education

Belief and faith in education and schooling, and devotion to them
Exaggeration
Disdain and distrust of foreigners, and feeling of superiority over them
Friendliness and sociability
Love of gain and pursuit of wealth
Good humor and kindliness
Gregariousness
Haste
Idealism
Ingenuity and inventiveness
Political isolationism
Laissez-fairism
Liberty, a fact and an ideal—devotion to it and faith in it
Materialism
Monotony
National conceit—desire for praise and unwillingness to stand criticism
Opportunity
Optimism
Instinct and aptitude for organization, and love of it
Interference with other people's affairs
Desire for peace and belief in it; disbelief in war
Absolute sovereignty of the people
Belief in the perfectability of man and the possibilities of human achievement
Periodical literature
Widespread interest in and knowledge of politics
Belief in private property and respect for it
The protective tariff
Racial heterogeneity—the "melting pot"
Restlessness
Sectionalism
Size and bigness
Universal suffrage
Tolerance
Variety, diversity, and contrasts
Dominance of women

Admittedly this study has made no startling revelations. It should, however, place renewed emphasis on the amazing diversity of American life and character, and consequently show the hazard involved in asserting that any trait is unqualifiedly American, to the exclusion of all opposing or modifying traits. With traditions as diverse as the races and nationalities that have made America, and with the accomplishment in a little more than a hundred years of a revolution so complete as the change from a pioneer farming country to the highly industrialized nation of today, perhaps the best that can be hoped for is a listing of whatever principles and tendencies can be found to run fairly consistently through the successive periods of American development, largely disregarding the contradictions which may be found to exist between concurrent principles and traits. Certainly there is ground for a wide divergence of opinion as to which are and which are not the essential American principles and characteristics.

Indeed, it may be that this very diversity can be shown to be the most fundamental of all American characteristics. Perhaps this is the reason that totalitarian theories have made so little progress in America. It may be that this explains why an American can still see a place for difference of opinion on all questions. Perhaps in today's world it is the most valuable trait Americans possess.

AS OTHERS HAVE SEEN US

II

INTRODUCTION II

In times past the American craving for definition was constantly fed, but never sated, by a host of foreign visitors who came on errands of inquiry to these shores. Many came to scoff, and some remained to praise; either way, whether sympathetic or censorious, their writings found an avid audience in the United States. Though their perceptions were more or less deeply colored by their preconceptions, the travelers from abroad held up a mirror in which Americans could see themselves as others saw them. The image provoked an occasional flurry of ruffled patriotism, yet on the whole young America's self-esteem was flattered by old Europe's attentions. What was said, even when derogatory, mattered less than the gratifying fact that Europeans found so much to say.

America figured ambiguously in the European imagination. To some onlookers it represented a primitive stage of culture in which the charms of agrarian innocence were mingled with the repugnant features of democratic barbarity. Observers like Mrs. Trollope, wife of the British novelist, were repelled by the adolescent braggadocio and uncultivated manners of rough-cut Jonathans who asserted their equality with any English "gent" by squirting tobacco juice indiscriminantly in public places. To other writers America appeared as Europe's lost paradise: it was the golden land of opportunity, the asylum of liberty, the new Garden of Eden beyond the western sea; its inhabitants, however unrefined their deportment, displayed the rudiments of natural nobility.

These dual versions of the theme of primitivism were linked together in J. Hector St. John de Crèvecoeur's *Letters from an American Farmer,* published in London in 1782. To his celebration of the simple pleasures of farming—the dominant stress of his account—Crèvecoeur coupled a disparaging report on the crudities of the forest frontier where "men appear to be no better than carnivorous animals of a superior rank," together with a horrified indictment of the cruelties of the slave system in the South. Two images stood side by side in striking contrast: in the idyl of innocence, a little boy rides happily upon his father's plow along the "odoriferous furrow"; in the portrait of barbarism, a Negro slave, found guilty of some unnamed offense, hangs caged and dying in the woods while rapacious birds, like Harpies, tear his flesh and peck out his eyes. America was thus depicted as the nearest modern approximation to the original state of nature, itself a highly ambivalent concept.

To numerous observers America prefigured the destiny of Western society: they located its significance in time to come rather than in time gone by. In fact, the primitivist and futurist visions were closely related. As Europe's fresh start, America was the place where the bonds of hoary tradition were relaxed, where the carapace of convention had not yet hardened, where things could be done over and done better. On this virgin ground, uncluttered by the debris of history, a fairer civilization might in time arise—but whether fair or foul, the career of the United States was portentous. Believing that the prospects of Europe were foreshadowed in America, many travelers came to learn what the New World republic was doing, where it was going, and what the Old World might have to hope or fear from its development.

That was why Alexis de Tocqueville, a young French aristocrat, passed several months in the United States in the early 1830s. His report, the two-volume *Democracy in America,* was published in 1835 and 1840. Tocqueville's method was bifocal: he brought to the inquiry a preconception of democracy, fashioned from the experience of France and polarized against an ideal-typical definition of aristocracy; he checked that concept by direct observation of the democratic example of Jacksonian America. Weaving together induction and deduction, he constructed a model of the democratic society; equalitarianism was its governing dogma and equality of conditions its primary attribute. Convinced that democracy was the wave of the future, Tocqueville hoped, by easing its advance in Europe, to forestall further revolutionary upheaval and fortify the elements of liberty against the antagonistic thrust, as he saw it, of the equalitarian principle. Though he was less interested in America for its own sake than in the monitory lessons that Europe might draw from the American record—"America," he remarked, "was only my framework; democracy was the subject"—*Democracy in America* ranks as the classic analysis of American political institutions and national character. The selection groups Tocqueville's reflections on the central themes of individualism and association, conformity and autonomy, mobility and materialism. It is taken from the original translation by the Englishman, Henry Reeve.

A half-century later, James Bryce came from England to survey the maturing American republic, publishing his *The American Commonwealth* in two volumes in 1888. A friendly critic whose judicious appraisal of American politics furnished ammunition for the reform movements of the period, Bryce found much to admire in America. Democracy, though its performance fell somewhat short of its promises, was no longer experimental, and the United States, whatever its defects, had arrived at "the highest level, not only of material well-being but of intelligence and happiness which the race has yet obtained." Insisting on rigorously empirical investigation and sharply critical of writers—Tocqueville among them—who, in his judgment, "preferred abstract speculation to the humble task of ascertaining and weighing the facts," Bryce worked close to the realities of American life. More than most foreigners, he was sensitive to the ways in which a peculiar historical experience had given a singular shape to the American character. Though Bryce's account was less apprehensive as well as less prophetic than Tocqueville's, their major findings ran so nearly parallel that the sagacity of the Frenchman's spacious conjectures was confirmed in important respects by the Englishman's observations.

For the student of American national character much of the value of the writings of Crèvecoeur, Tocqueville, and Bryce resides in their cosmopolitan scope. Each adopted an explicitly comparative method which, if not altogether free from diffractions of vision, gave exceptional clarity to the distinctive contours of American character. They did not disregard the diversities of American society, yet when viewed from a distance those diversities, disproportionately prominent to American eyes, tended to blur into a common form. Perhaps they overstated the elements of uniformity; nevertheless, their trans-national perspective helped to correct the myopia to which Americans, excepting a few (one thinks of Henry Adams, Henry James, and even James Fenimore Cooper) whose experience included a sojourn overseas, were generally subject. That the people of the United States possessed a *national* character these foreign observers had no doubt, and their cosmopolitan outlook lent authority to their descriptions of it.

J. HECTOR ST. JOHN DE CRÈVECOEUR

What Is an American?

I wish I could be acquainted with the feelings and thoughts which must agitate the heart and present themselves to the mind of an enlightened Englishman, when he first lands on this continent. He must greatly rejoice that he lived at a time to see this fair country discovered and settled; he must necessarily feel a share of national pride, when he views the chain of settlements which embellishes these extended shores. When he says to himself, this is the work of my countrymen, who, when convulsed by factions, afflicted by a variety of miseries and wants, restless and impatient, took refuge here. They brought along with them their national genius, to which they principally owe what liberty they enjoy, and what substance they possess. Here he sees the industry of his native country displayed in a new manner, and traces in their works the embrios of all the arts, sciences, and ingenuity which flourish in Europe. Here he beholds fair cities, substantial villages, extensive fields, an immense country filled with decent houses, good roads, orchards, meadows, and bridges, where an hundred years ago all was wild, woody and uncultivated! What a train of pleasing ideas this fair spectacle must suggest; it is a prospect which must inspire a good citizen with the most heartfelt pleasure. The difficulty consists in the manner of viewing so extensive a scene. He is arrived on a new continent; a modern society offers itself to his contemplation, different from what he had hitherto seen. It is not composed, as in Europe, of great lords who possess every thing, and of a herd of people who have nothing. Here are no aristocratical families, no courts, no kings, no bishops, no ecclesiastical dominion, no invisible power giving to a few a very visible one; no great manufacturers employing thousands, no great refinements of luxury. The rich and the poor are not so far removed from each other as they are in Europe. Some few towns excepted, we are all tillers of the earth, from Nova Scotia to West Florida. We are a people of cultivators, scattered over an immense territory, communicating with each other by means of good roads and navigable rivers, united by the silken bands of mild government, all respecting the laws, without dreading their power, because they are equitable. We are all animated with the spirit of an industry which is unfettered and unrestrained, because each person works for himself. If he travels through our rural districts he views not the hostile castle, and the haughty mansion, contrasted with the clay-built hut and miserable cabbin, where cattle and men help to keep each other warm, and dwell in meanness, smoke, and indigence. A pleasing uniformity of decent competence appears throughout our habitations. The meanest of our log-houses is a dry and comfortable habitation. Lawyer or merchant are the fairest titles our towns afford; that of a farmer is the only appellation of the rural inhabitants of our country. It must take some time ere he can reconcile himself to our dictionary, which is but short in words of dignity, and names of honour. There, on a Sunday, he sees a congregation of respectable farmers and their wives, all clad in neat homespun, well mounted, or riding in their own humble waggons. There is not among them an esquire, saving the unlettered magistrate. There he sees a parson as simple as his flock, a farmer who does not riot on the labour of others. We have no princes, for whom we toil, starve, and bleed: we are the most perfect society now existing in the world. Here man is free as he ought to be; nor is this pleasing equality so transitory as many others are. Many ages will not see the shores of our great lakes replenished with inland nations, nor the unknown bounds of North America entirely peopled. Who can tell how far it extends? Who can tell the millions of men whom it will feed and contain? for no European foot has as yet travelled half the extent of this mighty continent!

. . . .

In this great American asylum, the poor of Europe have by some means met together, and in consequence of various causes; to what purpose should they ask one another what countrymen they are? Alas, two thirds of them had no country. Can a wretch who wanders about, who works and starves, whose life is a continual scene of sore affliction or pinching penury; can that man call England or any other kingdom his country? A country that had no bread for him, whose fields procured him no harvest, who met with nothing but the frowns of the rich, the severity of the laws, with jails and punishments; who owned not a single foot of the extensive surface of this planet? No! urged by a variety of motives, here they came. Every thing has tended to regenerate them; new laws, a new mode of living, a new social system; here they are become men: in Europe they were as so many useless plants, wanting vegetative mould, and refreshing showers; they withered, and were mowed down by want, hunger, and war; but now by the power of transplantation, like all other plants they have taken root and flourished! Formerly they were not numbered in any civil lists of their country, except in those of the poor; here they rank as citizens. By what invisible power has this surprising metamorphosis been performed? By that of the laws and that of their industry. The laws, the indulgent laws, protect them as they arrive, stamping on them the symbol of adoption; they receive ample rewards for their labours; these accumulated rewards procure them lands; those lands confer on them the title of freemen, and to that title every benefit is affixed which men can possibly require. This is the great operation daily performed by our laws. From whence proceed these laws? From our government. Whence the government? It is derived from the original genius and strong desire of the people.

. . . .

What attachment can a poor European emigrant have for a country where he had nothing? The knowledge of the language, the love of a few kindred as poor as himself, were the only cords that tied him: his country is now that which gives him land, bread, protection, and consequence: *Ubi panis ibi patria,* is the motto of all emigrants. What then is the American, this new man? He is either an European, or the descendant of an European, hence that strange mixture of blood, which you will find in no other country. I could point out to you a family whose grandfather was an Englishman, whose wife was Dutch, whose son married a French woman, and whose present four sons have now four wives of different nations. *He* is an American, who leaving behind him all his ancient prejudices and manners, receives new ones from the new mode of life he has embraced, the new government he obeys, and the new rank he holds. He becomes an American by being received in the broad lap of our great *Alma Mater.* Here individuals of all nations are melted into a new race of men, whose labours and posterity will one day cause great changes in the world. Americans are the western pilgrims, who are carrying along with them that great mass of arts, sciences, vigour, and industry which began long since in the east; they will finish the great circle. The Americans were once scattered all over Europe; here they are incorporated into one of the finest systems of population which has ever appeared, and which will hereafter become distinct by the power of the different climates they inhabit. The American ought therefore to love this country much better than that wherein either he or his forefathers were born. Here the rewards of his industry follow with equal steps the progress of his labour; his labour is founded on the basis of nature, *self-interest;* can it want a stronger allurement? Wives and children, who before in vain demanded of him a morsel of bread, now, fat and frolicsome, gladly help their father to clear those fields whence exuberant crops are to arise to feed and to clothe them all; without any part being claimed, either by a despotic prince, a rich abbot, or a mighty lord. Here religion demands but little of him; a small voluntary salary to the minister, and gratitude to God; can he refuse these? The American is a new man, who acts upon new principles; he must therefore entertain new ideas, and form new opinions. From involuntary idleness, servile dependence, penury, and useless labour, he has passed to toils of a very different nature, rewarded by ample subsistence.—This is an American.

. . . .

Men are like plants; the goodness and flavour of the fruit proceeds from the peculiar soil and exposition in which they grow. We are nothing but what we derive from the air we breathe, the climate we inhabit, the government we obey, the system of religion we profess, and the nature of our employment. . . .

Those who live near the sea, feed more on fish than on flesh, and often encounter that boisterous element. This renders them more bold and enterprising; this leads them to neglect the confined occupations of the land. They see and converse with a variety of people; their intercourse with mankind becomes extensive. The sea inspires them with a love of traffic, a desire of transporting produce from one place to another; and leads them to a variety of resources which supply the place of labour. Those who inhabit the middle settlements, by far the most numerous, must be very different; the simple cultivation of the earth purifies them, but the indulgences of the government, the soft remonstrances of religion, the rank of independent freeholders, must necessarily inspire them with sentiments, very little known in Europe among people of the same class. What do I say? Europe has no such class of men; the early knowledge they acquire, the early bargains they make, give them a great degree of sagacity. As freemen they will be litigious; pride and obstinacy are often the cause of law suits; the nature of our laws and governments may be another. As citizens it is easy to imagine, that they will carefully read the newspapers, enter into every political disquisition, freely blame or censure governors and others. As farmers they will be careful and anxious to get as much as they can, because what they get is their own. As northern men they will love the chearful cup. As Christians, religion curbs them not in their opinions; the general indulgence leaves every one to think for themselves in spiritual matters; the laws inspect our actions, our thoughts are left to God. Industry, good living, selfishness, litigiousness, country politics, the pride of freemen, religious indifference, are their characteristics. If you recede still farther from the sea, you will come into more modern settlements; they exhibit the same strong lineaments, in a ruder appearance. Religion seems to have still less influence, and their manners are less improved.

Now we arrive near the great woods, near the last inhabited districts; there men seem to be placed still farther beyond the reach of government, which in some measure leaves them to themselves. How can it pervade every corner; as they were driven there by misfortunes, necessity of beginnings, desire of acquiring large tracks of land, idleness, frequent want of œconomy, ancient debts; the re-union of such people does not afford a very pleasing spectacle. When discord, want of unity and friendship; when either drunkenness or idleness prevail in such remote districts; contention, inactivity, and wretchedness must ensue. There are not the same remedies to these evils as in a long established community. The few magistrates they have, are in general little better than the rest; they are often in a perfect state of war; that of man against man, sometimes decided by blows, sometimes by means of the law; that of man against every wild inhabitant of these venerable woods, of which they are come to dispossess them. There men appear to be no better than carnivorous animals of a superior rank, living on the flesh of wild animals when they can catch them, and when they are not able, they subsist on grain. He who would wish to see America in its proper light, and have a true idea of its feeble beginnings and barbarous rudiments, must visit our extended line of frontiers where the last settlers dwell, and where he may see the first labours of settlement, the mode of clearing the earth, in all their different appearances; where men are wholly left dependent on their native tempers, and on the spur of uncertain industry, which often fails when not sanctified by the efficacy of a few moral rules. There, remote from the power of example, and check of shame, many families exhibit the most hideous parts of our society. They are a kind of forlorn hope, preceding by ten or twelve years the most respectable army of veterans which come after them. In that space, prosperity will polish some, vice and the law will drive off the rest, who uniting again with others like themselves will recede still farther; making room for more industrious people, who will finish their improvements, convert the loghouse into a convenient habitation, and rejoicing that the first heavy labours are finished, will change in a few years that hitherto barbarous country into a fine fertile, well regulated district. Such is our progress, such is the march of the Europeans toward the interior parts of this continent. In all societies there are off-casts; this impure part serves as our precursors or pioneers; my father himself was one of that class, but he came upon honest principles, and was therefore one of the few who held fast; by good conduct and temperance, he transmitted to me his fair inheritance, when not above one in fourteen of his contemporaries had the same good fortune.

Forty years ago this smiling country was thus inhabited; it is now purged, a general decency of manners prevails throughout, and such has been the fate of our best countries.

Exclusive of those general characteristics, each province has its own, founded on the government, climate, mode of husbandry, customs, and peculiarity of circumstances. Europeans submit insensibly to these great powers, and become, in the course of a few generations, not only Americans in general, but either Pennsylvanians, Virginians, or provincials under some other name. Whoever traverses the continent must easily observe those strong differences, which will grow more evident in time. The inhabitants of Canada, Massachuset, the middle provinces, the southern ones will be as different as their climates; their only points of unity will be those of religion and language.

. . . .

There is no wonder that this country has so many charms, and presents to Europeans so many temptations to remain in it. A traveller in Europe becomes a stranger as soon as he quits his own kingdom; but it is otherwise here. We know, properly speaking, no strangers; this is every person's country; the variety of our soils, situations, climates, governments, and produce, hath something which must please every body. No sooner does an European arrive, no matter of what condition, than his eyes are opened upon the fair prospect; he hears his language spoke, he retraces many of his own country manners, he perpetually hears the names of families and towns with which he is acquainted; he sees happiness and prosperity in all places disseminated; he meets with hospitality, kindness, and plenty every where; he beholds hardly any poor, he seldom hears of punishments and executions; and he wonders at the elegance of our towns, those miracles of industry and freedom. He cannot admire enough our rural districts, our convenient roads, good taverns, and our many accommodations; he involuntarily loves a country where every thing is so lovely. When in England, he was a mere Englishman; here he stands on a larger portion of the globe, not less than its fourth part, and may see the productions of the north, in iron and naval stores; the provisions of Ireland, the grain of Egypt, the indigo, the rice of China. He does not find, as in Europe, a crouded society, where every place is over-stocked; he does not feel that perpetual collision of parties, that difficulty of beginning, that contention which oversets so many. There is room for every body in America; has he any particular talent, or industry? he exerts it in order to procure a livelihood, and it succeeds. Is he a merchant? the avenues of trade are infinite; is he eminent in any respect? he will be employed and respected. Does he love a country life? pleasant farms present themselves; he may purchase what he wants, and thereby become an American farmer. Is he a labourer, sober and industrious? he need not go many miles, nor receive many informations before he will be hired, well fed at the table of his employer, and paid four or five times more than he can get in Europe. Does he want uncultivated lands? thousands of acres present themselves, which he may purchase cheap. Whatever be his talents or inclinations, if they are moderate, he may satisfy them. I do not mean that every one who comes will grow rich in a little time; no, but he may procure an easy, decent maintenance, by his industry. Instead of starving he will be fed, instead of being idle he will have employment; and these are riches enough for such men as come over here. The rich stay in Europe, it is only the middling and the poor that emigrate. Would you wish to travel in independent idleness, from north to south, you will find easy access, and the most chearful reception at every house; society without ostentation, good cheer without pride, and every decent diversion which the country affords, with little expence. It is no wonder that the European who has lived here a few years, is desirous to remain; Europe with all its pomp, is not to be compared to this continent, for men of middle stations, or labourers.

An European, when he first arrives, seems limited in his intentions, as well as in his views; but he very suddenly alters his scale; two hundred miles formerly appeared a very great distance, it is now but a trifle; he no sooner breathes our air than he forms schemes, and embarks in designs he never would have thought of in his own country. There the plenitude of society confines many useful ideas, and often extinguishes the most laudable schemes which here ripen into maturity. Thus Europeans become Americans.

ALEXIS DE TOCQUEVILLE

Democracy in America

Introduction

Among the novel objects that attracted my attention during my stay in the United States, nothing struck me more forcibly than the general equality of conditions. I readily discovered the prodigious influence which this primary fact exercises on the whole course of society, by giving a certain direction to public opinion, and a certain tenor to the laws; by imparting new maxims to the governing powers, and peculiar habits to the governed. I speedily perceived that the influence of this fact extends far beyond the political character and the laws of the country, and that it has no less empire over civil society than over the Government; it creates opinions, engenders sentiments, suggests the ordinary practices of life, and modifies whatever it does not produce. The more I advanced in the study of American society, the more I perceived that the equality of conditions is the fundamental fact from which all others seem to be derived, and the central point at which all my observations constantly terminated.

. . . .

It is evident to all alike that a great democratic revolution is going on among us; but there are two opinions as to its nature and consequences. To some it appears to be a novel accident, which as such may still be checked; to others it seems irresistible, because it is the most uniform, the most ancient, and the most permanent tendency which is to be found in history. . . .

. . . .

. . . Gradually the . . . ranks mingle; the divisions which once severed mankind are lowered; property is divided, power is held in common, the light of intelligence spreads, and the capacities of all classes are equally cultivated; the State becomes democratic, and the empire of democracy is slowly and peaceably introduced into the institutions and the manners of the nation. I can conceive a society in which all men would profess an equal attachment and respect for the laws of which they are the common authors; in which the authority of the State would be respected as necessary, though not as divine; and the loyalty of the subject to the chief magistrate would not be a passion, but a quiet and rational persuasion. Every individual being in the possession of rights which he is sure to retain, a kind of manly reliance and reciprocal courtesy would arise between all classes, alike removed from pride and meanness. The people, well acquainted with its true interests, would allow that in order to profit by the advantages of society it is necessary to satisfy its demands. In this state of things the voluntary association of the citizens might supply the individual exertions of the nobles, and the community would be alike protected from anarchy and from oppression.

I admit that, in a democratic State thus constituted, society will not be stationary; but the impulses of the social body may be regulated and directed forward; if there be less splendour than in the halls of an aristocracy, the contrast of misery will be less frequent also; the pleasures of enjoyment may be less excessive, but those of comfort will be more general; the sciences may be less perfectly cultivated, but ignorance will be less common; the impetuosity of the feelings will be repressed, and the habits of the nation softened; there will be more vices and fewer crimes. In the absence of enthusiasm and of an ardent faith, great sacrifices may be obtained from the members of a commonwealth by an appeal to their understandings and their experience; each individual will feel the same necessity for uniting with his fellow-citizens to protect his own weakness; and as he knows that if they are to assist he must co-operate, he will readily perceive that his personal interest is identified with the interest of the community. The nation, taken as a whole, will be less brilliant, less glorious, and perhaps less strong; but the majority of the citizens will enjoy a greater degree of prosperity, and the people will remain quiet, not because it despairs of amelioration, but because it is conscious of the advantages of its condition. If all the consequences of this state of things were not good or useful, society would at least have appropriated all such as were useful and good; and having once and forever renounced the social advantages of aristocracy, mankind would enter into possession of all the benefits which democracy can afford.

. . . .

. . . I confess that in America I saw more than America; I sought the image of democracy itself, with its inclinations, its character, its prejudices, and its passions, in order to learn what we have to fear or to hope from its progress.

Individualism and Association

I have shown how it is that in ages of equality every man seeks for his opinions within himself: I am now about to show how it is that, in the same ages, all his feelings are turned toward himself alone. Individualism is a novel expression, to which a novel idea has given birth. Our fathers were only acquainted with egotism. Egotism is a passionate and exaggerated love of self, which leads a man to connect everything with his own person, and to prefer himself to everything in the world. Individualism is a mature and calm feeling, which disposes each member of the community to sever himself from the mass of his fellow-creatures; and to draw apart with his family and his friends; so that, after he has thus formed a little circle of his own, he willingly leaves society at large to itself. Egotism originates in blind instinct: individualism proceeds from erroneous judgment more than from depraved feelings; it originates as much in the deficiencies of the mind as in the perversity of the heart. Egotism blights the germ of all virtue; individualism, at first, only saps the virtues of public life; but, in the long run, it attacks and destroys all others, and is at length absorbed in downright egotism. Egotism is a vice as old as the world, which does not belong to one form of society more than to another: individualism is of democratic origin, and it threatens to spread in the same ratio as the equality of conditions.

Among aristocratic nations, as families remain for centuries in the same condition, often on the same spot, all generations become, as it were, contemporaneous. A man almost always knows his forefathers, and respects them: he thinks he already sees his remote descendants, and he loves them. He willingly imposes duties on himself toward the former and the latter; and he will frequently sacrifice his personal gratifications to those who went before and to those who will come after him. Aristocratic institutions have, moreover, the effect of closely binding every man to several of his fellow-citizens. As the classes of an aristocratic people are strongly marked and permanent, each of them is regarded by its own members as a sort of lesser country, more tangible and more cherished than the country at large. As in aristocratic communities all the citizens occupy fixed positions, one above the other, the result is that each of them always sees a man above himself whose patronage is necessary to him, and below himself another man whose co-operation he may claim. Men living in aristocratic ages are therefore almost always closely attached to something placed out of their own sphere, and they are often disposed to forget themselves. It is true that in those ages the notion of human fellowship is faint, and that men seldom think of sacrificing themselves for mankind; but they often sacrifice themselves for other men. In democratic ages, on the contrary, when the duties of each individual to the race are much more clear, devoted service to any one man becomes more rare; the bond of human affection is extended, but it is relaxed.

Among democratic nations new families are constantly springing up, others are constantly falling away, and all that remain change their condition; the woof of time is every instant broken, and the track of generations effaced. Those who went before are soon forgotten; of those who will come after no one has any idea: the interest of man is confined to those in close propinquity to himself. As each class approximates to other classes, and intermingles with them, its members become indifferent and as strangers to one another. Aristocracy had made a chain of all the members of the community, from the peasant to the king: democracy breaks that chain, and severs every link of it. As social conditions become more equal, the number of persons increases who, although they are neither rich enough nor powerful enough to exercise any great influence over their fellow-creatures, have nevertheless acquired or retained sufficient education and fortune to satisfy their own wants. They owe nothing to any man, they expect nothing from any man; they acquire the habit of always considering themselves as standing alone, and they are apt to imagine that their whole destiny is in their own hands. Thus not only does democracy make every man forget his ancestors, but it hides his descendants, and separates his contemporaries from him; it throws him back forever upon himself alone, and threatens in the end to confine him entirely within the solitude of his own heart.

. . . .

The Americans have combated by free institutions the tendency of equality to keep men asunder, and they have subdued it. The legislators of America did not suppose that a general representation of the whole nation would suffice to ward off a disorder at once so natural to the frame of democratic society, and so fatal: they also thought that it would be well to infuse political life into each portion of the territory, in order to multiply to an infinite extent opportunities of acting in concert for all the members of the community, and to make them constantly feel their mutual dependence on each other. The plan was a wise one. The general affairs of a country only engage the attention of leading politicians, who assemble from time to time in the same places; and as they often lose sight of each other afterward, no lasting ties are established between them. But if the object be to have the local affairs of a district conducted by the men who reside there, the same persons are always in contact, and they are, in a manner, forced to be acquainted, and to adapt themselves to one another.

It is difficult to draw a man out of his own circle to interest him in the destiny of the state, because he does not clearly understand what influence the destiny of the state can have upon his own lot. But if it be proposed to make a road across the end of his estate, he will see at a glance that there is a connection between this small public affair and his greatest private affairs; and he will discover, without its being shown to him, the close tie which unites private to general interest. Thus, far more may be done by intrusting to the citizens the administration of minor affairs than by surrendering to them the control of important ones, toward interesting them in the public welfare, and convincing them that they constantly stand in need one of the other in order to provide for it. A brilliant achievement may win for you the favour of a people at one stroke; but to earn the love and respect of the population which surrounds you, a long succession of little services rendered and of obscure good deeds—a constant habit of kindness, and an established reputation for disinterestedness—will be required. Local freedom, then, which leads a great number of citizens to value the affection of their neighbours and of their kindred, perpetually brings men together, and forces them to help one another, in spite of the propensities which sever them.

In the United States the more opulent citizens take great care not to stand aloof from the people; on the contrary, they constantly keep on easy terms with the lower classes: they listen to them, they speak to them every day. They know that the rich in democracies always stand in need of the poor; and that in democratic ages you attach a poor man to you more by your manner than by benefits conferred. The magnitude of such benefits, which sets off the difference of conditions, causes a secret irritation to those who reap advantage from them; but the charm of simplicity of manners is almost irresistible: their affability carries men away, and even their want of polish is not always displeasing. This truth does not take root at once in the minds of the rich. They generally resist it as long as the democratic revolution lasts, and they do not acknowledge it immediately after that revolution is accomplished. They are very ready to do good to the people, but they still choose to keep them at arm's length; they think that is sufficient, but they are mistaken. They might spend fortunes thus without warming the hearts of the population around them—that population does not ask them for the sacrifice of their money, but of their pride.

It would seem as if every imagination in the United States were upon the stretch to invent means of increasing the wealth and satisfying the wants of the public. The best-informed inhabitants of each district constantly use their information to discover new truths which may augment the general prosperity; and if they have made any such discoveries, they eagerly surrender them to the mass of the people.

. . . .

It would be unjust to suppose that the patriotism and the zeal that every American displays for the welfare of his fellow-citizens are wholly insincere. Although private interest directs the greater part of human actions in the United States as well as elsewhere, it does not regulate them all. I must say that I have often seen Americans make great and real sacrifices to the public welfare; and I have remarked a hundred instances in which they hardly ever failed to lend faithful support to each other. The free institutions which the inhabitants of the United States possess, and the political rights of which they make so much use, remind every citizen, and in a thousand ways, that he lives in society. They every instant impress upon his mind the notion that it is the duty, as well as the interest of men, to make themselves useful to their fellow-creatures; and as he sees no particular ground of animosity to them, since he is never either their master or their slave, his heart readily leans to the side of kindness. Men attend to the interests of the public, first by necessity, afterward by choice: what was intentional becomes an instinct; and by dint of working for the good of one's fellow-citizens, the habit and the taste for serving them is at length acquired.

. . . .

. . . Americans of all ages, all conditions, and all dispositions, constantly form associations. They have not only commercial and manufacturing companies, in which all take part, but associations of a thousand other kinds—religious, moral, serious, futile, extensive or restricted, enormous or diminutive. The Americans make associations to give entertainments, to found establishments for education, to build inns, to construct churches, to diffuse books, to send missionaries to the antipodes; and in this manner they founded hospitals, prisons, and schools. If it be proposed to advance some truth, or to foster some feeling by the encouragement of a great example, they form a society. Wherever, at the head of some new undertaking, you see the Government in France, or a man of rank in England, in the United States you will be sure to find an association. . . .

. . . Aristocratic communities always contain, among a multitude of persons who by themselves are powerless, a small number of powerful and wealthy citizens, each of whom can achieve great undertakings single-handed. In aristocratic societies men do not need to combine in order to act, because they are strongly held together. Every wealthy and powerful citizen constitutes the head of a permanent and compulsory association, composed of all those who are dependent upon him, or whom he makes subservient to the execution of his designs. Among democratic nations, on the contrary, all the citizens are independent and feeble; they can do hardly anything by themselves, and none of them can oblige his fellow-men to lend him their assistance. They all, therefore, fall into a state of incapacity, if they do not learn voluntarily to help each other. If men living in democratic countries had no right and no inclination to associate for political purposes, their independence would be in great jeopardy; but they might long preserve their wealth and their cultivation: whereas if they never acquired the habit of forming associations in ordinary life, civilization itself would be endangered. A people among whom individuals should lose the power of achieving great things single-handed, without acquiring the means of producing them by united exertions, would soon relapse into barbarism.

. . . .

Feelings and opinions are recruited, the heart is enlarged, and the human mind is developed by no other means than by the reciprocal influence of men upon each other. I have shown that these influences are almost null in democratic countries; they must therefore be artificially created, and this can only be accomplished by associations.

When the members of an aristocratic community adopt a new opinion, or conceive a new sentiment, they give it a station, as it were, beside themselves, upon the lofty platform where they stand; and opinions or sentiments so conspicuous to the eyes of the multitude are easily introduced into the minds or hearts of all around. In democratic countries the governing power alone is naturally in a condition to act in this manner; but it is easy to see that its action is always inadequate, and often dangerous. A government can no more be competent to keep alive and to renew the circulation of opinions and feelings among a great people than to manage all the speculations of productive industry. No sooner does a government attempt to go beyond its political sphere and to enter upon this new track, than it exercises, even unintentionally, an insupportable tyranny; for a government can only dictate strict rules, the opinions which it favours are rigidly enforced, and it is never easy to discriminate between its advice and its commands. Worse still will be the case if the government really believes itself interested in preventing all circulation of ideas; it will then stand motionless, and oppressed by the heaviness of voluntary torpor. Governments, therefore, should not be the only active powers: associations ought, in democratic nations, to stand in lieu of those powerful private individuals whom the equality of conditions has swept away.

As soon as several of the inhabitants of the United States have taken up an opinion or a feeling that they wish to promote in the world, they look out for mutual assistance; and as soon as they have found each other out, they combine. From that moment they are no longer isolated men, but a power seen from afar, whose actions serve for an example, and whose language is listened to. The first time I heard in the United States that a hundred thousand men had bound themselves publicly to abstain from spirituous liquors, it appeared to me more like a joke than a serious engagement; and I did not at once perceive why these temperate citizens could not content themselves with drinking water by their own firesides. I at last understood that three hundred thousand Americans, alarmed by the progress of drunkenness around them, had made up their minds to patronize temperance. They acted just in the same way as a man of high rank who should dress very plainly, in order to inspire the humbler orders with a contempt of luxury. It is probable that if these hundred thousand men had lived in France, each of them would singly have memorialized the government to watch the public-houses all over the kingdom.

Nothing, in my opinion, is more deserving of our attention than the intellectual and moral associations of America. The political and industrial associations of that country strike us forcibly; but the others elude our observation, or if we discover them, we understand them imperfectly, because we have hardly ever seen anything of the kind. It must, however, be acknowledged that they are as necessary to the American people as the former, and perhaps more so. In democratic countries the science of association is the mother of science; the progress of all the rest depends upon the progress it has made. Among the laws that rule human societies there is one that seems to be more precise and clear than all others. If men are to remain civilized, or to become so, the art of associating together must grow and improve in the same ratio in which the equality of conditions is increased.

. . . .

Democracy does not attach men strongly to each other; but it places their habitual intercourse upon an easier footing. If two Englishmen chance to meet at the Antipodes, where they are surrounded by strangers whose language and manners are almost unknown to them, they will first stare at each other with much curiosity and a kind of secret uneasiness; they will then turn away, or, if one accosts the other, they will take care only to converse with a constrained and absent air upon very unimportant subjects. Yet there is no enmity between these men; they have never seen each other before, and each believes the other to be a respectable person. Why, then, should they stand so cautiously apart? We must go back to England to learn the reason.

When it is birth alone, independent of wealth, which classes men in society, every one knows exactly what his own position is upon the social scale; he does not seek to rise, he does not fear to sink. In a community thus organized, men of different castes communicate very little with each other; but if accident brings them together, they are ready to converse without hoping or fearing to lose their own position. Their intercourse is not upon a footing of equality, but it is not constrained. When moneyed aristocracy succeeds to aristocracy of birth, the case is altered. The privileges of some are still extremely great, but the possibility of acquiring those privileges is open to all: whence it follows that those who possess them are constantly haunted by the apprehension of losing them, or of other men's sharing them; those who do not yet enjoy them long to possess them at any cost, or, if they fail, to appear at least to possess them—which is not impossible. As the social importance of men is no longer ostensibly and permanently fixed by blood, and is infinitely varied by wealth, ranks still exist, but it is not easy clearly to distinguish at a glance those who respectively belong to them. Secret hostilities then arise in the community; one set of men endeavour by innumerable artifices to penetrate, or to appear to penetrate, among those who are above them; another set are constantly in arms against these usurpers of their rights; or rather the same individual does both at once, and while he seeks to raise himself into a higher circle, he is always on the defensive against the intrusion of those below him.

Such is the condition of England at the present time; and I am of opinion that the peculiarity before adverted to is principally to be attributed to this cause. An aristocratic pride is still extremely great among the English, and as the limits of aristocracy are ill defined, everybody lives in constant dread lest advantage should be taken of his familiarity. Unable to judge at once of the social position of those he meets, an Englishman prudently avoids all contact with them. Men are afraid lest some slight service rendered should draw them into an unsuitable acquaintance; they dread civilities, and they avoid the obtrusive gratitude of a stranger quite as much as his hatred. Many people attribute these singular anti-social propensities, and the reserved and taciturn bearing of the English, to purely physical causes. I may admit that there is something of it in their race, but much more of it is attributable to their social condition, as is proved by the contrast of the Americans.

In America, where the privileges of birth never existed, and where riches confer no peculiar rights on their possessors, men unacquainted with each other are very ready to frequent the same places, and find neither peril nor advantage in the free interchange of their thoughts. If they meet by accident, they neither seek nor avoid intercourse; their manner is therefore natural, frank, and open: it is easy to see that they hardly expect or apprehend anything from each other, and that they do not care to display, any more than to conceal, their position in the world. If their demeanour is often cold and serious, it is never haughty or constrained; and if they do not converse, it is because they are not in a humour to talk, not because they think it their interest to be silent. In a foreign country two Americans are at once friends, simply because they are Americans. They are repulsed by no prejudice; they are attracted by their common country. For two Englishmen the same blood is not enough; they must be brought together by the same rank. The Americans remark this unsociable mood of the English as much as the French do, and they are not less astonished by it. . . .

. . . .

It has been universally remarked that in our time the several members of a family stand upon an entirely new footing toward each other; that the distance which formerly separated a father from his sons has been lessened; and that paternal authority, if not destroyed, is at least impaired. Something analogous to this, but even more striking, may be observed in the United States. In America the family, in the Roman and aristocratic signification of the word, does not exist. All that remains of it are a few vestiges in the first years of childhood, when the father exercises, without opposition, that absolute domestic authority which the feebleness of his children renders necessary, and which their interest, as well as his own incontestable superiority, warrants. But as soon as the young American approaches manhood, the ties of filial obedience are relaxed day by day: master of his thoughts, he is soon master of his conduct. In America there is, strictly speaking, no adolescence: at the close of boyhood the man appears, and begins to trace out his own path. It would be an error to suppose that this is preceded by a domestic struggle, in which the son has obtained by a sort of moral violence the liberty that his father refused him. The same habits, the same principles which impel the one to assert his independence, predispose the other to consider the use of that independence as an incontestable right. The former does not exhibit any of those rancorous or irregular passions which disturb men long after they have shaken off an established authority; the latter feels none of that bitter and angry regret which is apt to survive a by-gone power. The father foresees the limits of his authority long beforehand, and when the time arrives he surrenders it without a struggle: the son looks forward to the exact period at which he will be his own master; and he enters upon his freedom without precipitation and without effort, as a possession which is his own and which no one seeks to wrest from him.

It may perhaps not be without utility to show how these changes which take place in family relations are closely connected with the social and political revolution which is approaching its consummation under our own observation. There are certain great social principles which a people either introduces everywhere or tolerates nowhere. In countries which are aristocratically constituted with all the gradations of rank, the Government never makes a direct appeal to the mass of the governed: as men are united together, it is enough to lead the foremost; the rest will follow. This is equally applicable to the family, as to all aristocracies which have a head. Among aristocratic nations, social institutions recognize, in truth, no one in the family but the father; children are received by society at his hands; society governs him, he governs them. Thus the parent has not only a natural right, but he acquires a political right, to command them: he is the author and the support of his family; but he is also its constituted ruler. In democracies, where the government picks out every individual singly from the mass, to make him subservient to the general laws of the community, no such intermediate person is required: a father is there, in the eye of the law, only a member of the community, older and richer than his sons.

When most of the conditions of life are extremely unequal, and the inequality of these conditions is permanent, the notion of a superior grows upon the imaginations of men: if the law invested him with no privileges, custom and public opinion would concede them. When, on the contrary, men differ but little from each other, and do not always remain in dissimilar conditions of life, the general notion of a superior becomes weaker and less distinct: it is vain for legislation to strive to place him who obeys very much beneath him who commands; the manners of the time bring the two men nearer to one another, and draw them daily toward the same level. . . .

When men live more for the remembrance of what has been than for the care of what is, and when they are more given to attend to what their ancestors thought than to think themselves, the father is the natural and necessary tie between the past and the present—the link by which the ends of these two chains are connected. In aristocracies, then, the father is not only the civil head of the family, but the oracle of its traditions, the expounder of its customs, the arbiter of its manners. He is listened to with deference, he is addressed with respect, and the love which is felt for him is always tempered with fear. When the condition of society becomes democratic, and men adopt as their general principle that it is good and lawful to judge of all things for one's self, using former points of belief not as a rule of faith but simply as a means of information, the power which the opinions of a father exercise over those of his sons diminishes as well as his legal power.

. . . .

Thus, at the same time that the power of aristocracy is declining, the austere, the conventional, and the legal part of parental authority vanishes, and a species of equality prevails around the domestic hearth. I know not, upon the whole, whether society loses by the change, but I am inclined to believe that man individually is a gainer by it. I think that, in proportion as manners and laws become more democratic, the relation of father and son becomes more intimate and more affectionate; rules and authority are less talked of; confidence and tenderness are oftentimes increased, and it would seem that the natural bond is drawn closer in proportion as the social bond is loosened. In a democratic family the father exercises no other power than that with which men love to invest the affection and the experience of age; his orders would perhaps be disobeyed, but his advice is for the most part authoritative. Though he be not hedged in with ceremonial respect, his sons at least accost him with confidence; no settled form of speech is appropriated to the mode of addressing him, but they speak to him constantly, and are ready to consult him day by day; the master and the constituted ruler have vanished—the father remains. Nothing more is needed, in order to judge of the difference between the two states of society in this respect, than to peruse the family correspondence of aistocratic ages. The style is always correct, ceremonious, stiff, and so cold that the natural warmth of the heart can hardly be felt in the language. The language, on the contrary, addressed by a son to his father in democratic countries is always marked by mingled freedom, familiarity, and affection, which at once show that new relations have sprung up in the bosom of the family.

A similar revolution takes place in the mutual relations of children. In aristocratic families, as well as in aristocratic society, every place is marked out beforehand. Not only does the father occupy a separate rank, in which he enjoys extensive privileges, but even the children are not equal among themselves. The age and sex of each irrevocably determine his rank, and secure to him certain privileges: most of these distinctions are abolished or diminished by democracy....

...Under democratic laws all the children are perfectly equal, and consequently independent: nothing brings them forcibly together, but nothing keeps them apart; and as they have the same origin, as they are trained under the same roof, as they are treated with the same care, and as no peculiar privilege distinguishes or divides them, the affectionate and youthful intimacy of early years easily springs up between them. Scarcely any opportunities occur to break the tie thus formed at the outset of life; for their brotherhood brings them daily together, without embarrassing them. It is not, then, by interest, but by common associations and by the free sympathy of opinion and of taste, that democracy unites brothers to each other. It divides their inheritance, but it allows their hearts and minds to mingle together....

Conformity and Autonomy

I know no country in which there is so little true independence of mind and freedom of discussion as in America. In any constitutional state in Europe every sort of religious and political theory may be advocated and propagated abroad; for there is no country in Europe so subdued by any single authority as not to contain citizens who are ready to protect the man who raises his voice in the cause of truth from the consequences of his hardihood. If he is unfortunate enough to live under an absolute government, the people is upon his side; if he inhabits a free country, he may find a shelter behind the authority of the throne, if he require one. The aristocratic part of society supports him in some countries, and the democracy in others. But in a nation where democratic institutions exist, organized like those of the United States, there is but one sole authority, one single element of strength and of success, with nothing beyond it.

In America, the majority raises very formidable barriers to the liberty of opinion: within these barriers an author may write whatever he pleases, but he will repent it if he ever step beyond them. Not that he is exposed to the terrors of an auto-da-fé, but he is tormented by the slights and persecutions of daily obloquy. His political career is closed forever, since he has offended the only authority which is able to promote his success. Every sort of compensation, even that of celebrity, is refused to him. Before he published his opinions he imagined that he held them in common with many others; but no sooner has he declared them openly than he is loudly censured by his overbearing opponents, while those who think like him, without having the courage to speak, abandon him in silence. He yields at length, oppressed by the daily efforts he has been making, and he subsides into silence, as if he was tormented by remorse for having spoken the truth.

Fetters and headsmen were the coarse instruments which tyranny formerly employed; but the civilization of our age has refined the arts of despotism, which seemed, however, to have been sufficiently perfected before. The excesses of monarchical power had devised a variety of physical means of oppression: the democratic republics of the present day have rendered it as entirely an affair of the mind as that will which it is intended to coerce. Under the absolute sway of an individual despot the body was attacked in order to subdue the soul, and the soul escaped the blows which were directed against it and rose superior to the attempt; but such is not the course adopted by tyranny in democratic republics; there the body is left free, and the soul is enslaved. The sovereign can no longer say, "You shall think as I do on pain of death"; but he says: "You are free to think differently from me, and to retain your life, your property, and all that you possess; but if such be your determination, you are henceforth an alien among your people. . . ."

. . . .

If great writers have not at present existed in America, the reason is very simply given in these facts; there can be no literary genius without freedom of opinion, and freedom of opinion does not exist in America. The Inquisition never has been able to prevent a vast number of anti-religious books from circulating in Spain. The empire of the majority succeeds much better in the United States, since it actually removes the wish of publishing them. Unbelievers are to be met with in America, but, to say the truth, there is no public organ of infidelity. Attempts have been made by some governments to protect the morality of nations by prohibiting licentious books. In the United States no one is punished for this sort of works, but no one is induced to write them; not because all the citizens are immaculate in their manners, but because the majority of the community is decent and orderly.

In these cases the advantages derived from the exercise of this power are unquestionable, and I am simply discussing the nature of the power itself. This irresistible authority is a constant fact, and its judicious exercise is an accidental occurrence.

The tendencies to which I have just alluded are as yet very slightly perceptible in political society, but they already begin to exercise an unfavourable influence upon the national character of the Americans. I am inclined to attribute the singular paucity of distinguished political characters to the ever-increasing activity of the despotism of the majority in the United States. . . .

. . . .

In that immense crowd which throngs the avenues to power in the United States I found very few men who displayed any of that manly candour and that masculine independence of opinion which frequently distinguished the Americans in former times, and which constitutes the leading feature in distinguished characters, wheresoever they may be found. It seems, at first sight, as if all the minds of the Americans were formed upon one model, so accurately do they correspond in their manner of judging. . . .

. . . .

. . . In the ages of aristocracy which preceded our own, there were private persons of great power, and a social authority of extreme weakness. The outline of society itself was not easily discernible, and constantly confounded with the different powers by which the community was ruled. The principal efforts of the men of those times were required to strengthen, aggrandize, and secure the supreme power; and, on the other hand, to circumscribe individual independence within narrower limits, and to subject private interests to the interests of the public. Other perils and other cares await the men of our age. Among the greater part of modern nations, the government, whatever may be its origin, its constitution, or its name, has become almost omnipotent, and private persons are falling, more and more, into the lowest stage of weakness and dependence. In olden society everything was different; unity and uniformity were nowhere to be met with. In modern society everything threatens to become so much alike, that the peculiar characteristics of each individual will soon be entirely lost in the general aspect of the world. Our forefathers were ever prone to make an improper use of the notion that private rights ought to be respected; and we are naturally prone, on the other hand, to exaggerate the idea that the interest of a private individual ought always to bend to the interest of the many. . . .

. . . .

I think that in no country in the civilized world is less attention paid to philosophy than in the United States. The Americans have no philosophical school of their own; and they care but little for all the schools into which Europe is divided, the very names of which are scarcely known to them. Nevertheless it is easy to perceive that almost all the inhabitants of the United States conduct their understanding in the same manner, and govern it by the same rules —that is to say, that without ever having taken the trouble to define the rules of a philosophical method, they are in possession of one, common to the whole people. To evade the bondage of system and habit, of family-maxims, class-opinions, and, in some degree, of national prejudices; to accept tradition only as a means of information, and existing facts only as a lesson used in doing otherwise and doing better; to seek the reason of things for one's self, and in one's self alone; to tend to results without being bound to means, and to aim at the substance through the form—such are the principal characteristics of what I shall call the philosophical method of the Americans. But if I go further, and if I seek among these characteristics that which predominates over and includes almost all the rest, I discover that in most of the operations of the mind each American appeals to the individual exercise of his own understanding alone. America is therefore one of the countries in the world where philosophy is least studied, and where the precepts of Descartes are best applied. Nor is this surprising. The Americans do not read the works of Descartes, because their social condition deters them from speculative studies; but they follow his maxims because this very social condition naturally disposes their understanding to adopt them. In the midst of the continual movement which agitates a democratic community the tie which unites one generation to another is relaxed or broken; every man readily loses the trace of the ideas of his forefathers or takes no care about them. Nor can men living in this state of society derive their belief from the opinions of the class to which they belong; for, so to speak, there are no longer any classes, or those which still exist are composed of such mobile elements that their body can never exercise a real control over its members. As to the influence which the intelligence of one man has on that of another, it must necessarily be very limited in a country where the citizens, placed on the footing of a general similitude, are all closely seen by each other; and where, as no signs of incontestable greatness or superiority are perceived in any one of them, they are constantly brought back to their own reason as the most obvious and proximate source of truth. It is not only confidence in this or that man which is then destroyed, but the taste for trusting the ipse dixit of any man whatsoever. Every one shuts himself up in his own breast, and affects from that point to judge the world.

The practice which obtains among the Americans of fixing the standard of their judgment in themselves alone, leads them to other habits of mind. As they perceive that they succeed in resolving without assistance all the little difficulties which their practical life presents, they readily conclude that everything in the world may be explained, and that nothing in it transcends the limits of the understanding. Thus they fall to denying what they can not comprehend; which leaves them but little faith for whatever is extraordinary, and an almost insurmountable distaste for whatever is supernatural. As it is on their own testimony that they are accustomed to rely, they like to discern the object which engages their attention with extreme clearness; they therefore strip off as much as possible all that covers it, they rid themselves of whatever separates them from it, they remove whatever conceals it from sight, in order to view it more closely and in the broad light of day. This disposition of the mind soon leads them to contemn forms, which they regard as useless and inconvenient veils placed between them and the truth.

The Americans, then, have not required to extract their philosophical method from books; they have found it in themselves. . . .

. . . .

A principle of authority must . . . always occur, under all circumstances, in some part or other of the moral and intellectual world. Its place is variable, but a place it necessarily has. The independence of individual minds may be greater, or it may be less: unbounded it can not be. Thus the question is, not to know whether any intellectual authority exists in the ages of democracy, but simply where it resides and by what standard it is to be measured.

I have shown . . . how equality of condition leads men to entertain a sort of instinctive incredulity of the supernatural, and a very lofty and often exaggerated opinion of the human understanding. The men who live at a period of social equality are not, therefore, easily led to place that intellectual authority to which they bow either beyond or above humanity. They commonly seek for the sources of truth in themselves, or in those who are like themselves. This would be enough to prove that at such periods no new religion could be established, and that all schemes for such a purpose would be not only impious but absurd and irrational. It may be foreseen that a democratic people will not easily give credence to divine missions; that they will turn modern prophets to a ready jest; and that they will seek to discover the chief arbiter of their belief within, and not beyond, the limits of their kind.

When the ranks of society are unequal, and men unlike each other in condition, there are some individuals invested with all the power of superior intelligence, learning, and enlightenment, while the multitude is sunk in ignorance and prejudice. Men living at these aristocratic periods are therefore naturally induced to shape their opinions by the superior standard of a person or a class of persons, while they are averse to recognize the infallibility of the mass of the people.

The contrary takes place in ages of equality. The nearer the citizens are drawn to the common level of an equal and similar condition, the less prone does each man become to place implicit faith in a certain man or a certain class of men. But his readiness to believe the multitude increases, and opinion is more than ever mistress of the world. Not only is common opinion the only guide which private judgment retains among a democratic people, but among such a people it possesses a power infinitely beyond what it has elsewhere. At periods of equality men have no faith in one another, by reason of their common resemblance; but this very resemblance gives them almost unbounded confidence in the judgment of the public; for it would not seem probable, as they are all endowed with equal means of judging, but that the greater truth should go with the greater number.

When the inhabitant of a democratic country compares himself individually with all those about him, he feels with pride that he is the equal of any one of them; but when he comes to survey the totality of his fellows, and to place himself in contrast to so huge a body, he is instantly overwhelmed by the sense of his own insignificance and weakness. The same equality which renders him independent of each of his fellow-citizens taken severally exposes him alone and unprotected to the influence of the greater number. The public has therefore among a democratic people a singular power, of which aristocratic nations could never so much as conceive an idea; for it does not persuade to certain opinions, but it enforces them, and infuses them into the faculties by a sort of enormous pressure of the minds of all upon the reason of each.

In the United States the majority undertakes to supply a multitude of ready-made opinions for the use of individuals, who are thus relieved from the necessity of forming opinions of their own. Everybody there adopts great numbers of theories, on philosophy, morals, and politics, without inquiry, upon public trust; and if we look to it very narrowly, it will be perceived that religion herself holds her sway there, much less as a doctrine of revelation than as a commonly received opinion. . . .

. . . In the principle of equality I very clearly discern two tendencies; the one leading the mind of every man to untried thoughts, the other inclined to prohibit him from thinking at all. And I perceive how, under the dominion of certain laws, democracy would extinguish that liberty of the mind to which a democratic social condition is favourable; so that, after having broken all the bondage once imposed on it by ranks or by men, the human mind would be closely fettered to the general will of the greatest number.

. . . .

Whenever social conditions are equal, public opinion presses with enormous weight upon the mind of each individual; it surrounds, directs, and oppresses him; and this arises from the very constitution of society, much more than from its political laws. As men grow more alike, each man feels himself weaker in regard to all the rest; as he discerns nothing by which he is considerably raised above them, or distinguished from them, he mistrusts himself as soon as they assail him. Not only does he mistrust his strength, but he even doubts of his right; and he is very near acknowledging that he is in the wrong, when the greater number of his countrymen assert that he is so. The majority do not need to constrain him—they convince him. In whatever way, then, the powers of a democratic community may be organized and balanced, it will always be extremely difficult to believe what the bulk of the people reject, or to profess what they condemn.

This circumstance is extraordinarily favourable to the stability of opinions. When an opinion has taken root among a democratic people, and established itself in the minds of the bulk of the community, it afterward subsists by itself and is maintained without effort, because no one attacks it. Those who at first rejected it as false, ultimately receive it as the general impression; and those who still dispute it in their hearts, conceal their dissent; they are careful not to engage in a dangerous and useless conflict. . . .

. . . .

The principle of equality, which makes men independent of each other, gives them a habit and a taste for following, in their private actions, no other guide but their own will. This complete independence, which they constantly enjoy toward their equals and in the intercourse of private life, tends to make them look upon all authority with a jealous eye, and speedily suggests to them the notion and the love of political freedom. Men living at such times have a natural bias to free institutions. Take any one of them at a venture, and search if you can his most deep-seated instincts; you will find that of all governments he will soonest conceive and most highly value that government whose head he has himself elected, and whose administration he may control. Of all the political effects produced by the equality of conditions, this love of independence is the first to strike the observing, and to alarm the timid; nor can it be said that their alarm is wholly misplaced, for anarchy has a more formidable aspect in democratic countries than elsewhere. As the citizens have no direct influence on each other, as soon as the supreme power of the nation fails, which kept them all in their several stations, it would seem that disorder must instantly reach its utmost pitch, and that, every man drawing aside in a different direction, the fabric of society must at once crumble away.

I am, however, persuaded that anarchy is not the principal evil that democratic ages have to fear, but the least. For the principle of equality begets two tendencies: the one leads men straight to independence, and may suddenly drive them into anarchy; the other conducts them by a longer, more secret, but more certain road, to servitude. Nations readily discern the former tendency, and are prepared to resist it; they are led away by the latter, without perceiving its drift; hence it is peculiarly important to point it out. For myself, I am so far from urging as a reproach to the principle of equality that it renders men untractable, that this very circumstance principally calls forth my approbation. I admire to see how it deposits in the mind and heart of man the dim conception and instinctive love of political independence, thus preparing the remedy for the evil which it engenders; it is on this very account that I am attached to it.

. . . .

. . . As in ages of equality no man is compelled to lend his assistance to his fellow-men, and none has any right to expect much support from them, every one is at once independent and powerless. These two conditions, which must never be either separately considered or confounded together, inspire the citizen of a democratic country with very contrary propensities. His independence fills him with self-reliance and pride among his equals; his debility makes him feel from time to time the want of some outward assistance, which he can not expect from any of them, because they are all impotent and unsympathizing. In this predicament he naturally turns his eyes to that imposing power which alone rises above the level of universal depression. Of that power his wants and especially his desires continually remind him, until he ultimately views it as the sole and necessary support of his own weakness. This may more completely explain what frequently takes place in democratic countries, where the very men who are so impatient of superiors patiently submit to a master, exhibiting at once their pride and their servility.

The hatred which men bear to privilege increases in proportion as privileges become more scarce and less considerable, so that democratic passions would seem to burn most fiercely at the very time when they have least fuel. I have already given the reason of this phenomenon. When all conditions are unequal, no inequality is so great as to offend the eye; whereas the slightest dissimilarity is odious in the midst of general uniformity: the more complete is this uniformity, the more insupportable does the sight of such a difference become. Hence it is natural that the love of equality should constantly increase together with equality itself, and that it should grow by what it feeds upon. This never-dying, ever-kindling hatred, which sets a democratic people against the smallest privileges, is peculiarly favourable to the gradual concentration of all political rights in the hands of the representative of the State alone. The sovereign, being necessarily and incontestably above all the citizens, excites not their envy, and each of them thinks that he strips his equals of the prerogative which he concedes to the crown. The man of a democratic age is extremely reluctant to obey his neighbour who is his equal; he refuses to acknowledge in such a person ability superior to his own; he mistrusts his justice, and is jealous of his power; he fears and he contemns him; and he loves continually to remind him of the common dependence in which both of them stand to the same master. Every central power which follows its natural tendencies courts and encourages the principle of equality; for equality singularly facilitates, extends, and secures the influence of a central power.

In like manner it may be said that every central government worships uniformity: uniformity relieves it from inquiry into an infinite number of small details which must be attended to if rules were to be adapted to men, instead of indiscriminately subjecting men to rules: thus the government likes what the citizens like, and naturally hates what they hate. These common sentiments, which, in democratic nations, constantly unite the sovereign and every member of the community in one and the same conviction, establish a secret and lasting sympathy between them. The faults of the government are pardoned for the sake of its tastes; public confidence is only reluctantly withdrawn in the midst even of its excesses and its errors, and it is restored at the first call. Democratic nations often hate those in whose hands the central power is vested; but they always love that power itself.

Thus by two separate paths I have reached the same conclusion. I have shown that the principle of equality suggests to men the notion of a sole, uniform, and strong government: I have now shown that the principle of equality imparts to them a taste for it. To governments of this kind the nations of our age are therefore tending. They are drawn thither by the natural inclination of mind and heart; and in order to reach that result, it is enough that they do not check themselves in their course. I am of opinion that, in the democratic ages which are opening upon us, individual independence and local liberties will ever be the produce of artificial contrivance; that centralization will be the natural form of government.

. . . .

I seek to trace the novel features under which despotism may appear in the world. The first thing that strikes the observation is an innumerable multitude of men all equal and alike, incessantly endeavouring to procure the petty and paltry pleasures with which they glut their lives. Each of them, living apart, is as a stranger to the fate of all the rest—his children and his private friends constitute to him the whole of mankind; as for the rest of his fellow-citizens, he is close to them, but he sees them not—he touches them, but he feels them not; he exists but in himself and for himself alone; and if his kindred still remain to him, he may be said at any rate to have lost his country. Above this race of men stands an immense and tutelary power, which takes upon itself alone to secure their gratifications, and to watch over their fate. That power is absolute, minute, regular, provident, and mild. It would be like the authority of a parent, if, like that authority, its object was to prepare men for manhood; but it seeks, on the contrary, to keep them in perpetual childhood: it is well content that the people should rejoice, provided they think of nothing but rejoicing. For their happiness such a government willingly labours, but it chooses to be the sole agent and the only arbiter of that happiness: it provides for their security, foresees and supplies their necessities, facilitates their pleasures, manages their principal concerns, directs their industry, regulates the descent of property, and subdivides their inheritances—what remains, but to spare them all the care of thinking and all the trouble of living? Thus it every day renders the exercise of the free agency of man less useful and less frequent; it circumscribes the will within a narrower range, and gradually robs a man of all the uses of himself. The principle of equality has prepared men for these things: it has predisposed men to endure them, and oftentimes to look on them as benefits.

After having thus successively taken each member of the community in its powerful grasp, and fashioned them at will, the supreme power then extends its arm over the whole community. It covers the surface of society with a network of small complicated rules, minute and uniform, through which the most original minds and the most energetic characters can not penetrate, to rise above the crowd. The will of man is not shattered, but softened, bent, and guided: men are seldom forced by it to act, but they are constantly restrained from acting: such a power does not destroy, but it prevents existence; it does not tyrannize, but it compresses, enervates, extinguishes, and stupefies a people, till each nation is reduced to be nothing better than a flock of timid and industrious animals, of which the government is the shepherd.

I have always thought that servitude of the regular, quiet, and gentle kind which I have just described might be combined more easily than is commonly believed with some of the outward forms of freedom; and that it might even establish itself under the wing of the sovereignty of the people. Our contemporaries are constantly excited by two conflicting passions; they want to be led, and they wish to remain free: as they can not destroy either one or the other of these contrary propensities, they strive to satisfy them both at once. They devise a sole, tutelary, and all-powerful form of government, but elected by the people. They combine the principle of centralization and that of popular sovereignty; this gives them a respite; they console themselves for being in tutelage by the reflection that they have chosen their own guardians. Every man allows himself to be put in leading-strings, because he sees that it is not a person or a class of persons, but the people at large, that holds the end of his chain....

Mobility and Materialism

In America the passion for physical well-being is not always exclusive, but it is general; and if all do not feel it in the same manner, yet it is felt by all. Carefully to satisfy all, even the least wants of the body, and to provide the little conveniences of life, is uppermost in every mind.... All the revolutions which have ever shaken or destroyed aristocracies, have shown how easily men accustomed to superfluous luxuries can do without the necessaries of life; whereas men who have toiled to acquire a competency can hardly live after they have lost it.

...When...the distinctions of ranks are confounded together and privileges are destroyed—when hereditary property is subdivided, and education and freedom widely diffused, the desire of acquiring the comforts of the world haunts the imagination of the poor, and the dread of losing them that of the rich. Many scanty fortunes spring up; those who possess them have a sufficient share of physical gratifications to conceive a taste for these pleasures—not enough to satisfy it. They never procure them without exertion, and they never indulge in them without apprehension. They are, therefore, always straining to pursue or to retain gratifications so delightful, so imperfect, so fugitive.

If I were to inquire what passion is most natural to men who are stimulated and circumscribed by the obscurity of their birth or the mediocrity of their fortune, I could discover none more peculiarly appropriate to their condition than this love of physical prosperity. The passion for physical comforts is essentially a passion of the middle classes: with those classes it grows and spreads, with them it preponderates. From them it mounts into the higher orders of society, and descends into the mass of the people. I never met in America with any citizen so poor as not to cast a glance of hope and envy on the enjoyments of the rich, or whose imagination did not possess itself by anticipation of those good things which fate still obstinately withheld from him. On the other hand, I never perceived among the wealthier inhabitants of the United States that proud contempt of physical gratifications which is sometimes to be met with even in the most opulent and dissolute aristocracies.

Most of these wealthy persons were once poor: they have felt the sting of want; they were long a prey to adverse fortunes; and now that the victory is won, the passions which accompanied the contest have survived it: their minds are, as it were, intoxicated by the small enjoyments which they have pursued for forty years. Not but that in the United States, as elsewhere, there are a certain number of wealthy persons who, having come into their property by inheritance, possess, without exertion, an opulence they have not earned. But even these men are not less devotedly attached to the pleasures of material life. The love of well-being is now become the predominant taste of the nation; the great current of man's passions runs in that channel, and sweeps everything along in its course.

. . . .

The especial taste that the men of democratic ages entertain for physical enjoyments is not naturally opposed to the principles of public order; nay, it often stands in need of order that it may be gratified. Nor is it adverse to regularity of morals, for good morals contribute to public tranquility and are favourable to industry. It may even be frequently combined with a species of religious morality: men wish to be as well off as they can in this world, without foregoing their chance of another. Some physical gratifications can not be indulged in without crime; from such they strictly abstain. The enjoyment of others is sanctioned by religion and morality; to these the heart, the imagination, and life itself are unreservedly given up; till, in snatching at these lesser gifts, men lose sight of those more precious possessions which constitute the glory and the greatness of mankind. The reproach I address to the principle of equality is not that it leads men away in the pursuit of forbidden enjoyments, but that it absorbs them wholly in quest of those which are allowed. By these means, a kind of virtuous materialism may ultimately be established in the world, which would not corrupt, but enervate the soul, and noiselessly unbend its springs of action.

. . . .

. . . In America I saw the freest and most enlightened men placed in the happiest circumstances that the world affords: it seemed to me as if a cloud habitually hung upon their brow, and I thought them serious and almost sad even in their pleasures. . . . It is strange to see with what feverish ardour the Americans pursue their own welfare; and to watch the vague dread that constantly torments them lest they should not have chosen the shortest path which may lead to it. A native of the United States clings to this world's goods as if he were certain never to die; and he is so hasty in grasping at all within his reach that one would suppose he was constantly afraid of not living long enough to enjoy them. He clutches everything, he holds nothing fast, but soon loosens his grasp to pursue fresh gratifications.

In the United States a man builds a house to spend his latter years in it, and he sells it before the roof is on: he plants a garden, and lets it just as the trees are coming into bearing: he brings a field into tillage, and leaves other men to gather the crops: he embraces a profession, and gives it up: he settles in a place, which he soon afterward leaves, to carry his changeable longings elsewhere. If his private affairs leave him any leisure, he instantly plunges into the vortex of politics; and if at the end of a year of unremitting labour he finds he has a few days' vacation, his eager curiosity whirls him over the vast extent of the United States, and he will travel fifteen hundred miles in a few days to shake off his happiness. Death at length overtakes him, but it is before he is weary of his bootless chase of that complete felicity which is forever on the wing.

At first sight there is something surprising in this strange unrest of so many happy men, restless in the midst of abundance. The spectacle itself is, however, as old as the world; the novelty is to see a whole people furnish an exemplification of it. Their taste for physical gratifications must be regarded as the original source of that secret inquietude that the actions of the Americans betray, and of that inconstancy of which they afford fresh examples every day. He who has set his heart exclusively upon the pursuit of worldly welfare is always in a hurry, for he has but a limited time at his disposal to reach it, to grasp it, and to enjoy it. The recollection of the brevity of life is a constant spur to him. Besides the good things which he possesses, he every instant fancies a thousand others which death will prevent him from trying if he does not try them soon. This thought fills him with anxiety, fear, and regret, and keeps his mind in ceaseless trepidation, which leads him perpetually to change his plans and his abode. If in addition to the taste for physical well-being a social condition be superadded, in which the laws and customs make no condition permanent, here is a great additional stimulant to this restlessness of temper. Men will then be seen continually to change their track, for fear of missing the shortest cut to happiness. It may readily be conceived that if men, passionately bent upon physical gratifications, desire eagerly, they are also easily discouraged: as their ultimate object is to enjoy, the means to reach that object must be prompt and easy, or the trouble of acquiring the gratification would be greater than the gratification itself. Their prevailing frame of mind, then, is at once ardent and relaxed, violent and enervated. Death is often less dreaded than perseverance in continuous efforts to one end.

The equality of conditions leads by a still straighter road to several of the effects which I have here described. When all the privileges of birth and fortune are abolished, when all professions are accessible to all, and a man's own energies may place him at the top of any one of them, an easy and unbounded career seems open to his ambition, and he will readily persuade himself that he is born to no vulgar destinies. But this is an erroneous notion, which is corrected by daily experience. The same equality which allows every citizen to conceive these lofty hopes renders all the citizens less able to realize them: it circumscribes their powers on every side, while it gives freer scope to their desires. Not only are they themselves powerless, but they are met at every step by immense obstacles, which they did not at first perceive. They have swept away the privileges of some of their fellow-creatures which stood in their way, but they have opened the door to universal competition: the barrier has changed its shape rather than its position. When men are nearly alike, and all follow the same track, it is very difficult for any one individual to walk quick and cleave a way through the dense throng which surrounds and presses him. This constant strife between the propensities springing from the equality of conditions and the means it supplies to satisfy them harasses and wearies the mind.

It is possible to conceive men arrived at a degree of freedom which should completely content them; they would then enjoy their independence without anxiety and without impatience. But men will never establish any equality with which they can be contented. Whatever efforts a people may make, they will never succeed in reducing all the conditions of society to a perfect level; and even if they unhappily attained that absolute and complete depression, the inequality of minds would still remain, which, coming directly from the hand of God, will forever escape the laws of man. However democratic, then, the social state and the political constitution of a people may be, it is certain that every member of the community will always find out several points about him that command his own position; and we may foresee that his looks will be doggedly fixed in that direction. When inequality of conditions is the common law of society, the most marked inequalities do not strike the eye: when everything is nearly on the same level, the slightest are marked enough to hurt it. Hence the desire of equality always becomes more insatiable in proportion as equality is more complete.

Among democratic nations men easily attain a certain equality of conditions: they can never attain the equality they desire. It perpetually retires from before them, yet without hiding itself from their sight, and in retiring draws them on. At every moment they think they are about to grasp it; it escapes at every moment from their hold. They are near enough to see its charms, but too far off to enjoy them; and before they have fully tasted its delights they die. To these causes must be attributed that strange melancholy that oftentimes will haunt the inhabitants of democratic countries in the midst of their abundance, and that disgust at life that sometimes seizes upon them in the midst of calm and easy circumstances. . . .

In democratic ages enjoyments are more intense than in the ages of aristocracy, and especially the number of those who partake in them is larger: but, on the other hand, it must be admitted that man's hopes and his desires are oftener blasted, the soul is more stricken and perturbed, and care itself more keen.

. . . .

. . . Among aristocratic nations every man is pretty nearly stationary in his own sphere; but men are astonishingly unlike each other—their passions, their notions, their habits, and their tastes are essentially different: nothing changes, but everything differs. In democracies, on the contrary, all men are alike and do things pretty nearly alike. It is true that they are subject to great and frequent vicissitudes; but as the same events of good or adverse fortune are continually recurring, the name of the actors only is changed, the piece is always the same. The aspect of American society is animated, because men and things are always changing, but it is monotonous, because all these changes are alike.

Men living in democratic ages have many passions, but most of their passions either end in the love of riches or proceed from it. The cause of this is, not that their souls are narrower, but that the importance of money is really greater at such times. When all the members of a community are independent of or indifferent to each other, the co-operation of each of them can only be obtained by paying for it: this infinitely multiplies the purposes to which wealth may be applied, and increases its value. When the reverence that belonged to what is old has vanished, birth, condition, and profession no longer distinguish men, or scarcely distinguish them at all: hardly anything but money remains to create strongly marked differences between them, and to raise some of them above the common level. The distinction originating in wealth is increased by the disappearance and diminution of all other distinctions. Among aristocratic nations money only reaches to a few points on the vast circle of man's desires—in democracies it seems to lead to all. The love of wealth is therefore to be traced, either as a principal or an accessory motive, at the bottom of all that the Americans do: this gives to all their passions a sort of family likeness, and soon renders the survey of them exceedingly wearisome. This perpetual recurrence of the same passion is monotonous; the peculiar methods by which this passion seeks its own gratification are no less so.

In an orderly and constituted democracy like the United States, where men can not enrich themselves by war, by public office, or by political confiscation, the love of wealth mainly drives them into business and manufactures. Although these pursuits often bring about great commotions and disasters, they can not prosper without strictly regular habits and a long routine of petty uniform acts. The stronger the passion is, the more regular are these habits, and the more uniform are these acts. It may be said that it is the vehemence of their desires which makes the Americans so methodical; it perturbs their minds, but it disciplines their lives.

The remark I here apply to America may indeed be addressed to almost all our contemporaries. Variety is disappearing from the human race; the same ways of acting, thinking, and feeling are to be met with all over the world. This is not only because nations work more upon each other, and are more faithful in their mutual imitation; but as the men of each country relinquish more and more the peculiar opinions and feelings of a caste, a profession, or a family, they simultaneously arrive at something nearer to the constitution of man, which is everywhere the same. Thus they become more alike, even without having imitated each other. Like travellers scattered about some large wood, which is intersected by paths converging to one point, if all of them keep their eyes fixed upon that point and advance toward it, they insensibly draw nearer together—though they seek not, though they see not, though they know not each other; and they will be surprised at length to find themselves all collected on the same spot. . . .

JAMES BRYCE

The American Character in the 1880s

National Character and Public Opinion

As the public opinion of a people is even more directly than its political institutions the reflection and expression of its character, we may begin the analysis of opinion in America by noting some of those general features of national character which give tone and colour to the people's thoughts and feelings on politics. There are, of course, varieties proper to different classes, and to different parts of the vast territory of the Union; but it is well to consider first such characteristics as belong to the nation as a whole, and afterwards to examine the various classes and districts of the country. And when I speak of the nation, I mean the native Americans. What follows is not applicable to the recent immigrants from Europe, and, of course, even less applicable to the Southern negroes.

The Americans are a good-natured people, kindly, helpful to one another, disposed to take a charitable view even of wrong-doers. Their anger sometimes flames up, but the fire is soon extinct. Nowhere is cruelty more abhorred. Even a mob lynching a horse thief in the West has consideration for the criminal, and will give him a good drink of whiskey before he is strung up. Cruelty to slaves was unusual while slavery lasted, the best proof of which is the quietness of the slaves during the war when all the men and many of the boys of the South were serving in the Confederate armies. As everybody knows, juries are more lenient to offences of all kinds but one, offences against women, than they are anywhere in Europe. The Southern "rebels" were soon forgiven; and though civil wars are proverbially bitter, there have been few struggles in which the combatants did so many little friendly acts for one another, few in which even the vanquished have so quickly buried their resentments. It is true that newspapers and public speakers say hard things of their opponents; but this is a part of the game, and is besides a way of relieving their feelings: the bark is sometimes the louder in order that a bite may not follow. Vindictiveness shown by a public man excites general disapproval, and the maxim of letting bygones be bygones is pushed so far that an offender's misdeeds are often forgotten when they ought to be remembered against him.

All the world knows that they are a humorous people. They are as conspicuously the purveyors of humour to the nineteenth century as the French were the purveyors of wit to the eighteenth. Nor is this sense of the ludicrous side of things confined to a few brilliant writers. It is diffused among the whole people; it colours their ordinary life, and gives to their talk that distinctively new flavour which a European palate enjoys. Their capacity for enjoying a joke against themselves was oddly illustrated at the outset of the Civil War, a time of stern excitement, by the merriment which arose over the hasty retreat of the Federal troops at the battle of Bull Run. When William M. Tweed was ruling and robbing New York, and had set on the bench men who were openly prostituting justice, the citizens found the situation so amusing that they almost forgot to be angry. Much of President Lincoln's popularity, and much also of the gift he showed for restoring confidence to the North at the darkest moments of the war, was due to the humorous way he used to turn things, conveying the impression of not being himself uneasy, even when he was most so.

That indulgent view of mankind which I have already mentioned, a view odd in a people whose ancestors were penetrated with the belief in original sin, is strengthened by this wish to get amusement out of everything. The want of seriousness which it produces may be more apparent than real. Yet it has its significance; for people become affected by the language they use, as we see men grow into cynics when they have acquired the habit of talking cynicism for the sake of effect.

They are a hopeful people. Whether or no they are right in calling themselves a new people, they certainly seem to feel in their veins the bounding pulse of youth. They see a long vista of years stretching out before them, in which they will have time enough to cure all their faults, to overcome all the obstacles that block their path. They look at their enormous territory with its still only half-explored sources of wealth, they reckon up the growth of their population and their products, they contrast the comfort and intelligence of their labouring classes with the condition of the masses in the Old World. They remember the dangers that so long threatened the Union from the slave power, and the rebellion it raised, and see peace and harmony now restored, the South more prosperous and contented than at any previous epoch, perfect good feeling between all sections of the country. It is natural for them to believe in their star. And this sanguine temper makes them tolerant of evils which they regard as transitory, removable as soon as time can be found to root them up.

They have unbounded faith in what they call the People and in a democratic system of government. The great States of the European continent are distracted by the contests of Republicans and Monarchists, and of rich and poor,—contests which go down to the foundations of government, and in France are further embittered by religious passions. Even in England the ancient Constitution is always under repair, and while some think it is being ruined by changes, others hold that further changes are needed to make it tolerable. No such questions trouble native American minds, for nearly everybody believes, and everybody declares, that the frame of government is in its main lines so excellent that such reforms as seem called for need not touch those lines, but are required only to protect the Constitution from being perverted by the parties. Hence a further confidence that the people are sure to decide right in the long run, a confidence inevitable and essential in a government which refers every question to the arbitrament of numbers. There have, of course, been instances where the once insignificant minority proved to have been wiser than the majority of the moment. Such was eminently the case in the great slavery struggle. But here the minority prevailed by growing into a majority as events developed the real issues, so that this also has been deemed a ground for holding that all minorities which have right on their side will bring round their antagonists, and in the long run win by voting power. If you ask an intelligent citizen why he so holds, he will answer that truth and justice are sure to make their way into the minds and consciences of the majority. This is deemed an axiom, and the more readily so deemed because truth is identified with common sense, the quality which the average citizen is most confidently proud of possessing.

This feeling shades off into another, externally like it, but at bottom distinct —the feeling not only that the majority, be it right or wrong, will and must prevail, but that its being the majoriy proves it to be right. This idea, which appears in the guise sometimes of piety and sometimes of fatalism, seems to be no contemptible factor in the present character of the people. . . .

The native Americans are an educated people, compared with the whole mass of the population in any European country except Switzerland, parts of Germany, Norway, Iceland, and Scotland; that is to say, the average of knowledge is higher, the habit of reading and thinking more generally diffused, than in any other country. They know the Constitution of their own country, they follow public affairs, they join in local government and learn from it how government must be carried on, and in particular how discussion must be conducted in meetings, and its results tested at elections. The Town Meeting was for New England the most perfect school of self-government in any modern country. In villages, men used to exercise their minds on theological questions, debating points of Christian doctrine with no small acuteness. Women in particular, pick up at the public schools and from the popular magazines far more miscellaneous information than the women of any European country possess, and this naturally tells on the intelligence of the men. Almost everywhere one finds women's clubs in which literary, artistic, and social questions are discussed, and to which men of mark are brought to deliver lectures.

That the education of the masses is nevertheless a superficial education goes without saying. It is sufficient to enable them to think they know something about the great problems of politics: insufficient to show them how little they know. The public elementary school gives everybody the key to knowledge in making reading and writing familiar, but it has not time to teach him how to use the key, whose use is in fact, by the pressure of daily work, almost confined to the newspaper and the magazine. So we may say that if the political education of the average American voter be compared with that of the average voter in Europe, it stands high; but if it be compared with the functions which the theory of the American government lays on him, which its spirit implies, which the methods of its party organization assume, its inadequacy is manifest. This observation, however, is not so much a reproach to the schools, which generally do what English schools omit—instruct the child in the principles of the Constitution—as a tribute to the height of the ideal which the American conception of popular rule sets up.

For the functions of the citizen are not, as has hitherto been the case in Europe, confined to the choosing of legislators, who are then left to settle issues of policy and select executive rulers. The American citizen is one of the governors of the Republic. Issues are decided and rulers selected by the direct popular vote. Elections are so frequent that to do his duty at them a citizen ought to be constantly watching public affairs with a full comprehension of the principles involved in them, and a judgment of the candidates derived from a criticism of their arguments as well as a recollection of their past careers. The instruction received in the common schools and from the newspapers, and supposed to be developed by the practice of primaries and conventions, while it makes the voter deem himself capable of governing, does not fit him to weigh the real merits of statesmen, to discern the true grounds on which questions ought to be decided, to note the drift of events and discover the direction in which parties are being carried. He is like a sailor who knows the spars and ropes of the ship and is expert in working her, but is ignorant of geography and navigation; who can perceive that some of the officers are smart and others dull, but cannot judge which of them is qualified to use the sextant or will best keep his head during a hurricane.

They are a moral and well-conducted people. Setting aside the *colluvies gentium* which one finds in Western mining camps, now largely filled by recent immigrants, and which popular literature has presented to Europeans as far larger than it really is, setting aside also the rabble of a few great cities and the negroes of the South, the average of temperance, chastity, truthfulness, and general probity is somewhat higher than in any of the great nations of Europe. The instincts of the native farmer or artisan are almost invariably kindly and charitable. He respects the law; he is deferential to women and indulgent to children; he attaches an almost excessive value to the possession of a genial manner and the observance of domestic duties.

They are also—and here again I mean the people of native American stock, especially in the Eastern and Middle States, on the whole, a religious people. It is not merely that they respect religion and its ministers, for that one might say of Russians or Sicilians, not merely that they are assiduous church-goers and Sunday-school teachers, but that they have an intelligent interest in the form of faith they profess, are pious without superstition, and zealous without bigotry. The importance which some still, though all much less than formerly, attach to dogmatic propositions, does not prevent them from feeling the moral side of their theology. Christianity influences conduct, not indeed half as much as in theory it ought, but probably more than it does in any other modern country, and far more than it did in the so-called ages of faith.

Nor do their moral and religious impulses remain in the soft haze of self-complacent sentiment. The desire to expunge or cure the visible evils of the world is strong. Nowhere are so many philanthropic and reformatory agencies at work. Zeal outruns discretion, outruns the possibilities of the case, in not a few of the efforts made, as well by legislation as by voluntary action, to suppress vice, to prevent intemperance, to purify popular literature.

Religion apart, they are an unreverential people. I do not mean irreverent,—far from it; nor do I mean that they have not a great capacity for hero-worship, as they have many a time shown. I mean that they are little disposed, especially in public questions—political, economical, or social—to defer to the opinions of those who are wiser or better instructed than themselves. Everything tends to make the individual independent and self-reliant. He goes early into the world; he is left to make his way alone; he tries one occupation after another, if the first or second venture does not prosper; he gets to think that each man is his own best helper and adviser. Thus he is led, I will not say to form his own opinions, for few are those who do that, but to fancy that he has formed them, and to feel little need of aid from others towards correcting them. There is, therefore, less disposition than in Europe to expect light and leading on public affairs from speakers or writers. Oratory is not directed towards instruction, but towards stimulation. Special knowledge, which commands deference in applied science or in finance, does not command it in politics, because that is not deemed a special subject, but one within the comprehension of every practical man. Politics is, to be sure, a profession, and so far might seem to need professional aptitudes. But the professional politician is not the man who has studied statesmanship, but the man who has practised the art of running conventions and winning elections.

Even that strong point of America, the completeness and highly popular character of local government, contributes to lower the standard of attainment expected in a public man, because the citizens judge of all politics by the politics they see first and know best,—those of their township or city,—and fancy that he who is fit to be selectman, or county commissioner, or alderman, is fit to sit in the great council of the nation. Like the shepherd in Virgil, they think the only difference between their town and Rome is in its size, and believe that what does for Lafayetteville will do well enough for Washington. Hence when a man of statesmanlike gifts appears, he has little encouragement to take a high and statesmanlike tone, for his words do not necessarily receive weight from his position. He fears to be instructive or hortatory, lest such an attitude should expose him to ridicule; and in America ridicule is a terrible power. Nothing escapes it. Few have the courage to face it. In the indulgence of it even this humane race can be unfeeling.

They are a busy people. I have already observed that the leisured class is relatively small, is in fact confined to a few Eastern cities. The citizen has little time to think about political problems. Engrossing all the working hours, his avocation leaves him only stray moments from this fundamental duty. It is true that he admits his responsibilities, considers himself a member of a party, takes some interest in current events. But although he would reject the idea that his thinking should be done for him, he has not leisure to do it for himself, and must practically lean upon and follow his party. It astonished me in 1870 and 1881 to find how small a part politics played in conversation among the best educated classes and generally in the cities. Since 1896 there has been a livelier and more constant interest in public affairs; yet even now business matters so occupy the mind of the financial and commercial classes, and athletic competitions the minds of the uneducated classes and of the younger sort in all classes, that political questions are apt, except at critical moments, to fall into the background.[1] In a presidential year, and especially during the months of a presidential campaign, there is, of course, abundance of private talk, as well as of public speaking, but even then the issues raised are largely personal rather than political in the European sense. But at other times the visitor is apt to feel—more, I think, than he feels anywhere in Britain—that his host has been heavily pressed by his own business concerns during the day, and that when the hour of relaxation arrives he gladly turns to lighter and more agreeable topics than the state of the nation. This remark is less applicable to the dwellers in villages. There is plenty of political chat round the store at the cross roads, and though it is rather in the nature of gossip than of debate, it seems, along with the practice of local government, to sustain the interest of ordinary folk in public affairs.[2]

The want of serious and sustained thinking is not confined to politics. One feels it even more as regards economical and social questions. To it must be ascribed the vitality of certain prejudices and fallacies which could scarcely survive the continuous application of such vigorous minds as one finds among the Americans. Their quick perceptions serve them so well in business and in the ordinary affairs of private life that they do not feel the need for minute investigation and patient reflection on the underlying principles of things. They are apt to ignore difficulties, and when they can no longer ignore them, they will evade them rather than lay siege to them according to the rules of art.

[1]The increased space given to athletics and games of all sorts in the newspapers marks a change in public taste no less striking here than it is in Britain. As it is equally striking in the British colonies, one may take it as a feature common to the modern English-speaking world, and to that world only, for it is scarcely discernible in Continental Europe.

[2]The European country where the common people best understand politics is Switzerland. That where they talk most about politics is, I think, Greece. I remember, for instance, in crossing the channel which divides Cephalonia from Ithaca, to have heard the boatmen discuss a recent ministerial crisis at Athens, during the whole voyage, with the liveliest interest and apparently some knowledge.

The sense that there is no time to spare haunts an American even when he might find the time, and would do best for himself by finding it.

Some one will say that an aversion to steady thinking belongs to the average man everywhere. True. But less is expected from the average man in other countries than from a people who have carried the doctrine of popular sovereignty further than it has ever been carried before. They are tried by the standard which the theory of their government assumes. In other countries statesmen or philosophers do, and are expected to do, the solid thinking for the bulk of the people. Here the people are supposed to do it for themselves. To say that they do it imperfectly is not to deny them the credit of doing it better than a European philosopher might have predicted.

They are a commercial people, whose point of view is primarily that of persons accustomed to reckon profit and loss. Their impulse is to apply a direct practical test to men and measures, to assume that the men who have got on fastest are the smartest men, and that a scheme which seems to pay well deserves to be supported. Abstract reasonings they dislike, subtle reasonings they suspect; they accept nothing as practical which is not plain, downright, apprehensible by an ordinary understanding. Although open-minded, so far as willingness to listen goes, they are hard to convince, because they have really made up their minds on most subjects, having adopted the prevailing notions of their locality or party as truths due to their own reflection.

It may seem a contradiction to remark that with this shrewdness and the sort of hardness it produces, they are nevertheless an impressionable people. Yet this is true. It is not their intellect, however, that is impressionable, but their imagination and emotions, which respond in unexpected ways to appeals made on behalf of a cause which seems to have about it something noble or pathetic. They are capable of an ideality surpassing that of Englishmen or Frenchmen.

They are an unsettled people. In no State of the Union is the bulk of the population so fixed in its residence as everywhere in Europe; in some it is almost nomadic. Except in the more stagnant parts of the South, nobody feels rooted to the soil. Here to-day and gone to-morrow, he cannot readily contract habits of trustful dependence on his neighbours. Community of interest, or of belief in such a cause as temperance, or protection for native industry, unites him for a time with others similarly minded, but congenial spirits seldom live long enough together to form a school or type of local opinion which develops strength and becomes a proselytizing force. Perhaps this tends to prevent the growth of variety in opinion. When a man arises with some power of original thought in politics, he is feeble if isolated, and is depressed by his insignificance, whereas if he grows up in favourable soil with sympathetic minds around him, whom he can in prolonged intercourse permeate with his ideas, he learns to speak with confidence and soars on the wings of his disciples. One who considers the variety of conditions under which men live in America may certainly find ground for surprise that there should be so few independent schools of opinion.

But even while an unsettled, they are nevertheless an associative, because a sympathetic people. Although the atoms are in constant motion, they have a strong attraction for one another. Each man catches his neighbor's sentiment more quickly and easily than happens with the English. That sort of reserve and isolation, that tendency rather to repel than to invite confidence, which foreigners attribute to the Englishman, though it belongs rather to the upper and middle class than to the nation generally, is, though not absent, yet less marked in America.[3] It seems to be one of the notes of difference between the two branches of the race. In the United States, since each man likes to feel that his ideas raise in other minds the same emotions as in his own, a sentiment or impulse is rapidly propagated and quickly conscious of its strength. Add to this the aptitude for organization which their history and institutions have educed, and one sees how the tendency to form and the talent to work combinations for a political or any other object has become one of the great features of the country. Hence, too, the immense strength of party. It rests not only on interest and habit and the sense of its value as a means of working the government, but also on the sympathetic element and instinct of combination ingrained in the national character.

They are a changeful people. Not fickle, for they are if anything too tenacious of ideas once adopted, too fast bound by party ties, too willing to pardon the errors of a cherished leader. But they have what chemists call low specific heat; they grow warm suddenly and cool as suddenly; they are liable to swift and vehement outbursts of feeling which rush like wildfire across the country, gaining glow, like the wheel of a railway car, by the accelerated motion. The very similarity of ideas and equality of conditions which makes them hard to convince at first makes a conviction once implanted run its course the more triumphantly. They seem all to take flame at once, because what has told upon one, has told in the same way upon all the rest, and the obstructing and separating barriers which exist in Europe scarcely exist here. Nowhere is the saying so applicable that nothing succeeds like success. The native American or so-called Know-nothing party had in two years from its foundation become a tremendous force, running, and seeming for a time likely to carry, its own presidential candidate. In three years more it was dead without hope of revival. Now and then as for instance in the elections of 1874–75, and again in those of 1890, there comes a rush of feeling so sudden and tremendous, that the name of Tidal Wave has been invented to describe it.

After this it may seem a paradox to add that the Americans are a conservative people. Yet any one who observes the power of habit among them, the tenacity with which old institutions and usages, legal and theological formulas, have been clung to, will admit the fact. Moreover, prosperity helps to make

[3] I do not mean that Americans are more apt to unbosom themselves to strangers, but that they have rather more adaptiveness than the English, and are less disposed to stand alone and care nothing for the opinion of others. It is worth noticing that Americans travelling abroad seem to get more easily into touch with the inhabitants of the country than the English do; nor have they the English habit of calling those inhabitants—Frenchmen, for instance, or Germans—"the natives."

them conservative. They are satisfied with the world they live in, for they have found it a good world, in which they have grown rich and can sit under their own vine and fig tree, none making them afraid. They are proud of their history and of their Constitution, which has come out of the furnace of civil war with scarcely the smell of fire upon it. It is little to say that they do not seek change for the sake of change, because the nations that do this exist only in the fancy of alarmist philosophers. There are nations, however, whose impatience of existing evils, or whose proneness to be allured by visions of a brighter future, makes them under-estimate the risk of change, nations that will pull up the plant to see whether it has begun to strike root. This is not the way of the Americans. They are no doubt ready to listen to suggestions from any quarter. They do not consider that an institution is justified by its existence, but admit everything to be matter for criticism. Their keenly competitive spirit and pride in their own ingenuity have made them quicker than any other people to adopt and adapt inventions: telephones were in use in every little town over the West, while in the city of London men were just beginning to wonder whether they could be made to pay. The Americans have doubtless of late years become, especially in the West, an experimental people, so far as politics and social legislation are concerned. Yet there is also a sense in which they are at bottom a conservative people, in virtue both of the deep instincts of their race and of that practical shrewdness which recognizes the value of permanence and solidity in institutions. They are conservative in their fundamental beliefs, in the structure of their governments, in their social and domestic usages. They are like a tree whose pendulous shoots quiver and rustle with the lightest breeze, while its roots enfold the rock with a grasp which storms cannot loosen.

The Pleasantness of American Life

I have never met a European of the middle or upper classes who did not express astonishment when told that America was a more agreeable place than Europe to live in. "For working men," he would answer, "yes; but for men of education or property, how can a new rough country, where nothing but business is talked and the refinements of life are only just beginning to appear, how can such a country be compared with England, or France, or Italy?"

It is nevertheless true that there are elements in the life of the United States which may well make a European of any class prefer to dwell there rather than in the land of his birth. Let us see what they are.

In the first place there is the general prosperity and material well-being of the mass of the inhabitants. In Europe, if an observer takes his eye off his own class and considers the whole population of any one of the greater countries, he will perceive that by far the greater number lead very laborious lives, and are, if not actually in want of the necessities of existence, yet liable to fall into want, the agriculturists when nature is harsh, the wage-earners when work is scarce. In England the lot of the labourer has been hitherto a hard one, incessant field toil, with rheumatism at fifty and the workhouse at the end of the vista; while the misery in such cities as London, Liverpool, and Glasgow is only too well known. In France there is less pauperism, but nothing can be more pinched and sordid than the life of the bulk of the peasantry. In the great towns of Germany there is constant distress and increasing discontent. The riots of 1886 in Belgium told an even more painful tale of the wretchedness of the miners and artisans there. In Italy the condition of the rural population of Venetia as well as of the southern provinces still gives cause for grave concern. Of Russia, with her ninety millions of peasants living in half-barbarism, there is no need to speak. Contrast any one of these countries with the United States, where the working classes are as well fed, clothed, and lodged as the lower middle class in Europe, and the farmers who till their own land (as nearly all do) much better, where a good education is within the reach of the poorest, where the opportunities for getting on in one way or another are so abundant that no one need fear any physical ill but disease or the results of his own intemperance. Pauperism already exists in some of the larger cities, where drink breeds misery, and where recent immigrants, with the shiftlessness of Europe still clinging round them, are huddled together in squalor. But outside these few cities one sees nothing but comfort. In Connecticut and Ohio the native American operatives in many a manufacturing town lead a life easier, and more brightened by intellectual culture and by amusements, than that of the clerks and shopkeepers of England or France. In places like Kansas City or Chicago one finds miles on miles of suburb filled with neat wooden houses, each with its tiny garden plot, owned by the shop assistants and handicraftsmen who return on the electric-cars in the evening from their work. All over the wide West, from Lake Ontario to the Upper Missouri, one travels past farms of one to two hundred acres, in every one of which there is a spacious farmhouse among orchards and meadows, where the farmer's children grow up strong and hearty on abundant food, the boys full of intelligence and enterprise, ready to push their way on farms of their own or enter business in the nearest town, the girls familiar with the current literature of England as well as of America. The life of the agricultural settler in the further West has its privations, but it is brightened by hope, and has a singular charm of freedom and simplicity. The impression which this comfort and plenty makes is heightened by the brilliance and keenness of the air, by the look of freshness and cleanness which even the cities wear, all of them except the poorest parts of those few I have referred to above. The fog and soot-flakes of an English town, as well as its squalor, are wanting; you are in a new world, and a world which knows the sun. It is impossible not to feel warmed, cheered, invigorated by the sense of such material well-being all around one, impossible not to be infected by the buoyancy and hopefulness of the people. The wretchedness of Europe lies far behind; the weight of its problems seems lifted from the mind. As a man suffering from depression feels the clouds roll away from his spirit when he meets a friend whose good humour and energy present the better side of things and point the way through difficulties, so the sanguine temper of the Americans, and the sight of the ardour with which they pursue their aims, stimulates a European and makes him think the world a better place than it had seemed amid the entanglements and sufferings of his own hemisphere.

To some Europeans this may seem fanciful. I doubt if any European can realize till he has been in America how much difference it makes to the happiness of any one not wholly devoid of sympathy with his fellow-beings, to feel that all round him, in all classes of society and all parts of the country, there exist in such ample measure so many of the external conditions of happiness: abundance of the necessaries of life, easy command of education and books, amusements and leisure to enjoy them, comparatively few temptations to intemperance and vice.

The second charm of American life is one which some Europeans will smile at. It is social equality. To many Europeans the word has an odious sound. It suggests a dirty fellow in a blouse elbowing his betters in a crowd, or an ill-conditioned villager shaking his fist at the parson and the squire; or, at any rate, it suggests obtrusiveness and bad manners. The exact contrary is the truth. Equality improves manners, for it strengthens the basis of all good manners, respect for other men and women simply as men and women, irrespective of their station in life. Probably the assertion of social equality was one of the causes which injured American manners fifty years ago, for that they were then bad among townsfolk can hardly be doubted in face of the testimony, not merely of sharp tongues like Mrs. Trollope's, but of calm observers like Sir Charles Lyell and sympathetic observers like Richard Cobden.[4] In those days there was an obtrusive self-assertiveness among the less refined classes, especially towards those who, coming from the Old World, were assumed to come in a patronizing spirit. Now, however, social equality has grown so naturally out of the circumstances of the country, has been so long established, and is so ungrudgingly admitted, that all excuse for obtrusiveness has disappeared. People meet on a simple and natural footing, with more frankness and ease than is possible in countries where every one is either looking up or looking down.[5] There is no servility on the part of the humbler, and if now and then a little of the "I am as good as you" rudeness be perceptible, it is

[4] Volney, who at the end of last century commented on the "incivilite nationale," ascribes it "moins à un système d'intentions qu'à l'independance mutuelle, à l'isolement, au dèfaut des besoins réciproques."

[5] A trifling anecdote may illustrate what I mean. Long ago in Spokane, then a small Far Western town, the stationmaster lent me a locomotive to run a few miles out along the railway to see a remarkable piece of scenery. The engine took me and dropped me there, as I wished to walk back, much to the surprise of the driver and stoker, for in America no one walks if he can help it. The same evening, as I was sitting in the hall of the hotel, I was touched on the arm, and turning round found myself accosted by a well-mannered man, who turned out to be the engine-driver. He expressed his regret that the locomotive had not been cleaner and better "fixed up," as he would have liked to make my trip as agreeable as possible, but the notice given him had been short. He talked with intelligence, and we had some pleasant chat together. It was fortunate that I had resisted in the forenoon the British impulse to bestow a gratuity.

likely to proceed from a recent immigrant, to whom the attitude of simple equality has not yet become familiar as the evidently proper attitude of one man to another. There is no condescension on the part of the more highly placed, nor is there even that sort of scrupulously polite coldness which one might think they would adopt in order to protect their dignity. They have no cause to fear for their dignity, so long as they do not themselves forget it. And the fact that your shoemaker or your factory hand addresses his employer as an equal does not prevent him from showing all the respect to which any one may be entitled on the score of birth or education or eminence in any walk of life.

This naturalness is a distinct addition to the pleasure of social intercourse. It enlarges the circle of possible friendship, by removing the *gêne* which in most parts of Europe persons of different ranks feel in exchanging their thoughts on any matters save those of business. It raises the humbler classes without lowering the upper; indeed, it improves the upper no less than the lower by expunging that latent insolence which deforms the manners of so many of the European rich. It relieves women in particular, who in Europe are specially apt to think of class distinctions, from that sense of constraint and uneasiness which is produced by the knowledge that other women with whom they come in contact are either looking down on them, or at any rate trying to gauge and determine their social position. It expands the range of a man's sympathies, and makes it easier for him to enter into the sentiments of other classes than his own. It gives a sense of solidarity to the whole nation, cutting away the ground for the jealousies and grudges which distract people so long as the social pretensions of past centuries linger on to be resented by the levelling spirit of a revolutionary age. And I have never heard native Americans speak of any drawbacks corresponding to and qualifying these benefits.

There are, moreover, other rancours besides those of social inequality whose absence from America brightens it to a European eye. There are no quarrels of churches and sects. Judah does not vex Ephraim, nor Ephraim envy Judah. No Established Church looks down scornfully upon Dissenters from the height of its titles and endowments, and talks of them as hindrances in the way of its work. No Dissenters pursue an Established Church in a spirit of watchful jealousy, nor agitate for its overthrow. One is not offended by the contrast between the theory and the practice of a religion of peace, between professions of universal affection in pulpit addresses and forms of prayer, and the acrimony of clerical controversialists. Still less, of course, is there that sharp opposition and antagonism of Christians and anti-Christians which lacerates the private as well as public life of France. Rivalry between sects appears only in the innocent form of the planting of new churches and raising of funds for missionary objects, while most of the Protestant denominations, including the four most numerous, constantly fraternize in charitable work. Between Roman Catholics and the more educated Protestants there is little hostility, and sometimes even co-operation for a philanthropic purpose. The sceptic is no longer under a social ban, and discussions on the essentials of Christianity and of theism are conducted with good temper. There is not a country in the world where Frederick the Great's principle, that every one should be allowed to go to heaven his own way, is so fully applied. This sense of religious peace as well as religious freedom all around one is soothing to the weary European, and contributes not a little to sweeten the lives of ordinary people.

I come last to the character and ways of the Americans themselves in which there is a certain charm, hard to convey by description, but felt almost as soon as one sets foot on their shore, and felt constantly thereafter. In purely business relations there is hardness, as there is all the world over. Inefficiency has a very short shrift. But apart from those relations they are a kindly people. Good nature, heartiness, a readiness to render small services to one another, an assumption that neighbours in the country, or persons thrown together in travel, or even in a crowd, were meant to be friendly rather than hostile to one another, seem to be everywhere in the air, and in those who breath it. Sociability is the rule, isolation and moroseness the rare exception. It is not that people are more vivacious or talkative than an Englishman expects to find them, for the Western man is often taciturn and seldom wreathes his long face into a smile. It is rather that you feel that the man next you, whether silent or talkative, does not mean to repel intercourse, or convey by his manner his low opinion of his fellow-creatures. Everybody seems disposed to think well of the world and its inhabitants, well enough at least to wish to be on easy terms with them and serve them in those little things whose trouble to the doer is small in proportion to the pleasure they give to the receiver. To help others is better recognized as a duty than in Europe. Nowhere is money so readily given for any public purpose; nowhere, I suspect, are there so many acts of private kindness done, such, for instance, as paying the college expenses of a promising boy, or aiding a widow to carry on her husband's farm; and these are not done with ostentation. People seem to take their own troubles more lightly than they do in Europe, and to be more indulgent to the faults by which troubles are caused. It is a land of hope, and a land of hope is a land of good humour. And they have also, though this is a quality more perceptible in women than in men, a remarkable faculty for enjoyment, a power of drawing more happiness from obvious pleasures, simple and innocent pleasures, than one often finds in overburdened Europe.

As generalizations like this are necessarily comparative, I may be asked with whom I am comparing the Americans. With the English, or with some attempted average of European nations? Primarily I am comparing them with the English, because they are the nearest relatives of the English. But there are other European countries, such as France, Belgium, Spain, in which the sort of cheerful friendliness I have sought to describe is less common than it is in America. Even in Germany and German Austria, simple and kindly as are the masses of the people, the upper classes have that *roideur* which belongs to countries dominated by an old aristocracy, or by a plutocracy trying to imitate aristocratic ways. The upper class in America (if one may use such an expression) has not in this respect differentiated itself from the character of the nation at large.

If the view here presented be a true one, to what causes are we to ascribe this agreeable development of the original English type, a development in whose course the sadness of Puritanism seems to have been shed off?

Perhaps one of them is the humorous turn of the American character. Humour is a sweetener of temper, a copious spring of charity, for it makes the good side of bad things even more visible than the bad side of good things; but humour in Americans may be as much a result of an easy and kindly turn as their kindliness is of their humour. Another is the perpetuation of a habit of mutual help formed in colonial days. Colonists need one another's aid more constantly than the dwellers in an old country, are thrown more upon one another, even when they live scattered in woods or prairies, are more interested in one another's welfare. When you have only three neighbours within five miles, each of them covers a large part of your horizon. You want to borrow a plough from one; you get another to help you to roll your logs; your children's delight is to go over for an evening's merrymaking to the lads and lasses of the third. It is much pleasanter to be on good terms with these few neighbours, and when others come one by one, they fall into the same habits of intimacy. Any one who has read those stories of rustic New England or New York life which delighted those who were English children in 1850—I do not know whether they delight children still, or have been thrown aside for more highly spiced food—will remember the warm-hearted simplicity and atmosphere of genial good-will which softened the roughness of peasant manners and tempered the sternness of a Calvinistic creed. It is natural that the freedom of intercourse and sense of interdependence which existed among the early settlers, and which have existed ever since among the pioneers of colonization in the West as they moved from the Connecticut to the Mohawk, from the Mohawk to the Ohio, from the Ohio to the Mississippi, should have left on the national character traces not effaced even in the more artificial civilization of our own time. Something may be set down to the feeling of social equality, creating that respect for a man as a man, whether he be rich or poor, which was described a few pages back; and something to a regard for the sentiment of the multitude, a sentiment which forbids any man to stand aloof in the conceit of self-importance, and holds up geniality and good fellowship as almost the first of social virtues. I do not mean that a man consciously suppresses his impulses to selfishness or gruffness because he knows that his faults will be ill regarded; but that, having grown up in a society which is infinitely powerful as compared with the most powerful person in it, he has learnt to realize his individual insignificance, as members of the upper class in Europe never do, and has become permeated by the feeling which this society entertains—that each one's duty is not only to accept equality, but also to relish equality, and to make himself pleasant to his equals. Thus the habit is formed even in natures of no special sweetness, and men become kindly by doing kindly acts.

Whether, however, these suggestions be right or wrong, there is no doubt as to the fact which they attempt to explain. I do not, of course, give it merely as the casual impression of European visitors, whom a singularly frank and ready hospitality welcomes and makes much of. I base it on the reports of European friends who have lived for years in the United States, and whose criticism of the ways and notions of the people is keen enough to show that they are no partial witnesses.

The Uniformity of American Life

To the pleasantness of American life there is one, and perhaps only one, serious drawback—its uniformity. Those who have been struck by the size of America, and by what they have heard of its restless excitement, may be surprised at the word. They would have guessed that an unquiet changefulness and turmoil were the disagreeables to be feared. But uniformity, which the European visitor begins to note when he has travelled for a month or two, is the feature of the country which Englishmen who have lived long there, and Americans who are familiar with Europe, most frequently revert to when asked to say what is the "crook in their lot."

. . . .

It is most clearly not with Europe, but with each of the leading European peoples that we must compare the people of America. So comparing them with the peoples of Britain, France, Germany, Italy, Spain, one discovers more varieties between individuals in these European peoples than one finds in America. Scotchmen and Irishmen are more unlike Englishmen, the native of Normandy more unlike the native of Provence, the Pomeranian more unlike the Wurtemberger, the Piedmontese more unlike the Neapolitan, the Basque more unlike the Andalusian, than the American from any part of the country is to the American from any other. Differences of course there are between the human type as developed in different regions of the country,—differences moral and intellectual as well as physical. You can generally tell a Southerner by his look as well as by his speech, and the South, as a whole, has a character of its own, propagated from the older Atlantic to the newer Western States. A native of Maine will probably differ from a native of Kentucky, a Georgian from an Oregonian. But these differences strike even an American observer much as the difference between a Yorkshireman and a Warwickshire man strikes the English, and is slighter than the contrast between a middle-class southern Englishman and a middle-class Scotchman, slighter than the differences between a peasant from Northumberland and a peasant from Dorsetshire. Or, to take another way of putting it: If at some great gathering of a political party from all parts of the United Kingdom you were to go round and talk to, say, one hundred, taken at random, of the persons present, you would be struck by more diversity between the notions and tastes and mental habits of the individuals comprising that one hundred than if you tried the same experiment with a hundred Americans of similar education and position, similarly gathered in a convention from every State in the Union.

I do not in the least mean that people are more commonplace in America than in England, or that the Americans are less ideal than the English. Neither of these statements would be true. On the contrary, the average American is more alive to new ideas, more easily touched through his imagination or his emotions, than the average Englishman or Frenchman. He has a keen sense of humour, and an unquenchable faith in the future. I mean only that the native-born Americans appear to vary less, in fundamentals, from what may be called the dominant American type than Englishmen, Germans, Frenchmen, Spaniards, or Italians do from any type which could be taken as the dominant type in any of those nations. Or, to put the same thing differently, it is rather more difficult to take any assemblage of attributes in any of these European countries and call it the national type than it is to do the like in the United States.

These are not given as the impressions of a traveller. Such impressions, being necessarily hasty, and founded on a comparatively narrow observation, would deserve little confidence. They sum up the conclusions of Europeans long resident in America, and familiar with different parts of the country. They are, I think, admitted by the most acute Americans themselves. I have often heard the latter dilate on what seems to them the one crowning merit of life in Europe—the variety it affords, the opportunities it gives of easy and complete changes of scene and environment. The pleasure which an American finds in crossing the Atlantic, a pleasure more intense than any which the European enjoys, is that of passing from a land of happy monotony into regions where everything is redolent with memories of the past, and derives from the past no less than from the present a wealth and a subtle complexity of interest which no new country can possess.

Life in America is in most ways pleasanter, simpler, less cumbered by conventions that in Europe; it floats in a sense of happiness like that of a radiant summer morning. But life in any of the great European centres is capable of an intensity, a richness blended of many elements, which has not yet been reached in America. There are more problems in Europe calling for solution; there is more passion in the struggles that rage round them; the past more frequently kindles the present with a glow of imaginative light. In whichever country of Europe one dwells, one feels that the other countries are near, that the fortunes of their peoples are bound up with the fortunes of one's own, that ideas are shooting to and fro between them. The web of history woven day by day all over Europe is vast and of many colours: it is fateful to every European. But in America it is only the philosopher who can feel that it will ultimately be fateful to Americans also; to the ordinary man the Old World seems far off, severed by a dissociating ocean, its mighty burden with little meaning for him.

Those who have observed the uniformity I have been attempting to describe have commonly set it down, as Europeans do most American phenomena, to what they call Democracy. Democratic government has in reality not much to do with it, except in so far as such a government helps to induce that deference of individuals to the mass which strengthens a dominant type, whether of ideas, of institutions, or of manners. More must be ascribed to the equality of material conditions, still more general than in Europe, to the fact that nearly every one is engaged either in agriculture, or in commerce, or in some handicraft, to the extraordinary mobility of the population, which, in migrating from one part of the country to another, brings the characteristics of each part into the others, to the diffusion of education, to the cheapness of literature and universal habit of reading, which enable every one to know what every one else is thinking, but above all, to the newness of the country, and the fact that four-fifths of it have been made all at a stroke, and therefore all of a piece, as compared with the slow growth by which European countries have developed. Newness is the cause of uniformity, not merely in the external aspect of cities, villages, farmhouses, but in other things also, for the institutions and social habits which belonged a century ago to a group of small communities on the Atlantic coast, have been rapidly extended over an immense area, each band of settlers naturally seeking to retain its customs, and to plant in the new soil shoots from which trees like those of the old home might spring up. The variety of European countries is due, not only to the fact that their race-elements have not yet become thoroughly commingled, but also that many old institutions have survived among the new ones; as in a city that grows but slowly, old buildings are not cleared away to make room for others more suited to modern commerce, but are allowed to stand, sometimes empty and unused, sometimes half adapted to new purposes. This scarcely happens in America. Doubtless many American institutions are old, and were old before they were carried across the Atlantic. But they have generally received a new dress, which, in adapting them to the needs of to-day, conceals their ancient character; and the form in which they have been diffused or reproduced in the different States of the Union is in all those States practically identical.

PERSPECTIVES, PAST AND PRESENT

III

INTRODUCTION III

In this section four historians and an anthropologist plot the developing design of the national character over the years from 1815 to the present day. The readings are noteworthy not only for what they have to say about the character of Americans but also for what they exhibit with respect to the shifting foci and advancing analytical sophistication of the study of national character.

Henry Adams concluded the ninth and final volume of his *History of the United States of America during the Administrations of Jefferson and Madison* in 1891 with a chapter, reproduced here in part, on the character of the American people at the close of the War of 1812, an event which has been aptly called the second war for American independence. Adams was the first professional historian to take cognizance of the national character as a legitimate subject for investigation. Disparaging the conventional themes of political, constitutional, diplomatic, and military history, he contended that, to write significantly, the historian should concern himself with the totality of an evolving culture. That was what Adams meant when he declared that "of all historical problems, the nature of a national character is the most difficult and the most important," and when he asserted that the study of national character was "more important than that of politics or economics." For a generation of historians who were trained in the German "scientific" school of Leopold von Ranke and who concurred with the English historian Edward A. Freeman that history was "past politics," Adams was breaking new ground, anticipating the extension of interest into the uncharted fields of social, intellectual, and cultural history.

Adams himself stopped short on the threshold of those unexplored regions. Boldly opening the first volume of the *History* with six chapters on the character of the nation in 1800, he presented a portrait of a people prosperous, industrious, ambitious, mobile, optimistic, intensely practical, and deeply conservative. The description might have been drawn from Tocqueville's *Democracy in America;* some two decades earlier, Adams had adopted Tocqueville's work as "the Gospel of my private religion." Adams faltered, however, at the close of his study. In contrast to the careful craftsmanship and penetrating erudition which marked his best work and set him in the front rank of American historians, the concluding essay on the American character was marred by hasty and superficial execution. To the traits of "intelligence, rapidity, and mildness" which, in his judgment, were "fixed in the national character as early as 1817," Adams gave inadequate definition and merely cursory examination. As a result, his observations were more suggestive than conclusive.

The reason was partly that Adams was first in the field: His inquiry was hampered by paucity of appropriate data. It was also partly, perhaps fundamentally, personal: The tragic suicide of his wife in 1885, during the writing of the *History,* cut his life in two. Six years later he told an intimate friend that the last two volumes had been composed "in a very different frame of mind from that in which the work was begun. . . . If you compare the tone of my first volume . . . with that of the ninth volume when it appears, you will feel that the light has gone out." And there was one other reason. In his autobiography, *The Education of Henry Adams,* the historian traced his futile search for "some great generalization which would finish one's clamor to be educated." As in his life, so in his *History:* He could neither discover nor contrive a formula to explain the shaping of American character. Adams' descriptions of that character were perceptive, but he was not content with mere description; he sought an organizing principle—and found it not. His discussion of causal factors was negative for the most part; it was mainly devoted to repudiation of those foreign observers who made "rapacity the accepted explanation of American peculiarities." But if the thesis of "rapacity" was not adequate or even accurate, what could be put in its place? Adams' inability to frame a satisfactory answer to that question was reflected in the insufficiency of his final assessment of the national character.

What Adams missed, Frederick Jackson Turner found. In a paper presented to the American Historical Association in 1893, just two years after the publication of the last volume of Adams' *History,* the younger historian from the Midwest discussed "The Significance of the Frontier in American History." The selection below, excerpted from that epoch-making essay and from Turner's article of 1910 entitled "Contributions of the West to American Democracy," offers a concise statement of the main elements of Turner's "frontier hypothesis" which dominated the interpretation of American history and character through the first four or five decades of the present century.

Turner regarded the frontier experience as the pre-eminent factor in the forming of an American character; he named the pioneer as the archetypical American. His interpretation, like Crèvecoeur's, was governed by the conjoined principles of environmentalism and exceptionalism, succinctly expressed in the magisterial dictum that "American democracy . . . was not carried in the *Susan Constant* to Virginia, nor in the *Mayflower* to Plymouth. It came out of the American forest, and it gained new strength each time it touched a new frontier." The distinctive features of the national character—indeed, its distinctively *national* features—were sculptured by the people's triumphant encounter with the western wilderness over the course of nearly three centuries. America possessed, and took possession of, what Europe lacked: an abundance of free or cheap land; it was the occupation of that land and the exploitation of its bounty that made Americans American.

In another way, also, Turner's exposition resembled Crèvecoeur's: The front of settlement advanced across the continent in cycles of regeneration wherein society was temporarily reduced, on the raw moving margins of civilization, to its bare essentials, subsequently to be reconstructed in novel, ever more characteristically American, patterns. The receding frontier was the place where institutions were dismantled and re-formed; where European and Eastern complexity yielded to elemental simplicity; where individuals were freed, however briefly, from social controls; where, in the outcome, the promise of America was fulfilled and an authentically American style came into being. Thus the primitivist thesis which Crèvecoeur had adumbrated was elaborated by Turner into a general formula of cultural transformation.

Thematic congruities aside, Turner broke company with Crèvecoeur at several major points, betokening the Americanization of the interpretation of American character. Where the Frenchman's European sensibilities led him to emphasize the continuity of land ownership over familial generations—his American husbandman aspired to no greater blessing than to cultivate his ancestral acres and bequeath them to his children after him—Turner stressed the restive mobility of the typical American farmer and his exploitative attitude toward the soil. Crèvecoeur's agrarian mystique bespoke the yearning of the European peasant rather than the acquisitive and wasteful enterprise of the westering Yankee who was not content to pin his life within the narrow domestic bounds of the parental fields. Crèvecoeur wrote harshly of the backwoodsmen whose manners compared unfavorably, to his eye, with those of the Indians; Turner presented a more sanguine appraisal. In short, Turner's pioneer was Crèvecoeur's "new man" responding to the attraction of a rich and accessible continent, shucking off his European garments as he entered the forest, and rejoicing to find his fortunes magnified, his stature enhanced, and his spirits rejuvenated by his movement through American space. The Pennsylvania farm which marked the *terminus ad quem* for Crèvecoeur's liberated peasant became the *terminus a quo* of Turner's newer and more American frontiersman.

By about 1930 the frontier hypothesis, embellished and extended by Turner's followers, had established a near monopoly of American historiography and acquired the sanctity of orthodox doctrine. Thereafter it came under mounting criticism from historians who sharply questioned its presuppositions, its scholarship, and its adequacy as a theory of American history and character.[1] Facts were turned up which did not fit the formula—nor could the formula be stretched to accommodate the facts. Especially strenuous objections were elicited by the inapplicability of the interpretation, as Turner himself admitted,

[1]Selections from the literature of controversy can be found in George Rogers Taylor (ed.), *The Turner Thesis* (Boston: D. C. Heath and Company, 1949). See also "Interpretations of the American West: A Descriptive Bibliography," annotated by Walter Rundell, Jr., in *Arizona and the West,* III (Spring, 1961; Summer, 1961), pp. 69–88, 148–68.

to the emergent industrial-urban complex of American life, by its exclusivist or isolationist connotations, and by its insufficient regard for the continuities of culture and the tough conservative character of institutions.

Alternative emphases and approaches were suggested by such scholars as Arthur M. Schlesinger, now professor emeritus of history at Harvard University, whose essay on American character, originally published in 1943, is reprinted here in full. While concurring with Turner in stressing the prime importance of "New World conditions"—"The undeveloped continent prescribed the conditions of living the new life, the mold within which the American character took shape"—Schlesinger insisted that due attention be given to "Old World influences" on American culture as well as to the formative significance of other frontiers than that of the land. His essay can be read as an expansion of Turner's thesis, as a qualification of it, and as a post-Turnerian inquiry into the modifications of character that occurred when "the primacy of rural life gave way to the rise of urbanism."[2]

Among Turner's most acute critics were historians who, acknowledging their debt to the master and attempting to salvage whatever was valid in his work, reinterpreted the frontier experience as a special case of some more general phenomenon of American life. Turner had defined the frontier as, among other things, the abundance of open land; by the 1950s historians were exploring the implications of abundance in general for the development of the national character.[3] Turner had stressed the movement of Americans across the face of the continent; later writers, drawing on the resources of sociology and psychology, developed a general theory of social mobility, both horizontal and vertical, in which the settlement of the West occupied an important but restricted place.[4] In the fourth selection, George W. Pierson, professor of history at Yale University, rings changes on that latter theme with some provocative comments on the relation of American character to the "M-Factor" of migration, mobility, and movement. Pierson's article was originally presented as a lecture at the University of Munich in 1961; it invites comparison with Tocqueville's observations on the same large topic of the American as man in motion.

In the frontier hypothesis the factor of vertical mobility was subordinated to the factor of horizontal mobility; movement on the ladder of social class was treated as a function or by-product of movement over land-space, and vertical mobility as an independent variable in the formation of American character received less than adequate attention from the Turnerians. By way of corrective, the concluding essay in this section examines the characterological

[2]For an extended statement of Schlesinger's "urban interpretation" see his essay, "The City in American Civilization," in *Paths to the Present* (New York: The Macmillan Company, 1949), chap. XI.

[3]See especially David M. Potter, *People of Plenty: Economic Abundance and the American Character* (Chicago: University of Chicago Press, 1954), chap. VII.

[4]See, e.g., Everett S. Lee, "The Turner Thesis Re-examined," *American Quarterly,* XIII (Spring, 1961), pp. 77–83.

significance of the American "race towards success" in which each generation strives to climb higher than its fathers. The author, Margaret Mead, is one of America's leading anthropologists. The book from which the reading is excerpted, *And Keep Your Powder Dry* (1943), commands a prominent position in the literature of national character as the pioneer application of culture-and-personality analysis to the character and culture of a complex modern nation.[5]

[5]For a theoretical discussion of the redefinition of national character in terms of culture-and-personality see Margaret Mead, "The Study of National Character," in Daniel Lerner and Harold D. Lasswell (eds.), *The Policy Sciences* (Stanford, Calif.: Stanford University Press, 1951), chap. 4.

HENRY ADAMS

The Shaping of National Character

Until 1815 nothing in the future of the American Union was regarded as settled. As late as January, 1815, division into several nationalities was still thought to be possible. Such a destiny, repeating the usual experience of history, was not necessarily more unfortunate than the career of a single nationality wholly American; for if the effects of divided nationality were certain to be unhappy, those of a single society with equal certainty defied experience or sound speculation. One uniform and harmonious system appealed to the imagination as a triumph of human progress, offering prospects of peace and ease, contentment and philanthropy, such as the world had not seen; but it invited dangers, formidable because unusual or altogether unknown. The corruption of such a system might prove to be proportionate with its dimensions, and uniformity might lead to evils as serious as were commonly ascribed to diversity.

The laws of human progress were matter not for dogmatic faith, but for study; and although society instinctively regarded small States, with their clashing interests and incessant wars, as the chief obstacle to improvement, such progress as the world knew had been coupled with those drawbacks. The few examples offered by history of great political societies, relieved from external competition or rivalry, were not commonly thought encouraging. War had been the severest test of political and social character, laying bare whatever was feeble, and calling out whatever was strong; and the effect of removing such a test was an untried problem.

In 1815 for the first time Americans ceased to doubt the path they were to follow. Not only was the unity of their nation established, but its probable divergence from older societies was also well defined. Already in 1817 the difference between Europe and America was decided. In politics the distinction was more evident than in social, religious, literary, or scientific directions; and the result was singular. For a time the aggressions of England and France forced the United States into a path that seemed to lead toward European methods of government; but the popular resistance, or inertia, was so great

From *History of the United States* by Henry Adams (Charles Scribner's Sons, 1890).

that the most popular party leaders failed to overcome it, and no sooner did foreign dangers disappear than the system began to revert to American practices; the national government tried to lay aside its assumed powers. When Madison vetoed the bill for internal improvements he could have had no other motive than that of restoring to the government, as far as possible, its original American character.

The result was not easy to understand in theory or to make efficient in practice; but while the drift of public opinion, and still more of practical necessity, drew the government slowly toward the European standard of true political sovereignty, nothing showed that the compromise, which must probably serve the public purpose, was to be European in form or feeling. As far as politics supplied a test, the national character had already diverged from any foreign type. Opinions might differ whether the political movement was progressive or retrograde, but in any case the American, in his political character, was a new variety of man.

The social movement was also decided. The war gave a severe shock to the Anglican sympathies of society, and peace seemed to widen the breach between European and American tastes. Interest in Europe languished after Napoleon's overthrow. France ceased to affect American opinion. England became an object of less alarm. Peace produced in the United States a social and economic revolution which greatly curtailed the influence of New England, and with it the social authority of Great Britain. The invention of the steamboat counterbalanced ocean commerce. The South and West gave to society a character more aggressively American than had been known before. That Europe, within certain limits, might tend toward American ideas was possible, but that America should under any circumstances follow the experiences of European development might thenceforward be reckoned as improbable. American character was formed, if not fixed.

The scientific interest of American history centered in national character, and in the workings of a society destined to become vast, in which individuals were important chiefly as types. Although this kind of interest was different from that of European history, it was at least as important to the world. Should history ever become a true science, it must expect to establish its laws, not from the complicated story of rival European nationalities, but from the economical evolution of a great democracy. North America was the most favorable field on the globe for the spread of a society so large, uniform, and isolated as to answer the purposes of science. There a single homogeneous society could easily attain proportions of three or four hundred million persons, under conditions of undisturbed growth.

In Europe or Asia, except perhaps in China, undisturbed social evolution had been unknown. Without disturbance, evolution seemed to cease. Wherever disturbance occurred, permanence was impossible. Every people in turn adapted itself to the law of necessity. Such a system as that of the United States could hardly have existed for half a century in Europe except under the protection of another power. In the fierce struggle characteristic of European society, systems were permanent in nothing except in the general law, that, whatever other character they might possess they must always be chiefly military.

The want of permanence was not the only or the most confusing obstacle to the treatment of European history as a science. The intensity of the struggle gave prominence to the individual, until the hero seemed all, society nothing; and what was worse for science, the men were far more interesting than the societies. In the dramatic view of history, the hero deserved more to be studied than the community to which he belonged; in truth, he was the society, which existed only to produce him and to perish with him. Against such a view historians were among the last to protest, and protested but faintly when they did so at all. They felt as strongly as their audiences that the highest achievements were alone worth remembering either in history or in art, and that a reiteration of commonplaces was commonplace. With all the advantages of European movement and color, few historians succeeded in enlivening or dignifying the lack of motive, intelligence, and morality, the helplessness characteristic of many long periods in the face of crushing problems, and the futility of human efforts to escape from difficulties religious, political, and social. In a period extending over four or five thousand years, more or less capable of historical treatment, historians were content to illustrate here and there the most dramatic moments of the most striking communities. The hero was their favorite. War was the chief field of heroic action, and even the history of England was chiefly the story of war.

The history of the United States promised to be free from such disturbances. War counted for little, the hero for less; on the people alone the eye could permanently rest. The steady growth of a vast population without the social distinctions that confused other histories,—without kings, nobles, or armies; without church, traditions, and prejudices,—seemed a subject for the man of science rather than for dramatists or poets. To scientific treatment only one great obstacle existed. Americans, like Europeans, were not disposed to make of their history a mechanical evolution. They felt that they even more than other nations needed the heroic element, because they breathed an atmosphere of peace and industry where heroism could seldom be displayed; and in unconscious protest against their own social conditions they adorned with imaginary qualities scores of supposed leaders, whose only merit was their faculty of reflecting a popular trait. Instinctively they clung to ancient history as though conscious that of all misfortunes that could befall the national character, the greatest would be the loss of the established ideals which alone ennobled human weakness. Without heroes, the national character of the United States had few charms of imagination even to Americans.

Historians and readers maintained Old World standards. No historian cared to hasten the coming of an epoch when man should study his own history in the same spirit and by the same methods with which he studied the formation of a crystal. Yet history had its scientific as well as its human side, and in

American history the scientific interest was greater than the human. Elsewhere the student could study under better conditions the evolution of the individual, but nowhere could he study so well the evolution of a race. The interest of such a subject exceeded that of any other branch of science, for it brought mankind within sight of its own end.

Travellers in Switzerland who stepped across the Rhine where it flowed from its glacier could follow its course among mediaeval towns and feudal ruins, until it became a highway for modern industry, and at last arrived at a permanent equilibrium in the ocean. American history followed the same course. With prehistoric glaciers and mediaeval feudalism the story had little to do; but from the moment it came within sight of the ocean it acquired interest almost painful. A child could find his way in a river-valley, and a hoy could float on the waters of Holland; but science alone could sound the depths of the ocean, measure its currents, foretell its storms, or fix its relations to the system of Nature. In a democratic ocean science could see something ultimate. Man could go no further. The atom might move, but the general equilibrium could not change.

Whether the scientific or the heroic view were taken, in either case the starting-point was the same, and the chief object of interest was to define national character. Whether the figures of history were treated as heroes or as types, they must be taken to represent the people. American types were especially worth study if they were to represent the greatest democratic evolution the world could know. Readers might judge for themselves what share the individual possessed in creating or shaping the nation; but whether it was small or great, the nation could be understood only by studying the individual. For that reason, in the story of Jefferson and Madison individuals retained their old interest as types of character, if not as sources of power.

. . . .

That the individual should rise to a higher order either of intelligence or morality than had existed in former ages was not to be expected, for the United States offered less field for the development of individuality than had been offered by older and smaller societies. The chief function of the American Union was to raise the average standard of popular intelligence and well-being, and at the close of the War of 1812 the superior average intelligence of Americans was so far admitted that Yankee acuteness, or smartness, became a national reproach; but much doubt remained whether the intelligence belonged to a high order, or proved a high morality. From the earliest ages, shrewdness was associated with unscrupulousness; and Americans were freely charged with wanting honesty. The charge could neither be proved nor disproved. American morality was such as suited a people so endowed, and was high when compared with the morality of many older societies; but, like American intelligence, it discouraged excess. Probably the political morality shown by the government and by public men during the first sixteen years of the century offered a fair gauge of social morality. Like the character of the popular inventions, the character of the morals corresponded to the wants of a growing democratic society; but time alone could decide whether it would result in a high or low national ideal.

Finer analysis showed other signs of divergence from ordinary standards. If Englishmen took pride in one trait more than in another, it was in the steady uniformity of their progress. The innovating and revolutionary quality of the French mind irritated them. America showed an un-English rapidity in movement. In politics, the American people between 1787 and 1817 accepted greater changes than had been known in England since 1688. In religion, the Unitarian movement of Boston and Harvard College would never have been possible in England, where the defection of Oxford or Cambridge, and the best educated society in the United Kingdom, would have shaken Church and State to their foundations. In literature the American school was chiefly remarkable for the rapidity with which it matured. The first book of Irving was a successful burlesque of his own ancestral history; the first poem of Bryant sang of the earth only as a universal tomb; the first preaching of Channing assumed to overthrow the Trinity; and the first paintings of Allston aspired to recover the ideal perfection of Raphael and Titian. In all these directions the American mind showed tendencies that surprised Englishmen more than they struck Americans. Allston defended himself from the criticism of friends who made complaint of his return to America. He found there, as he maintained, not only a growing taste for art, but "a quicker appreciation" of artistic effort than in any European land. If the highest intelligence of American society were to move with such rapidity, the time could not be far distant when it would pass into regions which England never liked to contemplate.

Another intellectual trait . . . was the disposition to relax severity. Between the theology of Jonathan Edwards and that of William Ellery Channing was an enormous gap, not only in doctrines but also in methods. Whatever might be thought of the conclusions reached by Edwards and [Samuel] Hopkins, the force of their reasoning commanded respect. Not often had a more strenuous effort than theirs been made to ascertain God's will, and to follow it without regard to weaknesses of the flesh. The idea that the nature of God's attributes was to be preached only as subordinate to the improvement of man, agreed little with the spirit of their religion. The Unitarian and Universalist movements marked the beginning of an epoch when ethical and humanitarian ideas took the place of metaphysics, and even New England turned from contemplating the omnipotence of the Deity in order to praise the perfections of his creatures.

The spread of great popular sects like the Universalists and Campbellites, founded on assumptions such as no Orthodox theology could tolerate, showed a growing tendency to relaxation of thought in that direction. The struggle for existence was already mitigated, and the first effect of the change was seen in the increasing cheerfulness of religion. Only when men found their actual world almost a heaven, could they lose overpowering anxiety about the world to come. Life had taken a softer aspect, and as a consequence God was no longer terrible. Even the wicked became less mischievous in an atmosphere where virtue was easier than vice. Punishments seemed mild in a society where every offender could cast off his past, and create a new career. For the first time in history, great bodies of men turned away from their old religion, giving no better reason than that it required them to believe in a cruel Deity, and rejected necessary conclusions of theology because they were inconsistent with human self-esteem.

The same optimism marked the political movement. Society was weary of strife, and settled gladly into a political system which left every disputed point undetermined. The public seemed obstinate only in believing that all was for the best, as far as the United States were concerned, in the affairs of mankind. The contrast was great between this temper of mind and that in which the Constitution had been framed; but it was no greater than the contrast in the religious opinions of the two periods, while the same reaction against severity marked the new literature. The rapid accumulation of wealth and increase in physical comfort told the same story from the standpoint of economy. On every side society showed that ease was for a time to take the place of severity, and enjoyment was to have its full share in the future national existence.

The traits of intelligence, rapidity, and mildness seemed fixed in the national character as early as 1817, and were likely to become more marked as time should pass. A vast amount of conservatism still lingered among the people; but the future spirit of society could hardly fail to be intelligent, rapid in movement, and mild in method. Only in the distant future could serious change occur, and even then no return to European characteristics seemed likely. The American continent was happier in its conditions and easier in its resources than the regions of Europe and Asia, where Nature revelled in diversity and conflict. If at any time American character should change, it might as probably become sluggish as revert to the violence and extravagances of Old-World development. The inertia of several hundred million people, all formed in a similar social mould, was as likely to stifle energy as to stimulate evolution.

With the establishment of these conclusions, a new episode in American history began in 1815. New subjects demanded new treatment, no longer dramatic but steadily tending to become scientific. The traits of American character were fixed; the rate of physical and economical growth was established; and history, certain that at a given distance of time the Union would contain so many millions of people, with wealth valued at so many millions of dollars, became thenceforward chiefly concerned to know what kind of people these millions were to be. They were intelligent, but what paths would their intelligence select? They were quick, but what solution of insoluble problems would quickness hurry? They were scientific, and what control would their science exercise over their destiny? They were mild, but what corruptions would their relaxations bring? They were peaceful, but by what machinery were their corruptions to be purged? What interests were to vivify a society so vast and uniform? What ideals were to ennoble it? What object, besides physical content, must a democratic continent aspire to attain? For the treatment of such questions, history required another century of experience.

FREDERICK JACKSON TURNER

The Frontier Experience

. . . In the settlement of America we have to observe how European life entered the continent, and how America modified and developed that life and reacted on Europe. . . . The frontier is the line of most rapid and effective Americanization. The wilderness masters the colonist. It finds him a European in dress, industries, tools, modes of travel, and thought. It takes him from the railroad car and puts him in the birch canoe. It strips off the garments of civilization and arrays him in the hunting shirt and the moccasin. It puts him in the log cabin of the Cherokee and Iroquois and runs an Indian palisade around him. Before long he has gone to planting Indian corn and plowing with a sharp stick; he shouts the war cry and takes the scalp in orthodox Indian fashion. In short, at the frontier the environment is at first too strong for the man. He must accept the conditions which it furnishes, or perish, and so he fits himself into the Indian clearings and follows the Indian trails. Little by little he transforms the wilderness, but the outcome is not the old Europe. . . . The fact is, that here is a new product that is American. At first, the frontier was the Atlantic coast. It was the frontier of Europe in a very real sense. Moving westward, the frontier became more and more American. As successive terminal moraines result from successive glaciations, so each frontier leaves its traces behind it, and when it becomes a settled area the region still partakes of the frontier characteristics. Thus the advance of the frontier has meant a steady movement away from the influence of Europe, a steady growth of independence on American lines. And to study this advance, the men who grew up under these conditions, and the political, economic, and social results of it, is to study the really American part of our history.

. . . .

. . . The frontier promoted the formation of a composite nationality for the American people. The coast was preponderantly English, but the later tides of continental immigration flowed across to the free lands. This was the case from the early colonial days. The Scotch-Irish and the Palatine Germans, or "Pennsylvania Dutch," furnished the dominant element in the stock of the colonial frontier. With these peoples were also the freed indented servants, or redemptioners, who at the expiration of their time of service passed to the frontier. Governor Spotswood of Virginia writes in 1717, "The inhabitants of our frontiers are composed generally of such as have been transported hither as servants, and, being out of their time, settle themselves where land is to be taken up and that will produce the necessarys of life with little labour." Very generally these redemptioners were of non-English stock. In the crucible of the frontier the immigrants were Americanized, liberated, and fused into a mixed race, English in neither nationality nor characteristics. The process has gone on from the early days to our own.

. . . .

From the conditions of frontier life came intellectual traits of profound importance. The works of travelers along each frontier from colonial days onward describe certain common traits, and these traits have, while softening down, still persisted as survivals in the place of their origin, even when a higher social organization succeeded. The result is that to the frontier the American intellect owes its striking characteristics. That coarseness and strength combined with acuteness and inquisitiveness; that practical, inventive turn of mind, quick to find expedients; that masterful grasp of material things, lacking in the artistic but powerful to effect great ends; that restless, nervous energy; that dominant individualism, working for good and for evil, and withal that buoyancy and exuberance which comes with freedom—these are traits of the frontier, or traits called out elsewhere because of the existence of the frontier.

. . . .

It was because Andrew Jackson personified these essential Western traits that in his presidency he became the idol and the mouthpiece of the popular will. In his assault upon the Bank as an engine of aristocracy, and in his denunciation of nullification, he went directly to his object with the ruthless energy of a frontiersman. For formal law and the subleties of State sovereignty he had the contempt of a backwoodsman. Nor is it without significance that this typical man of the new democracy will always be associated with the triumph of the spoils system in national politics. To the new democracy of the West, office was an opportunity to exercise natural rights as an equal citizen of the community. Rotation in office served not simply to allow the successful man to punish his enemies and reward his friends, but it also furnished the training in the actual conduct of political affairs which every American claimed as his birthright. Only in a primitive democracy of the type of the United States in 1830 could such a system have existed without the ruin of the State. National government in that period was no complex and nicely adjusted machine, and the evils of the system were long in making themselves fully apparent.

The triumph of Andrew Jackson marked the end of the old era of trained statesmen for the Presidency. With him began the era of the popular hero. Even Martin Van Buren, whom we think of in connection with the East, was born in a log house under conditions that were not unlike parts of the older

West. Harrison was the hero of the Northwest, as Jackson had been of the Southwest. Polk was a typical Tennesseean, eager to expand the nation, and Zachary Taylor was what Webster called a "frontier colonel." During the period that followed Jackson, power passed from the region of Kentucky and Tennessee to the border of the Mississippi. The natural democratic tendencies that had earlier shown themselves in the Gulf States were destroyed, however, by the spread of cotton culture, and the development of great plantations in that region. What had been typical of the democracy of the Revolutionary frontier and of the frontier of Andrew Jackson was now to be seen in the States between the Ohio and the Mississippi. As Andrew Jackson is the typical democrat of the former region, so Abraham Lincoln is the very embodiment of the pioneer period of the Old Northwest. Indeed, he is the embodiment of the democracy of the West. . . .

The pioneer life from which Lincoln came differed in important respects from the frontier democracy typified by Andrew Jackson. Jackson's democracy was contentious, individualistic, and it sought the ideal of local self-government and expansion. Lincoln represents rather the pioneer folk who entered the forest of the great Northwest to chop out a home, to build up their fortunes in the midst of a continually ascending industrial movement. In the democracy of the Southwest, industrial development and city life were only minor factors, but to the democracy of the Northwest they were its very life. To widen the area of the clearing, to contend with one another for the mastery of the industrial resources of the rich provinces, to struggle for a place in the ascending movement of society, to transmit to one's offspring the chance for education, for industrial betterment, for the rise in life which the hardships of the pioneer existence denied to the pioneer himself, these were some of the ideals of the region to which Lincoln came. The men were commonwealth builders, industry builders. Whereas the type of hero in the Southwest was militant, in the Northwest he was industrial. It was in the midst of these "plain people," as he loved to call them, that Lincoln grew to manhood. As Emerson says, "He is the true history of the American people in his time." The years of his early life were the years when the democracy of the Northwest came into struggle with the institution of slavery which threatened to forbid the expansion of the democratic pioneer life in the West. In President Eliot's essay on "Five American Contributions to Civilization," he instances as one of the supreme tests of American democracy its attitude upon the question of slavery. But if democracy chose wisely and worked effectively toward the solution of this problem, it must be remembered that Western democracy took the lead. The rail-splitter himself became the nation's President in that fierce time of struggle, and armies of the woodsmen and pioneer farmers recruited in the Old Northwest made free the Father of Waters, marched through Georgia, and helped to force the struggle to a conclusion at Appomattox. The free pioneer democracy struck down the slave-holding aristocracy on its march to the West.

The last chapter in the development of Western democracy is the one that deals with its conquest over the vast spaces of the new West. At each new stage of Western development, the people have had to grapple with larger areas, with bigger combinations. The little colony of Massachusetts' veterans that settled at Marietta received a land grant as large as the State of Rhode Island. The band of Connecticut pioneers that followed Moses Cleaveland to the Connecticut Reserve occupied a region as large as the parent State. The area which settlers of New England stock occupied on the prairies of northern Illinois surpassed the combined area of Massachusetts, Connecticut, and Rhode Island. Men who had become accustomed to the narrow valleys and the little towns of the East found themselves out on the boundless spaces of the West dealing with units of such magnitude as dwarfed their former experience. The Great Lakes, the Prairies, the Great Plains, the Rocky Mountains, the Mississippi and the Missouri, furnished new standards of measurement for the achievement of this industrial democracy. Individualism began to give way to cooperation and to governmental activity. Even in the earlier days of the democratic conquest of the wilderness, demands had been made upon the government for support in internal improvements, but this new West showed a growing tendency to call to its assistance the powerful arm of national authority. In the period since the Civil War, the vast public domain has been donated to the individual farmer, to States for education, to railroads for the construction of transportation lines.

Moreover, with the advent of democracy in the last fifteen years upon the Great Plains, new physical conditions have presented themselves which have accelerated the social tendency of Western democracy. The pioneer farmer of the days of Lincoln could place his family on a flatboat, strike into the wilderness, cut out his clearing, and with little or no capital go on to the achievement of industrial independence. Even the homesteader on the Western prairies found it possible to work a similar independent destiny, although the factor of transportation made a serious and increasing impediment to the free working-out of his individual career. But when the arid lands and the mineral resources of the Far West were reached, no conquest was possible by the old individual pioneer methods. Here expensive irrigation works must be constructed, cooperative activity was demanded in utilization of the water supply, capital beyond the reach of the small farmer was required. In a word, the physiographic province itself decreed that the destiny of this new frontier should be social rather than individual.

Magnitude of social achievement is the watchword of the democracy since the Civil War. From petty towns built in the marshes, cities arose whose greatness and industrial power are the wonder of our time. The conditions were ideal for the production of captains of industry. The old democratic admiration for the self-made man, its old deference to the rights of competitive individual development, together with the stupendous natural resources that opened to the conquest of the keenest and the strongest, gave such conditions of mobility as enabled the development of the large corporate industries which in our own decade have marked the West.

. . . If now in the way of recapitulation, we try to pick out from the influences that have gone to the making of Western democracy the factors which constitute the net result of this movement, we shall have to mention at least the following:—

Most important of all has been the fact that an area of free land has continually lain on the western border of the settled area of the United States. Whenever social conditions tended to crystallize in the East, whenever capital tended to press upon labor or political restraints to impede the freedom of the mass, there was this gate of escape to the free conditions of the frontier. These free lands promoted individualism, economic equality, freedom to rise, democracy. Men would not accept inferior wages and a permanent position of social subordination when this promised land of freedom and equality was theirs for the taking. Who would rest content under oppressive legislative conditions when with a slight effort he might reach a land wherein to become a co-worker in the building of free cities and free States on the lines of his own ideal? In a word, then, free lands meant free opportunities. Their existence has differentiated the American democracy from the democracies which have preceded it, because ever, as democracy in the East took the form of highly specialized and complicated industrial society, in the West it kept in touch with primitive conditions, and by action and reaction these two forces have shaped our history.

In the next place, these free lands and this treasury of industrial resources have existed over such vast spaces that they have demanded of democracy increasing spaciousness of design and power of execution. Western democracy is contrasted with the democracy of all other times in the largeness of the tasks to which it has set its hand, and in the vast achievements which it has wrought out in the control of nature and of politics. It would be difficult to overemphasize the importance of this training upon democracy. Never before in the history of the world has a democracy existed on so vast an area and handled things in the gross with such success, with such largeness of design, and such grasp upon the means of execution. In short, democracy has learned in the West of the United States how to deal with the problem of magnitude. The old historic democracies were but little states with primitive economic conditions.

But the very task of dealing with vast resources, over vast areas, under the conditions of free competition furnished by the West, has produced the rise of those captains of industry whose success in consolidating economic power now raises the question as to whether democracy under such conditions can survive. For the old military type of Western leaders like George Rogers Clark, Andrew Jackson, and William Henry Harrison have been substituted such industrial leaders as James J. Hill, John D. Rockefeller, and Andrew Carnegie.

The question is imperative, then, What ideals persist from this democratic experience of the West; and have they acquired sufficient momentum to sustain themselves under conditions so radically unlike those in the days of their origin? . . . Under the forms of the American democracy is there in reality evolving such a concentration of economic and social power in the hands of a comparatively few men as may make political democracy an appearance rather than a reality? The free lands are gone. The material forces that gave vitality to Western democracy are passing away. It is to the realm of the spirit, to the domain of ideals and legislation, that we must look for Western influence upon democracy in our own days.

. . . .

This, at least, is clear: American democracy is fundamentally the outcome of the experiences of the American people in dealing with the West. Western democracy through the whole of its earlier period tended to the production of a society of which the most distinctive fact was the freedom of the individual to rise under conditions of social mobility, and whose ambition was the liberty and well-being of the masses. This conception has vitalized all American democracy, and has brought it into sharp contrasts with the democracies of history, and with those modern efforts of Europe to create an artificial democratic order by legislation. The problem of the United States is not to create democracy, but to conserve democratic institutions and ideals. . . .

ARTHUR M. SCHLESINGER

What Then Is the American, This New Man?

The question which forms the title of this essay has never ceased to arouse interest since Crèvecoeur posed it in the last years of the Revolution. If we can learn why the American has come to be what he is, how he reacts instinctively to life, wherein he differs from other peoples, we shall have gained a deep insight into the springs of national behavior. Crèvecoeur's own answer, the considered opinion of a Frenchman long resident in the New World, may still be read with profit. The American, he said, "is either an European, or the descendant of an European, hence that strange mixture of blood which you will find in no other country. . . . *He* is an American, who leaving behind him all his ancient prejudices and manners, receives new ones from the new mode of life he has embraced, the new government he obeys, and the new rank he holds. . . . From involuntary idleness, servile dependence, penury, and useless labour, he has passed to toils of a very different nature.—This is an American."

I

Crèvecoeur, of course, was one of a long procession of Europeans who have tried to describe and appraise the American. Their writings, though of varying merit, possess the common advantage of presenting an outsider's point of view, free from the predilections and prepossessions which blur the American's vision of himself. Viewing the scene from a different background, they are also sensitive to national divergences of which the native-born are usually unaware. Though bias may influence the individual observer's judgment, the total number of visitors has been so great as to render far more significant their points of agreement.

The composite portrait that emerges deserves thoughtful consideration. The attributes most frequently noted are a belief in the universal obligation to work; the urge to move from place to place; a high standard of average comfort;

---

faith in progress; the eternal pursuit of material gain; an absence of permanent class barriers; the neglect of abstract thinking and of the aesthetic side of life; boastfulness; a deference for women; the prevalence of spoiled children; the general restlessness and hurry of life, always illustrated by the practice of fast eating; and certain miscellaneous traits such as overheated houses, the vice of spitting and the passion for rocking chairs and ice water.

This inventory, so far as it goes, reveals qualities and attitudes recognizably American. Moreover, the travelers express no doubt as to the existence of a distinctive national character. The native-born looking at their fellow countrymen readily identify them as New Englanders and Middle Westerners or Southerners, as products of old American stock or newcomers of immigrant origin; and they remember that at one period of their history the differences between Northerner and Southerner sharpened into a tragic war. But the detached observer from Europe has always been less impressed by these regional deviations than by the evidences of fundamental kinship, even in slavery times.

James Bryce, most perspicacious of the commentators, goes so far as to say, "Scotchmen and Irishmen are more unlike Englishmen, the native of Normandy more unlike the native of Provence, the Pomeranian more unlike the Wurtemberger, the Piedmontese more unlike the Neapolitan, the Basque more unlike the Andalusian, than the American from any part of the country is to the American from any other part." His conclusion is that "it is rather more difficult to take any assemblage of attributes in any of these European countries and call it the national type than it is to do the like in the United States." The preoccupation of American historians with local and sectional diversities has tended to obscure this underlying reality.

But the particular "assemblage of attributes" recorded by the travelers leaves much to be desired. Not only is the list incomplete, but it carelessly lumps the significant with the trivial. Since the typical European tried to cover as much ground as possible in a short time, his attention was caught by externals, with the result that annoying traits and ways assumed undue importance, much as dust in the eye of a wayfarer distorts the appearance of the landscape. The gospel of work, for example, hardly deserves to be equated with the addiction to spitting. Though the more thoughtful sought to correlate what they noticed with the avowed ideals of the people, they usually lacked sufficient knowledge of the deeper historical trends to grasp either the true import of the ideals or how they manifested themselves in action. Finally, the traveler gave little attention to the crucial problem of why the special combination of qualities and attitudes had become endemic within the borders of the United States.

Hence the judgment of these onlookers, though often clear-sighted and frequently valuable as a corrective, leaves ample room for the student of United States history to venture an answer to Crèvecoeur's question. If the native-born historian be suspect as a party in interest, he may at least strive to observe that counsel of objectivity which his professional conscience reveres.

II

What then is the American from a historian's point of view? The answer, briefly expressed, is so simple as to be a platitude. This "new man" is the product of the interplay of Old World influences and New World conditions. But just what heritage did the colonists bring with them from Europe, and why and how was it changed? Predominantly it involved that part of Europe's social experience in which they themselves had shared. The great bulk of the settlers, like the immigrants of later times, belonged to the poorer classes. They and their ancestors, whether in England or on the Continent, had been artisans, small tradesmen, farmers, day laborers—the broad foundation which supported the fine superstructure of European civilization. Shut out from a life of wealth, leisure and aesthetic enjoyment, they had tended to regard the ways of their social superiors with misgiving, if not resentment, and by the same token they magnified their own qualities of sobriety, diligence and thrift. Even when many of them, as notably in England, improved their economic position in the sixteenth and seventeenth centuries as a result of the great growth of commerce and industry, they continued to exalt the ancient proprieties.

This attitude found its classic spiritual expression in Calvinism. As Professor Tawney has said, Calvinism was "perhaps the first systematic body of religious teaching which can be said to recognize and applaud the economic virtues." It neatly fitted the glove of divine sanction to the hand of prudential conduct, thereby giving a sense of personal rectitude to the business of getting ahead in the world. But whether in Britain or elsewhere, whether in the religious groups directly concerned or those more remotely affected, Calvinism merely intensified a pre-existing bent. It is similarly true that the stringent code of morals often attributed to Calvinism, and more particularly to the Puritans, represented a lower-middle-class mentality long antedating the Geneva teachings.

This, then, was the type of humanity upon which the untamed New World wielded its influence. It has often been observed that plants and animals undergo modification when removed to America. These mutations arise from differences in climate and geography. But other factors as well affected transplanted people. One was the temperament of the settler, the fact that he was more adventurous, more ambitious or more rebellious against conditions at home than his fellows. It is not necessary to believe with William Stoughton in 1670 that "God sifted a whole Nation that he might send Choice Grain over into this Wilderness," but undoubtedly the act of quitting a familiar existence for a strange and perilous one demanded uncommon attributes of hardihood, self-reliance and imagination. Once the ocean was crossed, sheer distance from the old country and the challenge of new experiences further weakened the bonds of custom, evoked latent capacities and awakened the settler to possibilities of improvement hitherto unsuspected.

The undeveloped continent prescribed the conditions of living the new life, the mold within which the American character took shape. Farming was the primary occupation. At first resorted to to keep from starvation, it quickly became the mainstay of existence. The Revolution was fought by a people of whom nineteen out of twenty tilled the soil. With good land obtainable for more than a century after Independence, agriculture continued, though with gradually diminishing effect, to provide the pervasive atmosphere of American life and thought. "The vast majority of the people of this country live by the land, and carry its quality in their manners and opinions," wrote Ralph Waldo Emerson in 1844. Even when the hosts from Continental Europe began to swell the population after the middle of the nineteenth century, the rural temper of the nation remained pretty much unaltered, for many of the immigrants also turned to farming. This long apprenticeship to the soil made an indelible impress on the developing American character, with results which the modern age of the city has not wholly effaced.

Agriculture in the New World, however, differed from agriculture in the Old. This was the initial lesson which the colonists were compelled to learn. Those who had been farmers in their homelands found many of the traditional methods unsuitable. Those who had worked at urban occupations suffered an even greater handicap. Densely forested land must be cleared; the wildness taken out of the soil; a knowledge gained of indigenous plants and of the best means of growing them. The settlers of Jamestown were barely able to struggle through the early years. "There were never Englishmen left in a forreigne Country in such miserie as wee," wrote one of them. "Unsufferable hunger" caused them to eat horses, dogs, rats and snakes, and instances even of cannibalism are recorded. As is well known, the Plymouth colonists experienced similar trials. Yet in both cases the woods abounded with native fruits, berries, roots and nuts, game was plentiful, and near-by waters teemed with fish.

Had these courageous men been more readily adaptable, they could have enjoyed a gastronomic abundance beyond the dreams of the wealthiest classes at home. But they had never faced such an experience before, and reversion to a stage of civilization which the white man had long since outgrown was not easy. At the very first, all the early settlements actually imported food supplies; the Swedish colony on the Delaware did so for twenty years. A knowledge of self-sufficient farming came slowly and painfully, with untold numbers of men, women and children perishing in the process. In the long run, however, the settlers learned how to master their environment. Utilizing native crops and Indian methods of tillage, they abandoned the intensive cultivation required by the limited land resources of the Old World. It was simpler to move on to new fields when the fertility of the old was exhausted. The typical farm was a small one, worked by the owner and his family. Even when the system of staple production developed in the South, the small independent farmers considerably outnumbered the great slaveholding planters.

Though the colonial agriculturalist owed much to the savage, he had no wish to live like one. Accustomed in the old country to simple comforts and mechanical devices in the home and about the farm, he duplicated them in the wilderness. Every husbandman became a manufacturer and every farmhouse a small factory, producing flour, soap and candles, tanning skins, preparing the winter's meat supply, making nails, harness, hats, shoes and rugs, contriving tools, churns, casks, beds, chairs and tables. Such activities he supplemented with trapping, hunting and fishing. As cold weather closed in, he used his spare time getting out rough timber products, such as shingles and planks, or spent the long evenings before the open fireplace carving gunstocks or making brooms while his womenfolk knitted, spun or wove.

Under pressure of circumstances the farmer thus became a Jack-of-all-trades. As Chancellor Livingston wrote, "being habituated from early life to rely upon himself he acquires a skill in every branch of his profession, which is unknown in countries where labour is more divided." Take the case of a typical New Englander, John Marshall of Braintree, early in the eighteenth century. Besides tending his farm, he bought and sold hogs, was a painter, brickmaker and carpenter, turning out as many as three hundred laths in a day, and served as a precinct constable. The primitive state of society fostered a similar omnicompetence in other walks of life, as the career of Benjamin Franklin so well exemplifies. Lord Cornbury, the governor of New York, characterized Francis Makemie as "a Preacher, a Doctor of Physick, a Merchant, an Attorney, or Counsellor at Law, and," he ruefully added, "which is worse of all, a Disturber of Governments."

The pioneer farmer of later times was the colonial farmer reborn. Up and down the Mississippi Valley he faced the same difficulties and opportunities as his forefathers, and he dealt with them in much the same way. As time went on, to be sure, he managed to buy more and more of his tools and household conveniences. He also took advantage of new inventions like the iron plow and the reaper, while increasingly he raised crops for sale in a general market. Meanwhile along the Atlantic Seaboard similar changes occurred. But whether in the older or newer communities these innovations affected the surface rather than the substance of the traditional mode of life. Nor did the advent of cities at first do much to alter the situation. Mere islands in a sea of forests and farms, they long retained marked rural characteristics and depended for a large part of their growth on continued accessions from the countryside.

III

What elements of the national character are attributable to this long-time agrarian environment? First and foremost is the habit of work. For the colonial farmer ceaseless striving constituted the price of survival; every member of the community must be up and doing. When anyone failed to do his part, the authorities, whether Puritan, Anglican or otherwise, laid a heavy hand upon the culprit. The Virginia Assembly in 1619 ordered the slothful to be bound over to compulsory labor. A few years later the Massachusetts Bay Company instructed Governor John Endecott that "noe idle drone bee permitted to live amongst us," and the General Court followed this up in 1633 with a decree that "noe prson, howse houlder or othr, shall spend his time idlely or unproffitably, under paine of such punishmt as the Court shall thinke meete to inflicte." Such regulations had long existed in England, where it was hoped, vainly, they might combat the unemployment and vagrancy of a surplus laboring class; in America the object was to overcome a labor shortage—that exigent problem of every new country. Of course, most of the settlers, having been inured to toil in the homeland, needed no official prodding. They were the hardest-working people on earth, their only respite being afforded by strict observance of the Sabbath as demanded by both church and state.

The tradition of toil so begun found new sustenance as settlers opened up the boundless stretches of the interior. "In the free States," wrote Harriet Martineau in 1837, "labour is more really and heartily honoured than, perhaps, in any other part of the civilised world." Alonzo Potter voiced the general opinion of the American people when he asserted a few years later, "Without a definite pursuit, a man is an excrescence on society. . . . In isolating himself from the cares and employments of other men, he forfeits much of their sympathy, and can neither give nor receive great benefit." Even when the usual motives for work did not exist, the social compulsion remained. As William Ellery Channing put it, "The rich man has no more right to repose than the poor," for nobody should so live as to "throw all toil on another class of society."

One source of Northern antagonism to the system of human bondage was the fear that it was jeopardizing this basic tenet of the American creed. "Wherever labor is mainly performed by slaves," Daniel Webster told the United States Senate, "it is regarded as degrading to freemen"; and the Kentucky abolitionist David Rice pointed out that in the South "To labour, is to *slave;* to work, is *to work like a Negroe.*" After the Civil War, General W. T. Sherman found public occasion to thank God that now at long last Southern whites would have "to earn an honest living."

Probably no legacy from our farmer forebears has entered more deeply into the national psychology. If an American has no purposeful work on hand, the fever in his blood impels him nevertheless to some visible form of activity. When seated he keeps moving in a rocking chair. A European visitor in the 1890's saw more fact than fancy in a magazine caricature which pictured a foreigner as saying to his American hostess, "It's a defect in your country, that you have no leisured classes." "But we have them," she replied, "only we call them tramps." The traveler's own comment was: "America is the only country in the world, where one is ashamed of having nothing to do."

This worship of work has made it difficult for Americans to learn how to play. As Poor Richard saw it, "Leisure is the Time for doing something useful"; and James Russell Lowell confessed,

Pleasure doos make us Yankees kind o'winch,
Ez though 't wuz sunthin' paid for by the inch;
But yit we du contrive to worry thru,
Ef Dooty tells us thet the thing's to du.

The first mitigations of the daily grind took the form of hunting, fishing, barn-raisings and logrollings—activities that had no social stigma because they contributed to the basic needs of living. As the years went on, the great Southern planters, imitating the landed gentry in England, developed rural diversions of an elaborate sort; but their example, like that of the fashionable circles in the Northern cities, merely made the common man all the more self-conscious when he turned to recreation. Nor did the mid-nineteenth-century German and Irish immigrants, who indulged in spontaneous enjoyments when the day was over, have any other effect upon the native stock than to reinforce suspicions of the newcomers formed on other grounds. "The American," wrote the New Yorker, Henry T. Tuckerman, in 1857, "enters into festivity as if it were a serious business." And a serious business it has in considerable degree continued to be ever since.

Into it goes all the fierce energy that once felled the forests and broke the prairies. Americans play games not for fun but to win. They attend social gatherings grimly determined to have a "good time." Maxim Gorky said of Coney Island, "What an unhappy people it must be that turns for happiness here." The "rich gift of extemporizing pleasures," of taking leisure leisurely, seems alien to the national temper. It is significant that the English *Who's Who* includes the recreations of the notables listed, while the American does not.

The importance attached to useful work had the further effect of helping to make "this new man" indifferent to aesthetic considerations. To the farmer a tree was not a thing of beauty and a joy forever, but an obstacle to be replaced as quickly as possible with a patch of corn. In the words of an eighteenth-century American, "The Plow-man that raiseth Grain is more serviceable to Mankind, than the Painter who draws only to please the Eye. The Carpenter who builds a good House to defend us from the Wind and Weather, is more serviceable than the curious Carver, who employs his Art to please the Fancy." The cult of beauty, in other words, had nothing to contribute to the stern business of living; it wasn't "practical." The bias thus given to the national mentality lasted well into America's urban age. One result has been the architectural monotony and ugliness which have invariably offended travelers used to the picturesque charm of Old World cities.

IV

On the other hand, the complicated nature of the farmer's job, especially during the first two and a half centuries, afforded an unexcelled training in mechanical ingenuity. These ex-Europeans and their descendants became a race of whittlers and tinkers, daily engaged in devising, improving and repairing tools and other utensils until, as Emerson said, they had "the power and habit of invention in their brain." "Would any one but an American," asked one of Emerson's contemporaries, "have ever invented a milking machine? or a machine to beat eggs? or machines to black boots, scour knives, pare apples, and do a hundred things that all other peoples have done with their ten fingers from time immemorial?"

As population increased and manufacturing developed on a commercial scale, men merely turned to new purposes the skills and aptitudes that had become second nature to them. Thus Eli Whitney, who as a Massachusetts farm youth had made nails and hatpins for sale to his neighbors, later contrived the cotton gin and successfully applied the principle of interchangeable parts to the production of muskets; and Theodore T. Woodruff, a New York farm boy, won subsequent fame as the inventor of a sleeping car, a coffee-hulling machine and a steam plow. In this manner another trait became imbedded in the American character.

The farmer's success in coping with his multitudinous tasks aroused a pride of accomplishment that made him scorn the specialist or expert. As a Jack-of-all-trades he was content to be master of none, choosing to do many things well enough rather than anything supremely well. Accordingly, versatility became another outstanding American attribute. In public affairs the common man agreed with President Jackson that any intelligent citizen could discharge the duties of any governmental office. He had an abiding suspicion of the theorist or the "scholar in politics," preferring to trust his own quick perceptions and to deal from day to day with matters as they arose. In his breadwinning pursuits the American flitted from job to job in marked contrast to the European custom of following occupations which often descended from father to son.

The most casual scrutiny of the *Dictionary of American Biography* discloses countless instances reminiscent of John Marshall and Francis Makemie in colonial times. Thomas Buchanan Read, born on a Pennsylvania farm, was in turn a tailor's apprentice, grocer's assistant, cigar maker, tombstone carver, sign painter and actor before he became a portrait painter, novelist and poet. Another personage is listed as "ornithologist and wholesale druggist"; another as "preacher, railway president, author"; and still another as "physician, merchant, political leader, magazine editor, poet, and critic." The wonder is that, despite such a squandering of energies, they could yet gain sufficient distinction in any phase of their activities to be recalled by posterity.

Even in his principal occupation of growing food, the farmer encountered harsh criticism from foreign observers because of the way he wore out the land, neglected livestock and destroyed forest resources. But Old World agriculture rested on a ratio of man to land which in the New World was the reverse. It was as logical for the American farmer to "mine" the soil and move on to a virgin tract as it was for the European peasant to husband his few acres in the interest of generations unborn. Not till the opening years of the twentieth century, when the pressure of population dramatized the evils of past misuse, did the conservation of natural resources become a set national policy.

Meanwhile the tradition of wasteful living, bred by an environment of plenty, had fastened itself upon the American character, disposing men to condone extravagance in public as well as in private life. Even governmental corruption could be winked at on the ground that a wealthy country like the United States could afford it. In their daily living, Americans were improvident of riches that another people would have carefully preserved. One newcomer from England in the early nineteenth century wrote that the apples and peaches rotting in Ohio orchards were more "than would sink the British fleet." Another said of her neighbors that she wished "the poor people of England had the leavings of their tables, that goes to their dogs and hogs." A great national emergency like that of the Axis war reveals the extent to which the practice still prevails. People learned that, by responding to the government's appeal to salvage kitchen fats, old iron and other materials usually discarded, they could make a substantial contribution to the war effort.

Toward women the American male early acquired an attitude which sharply distinguished him from his brother in the Old World. As in every new country, women had a high scarcity value, both in the colonies and later in the pioneer West. They were in demand not only as sweethearts and wives, but also because of their economic importance, for they performed the endless work about the house and helped with the heavy farm labor. "The cry is everywhere for girls; girls, and more girls!" wrote a traveler in 1866. He noted that men outnumbered women in thirty-eight of the forty-five states and territories. In California the proportion was three to one; in Colorado, twenty to one. "Guess my husband's got to look after me, and make himself agreeable to me, if he can," a pretty Western girl remarked—"if he don't, there's plenty will." In the circumstances men paid women a deference and accorded them a status unknown in older societies. European observers attributed the high standard of sex morals largely to this fact, and it is significant that the most rapid strides toward equal suffrage took place in those commonwealths whose rural characteristics were strongest.

V

Since the agriculturalist regarded his farm as only a temporary abode—an investment rather than a home—he soon contracted the habit of being "permanently transitory." Distances that would have daunted the stoutest-hearted European deterred "this new man" not at all. Many an Atlantic Coast family migrated from place to place across the continent until the second or third generation reached the rim of the Pacific, then the next one began the journey back. "In no State of the Union," wrote James Bryce in 1888, "is the bulk of the population so fixed in its residence as everywhere in Europe; in many it is almost nomadic."

But for this constant mingling of people and ideas the spirit of sectionalism would have opened far deeper fissures in American society than it did, for the breadth of the land, the regional diversification of economic interests and the concentration of European immigrants in certain areas were all factors conducive to disaffection and disunity. Apart from the crisis of 1861, however, it has always been possible to adjust sectional differences peaceably. The war between North and South might itself have been avoided if the system of slave labor had not increasingly stopped the inflow of persons from other parts of the country as well as from Europe. Denied such infusions of new blood, the Southerners lived more and more to themselves, came to exalt their peculiarities over the traits they had in common with their fellow countrymen and, in the end, determined to establish an independent state.

As the nation grew older and its institutions took on a more settled aspect, the locomotive tendencies of the Americans showed no signs of abatement. According to a study in 1936, "over the last few decades mobility has been increasing rather than decreasing." The Department of Agriculture noted that the average farm family remained in the same place only five or six years and that nearly half the children ultimately abandoned the farm. Urban dwellers are no more likely to stay put, shifting about from city to city. On the principle of the man biting the dog, the *New York Times,* June 14, 1942, reported that a resident of Sebastapol, California, had lived in the same house for fifty years, though it admitted that his ten brothers and sisters had left the town.

With the advent of the low-priced automobile and the passion for long-distance touring, the rippling movement of humanity came to resemble the waves of the ocean. In 1940 the American people owned more motorcars than bathtubs. It seemed as though the pursuit of happiness had become the happiness of pursuit. Foreigners had earlier expressed amazement at the spectacle of dwellings being hauled along the streets from one site to another, but even before the late war, more than half a million Americans had discovered in the automobile trailer a means of living constantly on wheels.

Geographic or horizontal mobility, however, was a less fundamental aspect of American life than social or vertical mobility, though the two were not unrelated. The European conception of a graded society, with each class everlastingly performing its allotted function, vanished quickly amidst primitive surroundings that invited the humblest to move upward as well as outward. Instead of everybody being nobody, they found that anybody might become somebody. In the language of James Russell Lowell, "Here, on the edge of the forest, where civilized man was brought face to face again with nature and taught mainly to rely on himself, mere manhood became a fact of prime importance." This emancipation from hoary custom was "no bantling of theory, no fruit of forethought," but "a gift of the sky and of the forest."

Accordingly, there arose the ingrained belief in equality of opportunity, the right of all men to a free and fair start—a view which in one of its most significant ramifications led to the establishment of free tax-supported schools. This was far from being a dogma of enforced equality. To benefit from equality of opportunity a man must be equal to his opportunities, with the government serving principally as an umpire to supervise the game with a minimum of rules. The upshot was a conception of democracy rigorously qualified by individualism.

This individualistic bias sometimes assumed forms that defied government. The colonists in their relations with the mother country evaded unwelcome regulations and, prompted by their theologians and lawyers, insisted that acts of Parliament contrary to their "unalienable rights" were void. Within the colonies those who dwelt remote from centers of law and order adopted a like attitude toward the provincial authorities. The Scotch-Irish who illegally occupied Pennsylvania soil in the early eighteenth century contended "it was against the laws of God and nature, that so much land should be idle while so many Christians wanted it to labor on and to raise their bread." As a substitute for constituted authority the settlers sometimes created their own unofficial tribunals, which adjudicated property titles and punished offenders against the public peace. In other instances they resorted to the swifter retribution of individual gunplay, or of mob action and lynch law, for from taking the law into one's hands when it could not function it was but a step to taking the law into one's hands when it did not function as one wanted it to.

The tendency to violence so generated has continued to condition the national mentality to the present time. Thoreau, the great philosopher of individualism, knew of no reason why a citizen should "ever for a moment, or in the least degree, resign his conscience to the legislator," declaring that "we should be men first, and subjects afterward." A similar conviction undoubtedly inspired William H. Seward's flaming declaration to the proslavery Senators in 1850 that "there is a higher law than the Constitution," just as it actuated the thousands of churchgoing Northerners who secretly banded together to violate the Fugitive Slave Act. But generally it has been self-interest or convenience, rather than conscience, that has provided the incentive to lawbreaking, as in the case of the businessman chafing against legislative restrictions or of the motorist disobeying traffic regulations. Sometimes the attitude has paraded under such high-sounding names as states' rights and nullification. This lawless streak in the American character has often been directed to wrong purposes, but it has also served as a check on the abuse of governmental powers and as a safeguard of minority rights.

In still another aspect, the individualism of the pioneer farmer does much to explain the intense cultivation of the acquisitive spirit. In the absence of hereditary distinctions of birth and rank the piling up of wealth constituted the most obvious badge of social superiority, and once the process was begun, the inbred urge to keep on working made it difficult to stop. "The poor struggle to be rich, the rich to be richer," remarked an onlooker in the mid-nineteenth century. Thanks to equality of opportunity with plenty for all, the class struggle in America has consisted in the struggle to climb out of one class into a higher one. The zest of competition frequently led to sharp trading, fraud and chicanery, but in the popular mind guilt attached less to the practices than to being caught at them. Financial success was accepted as the highest success, and not till the twentieth century did a religious leader venture to advance the un-American doctrine that ill-gotten wealth was "tainted money," even when devoted to benevolent uses.

VI

It would be a mistake, however, to think of the American simply as a mechanism set in motion by dropping a coin in the slot. When President Coolidge made his famous remark, "The business of America is business," he quite properly added, "The chief ideal of the American people is idealism. I cannot repeat too often that America is a nation of idealists." This ambivalence puzzled foreign commentators, who found it difficult, for example, to reconcile worship of the Almighty Dollar with the equally universal tendency to spend freely and give money away. In contrast to Europe, America has had practically no misers, and one consequence of the winning of Independence was the abolition of primogeniture and entail. Harriet Martineau was among those who concluded that "the eager pursuit of wealth does not necessarily indicate a love of wealth for its own sake."

The fact is that, for a people who recalled how hungry and oppressed their ancestors had been through long centuries in the Old World, the chance to make money was like the sunlight at the end of a tunnel. It was the means of living a life of human dignity. It was a symbol of idealism rather than materialism. Hence "this new man" had an instinctive sympathy for the underdog, and even persons of moderate substance freely shared it with the less fortunate, helping to endow charities, schools, hospitals and art galleries and to nourish humanitarian undertakings which might otherwise have died a-borning.

The energy that entered into many of these causes was heightened by another national attitude: optimism. It was this quality that sustained the European men and women who with heavy hearts left ancestral homes to try their fortunes in a wild and far-off continent. The same trait animated the pioneer farmers confronted by the hardships, loneliness and terrors of the primeval forest, and served also to spur their successors who, though facing less dire conditions, were constantly pitted against both the uncertainties of the weather and the unpredictable demands of the market. When Thomas Jefferson remarked, "I steer my bark with Hope in the head, leaving Fear astern," he spoke for his compatriots. To doubt the future was to confess oneself a failure since the life history of almost any American documented the opposite view. A belief in progress blossomed spontaneously in such a soil.

If this belief made some men tolerant of present abuses in the confident expectation that time would provide the cure, it fired others with an apostolic zeal to hasten the happy day. As a keen observer in the middle of the last century said of his countrymen, "Americans are sanguine enough to believe that no evil is without a remedy, if they could only find it, and they see no good reason why they should not try to find remedies for all the evils of life." Not even fatalism in religion could long withstand the bracing atmosphere of the New World. This quality of optimism sometimes soared to dizzy heights, impelling men to strive for earthly perfection in communistic societies or to prepare to greet the imminent return of Christ.

It attained its most blatant expression, however, in the national addiction to bragging. At bottom, this habit sprang from pride in a country of vast distances and huge elevations plus an illimitable faith in its possibilities of being great as well as big. The American glorified the future in much the same spirit as the European glorified the past, both tending to exalt what they had the most of. And by a simple transition the American went on to speak of expected events as though they had already happened, being prompted perhaps by an urge to compensate for an inner sense of inferiority. This frame of mind led statesmen to cultivate spreadeagle oratory—a style which the *North American Review* in 1858 defined as "a compound of exaggeration, effrontery, bombast, and extravagance, mixed metaphors, platitudes, defiant threats thrown at the world, and irreverent appeals flung at the Supreme Being."

For the same reason the ordinary citizen resorted to hyperbole. In the thinly settled sections this manner of speech went by the name of tall talk, causing the backwoods to be known as a "paradise of puffers." A Frenchman, however, referred to a national, not a regional, trait when he said Americans seemed loath to admit that Christopher Columbus himself had not been an American, and it was an Easterner writing in an Eastern magazine who soberly averred, "It is easier, say the midwives, to come into this world of America . . . than in any other world extant." In business life this indulgent attitude toward truth lent itself to deliberate attempts to defraud, and made the land speculator with his "lithographed mendacity" the natural forerunner of the dishonest stock promoter of later times. Boastfulness is an attribute of youth which greater national maturity has helped to temper. Still the War Department in its manual of behavior for Yankee soldiers in England during the Axis war thought it prudent to admonish them: "Don't show off or brag or bluster."

This facility for overstatement has lent a distinctive quality to American humor. In the United States humor has never been part of a general gaiety of spirit. It has had to break through a crust of life thick with serious purpose. Hence it has had to be boisterous and bold, delighting in exaggeration, incongruities and farcical effects and reaching a grand climax in the practical joke. Out of a comic mood so induced arose such folk heroes as Mike Fink, Paul Bunyan, Pecos Bill and the myth-embroidered Davy Crockett, whose fabulous exploits flourished in oral tradition long before they were reduced to print. In deference to the national sobriety of temperament the most successful professional humorists have been those who told their yarns while preserving a decorous gravity of expression.

VII

If this analysis of national characteristics is well-founded, then certain modifications of the pattern were inevitable when the primacy of rural life gave way to the rise of urbanism. That change began to take place in the latter years of the nineteenth century. In 1860 only a sixth of the people lived in towns of eight thousand or more, but by 1900 a third dwelt in such communities and today well over half do. Along with urban concentration went a remarkable development of means of communication and transport—the telephone, rural free delivery, interurban electric transit, good roads, the automobile, the movie, the radio—that carried city ideas and ways to "the very finger-tips of the whole land." Though most of the historic traits continued to thrive in this new milieu, some were moderated and a few disappeared. The time is too short to gauge the full consequences, but several of the reversals of attitude are noteworthy.

One is the importance which Americans have come to attach to cultural achievement. The ancient prejudice against "useless" activities could not long withstand the compelling opportunities of the city. In the city were to be found the best schools and colleges, the best newspapers and magazines, and practically all the bookstores, libraries, publishing houses, concert halls, conservatories of music, art museums and theaters. There, too, America made closest contact with the vital thought of Europe. Stimulated by such an atmosphere, the writer or artist could also command an appreciative audience and financial support. Who can ever know how dreadful a toll the two and a half centuries of agricultural life exacted in terms of creative advances of the mind and spirit, how many a mute inglorious Milton succumbed to the unremitting struggle with Nature? For persons like these the city meant a glad release, giving them a chance to mature their powers, consort with kindred spirits and enter the lists for fame and fortune. Even in earlier times cultural stirrings had centered in the towns and cities. Now as the urban influence became uppermost, Americans commenced to make contributions to scholarship, science, literature and the fine arts that challenged comparison with the best Europe could offer.

As a necessary consequence, much of the former aversion to specialization of talent vanished. In a civilization rapidly growing more complex, men began to place a higher value on thoroughly mastering a skill or conquering a particular intellectual domain. The business of making a living tended to fall into compartments, with the men best equipped by training or experience reaping the greatest rewards. This trend characterized not only industry and trade but also the arts and sciences. Even in public life expert knowledge steadily played a larger part, notably in the administrative services of city, state and nation. The derisive references to the New Deal's "Brain Trust" came from political opponents who, however, did not intend to forgo the same advantage when they returned to power.

A further result of the altered aspect of American society has been the great impetus given to voluntary associative activity. In a country environment the gregarious instinct was constantly balked by the dearth of neighbors. The hunger for companionship could discover only occasional outlet, as at the county fair or in the agitated throng gathered from far and near for a camp meeting. Now, to the rural birthright of liberty and equality the city added the boon of fraternity. In a crowded community, like could find like. The reformer, the businessman, the wage earner, the intellectual worker, the sports lover, the ancestor worshiper—all these and many others gravitated into special groups to further interests held in common—and these local societies seldom failed to expand into nation-wide federations. Soon the population became divided between the organized and those who organized them, until, if the late Will Rogers is to be believed, "Americans will join anything in town but their own family. Why, two Americans can't meet on the street without one banging a gavel and calling the other to order." Thus the passion for associative activity came to be a sovereign principle of life.

Quite as noteworthy has been another effect of city growth: the discrediting of individualism as the automatic cure of social and economic ills. As the nineteenth century advanced, the increasing domination of the national economy by urban magnates of business and finance caused the farmers to demand that the government intercede to protect their right to a decent livelihood. In the cities the cramped living quarters, the growing wretchedness of the poor and the rise of difficult social problems also created doubts as to the sufficiency of the laissez-faire brand of democracy. Only the rich and powerful seemed now to profit from a reign of unbridled individualism. Though the solid core of ancient habit yielded stubbornly, the average man came gradually to believe that under the changed conditions it was the duty of the government of all to safeguard the opportunities of all. After the American fashion it was a doctrineless conviction, the product of an adjustment to new times for the sake of preserving the traditional spirit of self-reliance and free competition.

Though the gospel of work continued as unquestioned as ever, willing workers could no longer be certain of regular employment, particularly in the towns and cities. Every sudden jar to the nation's business structure rendered large numbers idle. Through no fault of his own, the laborer was being denied an essential part of his heritage. As early as 1893 the American Federation of Labor resolved that "the right to work is the right to life," and declared that "when the private employer cannot or will not give work the municipality, state or nation must." But it was not till the Great Depression destroyed the livelihood of people in all walks of life that this novel view became an article of American faith. The New Deal assumed the obligation not merely of succoring the hungry, but of creating jobs for the idle and of guarding against such hazards in the future by means of unemployment insurance, retirement pay for aged wage earners and special provisions for farmers. Thus what had started originally because of the community's need that all should work became transformed, first into a doctrine of the right to work, and then into the duty of society to provide the means of work.

VIII

The national character, as we at present know it, is thus a mixture of long-persisting traits tempered by some newly acquired ones. Based upon the solid qualities of those Europeans who planted the colonies, it assumed distinctive form under pressure of adaptation to the radically different situation. "Our ancestors sought a new continent," said James Russell Lowell. "What they found was a new condition of mind." The protracted tutelage to the soil acted as the chief formative influence, dispelling ancient inhibitions, freeing dormant energies, revamping mental attitudes. The rise of the city confirmed or strengthened many of the earlier characteristics while reshaping others. Probably no one of the traits is peculiar to the American people; some occasion apology rather than pride; but the aggregate represents a way of life unlike that of any other nation.

Just as the American character has undergone modification in the past, so it will doubtless undergo modification in the future. Nevertheless, certain of its elements seem so deeply rooted as to withstand the erosion of time and circumstance. Of this order are the qualities that made possible the development of the continent, the building of a democratic society and the continuing concern for the welfare of the underprivileged. These are attributes better suited to peace than to war, yet every great crisis has found the people ready to die for their conception of life so that their children might live it. The American character, whatever its shortcomings, abounds in courage, creative energy and resourcefulness, and is bottomed upon the profound conviction that nothing in the world is beyond its power to accomplish.

GEORGE W. PIERSON

The M-Factor in American History

Is there any such thing as "national character"? In particular, is there, or has there ever been, an American Character? Many critics question, or even deny the idea. Students of American civilization generally seem to start out by thinking there must be an American Character. But then they encounter great difficulties in defining this character—that is, they find too many different or contradictory types, none of the types unique, all of them appearing also in other cultures, a few of them perhaps unstable across the years. The result? Conscientious scholars are driven to despair, and decide that American society is neither consistent nor original nor completely different; therefore we have no distinctive character.

Now this, I submit, may be just a little foolish. For theoretically it isn't scientific, and practically it doesn't make sense. Theoretically, is it not a poor kind of science which says that, because you and I cannot wholly know a thing or exactly define it, it doesn't exist? Just because we cannot scientifically define Americanism would seem a quite insufficient reason for ignoring its existence. What has not existed, rather, may be that intuition of causes, that exact grasp of detail, that art of proportion, that science of social structure, which will enable us to say: this is, in a sum total way, different, *sui generis,* peculiar. After all, a combination does not have to be unique in all its elements, or even in a single one of these elements, to be different in sum total. I will assert that theoretically there may be an American Character, even though that character may have been composed of familiar elements, even though it is only the proportions which have been different, even though the resulting society may be mixed, contradictory, pluralistic, unjelled. The very indeterminism of a society may be a distinguishing mark. Theoretically, I see no barrier to believing that an American Character may exist.

On the contrary, on the grounds of common sense, I see many reasons to believe that there is and has been an American Character, for one thing because

Reprinted with permission from George W. Pierson, "The M-Factor in American History," *American Quarterly,* XIV (Summer, 1962, Supplement), pp. 275–89.

the most intelligent thinkers and observers have thought so, and have kept on thinking so, across the years. These observers may have differed in the labels they attached to us, they may have argued about the causes of our American peculiarities, but every one of them has thought that the Americans are a little odd in their psychology, and a little different in their social institutions. Crèvecoeur went so far as to call the American a "New Man." And he defined this new man as the Progressive: "He is an American who leaves behind his ancient prejudices and manners." But whatever the definition, from Crèvecoeur to Tocqueville to André Siegfried, from Dickens to Bryce to Denis Brogan, from Lieber to Keyserling or Robert Jungk, the most thoughtful commentators have asserted that there is and has been (and, alas, will continue to be) an American Character.

What caused this Americanism to emerge? Many things, no doubt; far too many even to list in this paper. So I shall confine my attention to a single prevailing characteristic of our people: the migration factor in our history, our excessive mobility. Yet before I take up the Moving American, allow me to recall some classic interpretations which have exercised a strong influence on the writing of American history, and on thinking about America generally.

How are Americans different? In the beginning was the Word, and the Word had it that we were a Chosen People, a seed sifted out of the populations of Europe, a community of saints destined to create a better society on this earth. Like the Israelites of old, we were a people under divine command. As we sang in the old hymn: "O God, beneath thy guiding hand our exiled fathers crossed the sea!"

After about one hundred and fifty years, there succeeded to this Biblical interpretation the thought that, if we were not always more holy, we were at least more free. As an independent nation, our destiny was to bring liberty, self-government, republicanism, the art of federal decentralization to the succor of oppressed mankind. So to the religious mission there succeeded a political mission—which was what Alexis de Tocqueville came to study.

From the beginning, also, there had always been an economic mission. America was El Dorado: the golden opportunity, the country of get-rich-quick, the land of the second chance, the asylum for the poverty-stricken. So, as foreign and native observers alike commented, America was (1) the land of goodness, (2) the land of liberty, and (3) the land of plenty.

For a long while these three national myths satisfied. Toward the end of the nineteenth century, however, there emerged a series of more sophisticated, or "scientific," explanations, and, in particular, one which has exercised enormous influence. What was it changed Europeans into Americans?

For historians of the past generation, the Frontier Hypothesis of Frederick Jackson Turner supplied the classic answer. It was the *frontier* experience which made us different. That is, it was our struggle with the wilderness—it was exploiting the vast free lands of the interior—it was freeing ourselves from the past, "breaking the cake of custom," leaving behind the fetters of settled society and the refinements of civilization to start over again in the woods—it was the lonely pioneers chopping out clearings on the road westward—it was getting together with other pioneers to rebuild a simpler, freer society—it was pulling up stakes and repeating the process—it was moving and moving again until in 1890 the free land and the West were all used up. On the frontier, said Turner, society became atomic, individualism flourished, democracy was generated, national legislation was encouraged. The opportunities of the West also opened a gate of escape for the oppressed of the East, and so contributed to the democratization and Americanization of the seaboard. The frontier also transformed personal character. As Turner phrased it:

> That coarseness and strength combined with acuteness and inquisitiveness; that practical, inventive turn of mind, quick to find expedients; that masterful grasp of material things, lacking in the artistic but powerful to effect great ends; that restless, nervous energy; that dominant individualism, working for good and evil, and withal that buoyancy and exuberance which comes with freedom—these are traits of the frontier, or traits called out elsewhere because of the existence of the frontier.

In effect, said Turner, it was primarily the molding influence of the Frontier which had transformed so many European materials into a new American amalgam. In his oft-quoted phrase, the frontier was "the line of most rapid and effective Americanization."

For a long while this satisfied. But about thirty years ago, when Turner died, and his imaginative idea was making its way into popular speech, and Franklin Delano Roosevelt was using the disappearance of the frontier to justify a welfare state, a number of people discovered political reasons for questioning the doctrine. Historians themselves grew uneasy. For one thing, the hypothesis seemed too nationalistic, too provincial. For another, the Frontier concept embraced too many overlapping or discordant influences. Again, the frontier cause seemed to be credited with inconsistent results: it made Americans both sectional and nationalistic, cooperative and individualistic, repetitive yet original. Once again, one wondered how many Americans could have been affected. And how were we to stay American after 1890, when the frontier dissappeared? In the upshot, the frontier theory seemed to explain far too much by far too little.

Yet, for all this, it was a difficult theory to discard. For if the frontier did not produce the effects ascribed to it, what did?

I believe we now have at least a small part of the answer. It has been hinted by many perceptive observers, not least by Tocqueville or by Francis Lieber or by Sarmiento. I call it the M-Factor in American history.

What made and kept us different was not just the wildness of the North American continent, nor its vast empty spaces, nor even its wealth of resources, powerful as must have been those influences. No. It was, first of all, the M-Factor: the factor of movement, migration, mobility. Colonization was one part of it; immigration, another; the westward movement itself was a fraction, but only a fraction, of the whole. This whole began with many old-world uprootings. It gathered force with the transatlantic passage. It flooded on to the farmlands of the mid-continent. But increasingly it meant movement also *away* from the frontier, from farm to town, from region to region, from city to city. Individuals, families, churches, villages, on occasion whole countrysides have participated—and continue to participate. Francis Lieber said that in America he felt as if tied to the arms of a windmill. To him, movement had become our "historical task." And Sarmiento was so staggered by our propensity for traveling around that he predicted that, if the trump of doom were suddenly to sound, it would surprise two-thirds of the Americans, out on the roads like ants.

In all this, I repeat, the frontier played an important but limited part. For if people moved to the frontier, they moved also before there was a frontier, moved behind and away from the frontier, and kept on moving even more enthusiastically when the frontier closed.

Let us put it this way: Frederick Jackson Turner was a great poet-historian, who more than half sensed the power that was in migration, but then imprisoned this giant in the rough homespun of the vanishing pioneers. So we of a later generation must once again return to the great question: What has made and still makes Europeans into restless Americans? I venture herewith some tentative speculations, in the hope that we will find in them ideas worth working out.

My basic proposition is obvious: Movement means change. To transfer is in some part to transform. *"Wanderung meint wandlung,"* as the Germans put it. And all forms of movement, from mass exodus to simple milling around, have shared in this subtle process of alteration.

Why should motion cause change? First, because *institutions* do not move easily. A few will be destroyed; many more are damaged; nearly all are shaken, and have to be pruned, simplified, or otherwise adjusted to survive the transplanting. To a degree *displacement* means *replacement* of institutions.

Why again should migration cause modification? Because the migrants are not average people. As a group they do not represent a fair cross-section of the society they are leaving; as individuals they tend toward exaggerations of one sort or another; as settlers they won't wish to reproduce the society they have left, or succeed in reproducing it even should they so desire.

This brings us to the third great reason for change, the new circumstances: that is, the hardships and accidents of the crossing, the strangers encountered on the road, the unaccustomed climate and geography of their new environment. Movement means exposure, and successive exposures compel unexpected changes.

It may be urged that more credit should go to the strangers and the new countries. Or it may be observed that migrations are often the result or the symptom of changes that have already taken place in the parent society. And with both these ideas I agree. On the one hand, many immigrants were Americanized only long after they got over. On the other, not a few American types, like the puritan and the businessman, had already appeared in sixteenth-century

Europe. So migration served both as prologue and as epilogue; it has been the means of change and the effect of change (as well as the cause). Yet no movement of people or institutions, however started or motivated, can take place without further alterations. For migration selects special types for moving; it subjects them to exceptional strains on the journey; and it then compels them to rebuild, with liberty to choose or refuse from the mail-order catalogue of Western experience. On top of all that, repeated movements, such as we in our country have known, seem to have a cumulative, or progressive, effect.

What parts of a civilization, what elements in a society, does the M-Factor attack? Apparently, all parts. Before his death Ellsworth Huntington, who was one of the earliest American scientists to become curious about this phenomenon, came to see in migration a selective force so strong that it affected the stock and temperament of a people as well as its culture. After some hesitations, I believe we will concur. For I believe it can be demonstrated that movement changes the physical population, the institutions and group structures, the social habits and traditions, the personal character and attitudes of the migrants.

Allow me to offer some random, familiar illustrations at this point.

The American population? It was formed and re-formed by migration. To begin with we were all immigrants. Moreover, because the Atlantic was open, people from many lands and nations came to these shores, until we were the leading conglomerate of the West, a Rainbow Division of Europe. Political scientists call us a pluralistic society. Sociologists find culture conflicts endemic.

Again because the migrants did not all come at once, but in intermittent surges, and because in free movements the later comers, as strangers, are handicapped and must enter the lower levels of their class and occupation, the natives or earlier-comers have repeatedly found themselves pushed upstairs, to the more skilled jobs, to the managerial posts, to the position of employers and capitalists. At the same time, moving upstairs was difficult, so difficult that the older stock felt it had to cut down on the number of its own children, if it was to graduate them into the higher levels of living—so difficult that the next-to-last comers tended to resent the labor competition of the newcomers and tried to exclude them. Thus the Yankees industrialized with the aid of other people's children. Meanwhile these laboring generations, as they matured, tried to keep the jobs for themselves and, whether as skilled artisans or later trade union bosses, as Know-Nothings in the 1850s or McCarthyites a century later, became the strongest champions of immigration restriction, the most suspicious of new foreigners, the uncompromising 100 percenters. So from 1820 to 1920 what ought to have been for the Anglo–American population a series of European additions became instead a progressive physical substitution. And after 1920 the freedom to immigrate was shut off by the votes of the very groups which had benefited from it earlier. But why did not and has not this stepladder movement of infiltration produced a stratified, hierarchical, skyscraper society? The answer is again the M-Factor, but this time internal migration. Inside, the freedom to move remained, and a man could get out of his cellar in town by building a one-story cabin up-country, or he could come off his eroded acres into Chicago, where the rising buildings and professions had elevators in them.

If we now turn from questions of nationality and occupation to the age and sex characteristics of our population, we find that here, too, the M-Factor has left deep marks. For three hundred years, or at least until the great depression, we were a young country. We boasted of it. Foreigners rarely failed to mention the childlike innocence, the boyish enthusiasm, the youthful drive and bustle and activity-for-activity's sake of these strange Americans. The youth of America, quipped Oscar Wilde, is its oldest tradition. And perhaps we were guilty of a certain "shortage of adults." At least the demographers have proved that our Constitution was made for adolescents—as late as 1820 the median age of the population was only 16 years, and it was not until well into the twentieth century that that median soared above 25. That is, it was only after preventive medicine had started to prolong the lives of the infirm, and immigration restriction had cut down on the annual influx of bachelors and young marrieds, that we first really began to feel middle-aged. How does the M-Factor figure in this? Well, students of migration have rediscovered the fact that it is overwhelmingly the young, between the ages of 15 and 25, who move—and in the first waves or pioneer phases, it is primarily the young men. The frontiers, whether of farm or factory, start emphatically male (*Oh Susannah, don't you cry for me!*).

Yet the men were not to have it all their own way, for the M-Factor can give things a sardonic twist. Migration has perennially represented rebellion against past tyrannies or authorities, against the father no less than against the lord or priest, against the husband no less than against the father. Thus, after the first settlements had been established, the open spaces and open opportunities of this country just invited the younger generation to leave home and strike out on their own, and the able young men accepted the invitation. Even today it is the rare son of ability who does not insist on leaving the town where he was born to try to make his way in a larger world. Meanwhile the pioneer women, being scarce as well as weak, found that they had inadvertently acquired a scarcity value. For them, as well as for the children, migration meant progressive emancipation—an emancipation eventually crowned by woman suffrage, Mother's Day and much symbolic statuary. Thus, as our lonely forefathers pushed relentlessly westward, and the idea of equality came galloping up behind, the Pioneer Mother replaced the Pilgrim Father on the sculptor's pedestal in the town square. (Whether the statuesque Miss America has now replaced her bronzed mother in the popular imagination I leave to braver men to say—we may note only the querulous complaints of our English and Continental friends that we are today a woman-run and child-dominated subcivilization.)

If we next pursue the M-Factor from our population to our economy, what will we find? An economy in which transportation has loomed extraordinarily large—witness the railroads, the automobile age and the airplane industry of today—witness also in our myths how prairie schooners and pony express, paddle wheelers and the long whistle of the trains, Ford cars and the Spirit of St. Louis have entered into the folklore of our people.

The wheels are singing on the railroad track
If you go, you can't come back.
Hear the whistle blow.

For Americans, it has been said, the automobile restates a national principle, since, after all, the settler was the first auto-mobile. In the U.S. a mile is something to put behind you. Where else would you find a place named Stillwater Junction?

More soberly, if our interest runs rather to our religious peculiarities, it might be observed that the need for settlers, and the ease of exit and entrance from one colony to the other, made toleration and disestablishment of churches almost inevitable from the start. The same ease of escape then long made it difficult for the states to impose adequate taxation, or any other really burdensome regulation, on their footloose citizens. A Virginian did not have to stay in Virginia. A Yorker could go to Michigan. If a business failed, or a marriage, the simplest thing was to decamp. Other states would welcome you. So, by and by, Reno became a monument to our vagrant fancies in matters matrimonial.

Again, politically our moving habits not only made possible but reinforced a decentralizing, federal tendency. Legally, the absence of customary law in the new settlements must have fostered the excessive American dependence on statute law. Migration also splintered our first establishments of higher education, in the sense that it led to the founding of many colleges instead of concentration on a few national universities. Thus my own institution, through the efforts of its migrating graduates, became a mother of colleges a full century before it could accumulate enough substance in New Haven to rival the great foundations of Europe. Finally, our peculiar instability of family homesite, and the lack of a national capital or home, shifted emotional loyalties to things that could be carried with us, such as declarations of principle and constitutional theories. And eventually, to bind ourselves together, we were forced to insist with an unusual, almost tyrannical, emphasis on such assimilative codes and social practices as are commonly summed up in that telltale phrase: "The American WAY of Life."

But enough of such random illustrations.

Let us now proceed to ask, on a more systematic basis, how, just how, have migration and movement acted to convert Europeans into something rich and strange?

Considering the matter first on a broad social scale, I would propose that the M-Factor has been (turn by turn or even all at once): (1) the great Eliminator; (2) the persistent Distorter; (3) an arch-Conservator; (4) an almost irresistible Disintegrator or Atomizer; (5) a heart Stimulant or Energizer; and (6) the prime source of Optimism in the American atmosphere, a never-failing ozone of hope. Also, (7) the Secularizer and Externalizer of our beliefs, and (8) the Equalizer and Democratizer of social classes. Indeed a little reflection will suggest still other ways in which migration has shaken its European ingredients into new patterns. But on this occasion let us consider merely some of these eight, with just a hint or two of historic events by way of illumination.

Migration was the great Eliminator? Nothing could be plainer. In theory you can't take everything with you when you move. Some goods are too bulky or delicate to be put on ship; some household possessions will fall out of the covered wagon. Again, in a free migration, not all elements in a society will wish to move; the dregs will be too spiritless and impoverished to emigrate unaided; the ruling classes entirely too successful and satisfied. Check this theory against history and what do we find? In the early colonization there came out of England the rising middle classes, with some admixture of the lowest elements, but with only a few aristocratic leaders. Ours started, therefore, as a decapitated society, virtually without nobles or bishops, judges or learned lawyers, artists, playwrights or great poets. Taking a hopeful view, a student of mine once maintained that settlement transferred the accent from *nobility* to *ability*. Considering the transfer culturally, however, one must recognize a tragic impoverishment. Despite all our gains of goodness or plenty or freedom, the men of the highest attainments and greatest skills had stayed home—and with them their arts and refinements, their leisure-class culture. The same process of abandonment, of flight from the elite and their standards, would be discernible later in the settlement of the West. Axiomatically, the fine arts, the theoretical sciences, the most advanced tools and machinery, are not found or produced on moving frontiers. Like war or fire or inflation, migration has been a great destroyer of inherited treasure.

At first glance such destruction may seem only temporary, to be replaced "when we have time." Yet meanwhile some elements are missing, the balance is changed, the old society has been distorted—and before long one may get reconciled to doing without. On top of this, the M-Factor has promoted distortion in an even more drastic way. For moving forces the reclassification of values. Why? Because the land of destination attracts more strongly for one or two presumed goods than for the others (as for economic opportunity perhaps, or political freedom, or the right to worship in one's own way). So if a family is to go, they have to believe, or persuade themselves, that the particular goods to be realized are more important to them than all the other social goods, which may be diminished, or even be left behind altogether. If similar movements are made by later generations for like reasons, then these cherished values may rise almost to the status of holy commandments or natural rights, and in the nineteenth century become the polar magnets in a new value system. By elimination and wilful distortion a moving people becomes a narrower society: thinner and shallower, yet in some things much more intense.

This calls attention to a third and almost paradoxical characteristic of migration: its conservatism. People moved to save as well as to improve. But when they found they couldn't take everything with them, then a curious thing often happened. They came to value even more highly what they had succeeded in preserving. Having suffered such privations, having sacrificed so many other possessions, they clung to what was saved with a fiercer passion. Witness the Puritans with their Wilderness Zion, the Mormons under Brigham Young, or even Turner's leapfrogging pioneers. For these last, as for so many others, it had become easier to move than to change their vocation, their habits, their antiquated methods. To put this bluntly, for them the cheap lands of the West made it easier to keep on with their soil-mining and strip-farming, and possible to avoid such painful changes as learning a proper care of the land, or the new crop rotation of the advanced parts of Europe and the East. So for the American farmer—or agriculturally speaking—the westward movement became the great postponement of American history. They profited personally, but it was a postponement nonetheless—just as in the flight of the New England textile industry to the South in our times. In France, before De Gaulle, the peasant and small shopkeeper clung stubbornly to his land or shop, but politically moved constantly to the left. That is, economically, he might be a selfish reactionary, and even vote for Poujade, but by changing the name of his party leftward he was sure he was making "progress." Did not some of our American pioneers give themselves the same feeling of progress by moving westward? Migration, I would suggest, could be a way of promoting change—and of avoiding it, too. Flight can be an escape from the future as well as from the past.

The M-Factor, we must next realize, was an almost irresistible Disintegrator or Atomizer. Few authoritarian institutions from Europe could stand the strain of Atlantic distances or the explosion of American space. So either they decentralized or died. Witness the early church. In Virginia the episcopal organization proved so little suited to the far-flung tobacco plantations that the Church of England almost withered away, whereas in New England the Puritan branch of the same church developed a localized or Congregational organization, and flourished. Then, later, when the Irish immigration poured life and vigor into American Catholicism, the hierarchy, intuitively recognizing that moving out on the lands might cripple the Church as well as weaken the individual's faith, did their best to hold the new arrivals in the seaport towns, at least until some interior communities could be effectively churched. Ultimately, I believe it will be found that our Catholics have moved less often, less widely and less soon than their Protestant neighbors, hence have missed certain corrosive acids and opportunities in the M-Factor.

One of these opportunities, of course, was to stand on your own feet, to make your own way, and if need be to move again. In our expanding settlements the arm of the State (like the authority of the bishops) shriveled, and a kind of physical individualism sprouted. On the trail, society tended to break down into chance parties of moving families or individuals. And at the destination everything was to be reconstructed. It took energy and courage to move, and more energy to make the move succeed. Hence migration was a great stimulant to action—and when such action repeatedly succeeded (or, as we may say, "worked"), then perhaps the beginnings of a habit of action had been established, both for oneself and for one's neighbor. The American reputation for activism, as for self-help and neighborly helpfulness, surely needs no underlining.

Migration was not only the Destroyer, Distorter, Conservator, Atomizer and Energizer of western society, but its most effective "Optimizer." First of all, out of the welter of old-world classes and temperaments it selected the up-and-coming and the hopeful. Pessimists didn't bother; you had to be an optimist to move. Next it required sacrifice and waiting, and so captured many believers, the men of faith. Finally, it rewarded the successful—and those who weren't lucky were given a second try. America the Golden was the land of the second chance. And from failure it offered a full timetable of escapes.

I realize that it is customary at this point to do a ritualistic dance around the statue of the golden calf—and credit our optimism or success primarily to the sheer wealth of the continent. But if we did become a "people of plenty," and if that plenty left its mark even on the size of our automobiles, let us not forget that the beginnings were almost invariably hard, and what the land long offered most of was tough places and violent weather. What kind of plenty was it converted the gravel patch of New England into smiling farms? Lots of hard work, I should say, and plenty of faith. Again, who but a lunkheaded optimist would grow wheat in western Kansas? Or who in his right mind would go settle in Dakota? No. The Black Hills gold and the U.S. farm bounties, these bonanzas were later and almost accidental discoveries. In my book, optimism made more states than vice versa. Many a town existed first, or only, in the imagination. "Boost, don't knock" has been the slogan of new communities just abuilding, and the booster is Mr. Johnny-come-lately. We began as migrants, that is, wishful thinkers, and each wave of immigration, each boatload from abroad, brought us fresh injections of this heart stimulant. For Europe's poor, the freedom to come changed "tomorrow" from a threat into a promise. For its men of faith, the act of moving and moving again substituted "the future" for "the heavenly hereafter." And with time the mission of American idealists came to be in and for this world. From infant damnation to the social gospel is but a long tramp.

I hope I may be forgiven if I now pass over the secularizing and externalizing influences of mobility (which Sorokin has explored) in favor of its equalitarian and leveling effects. For these democratic tendencies seem to me particularly important, and I have stumbled on some odd illustrations.

Here the theoretical argument would be that the M-Factors are often democratic in their consequences, first because for the lower classes emigration means *"getting out from under,"* the first step on the road up; secondly because the hardships of the journey are no respecters of birth (witness the miserable failure of the early "Gentlemen" of the Jamestown Colony in Virginia). In the third place, and most significantly, the process of resettlement is a process of making new mixtures, out of a gathering of strangers, each without authority, credentials, reputation or other priority than that of arrival. In a new community (frontier or town) family and past performance hardly count. Everyone has to make his own mark, and stands equal with his fellow-strangers. The social competition, as it were, starts over, with all the camaraderie and "gamesmanship" of a new catch-as-catch-can. Migration has been a great Mixmaster. And mixtures of anonymous elements are necessarily more democratic, at least at first. So much for doctrine. Now for my illustrations.

My first illustration, if you will allow the personal reference, comes out of an effort to understand my own university. How explain Yale College of the 1890s, a college that prided itself on its democracy? It is true there were a few Whitneys, Vanderbilts or Harknesses, with social pretensions and inordinate allowances. Yet evidently the game was wide open, and any self-help student from no matter how humble a background or obscure a school had a chance to show what he could do and rise to the top and be the honor man in the Senior Society elections, if he had what it took. Now how was it possible that a college like Yale, with almost two hundred years of tradition and family attachments, could still offer so fair and square an opportunity to all comers? Because Yale was, in a sense, an annually renewed community, and because its constituents came, not just from around New Haven or New England but from all over the country, without prior knowledge of each other or claims to authority. It was a skeptical Harvard professor, European born, who first taught me this truth. Listen to George Santayana:

> The relations of one Yale student to another are completely simple and direct. They are like passengers in a ship.... They live in a sort of primitive brotherhood with a ready enthusiasm for every good or bad project, and a contagious good humor.
>
> ...Nothing could be more American.... Here is sound, healthy principle, but no scrupulousness, love of life, trust in success, a ready jocoseness, a democratic amiability, and a radiant conviction that there is nothing better than oneself. It is a boyish type of character, earnest and quick in things practical, hasty and frivolous in things intellectual, but the boyishness is a healthy one, and in a young man, as in a young nation, it is perfection to have only the faults of youth.

What Yale College and the Frontier, and indeed much of the rest of America, had in common, Santayana suggests, was young Americans in a new mixture.

If this first illustration comes with a strange sound, let me hasten to propose my second. It concerns dogs. In France, on sabbatical a few years ago, I seemed to run into only two kinds of dogs. One was the pampered, pedigreed poodle, sitting with his mistress in the restaurants, even eating from her plate: the fine flower of canine aristocracy, and most grandly indifferent to strangers. The second type was nondescript and fierce, the savage watchdog at peasant doorway or château gate, guarding the family domain and inherited possessions, *"les situations acquises."* This character disliked strangers on sight, and promptly tried to chew them up. After one or two close calls with such receptionists, I came back to the States—and found dogs of all sorts of ancestry, chiefly mixed. But what they showed mostly was curiosity, and a sort of friendly expectancy. Their tails said: "Howdy, stranger." For they were not guarding any particular place. They belonged to traveling men, and had been around.

My third illumination, if we can call it that, concerns money. Foreigners still accuse us of being excessively money-minded, of measuring everything by the almighty dollar. Our defenders answer: it's not the money, it's the power and the achievement. You make a million to prove you're a man; then, like as not, you give it away. After all, you can't take it with you.

Yet can't you? As I was once thinking about the M-Factor, it suddenly came to me that on a journey, or in a new community, money was one of the few things that you could take along. Cash took the place of your pedigree or family letter of credit. It spoke with a certain authority, East or West. Money was power? Yes. But especially it was currency: the power that you could take with you. So on the moving frontier, in the new towns, it was differentiation by dollars that first disturbed the democracy of new mixtures.

Having got diverted by some of the social consequences of the M-Factor, I cannot do justice to some of the most interesting effects of all: the influence of migration on personal character and attitudes. In the moment remaining let me merely suggest possibilities.

Was it not the psychological imperatives of migration, even more than frontier land, that helped make and keep us a nation of optimists? Was it not the physical demands of colonization and resettlement, as well as Calvinism and middle-class origins, that made us into such a nation of workers, activists, materialists, instrumentalists? The difference between what André Siegfried calls "homo faber" or the American, and homo sapiens or the European, is it not perhaps that one of these characters has been sitting still? Whereas we, poor pilgrims, have itching feet. Restless to start with, we have become more so with repeated displacement. *Here today and gone tomorrow.* The wandering mania has got into our blood, our houses, our attention, our very ways of speech. *Come on! Get going! Don't be a stick-in-the-mud! You don't want to get left, do you? It's a good year to make the move. So long! I don't know where I'm going, but I'm on my way. Anywhere I hang my hat is home, sweet home, to me.*

In the revealing American vernacular it is impressive to observe how many things are defined in terms of movement. A man *on the road* to success is a *comer,* a *go-getter. That's going some,* we say—and by and by we listen for the magic words that we also have *arrived.* So also with failure. *He missed the bus.* Or, *he missed the boat. He is not getting anywhere. She got left in the lurch. He got bogged down with administration.* A man who is growing old is *slowing up,* and then by and by he reaches *the end of the trail.* Death itself used to be spoken of as *crossing the divide.*

Reinforcing the testimony of our vernacular are our social habits. Unable to stay put, thrown among fellow transients, having newcomers flood in about us, we have perforce become hospitable, and genial with strangers. Not knowing their ancestry, and caring less, first names have been all we needed. There is a fellowship in our country, known to some of you perhaps, where last names are absolutely prohibited. And, incidentally, this illustrates another American trait: our propensity for "joining." Lonely from disassociation, we will make ten lodges grow where but one *bierstube* stood before. Frightened and not quite able to bear our independence, we oscillate between assertiveness and timidity, between an almost violent aggression and an almost cowardly conformity. Imaginative and suggestible, we are notorious for our fads and our instability. Insecure in our values, we have become adept at inventing dogmas to comfort ourselves. Not quite sure that our abandonment of the old world and of the past was justified, we have long been haunted by ambivalent feelings: a mixture of scorn and guilt complex about the older civilizations of Europe.

"It is a complex fate, being an American," said Henry James, "and one of the responsibilities it entails is fighting against a superstitious valuation of Europe." Ralph Waldo Emerson felt the same way: "Can we never extract the tapeworm of Europe from the brain of our countrymen?"

Finally, because migration appealed for diverse reasons especially to extremists—to saints and real sinners, to fundamentalists and free thinkers, to dreamers and "tough bastards," to groupists and individualists side by side—our society has never received its fair share of balanced, equable, middle-of-the-road temperaments, but has been shot through with violent contradictions. Hence so many of our seeming inconsistencies, to this very day.

To me the migrant seems not a single or a simple character, but is he not recognizably different—and American?

Paradoxically, if we turn up the other side of the coin, there are the Europeans, fearful of becoming Americanized. Is this entirely out of weakness, or envy, or admiration? Hardly. Let us rather take note of a curious and unappreciated development. In the last generation mobility has swept the continent. With their *vacances payés,* their *campings,* their folkwagons, our cousins have found a new freedom. So, if today there is Americanization in Europe, and if our ways of life seem to be coming closer together, may it not be in part because the Old World societies are as never before in movement, and because Siegfried's "homo sapiens," too, is taking to the roads?

MARGARET MEAD

We Are All Third Generation

What then is this American character, this expression of American institutions and of American attitudes which is embodied in every American, in everyone born in this country and sometimes even in those who have come later to these shores? What is it that makes it possible to say of a group of people glimpsed from a hotel step in Soerabaja or strolling down the streets of Marseilles, "There go some Americans," whether they have come from Arkansas or Maine or Pennsylvania, whether they bear German or Swedish or Italian surnames? Not clothes alone, but the way they wear them, the way they walk along the street without awareness that anyone of higher status may be walking there also, the way their eyes rove as if by right over the façade of palaces and the rose windows of cathedrals, interested and unimpressed, referring what they see back to the Empire State building, the Chrysler tower, or a good-sized mountain in Montana. Not the towns they come from—Sioux City, Poughkeepsie, San Diego, Scotsdale—but the tone of voice in which they say, "Why, I came from right near there. My home town was Evansville. Know anybody in Evansville?" And the apparently meaningless way in which the inhabitant of Uniontown warms to the inhabitant of Evansville as they name over a few names of people whom neither of them know well, about whom neither of them have thought for years, and about whom neither of them care in the least. And yet, the onlooker, taking note of the increased warmth in their voices, of the narrowing of the distance which had separated them when they first spoke, knows that something has happened, that a tie has been established between two people who were lonely before, a tie which every American hopes he may be able to establish as he hopefully asks every stranger: "What's your home town?"

Americans establish these ties by finding common points on the road that all are expected to have traveled, after their forebears came from Europe one or two or three generations ago, or from one place to another in America, resting for long enough to establish for each generation a "home town" in which they grew up and which they leave to move on to a new town which will become the home town of their children. Whether they meet on the deck of an Atlantic steamer, in a hotel in Singapore, in New York or in San Francisco, the same expectation underlies their first contact—that both of them have moved on and are moving on and that potential intimacy lies in paths that have crossed. Europeans, even Old Americans whose pride lies not in the circumstance that their ancestors have moved often but rather in the fact that they have not moved for some time, find themselves eternally puzzled by this "home town business." Many Europeans fail to find out that in nine cases out of ten the "home town" is not where one lives but where one did live; they mistake the sentimental tone in which an American invokes Evansville and Centerville and Unionville for a desire to live there again; they miss entirely the symbolic significance of the question and answer which say diagrammatically, "Are you the same kind of person I am? Good, how about a coke?"

Back of that query lies the remembrance and the purposeful forgetting of European ancestry. For a generation, they cluster together in the Little Italies, in the Czech section or around the Polish Church, new immigrants clinging together so as to be able to chatter in their own tongue and buy their own kind of red peppers, but later there is a scattering to the suburbs and the small towns, to an "American" way of life, and this is dramatized by an over-acceptance of what looks, to any European, as the most meaningless sort of residence—on a numbered street in Chicago or the Bronx. No garden, no fruit trees, no ties to the earth, often no ties to the neighbors, just a number on a street, just a number of a house for which the rent is $10 more than the rent in the old foreign district from which they moved—how can it mean anything? But it does.

For life has ceased to be expressed in static, spatial terms as it was in Europe, where generation after generation tied their security to the same plot of ground, or if they moved to a city, acted as if the house there, with its window plants, was still a plot of ground anchored by fruit trees. On a plot of ground a man looks around him, looks at the filled spaces in the corner of the garden. There used to be plum trees there, but father cut them down when he was a child; now he has planted young peaches—the plot is filled up again. And he can lean over the wall and talk to the neighbor who has planted plums again—they are the same kind of people, with the same origins and the same future. Having the same origins and the same future, they can dwell in the present which is assumed to be part of one continuous way of life.

But for two Americans, chance met on a train or at adjacent desks in a big office building, working in a road gang or a munition plant or on the same ground crew at an airport, there are no such common origins or common expectations. It is assumed, and not mentioned, that grandparents likely were of different nationality, different religion, different political faith, may have fought on opposite sides of the same battles—that great-great-grandparents may have burned each other at the stake. . . .

. . . Each and every American has followed a long and winding road; if the roads started in the same spot in Europe, best forget that—that tie leads backwards to the past which is best left behind. But if the roads touched here, in this vast country where everyone is always moving, that is a miracle which brings men close together.

In our behavior, however many generations we may actually boast of in this country, however real our lack of ties in the old world may be, we are all third generation, our European ancestry tucked away and half forgotten, the recent steps in our wanderings over America immortalized and over-emphasized. When a rising man is given an administrative job and a chance to choose men for other jobs, he does not, if he is an American, fill those jobs with members of his family—such conduct is left to those who have never left their foreign neighborhoods, or to the first generation. He does not fill them exclusively with members of his own class; his own class is an accidental cross-section which wouldn't contain enough skills. He can't depend upon his golfing mates or this year's neighbors to provide him with the men he needs. Instead, he fills the jobs with men from somewhere along the road he has traveled, his home town, his home state, his college, his former company. They give him the same kind of assurance that a first-generation Hollywood producer felt when he put his cousins in charge of the accounts—their past and his past are one—at one spot anyway—just as in a kin-oriented society common blood assures men of each other's allegiance. The secretary, trying to shield her boss from the importunities of the office seeker, knows it's no use trying to turn away a man from that little North Dakota college that the boss went to. The door is always open to them, any one of them, any day. And a newspaper headline screams: "Rock of Chickamauga blood still flows in soldiers' veins."

European social scientists look at this picture of American intimacy and fail to understand it. In the first place, they cannot get inside it. An Englishman, who has never been in America before, arriving in Indianapolis and trying to establish relationships with an American who has never been in England, finds himself up against what seems to be a blank wall. He meets hearty greetings, eager hospitality, an excessive attempt to tie the visitor to the local scene by taking him rapidly over its civic wonders, an equally excessive attempt to tie in Uncle Josiah's trip to India with the fact that the guest was reared in the Punjab—and then blankness. But if the Englishman then takes a tour in the Northwest, spends a week in the town where his Indiana host lived as a boy and then returns to Indianapolis, he will find a very different greeting awaiting him, which he may mistakenly put down to the fact that this is a second meeting. Only if he is a very astute observer will he notice how the path he has taken across the United State has the power to thaw out any number of hosts at any number of dinner parties.

The wife of the European scientist, now living as a faculty wife in a small university town in Colorado, will find herself similarly puzzled. She doesn't seem to get anywhere with the other faculty wives. Their husbands and her husband have the same status, the same salary, perhaps the same degree of world-wide reputation. She has learned their standards of conspicuous consumption; she can make exactly the same kind of appetizers, set a bridge table out with prizes just as they do—and yet, there is no intimacy. Only when both have children can she and some faculty wife really get together. She thinks it is the common interest in the children which forms the tie; actually it is the common experience of the children, who have something in common which the two women will never have in the same way—the same home town, which provides the necessary link, so fragile, and from a European point of view so meaningless and contentless, and yet, for an American, so essential. Later, even if they have lived childlessly beside each other, should they meet again in Alaska or Mississippi, they would be friends—with no real accession of common interests that the European wife could see. For she does not realize that to Americans only the past can give intimacy, nor can she conceive how such an incredibly empty contact in the past can be enough.

. . . .

But it is impossible for all Americans who must work or play together to have a bit of identical past, to have lived, even in such rapidly shifting lives, within a few miles of the spot where the others have lived, at some different period for some different reason. Thin and empty as is the "home town" tie, substitutes for it must be found; other still more tenuous symbols must be invoked. And here we find the enthusiastic preferences for the same movie actor, the same brand of peaches, the same way of mixing a drink. Superficially it makes no sense at all that preference for one brand of cigarette over another may call forth the same kind of enthusiasm that one might expect if two people discovered that they had both found poetry through Keats or both nearly committed suicide on account of the same girl. Only by placing these light preferences against a background of idiosyncratic experience—by realizing that every American's life is different from every other American's; that nowhere, except in parts of the Deep South and similar pockets, can one find people whose lives and background are both identical or even similar—only then do these feverish grabs at a common theme make sense. English or Dutch residents in the colonies will spend hours sighing over the names of the shops or drinks of their respective Bond Streets, creating in their nostalgia a past atmosphere which they miss in the harsh tropical landscape about them. Americans, in a sense colonials in every part of America, but colonials who have come to have no other home, also create a common atmosphere within which to bask in the present as they criticize or approve the same radio program or moving picture actor.

There is also that other American method of forming ties, the association—the lodge, fraternity, club which is such a prominent feature of American life. Lloyd Warner has described our societies of veterans of past wars as comparable to a cult of the dead which binds a community together, with the veterans of the most distant war lowest in the social scale. Seen from the point of view which I have been discussing, each war creates a magnificent common past for large numbers of men. It is not surprising that those who have the fewest ties among themselves—those whose poverty-stricken way of life admits of few associations—cling longest to this common experience.

. . . .

Social scientists, taking their cues from Eastern colleges or from Sinclair Lewis, have been inclined to sneer at the American habit of "joining," at the endless meetings, the clasp of fellowship, the songs, the allegedly pseudo-enthusiasm with which "brothers" greet each other. Safe on the eminence of available intellectual ties and able to gossip together about the famous names and the scandals of their professions, they have failed to appreciate that these associational ties give not the pseudo-security which some European philosopher feels he would get out of them if he had to share in them, but very real security. Not until he has been marooned—his train missed, no taxi available—and driven sixty miles across bad roads in the middle of the night by someone who belongs to another chapter of the same national organization does he begin to realize that the tie of common membership, flat and without content as it is, bolstered up by sentimental songs which no one really likes to sing but which everyone would miss if they weren't sung, has an intensity of its own; an intensity measured against the loneliness which each member would feel if there were no such society.

If this then, this third-generation American, always moving on, always, in his hopes, moving up, leaving behind him all that was his past and greeting with enthusiasm any echo of that past when he meets it in the life of another, represents one typical theme of the American character structure, how is this theme reflected in the form of the family, in the upbringing of the American child? For to the family we must turn for an understanding of the American character structure. We may describe the adult American, and for descriptive purposes we may refer his behavior to the American scene, to the European past, to the state of American industry, to any other set of events which we wish; but to understand the regularity of this behavior we must investigate the family within which the child is reared. Only so can we learn how the newborn child, at birth potentially a Chinaman or an American, a Pole or an Irishman, becomes an American. By referring his character to the family we do not say that the family is the cause of his character and that the pace of American industry or the distribution of population in America are secondary effects, but merely that all the great configuration of American culture is mediated to the child by his parents, his siblings, his near relatives, and his nurses. He meets American law first in the warning note of his mother's voice: "Stop digging, here comes a cop." He meets American economics when he finds his mother unimpressed by his offer to buy another copy of the wedding gift he has just smashed: "At the 5 and 10 cent store, can't we?" His first encounter with puritan standards may come through his mother's "If you don't eat your vegetables you can't have any dessert." He learns the paramount importance of distinguishing between vice and virtue; that it is only a matter of which comes first, the pleasure or the pain. All his great lessons come through his mother's voice, through his father's laughter, or the tilt of his father's cigar when a business deal goes right. Just as one way of understanding a machine is to understand how it is made, so one way of understanding the typical character structure of a culture is to follow step by step the way in which it is built into the growing child. Our assumption when we look at the American family will be that each experience of early childhood is contributing to make the growing individual "all of a piece," is guiding him towards consistent and specifically American inconsistency in his habits and view of the world.

What kind of parents are these "third-generation" Americans? These people who are always moving, always readjusting, always hoping to buy a better car and a better radio, and even in the years of Depression orienting their behavior to their "failure" to buy a better car or a better radio. Present or absent, the better car, the better house, the better radio are key points in family life. In the first place, the American parent expects his child to leave him, leave him physically, go to another town, another state; leave him in terms of occupation, embrace a different calling, learn a different skill; leave him socially, travel if possible with a different crowd. Even where a family has reached the top and actually stayed there for two or three generations, there are, for all but the very, very few, still larger cities or foreign courts to be stormed. Those American families which settle back to maintain a position of having reached the top in most cases moulder there for lack of occupation, ladder-climbers gone stale from sitting too long on the top step, giving a poor imitation of the aristocracy of other lands. At the bottom, too, there are some without hope, but very few. Studies of modern youth dwell with anxiety upon the disproportion between the daydreams of the under-privileged young people and the actuality which confronts them in terms of job opportunities. In that very daydream the break is expressed. The daughter who says to her hard-working mother: "You don't know. I may be going to be a great writer," is playing upon a note in her mother's mind which accepts the possibility that even if her daughter does not become famous, she will at least go places that she, the mother, has never gone.

In old societies such as those from which their grandparents and great-grandparents came (and it is important to remember that Americans are oriented towards the Europe from which their ancestors emigrated, not to the Europe which exists today) parents had performed an act of singular finality when they married, before ever a child was born. They had defined its probable place in the sun. If they maintained the same status throughout the child's growing life, kept the necessary bit of ground or inheritance to start him off as befitted him, reared him to act and feel and believe in a way appropriate to "that state of life to which it has pleased God to call him," the parents had done their share. Their service to their child was majorly the maintenance of their own place in the world. His care, his food, his shelter, his education—all of these were by-products of the parents' position. But in America, such an attitude, such a concentration on one's own position makes one, in most cases, a bad parent. One is not just restaking the same old claim for one's child, nor can one stake out the child's new claim for him. All one can do is to make him strong and well equipped to go prospecting for himself. For proper behavior *in* that state of life to which it has pleased God to call one, is substituted proper behavior *towards* that state of life to which God, if given enough assistance, may call one's son and daughter. Europeans laugh at the way in which parents pick for their newborn babies colleges which they have never seen. It does, of course, make sense to plan one's affairs so that one's son goes to the same school one went to oneself; but this fantastic new choice—for a squirming bit of humanity which may after all not have the brains to get through the third grade—is inexplicable. Parenthood in America has become a very special thing, and parents see themselves not as giving their children final status and place, rooting them firmly for life in a dependable social structure, but merely as training them for a race which they will run alone.

With this orientation towards a different future for the child comes also the expectation that the child will pass beyond his parents and leave their standards behind him. . . .

By and large, the American father has an attitude towards his children which may be loosely classified as autumnal. They are his for a brief and passing season, and in a very short while they will be operating gadgets which he does not understand and cockily talking a language to which he has no clue. He does his best to keep ahead of his son, takes a superior tone as long as he can, and knows that in nine cases out of ten he will lose. If the boy goes into his father's profession, of course, it will take him a time to catch up. He finds out that the old man knows a trick or two; that experience counts as over against this new-fangled nonsense. But the American boy solves that one very neatly: he typically does not go into his father's profession, nor take up land next to his father where his father can come over and criticize his plowing. He goes somewhere else, either in space or in occupation. And his father, who did the same thing and expects that his son will, is at heart terrifically disappointed if the son accedes to his ritual request that he docilely follow in his father's footsteps and secretly suspects the imitative son of being a milksop. He knows he is a milksop—or so he thinks—because he himself would have been a milksop if he had wanted to do just what his father did.

This is an attitude which reaches its most complete expression in the third-generation American. His grandfather left home, rebelled against a parent who did not expect final rebellion, left a land where everyone expected him to stay. Come to this country, his rebellious adventuring cooled off by success, he begins to relent a little, to think perhaps the strength of his ardor to leave home was overdone. When his sons grow up, he is torn between his desire to have them succeed in this new country—which means that they must be more American than he, must lose entirely their foreign names and every trace of allegiance to a foreign way of life—and his own guilt towards the parents and the fatherland which he has denied. So he puts on the heat, alternately punishing the child whose low marks in school suggest that he is not going to be a successful American and berating him for his American ways and his disrespect for his father and his father's friends from the old country. When that son leaves home, he throws himself with an intensity which his children will not know into the American way of life; he eats American, talks American, dresses American, he will be American or nothing. In making his way of life consistent, he inevitably makes it thin; the overtones of the family meal on which strange, delicious, rejected European dishes were set, and about which low words in a foreign tongue wove the atmosphere of home, must all be dropped out. His speech has a certain emptiness; he rejects the roots of words—roots lead back, and he is going forward—and comes to handle language in terms of surfaces and clichés. He rejects half of his life in order to make the other half self-consistent and complete. And by and large he succeeds. Almost miraculously, the sons of the Polish day laborer and the Italian fruit grower, the Finnish miner and the Russian garment worker become Americans.

Second generation—American-born of foreign-born parents—they set part of the tone of the American eagerness for their children to go onward. They have left their parents; left them in a way which requires more moral compensation than was necessary even for the parent generation who left Europe. The immigrant left his land, his parents, his fruit trees, and the little village street behind him. He cut the ties of military service; he flouted the king or the emperor; he built himself a new life in a new country. The father whom he left behind was strong, a part of something terribly strong, something to be feared and respected and fled from. Something so strong that the bravest man might boast of a successful flight. He left his parents, entrenched representatives of an order which he rejected. But not so his son. He leaves his father not a part of a strong other-way of life, but bewildered on the shores of the new world, having climbed only halfway up the beach. His father's ties to the old world, his mannerisms, his broken accent, his little foreign gestures are not part and parcel of something strong and different; they are signs of his failure to embrace this new way of life. Does his mother wear a kerchief over her head? He cannot see the generations of women who have worn such kerchiefs. He sees only the American women who wear hats, and he pities and rejects his mother who has failed to become—an American. And so there enters into the attitude of the second-generation American—an attitude which again is woven through our folkways, our attitude towards other languages, towards anything foreign, towards anything European—a combination of contempt and avoidance, a fear of yielding, and a sense that to yield would be weakness. His father left a father who was the representative of a way of life which had endured for a thousand years. When he leaves his father, he leaves a partial failure; a hybrid, one who represents a step towards freedom, not freedom itself. His first-generation father chose between freedom and what he saw as slavery; but when the second-generation American looks at his European father, and through him, at Europe, he sees a choice between success and failure, between potency and ignominy. He passionately rejects the halting English, the half-measures of the immigrant. He rejects with what seems to him equally good reasons "European ties and entanglements." This second-generation attitude which has found enormous expression in our culture especially during the last fifty years, has sometimes come to dominate it —in those parts of the country which we speak of as "isolationist." Intolerant of foreign language, foreign ways, vigorously determined on being themselves, they are, in attitude if not in fact, second-generation Americans.

When the third-generation boy grows up, he comes up against a father who found the task of leaving his father a comparatively simple one. The second-generation parent lacks the intensity of the first, and his son in turn fails to reflect the struggles, the first against feared strength and the second against guiltily rejected failure, which have provided the plot for his father and grandfather's maturation. He is expected to succeed; he is expected to go further than his father went; and all this is taken for granted. He is furthermore expected to feel very little respect for the past. Somewhere in his grandfather's day there was an epic struggle for liberty and freedom. His picture of that epic grandfather is a little obscured, however, by the patent fact that his father does not really respect him; he may have been a noble character, but he had a foreign accent. The grandchild is told in school, in the press, over the radio, about the founding fathers, but they were not after all *his* founding fathers; they are, in ninety-nine cases out of a hundred, somebody else's ancestors. Any time one's own father, who in his own youth had pushed his father aside and made his own way, tries to get in one's way, one can invoke the founding fathers—those ancestors of the real Americans; the Americans who got here earlier—those Americans which father worked so very hard, so slavishly, in fact, to imitate. This is a point which the European observer misses. He hears an endless invocation of Washington and Lincoln, of Jefferson and Franklin. Obviously, Americans go in for ancestor worship, says the European. Obviously, Americans are longing for a strong father, say the psycho-analysts. These observers miss the point that Washington is not the ancestor of the man who is doing the talking; Washington does not represent the past to which one belongs by birth, but the past to which one tries to belong by effort. Washington represents the thing for which grandfather left Europe at the risk of his life, and for which father rejected grandfather at the risk of his integrity. Washington is not that to which Americans passionately cling but that to which they want to belong, and fear, in the bottom of their hearts, that they cannot and do not.

This odd blending of the future and the past, in which another man's great-grandfather becomes the symbol of one's grandson's future, is an essential part of American culture. "Americans are so conservative," say Europeans. They lack the revolutionary spirit. Why don't they rebel? Why did President Roosevelt's suggestion of altering the structure of the Supreme Court and the Third-Term argument raise such a storm of protest? Because, in education, in attitudes, most Americans are third generation, they have just really arrived. Their attitude towards this country is that of one who has just established membership, just been elected to an exclusive club, just been initiated into the rites of an exacting religion. Almost any one of them who inspects his own ancestry, even though it goes back many more generations than three, will find a gaping hole somewhere in the family tree. Campfire girls give an honor to the girl who can name all eight great-grandparents, including the maiden names of the four great-grandmothers. Most Americans cannot get this honor. And who was that missing great-grandmother? Probably, oh, most probably, not a grand-niece of Martha Washington.

We have, of course, our compensatory mythology. People who live in a land torn by earthquakes have myths of a time when the land was steady, and those whose harvests are uncertain dream of a golden age when there was no drought. Likewise, people whose lives are humdrum and placid dream of an age of famine and rapine. We have our rituals of belonging, our DAR's and our Descendants of King Philip's Wars, our little blue book of the blue-blooded Hawaiian aristocracy descended from the first missionaries, and our *Mayflower,* which is only equaled in mythological importance by the twelve named canoes which brought the Maoris to New Zealand. The mythology keeps alive the doubt. The impressive president of a patriotic society knows that she is a member by virtue of only one of the some eight routes through which membership is possible. Only one. The other seven? Well, three are lost altogether. Two ancestors were Tories. In some parts of the country she can boast of that; after all, Tories were people of substance, real "old families." But it doesn't quite fit. Of two of those possible lines, she has resolutely decided not to think. Tinkers and tailors and candlestick makers blend indistinctly with heaven knows what immigrants! She goes to a meeting and is very insistent about the way in which the Revolutionary War which only one-eighth of her ancestors helped to fight should be represented to the children of those whose eight ancestors were undoubtedly all somewhere else in 1776.

On top of this Old American mythology, another layer has been added, a kind of placatory offering, a gesture towards the Old World which Americans had left behind. As the fifth- and sixth- and seventh-generation Americans lost his zest which came with climbing got to the top of the pecking order[1]

[1]Pecking order is a very convenient piece of jargon which social psychologists use to describe a group in which it is very clear to everybody in it, just which bird can peck which, or which cow butt which other cow away from the water trough. Among many living creatures these "pecking orders" are fixed and when a newcomer enters the group he has to fight and scramble about until everybody is clear just where he belongs—below No. 8 chick, for instance, and above old No. 9.

in their own town or city and sat, still uncertain, still knowing their credentials were shaky, on the top of the pile, the habit of wanting to belong—to really belong, to be accepted absolutely as something which one's ancestors had NOT been—became inverted. They turned towards Europe, especially towards England, towards presentation at Court, towards European feudal attitudes. And so we have had in America two reinforcements of the European class attitudes—those hold-overs of feudal caste attitudes, in the newly-come immigrant who carries class consciousness in every turn and bend of his neck, and the new feudalism, the "old family" who has finally toppled over backwards into the lap of all that their remote ancestors left behind them.

When I say that we are most of us—whatever our origins—third-generation in character structure, I mean that we have been reared in an atmosphere which is most like that which I have described for the third generation. Father is to be outdistanced and outmoded, but not because he is a strong representative of another culture, well entrenched, not because he is a weak and ineffectual attempt to imitate the new culture; he did very well in his way, but he is out of date. He, like us, was moving forwards, moving away from something symbolized by his own ancestors, moving towards something symbolized by other people's ancestors. Father stands for the way things were done, for a direction which on the whole was a pretty good one, in its day. He was all right because he was on the right road. Therefore, we, his children, lack the mainsprings of rebellion. He was out of date; he drove an old model car which couldn't make it on the hills. Therefore it is not necessary to fight him, to knock him out of the race. It is much easier and quicker to pass him. And to pass him it is only necessary to keep on going and to see that one buys a new model every year. Only if one slackens, loses one's interest in the race towards success, does one slip back. Otherwise, it is onward and upward, *towards* the world of Washington and Lincoln; a world in which we don't fully belong, but which we feel, if we work at it, we some time may achieve.

AS THE TWIG IS BENT

IV

INTRODUCTION IV

Nearly fifteen years ago the American psychoanalyst Erik H. Erikson called attention to the need for studies of the upbringing of children in relation to the development of national character. "One may scan work after work on history, society, and morality and find little reference to the fact that all people start as children and that all peoples begin in their nurseries."[1] With Erikson, students of the interactions of personality and culture contend that national character cannot be defined or explained solely in reference to the experiences of adults, whether on the frontier or in the city, whether winning bread or striving for higher social status. The modes of adult response to experience—the sense that is made of it, the ways by which problems are met or evaded, the modifications or confirmations of character that occur in consequence—are so profoundly conditioned by upbringing that it can be affirmed, without exaggeration, that the basic elements of mature character are formed in the crib, in the bathroom, and on the playground—at every point, in short, where the malleable personalities of the young are shaped by the impress of culture, mediated by parents and peers.

When Erikson wrote in 1950, behavioral scientists had already recognized the relevance of child-training to national character. Freudian and other psychoanalytic theories had been deployed, with mixed effect, in the interpretation of national character, and anthropologists such as Margaret Mead, whose trail-blazing account of the *Coming of Age in Samoa* was published in 1928, had reported on the processes of personality formation among primitive peoples. Since Erikson wrote, the techniques of inquiry have been further refined, the conceptual apparatus of culture-and-personality analysis has been more fully developed, and promising efforts have been made to engage the resources of history with those of the behavioral sciences in interdisciplinary liaison.

Examples of progress in this field of study are furnished by the following selections from the exploratory work of a historian, David M. Potter of Stanford University, and an anthropologist, Francis L. K. Hsu of Northwestern University. No historian has done more than Potter to foster cooperation among disciplines in the investigation of American character. His book, *People of Plenty: Economic Abundance and the American Character* (1954), from which an excerpt is reprinted, persuasively argues the case for abundance as a key factor in the shaping of personality in the United States. The second selec-

[1]*Childhood and Society* (New York: W. W. Norton & Company, 1950), p. 12.

tion comes from Hsu's *Americans and Chinese: Two Ways of Life* (1953), one of the few systematic transnational studies which has been published. Born and brought up in China before World War II and now an American citizen, the author calls himself a "marginal man" in whom two contrasting cultures meet: "He paces the border where they confront each other within himself, and he can reach out to touch them both." Hsu's reflections on differences in child training in these two cultures illustrate the utility of comparative analysis of national character.

Potter's observations are also framed in comparative terms. His essay speaks to the following questions: "What, if anything, does the factor of abundance have to do with the process of personality formation (in so far as this process is understood) in the United States? How does the process differ from that in countries where the measure of abundance is not so great?"

DAVID M. POTTER

Economic Abundance and the Formation of American Character

To these questions, I believe, some highly explicit answers are possible. Let us therefore be entirely concrete. Let us consider the situation of a six-month-old American infant, who is not yet aware that he is a citizen, a taxpayer, and a consumer.

This individual is, to all appearances, just a very young specimen of *Homo sapiens,* with certain needs for protection, care, shelter, and nourishment which may be regarded as the universal biological needs of human infancy rather than specific cultural needs. It would be difficult to prove that the culture has as yet differentiated him from other infants, and, though he is an American, few would argue that he has acquired an American character. Yet abundance and the circumstances arising from abundance have already dictated a whole range of basic conditions which, from his birth, are constantly at work upon this child and which will contribute in the most intimate and basic way to the formation of his character.

To begin with, abundance has already revolutionized the typical mode of his nourishment by providing for him to be fed upon cow's milk rather than upon his mother's milk, taken from the bottle rather than from the breast. Abundance contributes vitally to this transformation, because bottle feeding requires fairly elaborate facilities of refrigeration, heating, sterilization, and temperature control, which only an advanced technology can offer and only an economy of abundance can make widely available. I will not attempt here to resolve the debated question as to the psychological effects, for both mother and child, of bottle feeding as contrasted wih breast feeding in infant nurture. But it is clear that the changeover to bottle feeding has encroached somewhat upon the intimacy of the bond between mother and child. The nature of this

Reprinted from *People of Plenty: Economic Abundance and the American Character* by David M. Potter, by permission of The University of Chicago Press.

bond is, of course, one of the most crucial factors in the formation of character. Bottle feeding also must tend to emphasize the separateness of the infant as an individual, and thus it makes, for the first time, a point which the entire culture reiterates constantly throughout the life of the average American. In addition to the psychic influences which may be involved in the manner of taking the food, it is also a matter of capital importance that the bottle-fed baby is, on the whole, better nourished than the breast-fed infant and therefore likely to grow more rapidly, to be more vigorous, and to suffer fewer ailments, with whatever effects these physical conditions may have upon his personality.

It may be argued also that abundance has provided a characteristic mode of housing for the infant and that this mode further emphasizes his separateness as an individual. In societies of scarcity, dwelling units are few and hard to come by, with the result that high proportions of newly married young people make their homes in the parental ménage, thus forming part of an "extended" family, as it is called. Moreover, scarcity provides a low ratio of rooms to individuals, with the consequence that whole families may expect as a matter of course to have but one room for sleeping, where children will go to bed in intimate propinquity to their parents. But abundance prescribes a different regime. By making it economically possible for newly married couples to maintain separate households of their own, it has almost destroyed the extended family as an institution in America and has ordained that the child shall be reared in a "nuclear" family, so-called, where his only intimate associates are his parents and his siblings, with even the latter far fewer now than in families of the past. The housing arrangements of this new-style family are suggested by census data for 1950. In that year there were 45,983,000 dwelling units to accommodate the 38,310,000 families in the United States, and, though the median number of persons in the dwelling unit was 3.1, the median number of rooms in the dwelling unit was 4.6. Eighty-four per cent of all dwelling units reported less than one person per room.[1] By providing the ordinary family with more than one room for sleeping, the economy thus produces a situation in which the child will sleep either in a room alone or in a room shared with his brothers or sisters. Even without allowing for the cases in which children may have separate rooms, these conditions mean that a very substantial percentage of children now sleep in a room alone, for, with the declining birth rate, we have reached a point at which an increasing proportion of families have one child or two children rather than the larger number which was at one time typical. For instance, in the most recent group of mothers who had completed their childbearing phase, according to the census, 19.5 per cent had had one child and 23.4 had had two. Thus almost half of

[1]Data from United States Department of Commerce, *Census of Housing: 1950,* Vol. I, Part I (Washington: Government Printing Office, 1953), p. xxx. For purposes of enumeration kitchens were counted as rooms, but bathrooms, hallways, and pantries were not. Many dwelling units were, of course, occupied by single persons or others not falling under the definition of a family, but the number of households—43,468,000—was also less than the number of dwelling units.

all families with offspring did not have more than two children throughout their duration. In the case of the first group, all the children were "only" children throughout their childhood, and in the second group half of the children were "only" children until the second child was born. To state this in another, and perhaps a more forcible, way, it has been shown that among American women who arrived at age thirty-four during the year 1949 and who had borne children up to that time, 26.7 per cent had borne only one child, and 34.5 per cent had borne only two.[2] If these tendencies persist, it would mean that, among families where there are children, hardly one in three will have more than two children.

The census has, of course, not got around to finding out how the new-style family, in its new-style dwelling unit, adjusts the life-practice to the space situation. But it is significant that America's most widely circulated book on the care of infants advises that "it is preferable that he [the infant] not sleep in his parents' room after he is about 12 months old," offers the opinion that "it's fine for each [child] to have a room of his own, if that's possible," and makes the sweeping assertion that "it's a sensible rule not to take a child into the parents' bed for any reason."[3] It seems clear beyond dispute that the household space provided by the economy of abundance has been used to emphasize the separateness, the apartness, if not the isolation, of the American child.

Not only the nourishment and housing, but also the clothing of the American infant are controlled by American abundance. For one of the most sweeping consequences of our abundance is that, in contrast to other peoples who keep their bodies warm primarily by wearing clothes, Americans keep their bodies warm primarily by a far more expensive and even wasteful method: namely, by heating the buildings in which they are sheltered. Every American who has been abroad knows how much lighter is the clothing—especially the underclothing—of Americans than of people in countries like England and France, where the winters are far less severe than ours, and every American who can remember the conditions of a few decades ago knows how much lighter our clothing is than that of our grandparents. These changes have occurred because clothing is no longer the principal device for securing warmth. The oil furnace has not only displaced the open fireplace; it has also displaced the woolen undergarment and the vest.

This is a matter of considerable significance for adults but of far greater importance to infants, for adults discipline themselves to wear warm garments,

[2]Clyde V. Kiser, "Fertility Trends in the United States," *Journal of the American Statistical Association,* XLVII (1952), 31–33. Figures given by Kiser, based on research by P. K. Whelpton, also include childless women; but my concern here is with the sibling relationships of children and not with the fertility of women, and I have therefore based my statements upon the record of women who have borne children rather than upon women of childbearing age. My statement has no way of allowing for half-brothers and sisters born of different mothers or for differentiating the number of children who survive from the number born.

[3]Benjamin Spock, *The Pocket Book of Baby and Child Care* (New York: Pocket Books, Inc., 1946), pp. 96–97.

submitting, for instance, to woolen underwear more or less voluntarily. But the infant knows no such discipline, and his garments or bedclothes must be kept upon him by forcible means. Hence primitive people, living in outdoor conditions, swaddle the child most rigorously, virtually binding him into his clothes, and breaking him to them almost as a horse is broken to the harness. Civilized peoples mitigate the rigor but still use huge pins or clips to frustrate the baby's efforts to kick off the blankets and free his limbs. In a state of nature, cold means confinement and warmth means freedom, so far as young humans are concerned. But abundance has given the American infant physical freedom by giving him physical warmth in cold weather.

In this connection it may be surmised that abundance has also given him a permissive system of toilet training. If our forebears imposed such training upon the child and we now wait for him to take the initiative in these matters himself, it is not wholly because the former held a grim Calvinistic doctrine of child-rearing that is philosophically contrary to ours. The fact was that the circumstances gave them little choice. A mother who was taking care of several babies, keeping them clean, making their clothes, washing their diapers in her own washtub, and doing this, as often as not, while another baby was on the way, had little choice but to hasten their fitness to toilet themselves. Today, on the contrary, the disposable diaper, the diaper service, and most of all the washing machine, not to mention the fact that one baby seldom presses upon the heels of another, make it far easier for the mother to indulge the child in a regime under which he will impose his own toilet controls in his own good time.

Thus the economy of plenty has influenced the feeding of the infant, his regime, and the physical setting within which he lives. These material conditions alone might be regarded as having some bearing upon the formation of his character, but the impact of abundance by no means ends at this point. In so far as it has an influence in determining what specific individuals shall initiate the infant into the ways of man and shall provide him with his formative impressions of the meaning of being a person, it must be regarded as even more vital. When it influences the nature of the relationships between these individuals and the infant, it must be recognized as reaching to the very essence of the process of character formation.

The central figures in the dramatis personae of the American infant's universe are still his parents, and in this respect, of course, there is nothing peculiar either to the American child or to the child of abundance. But abundance has at least provided him with parents who are in certain respects unlike the parents of children born in other countries or born fifty years ago. To begin with, it has given him young parents, for the median age of fathers at the birth of the first child in American marriages (as of 1940) was 25.3 years, and the median age of mothers was 22.6 years. This median age was substantially lower than it had been in the United States in 1890 for both fathers and mothers. Moreover, as the size of families has been reduced and the wife no longer continues to bear a succession of children throughout the period of her fertility, the median age of mothers at the birth of the last child has declined from 32 years (1890) to 27 years (1940). The age of the parents at the birth of both the first child and the last child is far lower than in the case of couples in most European countries. There can be little doubt that abundance has caused this differential, in the case of the first-born by making it economically possible for a high proportion of the population to meet the expenses of homemaking at a fairly early age. In the case of the last-born, it would also appear that one major reason for the earlier cessation of child-bearing is a determination by parents to enjoy a high standard of living themselves and to limit their offspring to a number for whom they can maintain a similar standard.

By the very fact of their youth, these parents are more likely to remain alive until the child reaches maturity, thus giving him a better prospect of being reared by his own mother and father. This prospect is further reinforced by increases in the life-span, so that probably no child in history has ever enjoyed so strong a likelihood that his parents will survive to rear him. Abundance has produced this situation by providing optimum conditions for prolonging life. But, on the other hand, abundance has also contributed much to produce an economy in which the mother is no longer markedly dependent upon the father, and this change in the economic relation between the sexes has probably done much to remove obstacles to divorce. The results are all too familiar. During the decade 1940–49 there were 25.8 divorces for every 100 marriages in the United States, which ratio, if projected over a longer period, would mean that one marriage out of four would end in divorce. But our concern here is with a six-month-old child, and the problem is to know whether this factor of divorce involves childless couples predominantly or whether it is likely to touch him. The answer is indicated by the fact that, of all divorces granted in 1948, no less than 42 per cent were to couples with children under eighteen, and a very large proportion of these children were of much younger ages. Hence one might say that the economy of abundance has provided the child with younger parents who chose their role of parenthood deliberately and who are more likely than parents in the past to live until he is grown, but who are substantially less likely to preserve the unbroken family as the environment within which he shall be reared.

In addition to altering the characteristics of the child's parents, it has also altered the quantitative relationship between him and his parents. It has done this, first of all, by offering the father such lucrative opportunities through work outside the home that the old agricultural economy in which children worked alongside their fathers is now obsolete. Yet, on the other hand, the father's new employment gives so much more leisure than his former work that the child may, in fact, receive considerably more of his father's attention. But the most vital transformation is in the case of the mother. In the economy of scarcity which controlled the modes of life that were traditional for many centuries, an upper-class child was reared by a nurse, and all others were normally reared by their mothers. The scarcity economy could not support many nonproductive members, and these mothers, though not "employed," were most decidedly hard workers, busily engaged in cooking, washing, sewing, weaving, preserving, caring for the henhouse, the garden, and perhaps the cow, and in general carrying on the domestic economy of a large family. Somehow they also attended to the needs of a numerous brood of children, but the mother was in no sense a full-time attendant upon any one child. Today, however, the economy of abundance very nearly exempts a very large number of mothers from the requirement of economic productivity in order that they may give an unprecedented share of their time to the care of the one or two young children who are now the usual number in an American family. Within the home, the wide range of labor-saving devices and the assignment of many functions, such as laundering, to service industries have produced this result. Outside the home, employment of women in the labor force has steadily increased, but the incidence of employment falls upon unmarried women, wives without children, and wives with grown children. In fact, married women without children are two and one-half times as likely to be employed as those with children. Thus what amounts to a new dispensation has been established for the child. If he belongs to the upper class, his mother has replaced his nurse as his full-time attendant. The differences in character formation that might result from this change alone could easily be immense. To mention but one possibility, the presence of the nurse must inevitably have made the child somewhat aware of his class status, whereas the presence of the mother would be less likely to have this effect. If the child does not belong to the upper class, mother and child now impinge upon each other in a relationship whose intensity is of an entirely different magnitude from that which prevailed in the past. The mother has fewer physical distractions in the care of the child, but she is more likely to be restive in her maternal role because it takes her away from attractive employment with which it cannot be reconciled.

If abundance has thus altered the relationship of the child with his parent, it has even more drastically altered the rest of his social milieu, for it has changed the identity of the rest of the personnel who induct him into human society. In the extended family of the past, a great array of kinspeople filled his cosmos and guided him to maturity. By nature, he particularly needed association with children of his own age (his "peers," as they are called), and he particularly responded to the values asserted by these peers. Such peers were very often his brothers and sisters, and, since they were all members of his own family, all came under parental control. This is to say that, in a sense, the parents controlled the peer group, and the peer group controlled the child. The point is worth making because we frequently encounter the assertion that parental control of the child has been replaced by peer-group control; but it is arguable that what is really the case is that children were always deeply influenced by the peer group and that parents have now lost their former measure of control over this group, since it is no longer a familial group. Today the nursery school replaces the large family as a peer group, and the social associations, even of young children, undergo the same shift from focused contact with family to diffused contact with a miscellany of people, which John Galsworthy depicted for grown people in the three novels of the *Forsyte Saga*. Again, the effects upon character may very well be extensive.

Abundance, then, has played a critical part in revolutionizing both the physical circumstances and the human associations which surround the American infant and child. These changes alone would warrant the hypothesis that abundance has profoundly affected the formation of character for such a child. But to extend this inquiry one step further, it may be worth while to consider how these altered conditions actually impinge upon the individual. Here, of course, is an almost unlimited field for investigation, and I shall only attempt to indicate certain crucial points at which abundance projects conditions that are basic in the life of the child.

One of these points concerns the cohesive force which holds the family together. The family is the one institution which touches all members of society most intimately, and it is perhaps the only social institution which touches young children directly. The sources from which the family draws its strength are, therefore, of basic importance. In the past, these sources were, it would seem, primarily economic. For agrarian society, marriage distinctively involved a division of labor. Where economic opportunity was narrowly restricted, the necessity for considering economic ways and means in connection with marriage led to the arrangement of matches by parents and to the institution of the dowry. The emotional bonds of affection, while always important, were not deemed paramount, and the ideal of romantic love played little or no part in the lives of ordinary people. Where it existed at all, it was as an upper-class luxury. (The very term "courtship" implies this upper-class orientation.) This must inevitably have meant that the partners in the majority of marriages demanded less from one another emotionally than do the partners of romantic love and that the emotional factor was less important to the stability of the marriage. Abundance, however, has played its part in changing this picture. On the American frontier, where capital for dowries was as rare as opportunity for prosperous marriage was plentiful, the dowry became obsolete. Later still, when abundance began to diminish the economic duties imposed upon the housewife, the function of marriage as a division of labor ceased to seem paramount, and the romantic or emotional factor assumed increasing importance. Abundance brought the luxury of romantic love within the reach of all, and, as it did so, emotional harmony became the principal criterion of success in a marriage, while lack of such harmony became a major threat to the existence of the marriage. The statistics of divorce give us a measure of the loss of durability in marriage, but they give us no measure of the factors of instability in the marriages which endure and no measure of the increased focus upon emotional satisfactions in such marriages. The children of enduring marriages, as well as the children of divorce, must inevitably feel the impact of this increased emphasis upon emotional factors, must inevitably sense the difference in the foundations of the institution which holds their universe in place.

In the rearing of a child, it would be difficult to imagine any factors more vital than the distinction between a permissive and an authoritarian regime or more vital than the age at which economic responsibility is imposed. In both these matters the modern American child lives under a very different dispensation from children in the past. We commonly think of these changes as results of our more enlightened or progressive or humanitarian ideas. We may even think of them as results of developments in the specific field of child psychology, as if the changes were simply a matter of our understanding these matters better than our grandparents. But the fact is that the authoritarian discipline of the child, within the authoritarian family, was but an aspect of the authoritarian social system that was linked with the economy of scarcity. Such a regime could never have been significantly relaxed within the family so long as it remained diagnostic in the society. Nor could it have remained unmodified within the family, once society began to abandon it in other spheres.

Inevitably, the qualities which the parents inculcate in a child will depend upon the roles which they occupy themselves. For the ordinary man the economy of scarcity has offered one role, as Simon N. Patten observed many years ago, and the economy of abundance has offered another. Abundance offers "work calling urgently for workmen"; scarcity found the "worker seeking humbly any kind of toil."[4] As a suppliant to his superiors, the worker under scarcity accepted the principle of authority; he accepted his own subordination and the obligation to cultivate the qualities appropriate to his subordination, such as submissiveness, obedience, and deference. Such a man naturally transferred the principle of authority into his own family and, through this principle, instilled into his children the qualities appropriate to people of their kind—submissiveness, obedience, and deference. Many copybook maxims still exist to remind us of the firmness of childhood discipline, while the difference between European and American children—one of the most clearly recognizable of all national differences—serves to emphasize the extent to which Americans have now departed from this firmness.

This new and far more permissive attitude toward children has arisen, significantly, in an economy of abundance, where work has called urgently for the workman. In this situation, no longer a suppliant, the workman found submissiveness no longer a necessity and therefore no longer a virtue. The principle of authority lost some of its majesty, and he was less likely to regard it as the only true criterion of domestic order. In short, he ceased to impose it upon his children. Finding that the most valuable trait in himself was a capacity for independent decision and self-reliant conduct in dealing with the diverse op-

[4]Simon Nelson Patten, *The New Basis of Civilization* (New York: Macmillan Co., 1907), pp. 187–88. I am indebted to Arthur Schlesinger, Jr., for calling my attention to Patten's important observations on this subject.

portunities which abundance offered him, he tended to encourage this quality in his children. The irresponsibility of childhood still called for a measure of authority on one side and obedience on the other, but this became a means to an end and not an end in itself. On the whole, permissive training, to develop independent ability, even though it involves a certain sacrifice of obedience and discipline, is the characteristic mode of child-rearing in the one country which most distinctively enjoys an economy of abundance. Here, in a concrete way, one finds something approaching proof for Gerth and Mills's suggestion that the relation of father and child may have its importance not as a primary factor but rather as a "replica of the power relations of society."

If scarcity required men to "seek humbly any kind of toil," it seldom permitted women to seek employment outside the home at all. Consequently, the woman was economically dependent upon, and, accordingly, subordinate to, her husband or her father. Her subordination reinforced the principle of authority within the home. But the same transition which altered the role of the male worker has altered her status as well, for abundance "calling urgently for workmen" makes no distinctions of gender, and, by extending economic independence to women, has enabled them to assume the role of partners rather than of subordinates within the family. Once the relation of voluntarism and equality is introduced between husband and wife, it is, of course, far more readily extended to the relation between parent and child.

If abundance has fostered a more permissive regime for the child, amid circumstances of democratic equality within the family, it has no less certainly altered the entire process of imposing economic responsibility upon the child, hence the process of preparing the child for such responsibility. In the economy of scarcity, as I have remarked above, society could not afford to support any substantial quota of nonproductive members. Consequently, the child went to work when he was as yet young. He attended primary school for a much shorter school year than the child of today; only a minority attended high school; and only the favored few attended college. Even during the brief years of schooling, the child worked, in the home, on the farm, or even in the factory. But today the economy of abundance can afford to maintain a substantial proportion of the population in nonproductive status, and it assigns this role, sometimes against their will, to its younger and its elder members. It protracts the years of schooling, and it defers responsibilities for an unusually long span. It even enforces laws setting minimal ages for leaving school, for going to work, for consenting to sexual intercourse, or for marrying. It extends the jurisdiction of juvenile courts to the eighteenth or the twentieth year of age.

Such exemption from economic responsibility might seem to imply a long and blissful youth free from strain for the child. But the delays in reaching economic maturity are not matched by comparable delays in other phases of growing up. On the contrary, there are many respects in which the child matures earlier. Physically, the child at the lower social level will actually arrive at adolescence a year or so younger than his counterpart a generation ago, because of improvement in standards of health and nutrition.[5] Culturally, the child is made aware of the allurements of sex at an earlier age, partly by his familiarity with the movies, television, and popular magazines, and partly by the practice of "dating" in the early teens. By the standards of his peer group, he is encouraged to demand expensive and mature recreations, similar to those of adults, at a fairly early age. By reason of the desire of his parents that he should excel in the mobility race and give proof during his youth of the qualities which will make him a winner in later life, he is exposed to the stimuli of competition before he leaves the nursery. Thus there is a kind of imbalance between the postponement of responsibility and the quickening of social maturity which may have contributed to make American adolescence a more difficult age than human biology alone would cause it to be. Here, again, there are broad implications for the formation of character, and here, again, abundance is at work on both sides of the equation, for it contributes as much to the hastening of social maturity as it does to the prolongation of economic immaturity.

Some of these aspects of the rearing of children in the United States are as distinctively American, when compared with other countries, as any Yankee traits that have ever been attributed to the American people. In the multiplicity which always complicates social analysis, such aspects of child-rearing might be linked with a number of factors in American life. But one of the more evident and more significant links, it would seem certain, is with the factor of abundance. Such a tie is especially pertinent in this discussion, where the intention of the whole book has been to relate the study of character, as the historian would approach it, to the same subject as it is viewed by the behavioral scientist. In this chapter, especially, the attempt has been made to throw a bridge between the general historical force of economic abundance and the specific behavioral pattern of people's lives. Historical forces are too often considered only in their public and over-all effects, while private lives are interpreted without sufficient reference to the historical determinants which shape them. But no major force at work in society can possibly make itself felt at one of these levels without also having its impact at the other level. In view of this fact, the study of national character should not stand apart, as it has in the past, from the study of the process of character formation in the individual. In view of this fact, also, the effect of economic abundance is especially pertinent. For economic abundance is a factor whose presence and whose force may be clearly and precisely recognized in the most personal and intimate phases of the development of personality in the child. Yet, at the same time, the presence and the force of this factor are recognizable with equal certainty in the whole broad, general range of American experience, American ideals, and American institutions. At both levels, it has exercised a pervasive influence in the shaping of the American character.

[5] Alfred C. Kinsey *et al.*, *Sexual Behavior in the Human Male* (Philadelphia: W. B. Saunders Co., 1948), p. 397.

FRANCIS L. K. HSU

Americans and Chinese: The Beginnings of Contrast

How have Chinese and Americans acquired their contrasting ways of life? I am convinced that the most plausible and probable answer to this question must be broadly Freudian. That is, these contrasts are to be found first and foremost in the family, the first external mold of the vast majority of mankind.

All students of man today accept the general theorem that, except for extreme cases such as geniuses and idiots, personality is chiefly the result of conditioning by culture. Personality is the sum total of the individual's characteristic reactions to his environment, while culture consists of the accepted patterns of behavior in every society. The contrasts between Chinese and American ways of life may be viewed, therefore, as contrasts between the sum totals in their respective personality and culture.

The personality of the individual and the culture of his society are by no means identical. No individual is an automaton, just as no society is without variation. However, each society offers rewards to those of its members who act according to its accepted pattern of behavior and it punishes those who do not.

Since cultural conditioning begins in the family, it is logical for us to inquire first into the broad contrasts in the family systems in which the two ways of life are taught and propagated.

In doing so, however, we must exercise great restraint. There is ample temptation to stretch Freudian theory to absurd lengths. Gregory Bateson, a British anthropologist, suggested, for example, that British and American attitudes toward their respective colonies are copies of the respective parent-child relationships in the two countries. The American parents encourage in their children "certain sorts of boastful and exhibitionistic behavior, while still in a position somewhat subordinate to and dependent upon the parents," but in England the parent-child relationship is characterized by "dominance and succoring." The American parent-child relationship "contains within itself factors for psychologically weaning the child, while in England, among the upper classes,

Reprinted from *Americans and Chinese: Two Ways of Life* by Francis L. K. Hsu, by permission of Abelard-Schuman Ltd.

the analogous breaking of the succoring dependent link has to be performed by . . . the boarding school." Since "colonies cannot be sent to a boarding school . . . England has very great difficulty in weaning her non-Anglo Saxon colonies, while these colonies have had corresponding difficulty in attaining maturity—in sharp contrast with the history of the Philippines."[1]

Geoffrey Gorer, another British anthropologist, is equally daring. He considers America's two houses of Congress as a sort of extension of a certain sibling relationship in the American family. The House, being the younger brother of the family, is erratic and less responsible in its actions, knowing full well that the Senate, its older brother, will come to its rescue.[2]

Neither of these are examples of true science or even of sound logic. To avoid such pitfalls, we shall, instead of concentrating on details (which tend to vary because of geography, class, occupation, and many other factors), look at the broader phases of the family pattern in which the two peoples differ greatly, but consistently.

The Home

Let us begin with Chinese and American homes. An American house usually has a yard, large or small. It may have a hedge, but rarely is there a wall so high that a passer-by cannot see the windows. The majority of American houses have neither hedge nor wall whatsoever. Usually the interior is shielded from exterior view only by window curtains or blinds, and then during but part of the day.

The majority of Chinese houses are, in the first place, surrounded by such high walls that only the roofs are visible from the outside, and solid gates separate the interior grounds from the outside world. In addition there is usually a shadow wall placed directly in front of the gates on the other side of the street[3] as well as a four-leafed wooden screen standing about five feet behind the gates. The outside shadow wall keeps the home from direct exposure to the unseen spirits. The inside wooden screen shields the interior courtyard from pedestrians' glances when the gates are ajar.

Inside the home, the contrast between China and America is reversed. The American emphasis within the home is on privacy. There are not only doors to the bathrooms but also to the bedrooms, to the living room, and even to the kitchen. Space and possessions are individualized. Thus parents have little liberty in the rooms of the children, and children cannot do what they want in those parts of the house regarded as pre-eminently the domain of the parents. Among some sections of the American population this rule of privacy extends to the husband and wife, so that each has a separate bedroom.

[1]Gregory Bateson, "Some Systematic Approaches to the Study of Culture and Personality," in *Character and Personality,* 11:76-82, 1942, reprinted in D. Haring, *Personal Character and Social Milieu,* 1949, pp. 110-16.

[2]Geoffrey Gorer, *The American People,* N.Y., 1949.

[3]Many streets are lined with houses on one side only. Where both sides of the street are occupied, it is still possible to erect shadow walls since home entrances do not as a rule directly face each other.

Within the Chinese home, on the other hand, privacy hardly exists at all, except between opposite sexes who are not spouses. Chinese children, even in the homes which have ample room, tend to share the same chambers with their parents until they reach adolescence. Not only do parents have freedom of action with reference to the children's belongings, but the youngsters can also use the possessions of the parents if they can lay their hands on them. If children damage their parents' possessions they are scolded not because they touched things that were not theirs but because they are too young to handle them with proper care.

The lack of privacy within the home finds its extreme expression in many well-to-do families of North China. Here the rooms are arranged in rows like the cars of a train. But instead of each room having a separate entrance, all the rooms are arranged in sequence, one leading into another. Thus, if there are five rooms, the front door of the house opens into the center room, which serves as the kitchen and dining room. There are two doors on opposite walls of the kitchen, each leading into a room which has in turn another door opening into the end rooms. Beginning at one end of the house, call it room A, one can walk in a straight line from there to room B, into the kitchen-dining room C, into room D, and finally into room E. The parents will occupy room B, nearest the kitchen, leaving room A free for a married daughter when she and her children come for a prolonged visit. If the family has two married sons, the older brother and his wife and children will occupy room D, while the younger brother and his wife will occupy room E. The occupants of rooms A and E will have to cross, respectively, rooms B and D in order to go in and out of the house. Actual arrangements vary somewhat from family to family, but this simplified picture is generally true.

Such an arrangement in living quarters would be very offensive to Americans. For even within the family Americans hew to the line as to what is yours and what is mine. But many Chinese adhere to a variation of the common linear arrangement even when they have more rooms in which to spread out. For they consider all within the four walls as being one body. The American child's physical environment establishes strong lines of individual distinction within the home but there is very little stress on separation of the home from the community. The Chinese child's environment is exactly the reverse. He finds a home with few demarcation lines within it but separated by high walls and multiple gates from the outside world.

Parents and Children

The difference between Chinese and American homes reflects their contrasting patterns of behavior in the family. In no country on earth is there so much attention paid to infancy[4] and so much privilege accorded childhood

[4]The attention-attracting value of children's photographs, recognized both by advertisers and the proverbial baby-kissing politician, is confirmed as well by newspaper readership surveys. In September 1947, the Journalism Quarterly published figures on reader re-

as in the United States. From every point of view this country is a paradise on earth for children. In contrast, it may be said without exaggeration that China is a country in which children come last.

The contrast can be seen in a myriad of ways. Americans are very verbal about their children's rights. There is not only state and federal legislation to protect the young ones, but there are also various juvenile protective associations to look after their welfare. Not only is infanticide treated like murder, but parents can get into legal trouble if they discipline their children with some enthusiasm.

In China parents have a completely free hand with their children. Popular misconception notwithstanding, infanticide has always been rare in China, and certainly no parents would brag about it. Yet even in modern times parents who have committed infanticide have almost always been free from legal action. It is literally true that from the viewpoint of American children, parents have practically no rights; but from the viewpoint of Chinese parents, children have little reason to expect protection from their elders. If an American were to point with justifiable pride to his country's many child protective associations, a Chinese would simply counter with an equally proud boast about his nation's numerous "societies for saving papers with written characters on" or "societies for giving away coffins."

American parents are so concerned with the welfare of their children, and they are so determined to do the right thing, that they handsomely support a huge number of child specialists, scientific or quack, to supply them with advice on what children like best. Chinese parents have taken their children so much for granted that pediatrics as a separate branch of medicine was unknown until modern times. As far as I know there is no piece of traditional literature aimed at making the Chinese better parents, and even during the days of the Republic there was hardly any scientific inquiry into what the children might think and desire. Articles on how to treat children appeared only sporadically in a few Chinese newspapers and magazines.

But Americans do not only study their children's behavior—they glorify it. Chinese do not only take their children for granted—they minimize them. The important thing to Americans is what parents should do for their children; to Chinese, what children should do for their parents.

The American emphasis on children has gone so far that even strangers can interfere with parents without regard to the circumstances. An Eastern

---

action to 2,200 general news photographs published in newspapers from coast to coast. Among males, pictures in the "children and baby" category caught the attention of 59 percent, which was a slightly higher response than that produced by the photo categories of "beauty queens and glamor girls," "international and general news," "accidents and disasters" (each 58 percent), and even "sports" (57 percent). Among women, the children's photos attracted the attention of 77 percent, slightly lower than the "weddings and engagements" classification (79 percent) but somewhat above the "society and club news" category (76 percent).

European immigrant friend of mine once related to me the following experience. He was riding in an elevated train with his six-year-old son. The youngster continued to ignore his cautions against standing close to the entrance. He cuffed the boy a few times. Thereupon another passenger arose, advanced menacingly and said angrily: "If you dare to strike that child again I'll have you arrested."

The extent to which some American parents go to suit the convenience of their children is exemplified by a mid-Western couple I know. To make their little ones happy, they installed a fancy slide in their living room. Guests entered the apartment by bending under it, and then they attempted to enjoy a conversation within reach of the boisterous sideshow provided by the young ones going up and down.

That this is unusual even for the United States is indicated by the fact that this couple felt compelled to justify their action every time they had a visitor and by the fact that their friends remarked about it. On the other hand, no Chinese parents could have kept the respect of the community if they permitted anything remotely resembling this.

For many centuries Chinese were both entertained and instructed by some tales known as "The Twenty-Four Examples of Filial Piety." These stories were illustrated in paintings, dramatized on the stage, recited by story-tellers in tea houses and in market places all over the country. Here is one of these "examples":

> A poor man by the name of Kuo and his wife were confronted with a serious problem. His aged mother was sick in bed. She needed both medicine and nourishment which Kuo could ill afford. After consultation between themselves, Kuo and his wife decided that the only way out was to get rid of their three-year-old only son. For Kuo and his wife said to each other, 'We have only one mother, but we can always get another child.' Thereupon the two went out to the field to dig a pit for the purpose of burying their child alive. But shortly after the man had started to dig he suddenly struck gold. It transpired that the gods were moved by the spirit of their filial piety, and this was their reward. Both the child and the mother were amply provided for and the family thrived happily ever after.

To the Chinese this story dramatized their most important cultural ideal, that support of the parents tops all other obligations and that this obligation must be fulfilled even at the expense of the children.

Economic support is not, however, the only way in which Chinese children are obligated to their parents. Their social duty toward their parents is even more striking. The son not only has to follow the Confucian dictum that "parents are always right," but at all times and in all circumstances he must try to satisfy their wishes and look after their safety. If the parents are indisposed, the son should spare no trouble in obtaining a cure for them. If a parent is sentenced to prison, the son must arrange to take that parent's place. If the parents are displeased with their daughter-in-law, the good son does not hesitate to think about divorce. In the service of the elders, no effort is too extraordinary or too great.

Here again folktales are useful indications of the actual values. One classical story tells how a man gave up his hard-won official post in order to walk many miles in search of his long-lost mother. Another tells how a youngster of fourteen jumped on and strangled a tiger when the beast was about to devour his father. In a third story, a man cut a piece of flesh from his arm and boiled it in the pot with his father's medicine, believing that the soup would help the elder to recover from his long illness. Yet another tells us:

> When the mother of the dutiful Wang Low was still alive in the days of the Wei dynasty, she was greatly afraid of thunder. After her death she was buried in a mountain forest. Whenever Low heard a thunderstorm he immediately ran to the graveyard, kneeled, and tearfully said: 'Low is here, Mother, do not be afraid.'

Moreover, many Chinese stories did not remain mere literature but were sometimes copied to the letter by over-filial sons. In the thousands of volumes of district histories and genealogical records to be found in every part of the country are many individual biographies of local greats. After a cursory reading of about fifty of them, I found at least five instances in which men and women were said to have sliced flesh from their arms to be boiled in the medicine pot of one or another of their parents. One man did this twice during one of his father's illnesses. Because the elder's condition remained serious, the filial son decided to take a more drastic course of action. He cut out a piece of what he thought was his "liver" instead. Both he and his father died shortly afterwards. Hundreds of other biographies contain less dramatic episodes, but all are variations on the same theme.

It is not suggested that all Chinese youngsters are indoctrinated in filial piety on the day of their birth, or that more than a handful of American parents have ever had occasion to be rebuked by strangers for the way they handled their own children. It is important to realize, however, that incidents and lore like the ones given are symptomatic of the different social climates in which parents and children in the two countries react to one another.

Given the American type of atmosphere, parents do not only wish to help their children according to the parents' experiences. They must try to find out by elaborate research what the youngsters really want, so that the elders can better satisfy the youngsters' individual predilections. Although it is true that children all over the world are inclined to play, American parents do not stop at giving their children every conceivable kind of toy. They feel compelled to reduce even the rudiments of a child's education to a matter of fun. Recently I came across two books advertised as *Playbooks That Teach Your Child to Dress,* one for boys and one for girls.

The toy industry of America rose from an annual business of a mere $150,000,000 in 1939 to $750,000,000 in 1951. We may expect that this figure will increase in the next decade because of the increasing number of commercially profitable events such as local "baby weeks," the acceleration of learning by playing, and the coming and going of fashions in playthings as in other products. The annual business catering to all infant needs has reached, in 1951, an astronomical $5,000,000,000. Television today, as has radio for years, has scores of programs designed for children. Their announcers advise the kiddies to tell parents that they will eat nothing but "Snapcrackles" for breakfast. The children do so, and most parents obey by purchasing the desired product.

The relations of Chinese parents and children exhibit none of these tendencies. Chinese parents are amused by infantile behavior and youthful exuberance, but the measure of their children's worth is determined primarily by the degree to which they act like adults. The sooner they do so the better. Chinese parents are rather proud of a child who acts "older than his age" where American parents are likely to take a similar child to a specialist. Or Chinese parents are apt to be upset by certain aspects of a child's behavior which would bring joy to American parents.

Take toys again for an example. Chinese children occasionally receive a toy. When I was six years of age my mother bought me a cart made of tinfoil. Soldered above the entrance to the cart was an ornamental rectangle. Having seen movable curtains on real carts, I attempted to lower the curtain at the entrance of my toy cart and yanked the stationary ornament out of place. An American mother would have gloated over the creative impulse of her "budding genius"; but my mother was very much displeased because she thought me destructive and temperamental. Had I acted the model child that the Chinese mother hoped for, by nursing one old toy for a couple of years, an American mother might have worried about the retarded or warped state of my mind.

The specific mechanisms through which Chinese and American children begin their contrasting ways of life are many. To begin with, the average size of the Chinese family is, contrary to popular belief, about five persons. The average number in an American family is three. More important than size is the fact that when an American speaks of a family he refers to a group composed of parents and unmarried children, whereas the Chinese term for family includes grandparents and in-laws. Even if Chinese grandparents and in-laws do not live under the same roof, they usually reside in the same village, a neighboring village, or at the farthest a neighboring district. On the other hand, Americans related by blood or legal bonds usually live so far from one another that this broader group does not come together except on such occasions as Easter, Thanksgiving, Christmas, or other holidays.

These differences mark the point of departure in the early experiences of Chinese and American children. The Chinese child grows up amidst continuing or frequent contacts with a number of related individuals besides his own parents and siblings, but his American counterpart grows up in much greater physical isolation. Very early in life the former is conditioned to appreciate the importance of getting along with a wide circle of relatives while the latter is not.

Far more crucial, however, is the manner of interaction between the growing child and individuals other than those making up his immediate family. American parents are the sole agents of control over their children until the latter are of age. The grandparents and in-laws do not ordinarily occupy a disciplinary role, whether they live in the same house or not. Even when grandparents take over during an emergency such as sickness or childbirth, the older people are supposed to do no more than administer things according to the laws laid down by the younger couple, more likely by the younger woman. The usual response of an American elder to any request made by his or her little grandchild is, "Does your mother want you to?" When control is exercised over an American child, it is the parental arm that does so, no other.

Chinese parents have much less exclusive control over their children. In cases where grandparents do not share the same roof with them, during a brief visit the older couple can do almost anything that they see fit in regard to the children, even if it means going over the parents' heads. The liberty taken by most Chinese aunts, uncles, and in-laws might break up most American families. Furthermore, while an American mother exhibits her displeasure with an over-indulgent grandmother and is considered right by others, a Chinese mother doing the same thing is an object of censure rather than sympathy. The strength of the Chinese parental authority, far from being overpowering, usually varies with circumstances.

The inevitable result of the omnipresent and exclusive control of American parents over their children is greater and deeper emotional involvement. Since parents are all-powerful, their images in the mind of the growing child naturally are elevated above all else. To the extent that they are the only objects of worship, they also are liable to become the only oppressors. Accordingly, when an American child likes his parents, they are his idols. When he dislikes them, they are his enemies. A conscious or unconscious attachment to one parent at the expense of the other, a situation which gave Freud ground for postulating his famed Oedipus complex, is the extreme expression of this situation.

Not knowing the American kind of close and exclusive relationship, the mutual affection of Chinese parents and children is toned down. Since parental authority varies with circumstances, the parental image in the mind of the growing child must necessarily share the spotlight with men and women held in much higher esteem, such as grandparents, and with those regarded as the equals of the parents, such as uncles and aunts. The feeling toward parents being divided and diluted, the child does not develop a paralyzing attachment to, or strong repulsion against, the elders. There is still less reason for the emergence of the Oedipal triangle, in which the child is allied to one parent against the other. Consequently, when the Chinese child likes his parents he fails to raise them to high heaven; when he dislikes them he still vents his displeasure with great reserve.

Contrary to popular belief, it is a fact that Chinese parents, though much more respected, revered, or even feared by their children than are American parents by theirs, actually leave much less of an impression on the character of their progeny, since the parent-child relationship is neither so close nor so emotionally charged.

The beginnings of the contrasts between the two ways of life now become apparent. In the American scene the child soon learns to follow his own predilections. For his environment is sensitive to *him*. In the Chinese scene the child soon learns to appreciate the importance of changing circumstances. For he is obliged to be sensitive to his *environment*.

Similarly, the American child tends to develop strong feelings of love or hate. For the exclusive parent-child bond inevitably concentrates emotions at a few points. The Chinese child tends to moderate his feelings in general. For his diffused relationship with parents and relatives likewise tempers his emotional involvements.

As Chinese and American children grow older the contrast between their experiences is intensified. American parents encourage their children to do things for themselves. At the age of three or four, American children are exhorted to be big boys and girls, to dress themselves, feed themselves, and defend themselves against bullies.

Chinese parents are pleased if their children can do any of these or similar things. They do not, however, make a point of encouraging them or bragging about them. As to defending themselves, the characteristic advice to Chinese children is "don't get into trouble outside, and run home if there is danger."

Yet, though consciously encouraging their children to grow up in some ways, American parents firmly refuse to let the youngsters enter the real world of the adults. For one thing, they leave their children with sitters when they go to parties. If they entertain at home they put the youngsters to bed before the guests arrive. Children have no part in parents' social activities.

Chinese parents take their children with them not only to wedding feasts, funeral breakfasts, and religious celebrations, but also to purely social or business gatherings. A father in business thinks nothing of bringing his boy of six or seven to an executives' conference.

This pattern is still adhered to by the majority of second, third and fourth generation Chinese-Americans in Hawaii. Like their Caucasian neighbors, Chinese organizers in Hawaii also resort to "family picnics" and "family evenings" and even athletics for the purpose of maintaining or increasing club or church enrollment. But, unlike their Caucasian neighbors, Chinese parents in Hawaii take their very young children with them on many more occasions, for example on social and business visits which regularly last until late at night.

The result is that while Chinese youngsters unobtrusively enter into the world of the adults, American youngsters tend to develop a world of their own. This is further accentuated by the Chinese parents' insistence on complete community of interests with children, as much as by the American parents' insistence on privacy for all individuals.

The business of American parents, social and commercial, is their private reserve, and no trespassing by children is allowed except on those rare and eventful occasions when an explicit invitation is extended. Newspaper "psychologists" frequently advise that a well-adjusted personality will result if parents do not burden their children with adult difficulties. By the same token, parents are also supposed to refrain from entering into the doings of their youngsters. These same advisors admonish worried mothers to disappear when their teen-age daughters entertain at home.

Not so among the Chinese. Chinese children consider it a matter of course to witness or even participate in adult negotiations, exactly as Chinese adults think nothing about joining in their children's activities. This reciprocity goes so far that neither has any qualms about opening letters addressed to the other.

Nothing is more strikingly symbolic of these profound differences than the fact that American children celebrate their birthdays among themselves, their parents being assistants or servants, while Chinese children's birthdays are occasions for adult celebration, in which children may be present, like in wedding or funeral feasts, but they are certainly not the center of attraction.

The line of demarcation between the adult and the child worlds is drawn in many other ways. For instance, many American parents may be totally divorced from the church, or entertain grave doubts about the existence of God, but they send their children to Sunday schools and help them to pray. American parents struggle in a world of tough competition where sheer cunning and falsehood are often rewarded and respected, but they feed their children with nursery tales in which the morally good is pitted against the bad, and in the end the good is invariably rewarded and the bad inevitably punished. When American parents are in serious domestic trouble, they maintain a front of sweetness and light before their children. Even if American parents suffer a major business catastrophe, they feel obliged to turn their tearful eyes to their children and fake a smile, saying, "Honey, everything is all right." This American desire to maintain the children's world separate from that of the adults is exemplified also by the practice of delaying transmission of the news to children when their parents have been killed in an accident, or concealing the facts from them when one of the parents goes to jail. Thus, in summary, American parents face a world of reality while their children live in the near ideal realm of the fairy tales where the rules of the parental world do not apply, are watered down, or are even reversed.

Chinese children, however, share the same world with their parents. While there is not complete accord between what Chinese parents teach and what they do, for all human beings are prone to leave some gap between the lesson and the deed, parents make little effort to hide their problems and real selves from their children. In triumph the children celebrate with the adults; in disaster the little ones suffer with them. Very early in life Chinese children learn that reward and punishment are not necessarily consistent with the established rules of conduct, and that justice and love do not always prevail. Yet at the same time they are more likely than American children to become conscious of the power exercised by the environment. For theirs is an environment that is very exposed, and young eyes without blinkers see their parents' faults as well as their virtues. From the beginning they see their parents not as giants astride the earth, moving mountains and slaying dragons, which is the American child's Bunyanesque interpretation of the scene, but as ordinary mortals succeeding at times but failing at others, following inevitably the paths marked by custom and tradition.

Thus the American child is not only increasingly convinced of the importance of his individual predilections, he is equally sure that no eventuality can deter him, the invincible individual, from realizing them in thought or action. In his restricted and comforting world he has experienced few irreparable setbacks and known few situations in which he is entirely frustrated by reality. Just as joy and good proceed from the parents, who focus upon themselves all attention and draw to themselves all power, it is they alone who can impose restrictions that the child may see as barriers to his own advancement.

The Chinese child is not only fully aware that he should obey his parents and other seniors, but even when he succeeds in circumventing them he still faces the hurdles presented by custom and tradition. Through his active observation of and participation in adult activities, he is already well versed, by hard knocks on the head, in his own shortcomings and the real nature of his society. The foci of attention and power being many, the restrictions imposed upon the individual come not from the parents, but the society at large. Even if he resents these barriers he can still see no point at which to center his attack, for they are too numerous and too diffuse.

. . . .

Chinese school children . . . are not shocked by injustice, slights, or untruths because they have experienced or learned to expect these trials. At 12 or 14 most of them are not merely acquainted with their future places and problems in society—they are already full-fledged members of society and have known its tribulations and disappointments.

This realistic orientation is assisted further by the Chinese ideal of mutual dependence, which is the exact opposite of the American spirit of self-reliance. In a previous connection we noted that the Chinese son has to support his father. We must now point out that the Chinese father is no less bound to the support of his son. This reciprocal obligation is a social contract that lasts for life. The idea of a legal "will" is alien to Chinese thought. A Chinese father's assets, no less than his liabilities, automatically and equally go to his several sons before or after his death.[5]

[5]This pattern survives today in spite of laws to the contrary. Even as late as 1944 villagers could not dispose of their property without consent of their adult male children.

The Chinese child learns about this in diverse ways. For one thing, he never has to manage an allowance.[6] He is free to spend whatever he can get out of his parents. The idea of earning money from one's parents is considered laughable by Chinese. Consequently, while necessity causes poor Chinese children to learn the value of money, youngsters from wealthier families have little financial worry in sight.

The social tie between Chinese parents and sons is equally automatic, irretrievable, and lasting for the lifetime of all parties. A proverb truly expresses the essence of the pattern: "First thirty years, one looks at the father and respects the son; second thirty years, one looks at the son and respects the father." That is to say, while the son is young the father's social status determines that of the son; but later the son's social status determines that of the father.

For this reason the sons of the powerful, however young, are as powerful as their fathers, while the fathers can, even after retirement, always wield the authority derived from the position of their sons. Thus the son of a Chinese warlord always commanded, and was respected, as a little warlord, just as the father of a Chinese emperor was unquestionably a sort of super-emperor.

Furthermore, while the American father who basks in his son's glory or the son who profits from his father's fame will always object to any suggestion that this is the real situation, a similarly situated Chinese father or son has no such desire to conceal his source of strength. In case the identity of such an individual is temporarily obscured, he is likely to glorify it in just so many words. Karl Eskelund, a Danish news reporter, in his book, *My Chinese Wife* (N.Y., 1945), tells of a fight he had one night in Chungking during World War II. Instead of returning blow for blow, his young Chinese opponent shouted: "Do you know who I am? I am Chiang Ching-Kuo—the Generalissimo's son!"

The performance of Chiang's offspring may seem cowardly to most Americans. But most Chinese would understand that it befitted the exalted station of his father. In fact, he did not even have to be the Generalissimo's son. The Generalissimo's nephews, or remoter relatives, if there were any, could also act similarly.

Thus the Chinese pattern of mutual dependence, instead of encouraging self-reliance, induces satisfaction in reliance. For the parent-child ties are permanent rather than transitory. It is taken for granted that they are immutable, and so not subject to individual acceptance or rejection. Secure in the shadow of their ancestors, Chinese youngsters at school age have no great psychological urge to seek any alliance outside the kin group.

For Chinese youngsters, therefore, the call of the gang possesses none of the dictatorial compulsion that it has for their American brethren. It is not that Chinese boys and girls will purposely differ from their schoolmates or

---

[6] In some parts of China, married sons each have a yearly allowance from the head of the family called something like "clothes money." This sum meets the clothing and other pocket expenses of the man and his wife. But if there is only one son in the family, he may spend as much as the family can afford.

friends. But they seem to get along with their play groups without having to part with the things their parents represent. My own experience illustrates the point. When my parents moved their home from a South Manchurian village to an East Manchurian town I was for the first time in my life confronted with a dialect difference. My first grade schoolmates spoke a dialect considerably different from mine. Within six weeks I had changed over to the speech prevailing in school, but at home I spoke in my original tongue, although my parents never suggested that I do so. This transition occurred again when I went to Peking and once more when I went to Shanghai. Each time I acquired a new dialect. But each new dialect was merely added to the list of those at my command. This pattern was true of all Chinese youngsters whom I knew, even with reference to entirely foreign languages, for Russian and Japanese were widely known in Manchuria, French in Yunnan, and English in the rest of China. Furthermore, this pride in individual achievement in foreign languages prevailed even at the height of anti-British or anti-Japanese feeling.

Chinese parents, on their part, have little reason for anxiety as their children grow older. First, never having been complete masters of their children, they do not feel rejected when the youngsters become more independent. Second, the Chinese parent-child relationship is permanent. A father is always a father, whether or not he is loving or kind. A son is always a son; rarely is he disowned because he is not dutiful. Lastly, Chinese social organization is such that age, far from being a defect, is a blessing. Chinese parents have no reason to regret their children's coming of age, for it assures not a lesser role but a more respected place for themselves.

The Chinese pattern of mutual dependence thus forms the basis of a psychological security for both the old and the young. When children have little urge to depart, parents have little need to hold. The result is a way of life in which individual predilections are minimized not because there is strong restraint that demands conformity, but because the emotions of the individual are neutralized when he is satisfied with things as they are.

AMERICAN VALUES

V

INTRODUCTION V

Since 1944, when the Swedish social analyst Gunnar Myrdal, exploring the problem of race relations in the United States, essayed a tentative summary of "the American Creed,"[1] behavioral scientists and historians have devoted systematic attention to the task of identifying, validating, classifying, and interpreting those values or configurations of values which may be said to be characteristically American. Formerly regarded as supplemental to the study of personality traits, behavioral patterns, and institutional structures, the examination of values has now been widely accepted as a coordinate approach in national character analysis; many scholars have found in it a key to aspects of the American character which are less accessible by other avenues of investigation. The readings in this section sample the results of the inquiry into values and constitute a report on its progress. They also point to certain difficulties that have been encountered in the attempt to define the values of a nation as complex and various as the United States.

Prominent among those difficulties is the problem of tracing a coherent pattern of demonstrably *national* values, a problem that divides the ranks of social science into camps which may be loosely characterized as pluralist and monist. The difference between the two positions is essentially a matter of emphasis: While it is generally agreed that the system of values is not altogether uniform or harmonious, opinions differ in regard to the *degree* of integration in the system. The pluralists stress the evidences of diversity; the monists accent the elements of consensus. Numerous observers have been deeply impressed by the inner tensions, inconsistencies, and unresolved contradictions which they detect in the structure of American values, while others, discerning a "strain toward consistency" and impatient of paradoxes and polarities which they judge to be more apparent than real, have identified certain "core" or "focal" values by which the value system—or substantial portions of it—is ordered and unified. Both positions are represented in the readings.

The pluralist emphasis appears in the selection from the work of Robin M. Williams, Jr., professor of sociology at Cornell University, and John Gillin, professor of anthropology at the University of North Carolina. "American society," according to Williams, "does not have a completely consistent and integrated value-structure. We do not seem to find a neatly unified 'ethos' or an irresistible 'strain toward consistency.' Rather, the total society is characterized by diversity

[1]*An American Dilemma: The Negro Problem and Modern Democracy* (New York: Harper & Bros., 1944), ch. 1.

and change in values."[2] Though he discovers significant linkages within the value system and though he closes his schematic survey of major value-orientations with a suggestive description of "a basic moral orientation" in American culture, Williams places the dominant stress on the heterogeneity of American values. The essay by Gillin deals with national uniformities and regional diversities in the value system. Like Williams, Gillin finds a wide range of variation, as well as substantial areas of consensus, in the values which Americans profess.

The monistic position reflects the tendency of social scientists to seek reductive formulas for complicated phenomena. "What we need to see," declares a leading American anthropologist, "is that the contradictory American 'values' noted by the sociologists, psychologists, and historians are but manifestations of one core value."[3] This dictum, though it may state the monist contention too emphatically, bespeaks the principle of *e pluribus unum* to which the logic of the social sciences is keyed and expresses the "strain toward consistency" which governs the monistic analysis of values. What the "core value" or central cluster of related values may be—whether, as various writers have suggested, it is self-reliance or individualism or competitive achievement or equality of opportunity or some other—is matter for further study.

The monistic stress is evident in the essays by Cora Du Bois, professor of anthropology at Harvard and Radcliffe College, and the historian David M. Potter, whose discussion of the effects of economic abundance on the rearing of American children appears in the previous section. Miss Du Bois describes "The Dominant Value Profile of American Culture" in terms of the "focal" middle-class values of "effort-optimism," material well-being, and conformity. Potter reflects upon the contrasting images of the American as individualist and idealist (depicted by Turner and Jefferson) and as materialist and conformist (Tocqueville). He suggests that these apparently contrary appraisals of the national character may in fact be variant expressions of the central value of American equalitarianism.

Though it seems improbable that the differences of emphasis between monists and pluralists will be altogether resolved in the foreseeable future, if ever, those differences are not entirely to be deplored. They witness to the vitality of the undertaking, and they furnish incentives to more intensive and extensive exploration in an important field. The inquiry into values ranks high on the agenda of unfinished business in the study of American character; many scholars would place it at the very top of the agenda. Much has been accomplished, as these four readings show, and much remains to be done, especially along the line of

---

[2]*American Society: A Sociological Interpretation* (2nd ed. rev.; New York: Alfred A. Knopf, Inc., 1960), pp. 413–14. The problem of change and continuity in values will be treated in Section VI of this collection.

[3]Francis L. K. Hsu, "American Core Value and National Character," in Hsu (ed.), *Psychological Anthropology: Approaches to Culture and Personality* (Homewood, Ill.: The Dorsey Press, Inc., 1961), pp. 216–17.

empirical investigation and comparative, transnational analysis. Future progress depends in large part on the sharpening of methodological instruments and the harnessing of the several disciplines, the humanities as well as the social sciences, which share a concern for the study of values.

ROBIN M. WILLIAMS, JR.

Values and Beliefs in American Society

Our next step is to describe the major patterns of values that can be identified in American society. Of course, "American values" are not values necessarily exclusive to, or even peculiar to, the United States, nor do all Americans share them. We wish to discover the extent to which any particular value or value complex is in fact present in this society.

There are, however, important grounds for expecting American culture to be characterized by a value system appreciably different from other cultures. Most obvious perhaps is the different environment—different location, physical surroundings, climate, resources, and so on. Equally impressive are the many diverse cultural strains and the subsequent crosscultural contacts within the American aggregate. Aside from these, and from any possible genetic selectivity, we know that a society separated from others by spatial and sociopolitical barriers will, over a period of time, develop a relatively distinctive culture.

The data cited in following pages indicate that in a broad comparative view, American culture does bear out this proposition. The real problem, however, is to identify and appraise the value patterns that are relatively most distinctive and important.

. . . .

WHAT IS MEANT BY VALUE?

It is essential . . . that we secure a clear conception of what values are and of how we may recognize and analyze their role in a system of motivated social action. We are concerned with values as observable variables in human conduct, not with an appraisal of various values as being better or worse than others, nor with the meaning and ontological status of value as a concept, however important these problems may be. For our purposes, we must seek a conception of value that can be referred to definite evidence.

Reprinted from *American Society: A Sociological Interpretation,* 2nd ed. rev. by Robin M. Williams, Jr., by permission of Alfred A. Knopf, Inc.

A common notion is that value refers to any aspect of a situation, event, or object that is invested with a *preferential interest* as being "good," "bad," "desirable," and the like. This conception is not enough for present purposes. Any formal definition of value is likely to be too general to be of great use to a sociological analysis, and a general definition seems to involve an inevitable circularity—to define value as "interest" is only another way of saying value. It is enough here if we circumscribe the boundaries of value. What are experienced by individuals as values have these qualities: (1) They have a conceptual element—they are more than pure sensations, emotions, reflexes, or so-called needs. Values are abstractions drawn from the flux of the individual's immediate experience. (2) They are affectively charged: they represent actual or potential emotional mobilization. (3) Values are not the concrete goals of action, but rather the *criteria* by which goals are chosen. (4) Values are important, not "trivial" or of slight concern. (Although this statement is circular, it suggests the possibility of studying values through the study of choices.)

. . . .

Empirically considered, value is not an all-or-none matter, but a continuum. At one pole, we find those intense moral values that are true matters of conscience. Values of this order are present when the individual who violates them shows a reaction of strong guilt or overwhelming shame and the group imposes strong censure upon the offender, or when the person who acts in accord with an accepted standard of evaluation experiences gratification, a clear conscience, and an enhanced self-image, and is rewarded and honored by his fellows. Such moral values are the core of the individual's internalized conscience. They also define the central institutional structure of the society —although the accepted mores do not necessarily coincide wih the "highest" social ethics and the ethical position of any given individual may not be identical with either the mores or the highest ethics. From the point on the value continuum at which the moral quality is emphasized, values shade off into those evoking less intense guilts and less severe social sanctions—for example, esthetic standards, conventional proprieties, and simple norms of expediency or technical efficiency. Only careful research testing can establish the position of any "alleged" value along this continuum in the actual functioning of a society.

We are reasonably content in the pages that follow to conceive of values as affective conceptions of the desirable—of the desirable qualities of objects, behavior, or social structures, and systems.[1] It is implied by this that values emerge in the experience of people in evaluating objects of desire; hence, values are to be found in the relation between a human actor and the objects that are of concern to him. Our treatment will have to neglect esthetic and expressive values in the interest of describing those values (and beliefs) which

[1]Cf. Clyde Kluckhohn, "Values and Value-orientations in the Theory of Action: An Exploration in Definition and Classification," in Talcott Parsons and Edward A. Shils (eds.), *Toward a General Theory of Action* (Cambridge, Mass., 1951), pp. 388–433.

most clearly characterize the main institutions of the society. For this purpose, we do not need to argue the ancient questions concerning the objectivity of values nor their quality of absoluteness or lack of it.[2] Our basic questions are: (1) what, in fact, are the conceptions of the desirable to be found in this society; and (2) what does the presence of these values tell us about the actual functioning of the social system? It will be necessary to deal with some clusters of belief-and-value which are diffuse and vague, as well as with highly generalized and explicit value-orientations.[3] Throughout we must be watchful to distinguish values, as criteria, from the evaluations of social conditions and processes; it is hoped that the context of the discussion will keep us on the right path.[4]

. . . .

WHAT ARE "DOMINANT VALUES"?

Upon leaving the United States after an extended visit, Sir William Beveridge observed that there were "six Americas in search of a faith." In a social order of the flux, variety, and groping suggested by this statement, can anything be said as to its hierarchy of values? Are there any focal values that can be held to be "dominant" in the American scene? Which values are *common* (shared), which are intense or less intense, which are persistent or transitory, which take precedence over others? To be at all specific about the structure of American value-systems, some concrete tests of value dominance are obviously needed.

Dominant and subordinate values *for a group or social system as a whole* can be roughly ordered to these criteria:

1. *Extensiveness* of the value in the total activity of the system. What proportion of a population and of its activities manifest the value?

2. *Duration* of the value. Has it been persistently important over a considerable period of time?[5]

3. *Intensity* with which the value is sought or maintained, as shown by: effort, crucial choices, verbal affirmation, and by reactions to threats to the value—for example, promptness, certainty, and severity of sanctions.

---

[2]For a viewpoint different from our own see Franz Adler, "The Value Concept in Sociology," *The American Journal of Sociology,* Vol. LXIII, No. 3 (November 1956), pp. 272–79.

[3]Kluckhohn in *Toward a General Theory of Action* defines value-orientations as ". . . those value notions which are (a) general, (b) organized, and (c) include definitely existential judgments" (p. 490).

[4]In an unpublished paper ("A Tentative Outline of American Values"), Talcott Parsons regards values as the generalized principles from which more specific rules and evaluations can be derived. This conception seems close to Kluckhohn's idea of value-orientations. The present analysis is not limited to the highly generalized value-principles, although something will be said about them at various points.

[5]Or has it been thought important through time by the population in question? Not antiquity as objective fact, but antiquity as belief may be the more significant factor. This observation was suggested to the writer by R. Lauriston Sharp.

4. *Prestige of value carriers*—that is, of persons, objects, or organizations considered to be bearers of the value. Culture heroes, for example, are significant indexes of values of high generality and esteem.

. . . .

MAJOR VALUE-ORIENTATIONS IN AMERICA

We can now outline certain major value-configurations in American culture. For convenience, we will proceed by abstracting certain dominant themes from the many important regional, class, and other intracultural variations. The simplified picture that results will, of course, be inaccurate in every concrete detail—it will be a series of ideal types, subject to numerous exceptions. Nevertheless, these abstracted patterns will serve as working models against which variations and contradictions can be more clearly seen; the value configurations thus identified will represent *tendencies* only, but they will bring out certain regularities that would not otherwise be easily seen. As a first approximation, we can use these tentative formulations in each instance as test cases. For each alleged value-pattern let us ask: Is it actually an important value in American society? How do we know whether it is or not? Where does it stand in relation to other values? Within the total society, what groups or subcultures are the main bearers of the value, and what groups or subcultures are indifferent or opposed? How do the mutually supporting or antagonistic value-systems work toward or against the integration of the culture as a whole?

Such systematic questioning will help us avoid naïve acceptance or rejection of the broad descriptive generalizations that follow. Reasonably adequate documentation is provided in the references cited, but limited space makes it impossible to present here anything like the full evidence pro and con. . . . We will list a value or theme frequently observed in the American scene, cite a few illustrations, and comment briefly upon the nature and significance of the alleged value-pattern. Nearly every statement will bring up unsolved problems and gaps in existing knowledge, but some firm knowledge we do have. Many major themes in American culture have been identified. From them, we may secure clues concerning values themselves. . . .

"Achievement" and "Success"

First, American culture is marked by a central stress upon personal achievement, especially secular occupational achievement. The "success story" and the respect accorded to the self-made man are distinctly American, if anything is. Our society has been highly competitive—a society in which ascribed status in the form of fixed, hereditary social stratification has been minimized. It has endorsed Horatio Alger and has glorified the rail splitter who becomes president: "Periodic public opinion polls are not needed to justify the selection of Abe Lincoln as the culture hero who most fully embodies the cardinal American virtues. . . . Even the inevitable schoolboy knows that Lincoln was thrifty, hard-working, eager for knowledge, ambitious, devoted to the rights of the average man, and eminently successful in climbing the ladder of opportunity from the lowermost rung of laborer to the respectable heights of merchant and lawyer. . . ."[6]

Emphasis upon achievement must be distinguished from the broader valuation of personal excellence. All societies have standards of character and proficiency, and accord rewards to those best meeting whatever standards are most highly appraised, whether of military prowess, ritual knowledge, asceticism, piety, or what not. The comparatively striking feature of American culture is its tendency to identify standards of personal excellence with competitive occupational achievement. In the pure type, the value attached to achievement does not comprehend the person as a whole, but only his accomplishments, emphasizing the objective results of his activity. Because of the preoccupation with business, the most conspicuous achievements have been those centered in business enterprise. We can say, with Laski and many others, that the "values of the business man" dominate and permeate national life. Yet achievement has never been completely identified with sheer business success; for example, such an assumption does not account for the respect and prestige accorded to the professions. Seen in the context of other major value themes,[7] business success seems to be a dominant focus, but not the dominant value-pattern, in American society.

However, as already noted, economic success has been so heavily stressed in certain parts of our society as to impose a widespread and persistent strain upon institutional regulation of means used to attain this goal. At the extreme, only questions of technical effectiveness enter into the choice of means—thus, the "Robber Barons," "business is business," and much organized crime, vice and racketeering. Perhaps the apogee of largely unrestrained economic acquisition was reached in the period of "business baroque" from about 1890 to 1912, when the leaders of business "exulted openly in power and riches, won by national centralization. . . ."[8]

Adequate research evidence is not as yet available to allow an accurate appraisal of the extent to which success rather than achievement has moved to the center of the values of our culture. Such evidence is greatly needed, for the question thus raised is fundamental to any real diagnosis of the current value-system. Whereas achievement refers to valued accomplishments, success lays the emphasis upon rewards. Amoral success-striving may not have gone

[6]Robert K. Merton, "The Self-Fulfilling Prophecy," *The Antioch Review* (Summer 1948), p. 199.

[7]The so-called success philosophy attains its full cultural meaning only along with a particular kind of moral individualism. See Cuber and Harper, *Problems of American Society,* p. 356: "The basic premise of this philosophy is that individuals, not classes, are the real competing units. A man is said to reap his reward by 'his own' efforts, skills, and perseverance."

[8]Miriam Beard, *A History of the Business Man* (New York, 1938), p. 641. For a similar period in the ancient world see Gilbert Murray, *Five Stages of Greek Religion* (London, 1935), p. 79. Compare also pp. 115 ff. for an analysis of the way in which the Good becomes assimilated to success (wealth and power) in a certain type of social order.

to the lengths suggested by some observers,[9] but the important point is that once success goals are divorced from the ultimate values of society, the way is opened for a corrosion of regulative norms.[10] In the United States, the available evidence suggests that, even though success is often regarded as an end in itself and sometimes there is almost no positive relation between success and moral virtue, yet the success pattern is still linked to achievement, achievement is still associated with work, and work is still invested with an almost organic complex of ethical values. Thus, success is still not a primary criterion of value in its own right, but rather a derivative reward *for* active, instrumental performance. There is growing evidence that performance in consumption is partly replacing performance in work: how one spends his income, rather than what he did to earn it appears increasingly to be a mark of "achievement."[11] Nevertheless, as Wecter has suggested, the American heroes are not merely successful—they must be successful within a certain ethical framework: they must be, or appear to be, "self-respecting, decent, honorable, with a sense of fair play; no Machiavelli nor Mussolini need apply."[12] The belief that virtue will be rewarded and that success attends upon effort dies hard; and in our culture failure is still more likely to be charged to defect of character than to blind fate, capricious accident, or impersonalized social and economic forces, and the wealthy and powerful still either desire or find it expedient to justify their position in the name of "service" and "stewardship."

The dimensions of success values may perhaps be clarified by an examination of the place of wealth and its attainment in the culture. Many foreign and native observers have viewed American society as grossly acquisitive and materialistic, as naïvely impressed by bigness, speed, wealth, and power. Such a view is too simple, as an examination of American attitudes toward money will illustrate.

We may begin by eliminating any interpretation such as "of course money is wanted because it is the universal agency for satisfying any desires that can be met by purchasable goods."[13] For many profitable activities are socially

---

[9]Geoffrey Gorer, *The American People: A Study in National Character* (New York, 1948), pp. 169 and 172.

[10]Some of the more important personality strains engendered by high levels of aspiration in a competitive order have been compactly analyzed by Karen Horney in several works; see, for example, *The Neurotic Personality of Our Time* (New York, 1937).

[11]See, for example: Eli Chinoy, *Automobile Workers and the American Dream* (Garden City, N.Y., 1955); David Riesman, "The Suburban Sadness," in William M. Dobriner (ed.), *The Suburban Community* (New York, 1958).

[12]Dixon Wecter, *The Hero in America* (New York, 1941), p. 482. (This comment has to be qualified to take into account a Huey Long and an Al Capone, as well as the hero worship of the movie stars who are presented as living in opulent success as the result of pure accident—unrelated to personal virtues.)

[13]The American sociologist Charles Horton Cooley pointed out as long ago as the turn of the century that "wealth as an object of ambition and a measure of success owes its ascendency to its social implications, and the pursuit of it is by no means a proof of materialism or sensuality. . . . The fact that a man desires it, throws little or no light upon the real object of his ambition."—*Sociological Theory and Social Research* (New York, 1930), p. 222; the quotation is from the essay "Personal Competition," which first appeared as an article in 1899.

condemned and not widely carried on; and people strive intensely for wealth long after their basic physical needs have been met or even after they have achieved nearly every conceivable means for satisfying their desires. Santayana's insight has more accurately indicated the central function of money in the American value system: "It is the symbol and measure he (the American) has at hand for success, intelligence, and power; but as to money itself he makes, loses, spends and gives it away with a very light heart."[14] In a society of relatively high social mobility, in which position in the scale of social stratification basically depends upon occupational achievement, wealth is one of the few obvious signs of one's place in the hierarchy. Achievement is difficult to index, in a highly complex society of diverse occupations, because of the great differences in abilities and effort required for success in various fields. At the same time, the central type of achievement is in business, manufacturing, commerce, finance; and since traditionalized social hierarchies, fixed estates, and established symbols of hereditary rank have had only a rudimentary development, there is a strong tendency to use money as a symbol of success. Money comes to be valued not only for itself and for the goods it will buy, but as symbolic evidence of success and, thereby, of personal worth.

Much the same type of analysis applies to the so-called American love of bigness. It is said that Americans are impressed by size *qua* size; "bigger and better" is a childish love of quantity as such. Actually the important thing is that "better" is presumed to be *implied* by "bigger." Things are good not so much because they are big, but because goodness is assumed and bigness therefore means more of something already considered valuable. Again Santayana has well expressed the essential point: "Respect for quantity is accordingly more than the childish joy and wonder at bigness; it is the fisherman's joy in a big haul, the good uses of which he can take for granted."[15] Unquestionably, we are dealing here with a culture that values action and the mastery of the physical world,[16] and its whole history has been, in the main, an experience of expansionism and mastery: increasing population, increasing territory, increased levels of living, and so on indefinitely. Given the definition of such things as good, respect for quantity directly follows.

"Activity" and "Work"

In the United States is to be found what is almost the ideal type of a culture that stresses activity; it is no accident that the business so characteristic of the culture can also be spelled "busyness." Although one might quibble over Laski's flat statement that few Americans "find it easy to be happy unless they

[14]*Character and Opinion in the United States* (New York, 1920), p. 185. Cf. Gorer: *The American People,* p. 177: "It can be said that, as a general rule, the acquisition of money is very important to Americans, but its retention relatively unimportant."

[15]*Character and Opinion in the United States,* p. 182.

[16]Cf. Laski, *The American Democracy,* p. 42: "No attempt to grasp the nature of the American spirit can be complete which does not emphasize the degree to which action is of its essence."

are doing something,"[17] we know that a notable series of observers have overwhelmingly agreed that America is the land of haste and bustle, of strenuous competition, of "ceaseless activity and agitation."[18] In this culture the individual tends to "face outward"—to be interested in making things happen in the external world. In ideal type, he seeks to dominate the world of nature, to subdue and exploit the physical world around him. This pattern—which forms a *leit motif* in American history—may be explained historically, of course, as developing out of religious tradition, frontier experience,[19] ceaseless change, vast opportunity, and fluid social structure. Whatever its sources, the sheer fact of this emphasis on "action" is enough for present purposes.[20]

Directed and disciplined activity in a regular occupation is a particular form of this basic orientation. If Justice Holmes could say that the purpose of life "is to function," the resonance his words aroused in the culture applied particularly to *work* in a full time vocation. This high evaluation of work has been called typical of the culture by many students of the American scene.[21]

A strong cultural emphasis upon disciplined productive activity was to be expected in America during the first two centuries in which value systems were being generalized out of experience.[22] Work was required for *group* survival along the moving frontier from the first settlements until the continent had been won. The rule "he who does not work shall not eat" expressed the deadly struggles of the early settlement period. To this compulsion was added the dawning sense of the rich rewards to be had in a land of relatively unappropriated resources. Furthermore, the population was mainly recruited from the working classes of Britain and Europe;[23] except in a few areas of the South and New England, there was no aristocratic class to give prestige to leisure and to stigmatize manual labor and trade. Finally, there was the influence of the so-called Puritan tradition—that is, of all those varieties of Protestantism in which secular occupational activity was invested with religious sanction and in which successful works became a sign of grace. This "metaphysical drive

---

[17]Laski, *The American Democracy,* p. 15.

[18]See the summary in Lee Coleman, "What Is American?" pp. 492–99; also, Henry Steele Commager, *America in Perspective* (New York, 1947), p. xii.

[19]Cf. Constance Rourke's characterization of the man of the frontier: "Strength was his obsession—size, scale, power: he seemed obliged to shout their symbols as if after all he were not wholly secure in their possession." *American Humor: A Study of the National Character* (New York, 1931), p. 36.

[20]For interpretations of this theme in literature see: Vernon L. Parrington, *Main Currents in American Thought* (New York, 1930); Henry A. Myers, *Are Men Equal?* (New York, 1945); Henry B. Parkes, *The American Experience* (New York, 1947).

[21]Lee Coleman, "What Is American?" *Social Forces,* Vol. XIX, No. 4, (May 1941), pp. 492–99; Tufts, *America's Social Morality,* pp. 38–43.

[22]Cf. E. T. Hiller, *Social Relations and Structures* (New York, 1947), p. 313.

[23]Max Savelle, *Seeds of Liberty* (New York, 1948), p. 219. "From the beginning, America was made up of what they call in England the middle and laboring classes, and it has always remained so. This is, in fact, one of the important points about it."—James Truslow Adams, *The American: The Making of a New Man* (New York, 1943), p. 49.

to work"[24] permeated the older agrarian culture of this country[25] and exists even today in rural areas and among certain other subgroups that have not yet fully assimilated the more recent cult of success and conspicuous consumption.

In short, the emphasis upon work as an end in itself represented a convergence of factors all operating in one direction—a mutual reinforcement of self-interest, social recognition, and ethical and religious precepts; "work" therefore became a value incorporated into the ego ideal of the representative personality types of the culture and often approached the intensity of a true matter of conscience. If distinctive foci of values can be found in this complicated culture, it seems that one should look into the strong positive appreciation of the support for *worldly, instrumental activism.*[26] From this emphasis follows the stress upon universal standards of performance. And this in turn (logically and in fact) implies a concern with universalizing opportunity for performance to a high degree, and with encouraging the maintenance of the full capacities of individuals for valued performance. So it is that efforts to improve health conditions and extend educational opportunities are often approved on these grounds.[27] Consistent with the main values also are the high evaluations placed upon teamwork and upon executive or managerial roles, the approval of technology (as "control of the world"), and the distinctive form of individualism in which the emphasis is upon permissiveness for a wide variety of achievements.

Although, as later discussion will show, work as an end in itself has lost a great deal of its earlier potency, it is still important to remember that it has formed one of the core elements in the historic culture. It was, however, closely linked to an agrarian social structure in which the independent farmer and the small business man were representative social types. In such a society, work was embedded in the wider meanings attached to these statuses. As the social structure has become more and more differentiated, as manual labor has lost its connection with the control of private property, and as differentials of wealth and power have become crystallized, work as such has been devalued. The focus of positive valuation is now shifting to certain patterns of achievement and success.

"Moral Orientation"

A third major value-configuration relates to a particular type of ethical quality in the total cultural orientation. Authoritative observers from Tocqueville, through Bryce, Siegfried, and others, down to such recent studies as

---

[24]The phrase used by Goetz Briefs, *The Proletariat* (New York, 1937).

[25]For a clear description see James M. Williams, *Our Rural Heritage* (New York, 1925).

[26]Talcott Parsons, *The Social System* (Glencoe, Ill., 1959), pp. 180–200.

[27]Notice how often public support for "health and welfare" measures is sought on the ground that we are "wasting our human resources" if we do not support efforts to increase capacities for performance.

those of Vernon L. Parrington, Margaret Mead, Gunnar Myrdal, and Harold Laski, have agreed on at least one point: Americans tend to "see the world in moral terms." They do not mean mere conformity to the detailed prescriptions of a particular moral code, but rather to a systematic moral orientation by which conduct is *judged*. It is asserted that the quasi-mythical figure, the "typical American," thinks in terms of right or wrong, good or bad, ethical or unethical. This attitude goes beyond questions of expediency or immediate utility—and beyond purely traditional or customary criteria of behavior—to test conduct against some systematic ethical principles. For example, Mead cites the query of a student who asked whether we *ought* to have a conscience.[28] And Myrdal says explicitly: "The conflict in the American concept of law and order is only one side of the 'moral overstrain' of the nation. America believes in and aspires to something much higher than its plane of actual life."[29] The presence of an element of moral overstrain in our culture seems to be established. This has a wide range of consequences, including ritualism, vacillating or compensatory behavior, "split between theory and practice," so-called "hypocrisy," and so on. Individuals facing severe tension between their incorporated ethics and current social "realities" may resolve the conflict by developing a militant reform mentality[30] or becoming "cynical"—we often suspect that the self-styled cynic is a highly moral person who is reacting to loss of faith in the efficacy of his code. Often ideals are insulated from action or restricted to limited groups and narrowly circumscribed situations.

The central themes of morality in America have undoubtedly had a common base and unified direction, derived from Judaic-Christian ethics. Of special importance has been the so-called Puritan ethic. Beginning as a rigidly theocratic system, it has gone through drastic modifications. At first it was markedly averse to traditionalistic forms and uncompromising toward the profane world. When works came to be interpreted as a sign of grace assuring salvation, it turned to a morality in which economic success became *prima facie* evidence of moral correctness.[31] In Laski's words: "What begins as a theocratic principle ends by becoming a tradition that it is not very easy to distinguish from utilitarianism. . . . To work hard, to lead an orderly life, to have a name for integrity and fair dealing, not to spend one's substance in reckless display, to have the resolution to carry out the purposes you under-

[28]Margaret Mead, *And Keep Your Powder Dry* (New York, 1942), Chap. 6.

[29]Myrdal, *et al., An American Dilemma,* Vol. I, p. 21. This phrase, however, is question-begging formulation, as we shall see in more detail later. "Overstrain" is itself a value-laden concept. However, it does suggest a strong tension between nominally dominant ethical principles and the pragmatic codes and exigencies of actual social life.

[30]Thus Harold D. Lasswell has suggested that anxiety from severe conscience assumed to be typical of much of middle-class America often leads to the attempt to enforce moralistic legislation upon others: "Emotional fixation upon the unqualified reaffirmation of 'principles' is one result of the anxieties generated by the threatened conscience." *World Politics and Personal Insecurity* (New York, 1935), p. 226.

[31][Footnote 31 has been omitted.]

take—it is, roughly, to an ethic such as this that the religion of America had been shaped when the basic tradition was formed."[32]

"Humanitarian Mores"

We shall use the term "humanitarianism" to refer to another important value cluster in American society, meaning by it, emphasis upon any type of disinterested concern and helpfulness, including personal kindliness, aid and comfort, spontaneous aid in mass disasters, as well as the more impersonal patterns of organized philanthropy. Do these things represent important values in America?

It would be easy to amass contrary evidence. We could cite the expulsion and extermination of the Indians, the harsher aspects of slavery, the sweatshop pattern in industry, and a long catalog of child labor, lynching, vigilantes, and social callousness in many forms. Probably few peoples have so copiously documented and analyzed what they themselves consider to be the "bad" aspects of their history—a revealing fact in itself, for it was broadly the same culture that produced the behavior, and then pronounced it undesirable or wrong. Even so, the evidences of humanitarian values meet all our tests for a major value. For one thing it is striking that failures to follow the standards of concern and helpfulness have not been defended as legitimate in themselves; they have been interpreted as *deviance from* a criterion which is not basically challenged, or "justified" in terms of other, allegedly more vital values. Certain patterns of mutual helpfulness and generosity were already apparent in colonial America—despite the stern theology and stringently disciplined individualism—and have persisted to an important extent down to the present time. Of course, it is only in a wide comparative perspective that the importance of the humanitarian mores can clearly be seen, making probable such hypotheses as "Americans are especially likely to identify with the 'underdog' rather than the 'bully.'" This identification is indicated in a quick, impulsive sympathy for people who are in distress "by no fault of their own"; in anger at the overbearing individual, group, or nation; in pride in America as a haven for the downtrodden and oppressed.[33] The proverbial generosity of American people toward other societies facing mass disaster—for example, earthquakes, floods, fire, famine—has elements of exaggeration and myth; but it does index a real and persistent theme broadly based on religious or quasi-religious ideas of brotherhood, even though it has often been overridden by dividing interests and competing values. The enormous range of relatively disinterested humanitarian activities in America—the commonplace Community Chest, the "service

[32]Harold Laski, *The American Democracy* (New York, 1948), p. 27.

[33]As in many other instances, the orientation has not been constant, and there are indications that the welcoming symbolism of the Statue of Liberty has lost much of its appeal for a world power in a time of international tension and crisis. Once again we must remind ourselves that values are subject to fluctuations and trends. Cf. Tufts, *America's Social Morality,* p. 35: "To speak of any single interest or end, as though the mind of the people were one and were settled upon the same objective throughout a period, is to assume too much unity and stability."

club" activities, the public welfare agencies, the numerous private philanthropies, and so on[34]—stands in striking contrast to the treatment meted out to "the poor" and the "sturdy beggars" in many other parts of Western society within the past two centuries.

As always, however, this value pattern does not stand alone but is reinforced and complemented, or checked and limited, by other values. Humanitarianism is closely related to the cluster of values implicit in the conception of a progressing equalitarian democracy. In the form of what might be called pseudo-humanitarian philanthropy, on the other hand, the pattern sometimes has lent itself to the justification of economic inequalities. Throughout American history, the humanitarian theme has clashed in a variety of ways with the conception of rugged individualism. Parrington has compactly summarized for an early period the conflict that still remains a prominent element in the shaping of the total value system:

> At the beginning of our national existence two rival philosophies contended for supremacy in America: the humanitarian philosophy of the French Enlightenment, based on the conception of human perfectibility and postulating as its objective an equalitarian democracy in which the political state should function as the servant to the common well-being; and the English philosophy of *laissez faire,* based on the assumed universality of the acquisitive instinct and postulating a social order answering the needs of an abstract "economic man," in which the state should function in the interest of trade.[35]

Efficiency and Practicality

American emphasis upon *efficiency* has consistently impressed outside observers. The Germans even coined the term *Fordismus* to refer to the standardization, mass production, and "streamlined" efficiency of American industrialism personified on the Continent by the name of Ford. "Efficient" is a word of high praise in a society that has long emphasized adaptability, technological innovation, economic expansion, up-to-dateness, practicality, expediency, "getting things done." The mere listing of these words and phrases serves to bring out the multiple extensions of efficiency as a standard against which activity is judged. Such a standard is premised in the first place upon that active orientation to the world of the here and now, so characteristic of our culture. As we have emphasized, this crucially important canalization of interest at once sets this society apart from societies placing greater emphasis upon esthetic, contemplative, ritualistic, mystical, or otherworldly concerns.

That being active is emphasized, however, tells us nothing about the kind of activity sanctioned. Even a culture centering its interest upon purposive

[34]The phenomenon of the "volunteer worker" is further evidence. There are reputed to be some thirty million persons in the United States who give unpaid help to various religious, social, political, civic, and service organizations. *Survey Graphic* (March 1949), p. 137.

[35]Vernon L. Parrington, *Main Currents in American Thought* (New York, Harcourt, Brace and Company, Inc., 1930), Book III, p. xxiii.

technical mastery of its physical environment (and, to some degree, of its social problems also) might conceivably act in relatively traditionalistic ways. The Western world generally, however, has tended to unite activity and substantive rationality, focusing upon a choice of the most effective means for a given end. Since systematic wealth-getting, technological achievement, and productive organization of effort have been strongly sanctioned, pressure has been created to search for "better methods," with the result that America epitomizes high regard for efficiency in techniques. In this kind of social climate, there is high sensitivity to such epithets as "backward," "inefficient," "useless." "Technical values" are greatly appreciated; especially in skilled trades, technical, quasi-professional, and professional vocations there is systematic indoctrination in the standards of "doing a good job"—the difference between a skilled and an unskilled performance. Despite the continual pressure of pecuniary or profit-making considerations, the values of good technical performance certainly have a measure of independent influence.[36]

The elevation of sheer technique into something closely approaching a value in its own right involves the familiar tendency to turn means-values into goal-values through a gradual withdrawal of attention and affect from the original ends[37]—a development that is re-enforced in so far as immediate interests and short-run goals are stressed. A culture that in the first place tends toward an ahistorical and utilitarian orientation will be especially likely to encourage just those behavior patterns in which technical efficiency can become valued for its own sake.

Although efficiency can and has become in this way a standard for evaluation, in certain areas of our culture it is a derivation rather than a basic theme. In economic activities and other fields that have acquired considerable autonomy apart from the ultimate-value systems of the society, the stress upon efficiency is a complex derivation from the values attached to action, to material comfort, and perhaps especially, to mastery over nature and disorder. For efficiency—like cleanliness, work, and systematic-universal ethics—is a *discipline,* and its meaning depends finally upon the broader meanings of the primary "orderliness" that underlies it.

Emphasis upon efficiency is obviously related to the high place accorded science (especially as translated into technology) and to the overweening importance attributed to practicality.[38] One of the blackest public curse-words we have is "impractical"—in the culture at large, the practical man is the good man, an embodiment of a major value. Although we could trace this interrelated set of attitudes back to the frontier tradition, there are more immediate influences in the contemporary culture contributing to its survival.

---

[36]On the psychological side, closely related to Gordon W. Allport's "autonomy of motives."

[37]Robert K. Merton, "The Unanticipated Consequences of Purposive Social Action," *American Sociological Review,* Vol. I, No. 6 (December 1936), pp. 891–904.

[38]Laski, *The American Democracy,* p. 12.

"Practical" (pragmatic) orientation is basically short-range adjustment to immediate situations. The practical man concentrates upon goals attainable in the given situation and solves immediate problems as they arise, leaving to others the more abstract and long-range problems. Thus it seems clear that practicality as a positive value involves very important presuppositions as to other values. For instance, it typically assumes the worth of the basic social order within which action occurs. It characteristically rests on a whole set of implicit premises, among which are the stress on *activity* and *rationality* already mentioned above.

Standards of pure efficiency can of course apply to any kind of human behavior; there is a technique for mysticism as well as a technique for producing automobiles. However, there is nothing practical, in the American meaning, in a dominant concern with purely esthetic or intellectual interests, nor in veneration of the past; asceticism, philosophic withdrawal, pessimistic quietism have never very long or very greatly stamped the American ethos; such tendencies have been confined to depressed or oppressed cultural enclaves, to small sectarian movements, or to individuals alienated from the main currents of national life. In part this view of practicality lies back of the attitude caricatured in Henry Ford's dictum: "History is bunk." Americans have been called, not with entire justification, a people without a sense of history, but it is significant that they generally have not been overly troubled by such comments.[39]

The practicality theme represents at least three quite different although closely related dimensions: (1) the nature of the immediate ends for activity; (2) the guiding criteria for arranging ends into a hierarchy of value; (3) the implicit conceptual framework—the absolute social logics—within which values are perceived. With respect to the sanctioned immediate ends of conduct, we have already seen a convergence upon the goals of certain kinds of success. Practicality as to concrete goals of actions correspondingly has meant the canalizing of action in the service of those specific life-models most highly approved in the general culture—broadly speaking, rational, strenuous, competitive striving for personal validation through occupational success. In so far as this definition of the situation has been accepted, only those things have been considered practical that contributed to this end. Second, as a guiding principle for arranging value priorities, practicality represents a particular form of what Max Weber called *Zweckrationalität* as over against *Wertrationalität*—the rational weighting of values in a pluralistic framework rather than overwhelming concern with a single value or end. In the latter case, all other considerations except the achievement of that end become irrelevant; in prototype this is the stand of the political or religious fanatic, the insatiable hedonist, the monomaniacal economic man. American standards of practicality

[39]The idea that America is a historyless civilization is, in fact, largely an illusion of observers who have not understood the basic world-view of the culture, especially its future orientation.

seem to have led mainly in the direction of a multifaceted balancing of values. Finally, practicality affects the conceptual schemes (explicit and implicit) that broadly characterize the culture. Even American philosophy displays a practical and critical cast and has been in various ways pragmatic, instrumental, relativistic.[40]

Thus, the theme of practicality points us again to activistic, rational, and secular (but "ethical") emphases of the culture; at the same time, it hints of possible tendencies toward the dissipation of the content of "ultimate" values in favor of immediate adaptability to immediate interests and satisfactions. As a highly derivative pattern, practicality does not provide in itself any sure anchorage for continuing organization and integration of individual activity. It is not a basic value. In common with the emphasis on *procedure* in American concepts of freedom and democracy, the emphasis upon practicality indicates a society that has tended to take for granted the implicit value framework within which practical action acquires meaning and rationale.

"Progress"

From the society's earliest formation there has been a diffuse constellation of beliefs and attitudes that may be called the cult of progress. This broad theme has no unitary value such as would tangibly regulate specific individual behavior, but is rather a certain "set" toward life that has permeated a wide range of behavior patterns. Various aspects of this complex are those allegedly typical American traits discussed earlier—"optimism," an emphasis upon the future rather than the past or present, "boosterism," receptivity to change, faith in the perfectibility of the common man.[41] At least in the enterprising middle classes, progress has been a prime article of faith. Our rich vocabulary of epithets ("backward," "outmoded," "old-fashioned," "stagnant," and the like) can be understood *as epithets* only against the unquestioning assumption that the new is the better—that "forward" is better than "backward."

From Tocqueville to Laski, inquiring foreign observers have been impressed with the faith in progress and the high evaluation of the future in the United States as contrasted with Europe. Americans have felt their present to be better than their past and have felt adequate to deal with a future that will be still better.

"Throughout their history Americans have insisted that the best was yet to be. . . . The American knew that nothing was impossible in his brave new world. . . . Progress was not, to him, a mere philosophical ideal but a commonplace of experience. . . ."[42]

The importance of the idea of progress is in part brought out by the ex-

---

[40]Charles A. Beard and Mary R. Beard, *The American Spirit* (New York, 1942), pp. 661–70.

[41]Coleman reports this general complex among the traits upon which writers on America have usually agreed.

[42]Henry Steele Commager (ed.), *America in Perspective* (New York, Random House, Inc., 1947), pp. xi and xiv.

amples of contrasting societies in which it has been, or is, absent. As John B. Bury has shown in a classic work,[43] the concept of progress has emerged only recently in history. For example, the ancient Greeks apparently believed in eternally recurring cycles, or else placed the Golden Age in the past. Medieval times tended to devalue radically the life of the present in favor of a static conception of society as far less significant than the supernatural world and the afterlife. Only with the breakdown of the feudal order and the emergence of a new society in western Europe did the idea become established that human nature is subject to continuous improvement and that society as a whole is inevitably moving toward a better order of life. This orientation, at first largely restricted to small circles of intellectuals in Europe, was made to order for the formative years of the United States. In the beginning America was promise, rather than past; hope, rather than accomplishment. For a long period the promise was kept and the hope was fulfilled to a remarkable degree.[44] Belief in progress involves acceptance of changes, the idea that changes are tending in a definite direction, and the belief that the direction is good. To generations of Americans all three components seemed verified: things were changing, they were moving in a central direction, they were getting better.

In the form in which it had been molded by the Enlightenment, progress was conceived as the beneficent unfolding of man's capacities for reason and goodness. In the course of its later development, however, the idea picked up dominant overtones of Social Darwinism ("the survival of the fittest") at about the same time that its application was being more and more restricted to economic and technological realms. By the late nineteenth century, the concept had been largely assimilated to the values of a complex and expanding industrial order. Progress could now become a slogan to defend the course of technological innovation and economic rationalization and concentration. If small entrepreneurs, farmers, or urban workers felt economic distress, their condition could be considered a regrettable but necessary and temporary byproduct of the triumphant march of progress. Progress became identified with "free private enterprise," in fact, at a time when the individual entrepreneur was already clearly certain to be supplemented by vast economic organizations the development of which was to change the traditional laissez faire concepts of "private property" and "economic freedom."

Material Comfort

In the twenties during the triumph of the so-called New Era (of Permanent Prosperity), a highly critical French observer could say of Americans

[43] *The Idea of Progress* (New York, 1932).

[44] For the eighteenth century, Savelle comments: "The belief in self-help, and the faith in progress . . . sprang from the American's actual daily experience; they were true and valid because the individual and social achievements, repeated over and over again, had proved them so."—*Seeds of Liberty* (New York, Alfred A. Knopf, Inc., 1948), p. 220.

that they "consider it only natural that their slightest whim should be gratified."[45] Even during this period there were millions of Americans who would have considered themselves fortunate to secure basic necessities for nutrition and shelter; yet notwithstanding its exaggeration, Siegfried's comment points attention to the value placed upon a *high level of material comfort.* Even before the Second World War, the United States undoubtedly had one of the highest material levels of living in the world, as judged by such criteria as adequacy of nutrition, medical care, facilities for shelter, transportation and communication, and so on.

The fact that material comfort undoubtedly is highly approved and sought after in the culture[46] tells us very little in itself about what specific values are involved; the "American standard of living" has its undertones and overtones of meanings—from nationalistic identification, to symbol of success, competence, and power and from a token of moral excellence to something very close to a terminal goal at the level of hedonistic gratification.

There is some criticism that passive gratification elements in American society have been receiving increased emphasis in recent decades. The most obvious although probably not the most important index of this trend is provided by commercial advertising that emphasizes comfort and effortless gratification: eat this, chew this, drink that; take a vacation; be catered to; and so on. The major focus is upon receiving, looking at, being catered to, in short, maximum pleasurable sensation with minimum effort or activity. Television and motion pictures are perhaps the clearest examples. "Spectator" sports fit the same pattern—huge audiences watch others perform.

The gratification motif appears in modern mass entertainment with all the clarity of a caricature. For motion pictures, Dorothy Jones's analysis of a hundred films appearing in 1941–42 showed a predominance of the "happy ending"—at the end of the picture, about 60 per cent of all major characters were indulged with respect to all of their wants; about 10 per cent were deprived as to all of their wants; about 14 per cent were indulged as to some wants and deprived as to others.[47]

Lowenthal's study of biographies appearing in two mass circulation magazines from 1901–41 gives another illustration of the value stimuli to which Americans are exposed. He suggests that there has thus been a shift from the "idols of production" to the "idols of consumption"—from attention focused on substantial achievement in social organization and economic production to the people who embellish leisure time. "The first quarter of the century cherishes biography in terms of an open-minded liberal society which really wants to know something about its own leading figures on the decisive social,

---

[45]André Siegfried, *America Comes of Age* (New York, 1927).

[46]Cf. Laski, "No church which urged the desirability of asceticism had any hope of influence or much hope of survival." *The American Democracy,* p. 13.

[47]Dorothy B. Jones, "Quantitative Analysis of Motion Picture Content," *Public Opinion Quarterly,* Vol. VI, No. 3 (Fall 1942), pp. 411–28.

commercial, and cultural fronts."[48] But by 1940–41 the heroes are figures from the world of entertainment and sport—a "dream world" of leisure-time activities. Even within the general category of entertainment, the proportion from serious arts (fine arts, theater, music, etc.) declined from 77 per cent in 1901–14 to 9 per cent in 1940–41. Furthermore, in their content the more recent biographies emphasized the private lives and consumption of the subjects. "It is neither a world of 'doers' nor a world of 'doing' for which the biographical curiosity of a mass public is evoked. . . . Instead of the 'givers' we are faced with the 'takers.' "[49] Although the biographies approved in general of "doing things," success seems to be treated as something that merely happens—an accidental, lucky event—not a rational outcome of integrated effort.

The American experience gives some support to the hypothesis that in so far as a group or society is able to attain a high plane of material comfort, it will tend increasingly to emphasize the "hedonistic values," unless checked by internal social danger or outside threat. Apparently, at least in Western societies, the objective opportunity to secure material comforts elicits, in the long run, a desire for them. Once a high standard of living has been enjoyed, however, it is extremely difficult to reduce the level of sensation. As new wants emerge and are satisfied over a period of time, they become accepted, expected, "normal," and in this process they at the same time come to be felt as rights to which one has a moral claim. When the level of material comfort of a whole people has been rising over a considerable period of time, it will be reduced only reluctantly even under the duress of great social emergency.

But the picture just sketched is highly incomplete. First, it does not take into account the large amount of participation in active sports, the vast activity of vacation travel, or the millions of home workshops and the popularity of "do-it-yourself" hobbies. Nor does it give enough weight to the millions of amateur painters, actors, writers, and other artists. One must remember also the large audiences who actively appreciate serious concerts and the theater. (Americans spend more money for admissions to concerts than to baseball games.) Although passive entertainment predominates, it has not displaced the active and purposive use of leisure time. Second, the newer emphasis upon consumption and leisure does not necessarily indicate a basic change in values. There certainly is more leisure time and there are more consumer goods and services available to the American people than ever before. And, although the evidence is impressionistic, there probably is some real alteration in the emphasis upon and arrangement of traditional evaluations, e.g.: lessened evaluation of asceticism, coupled with a lessened future-time orientation, leads to the enjoyment of leisure without the guilt and ambivalence it carried in a "puritan" ethos.[50] In the absence of convincing data, however, it is best to hold

[48]Leo Lowenthal, "Biographies in Popular Magazines," in Paul F. Lazarsfeld and Frank N. Stanton (eds.), *Radio Research, 1942–1943* (New York, 1944), pp. 512–13.

[49]*Ibid.*, p. 527.

[50]Cf. Clyde Kluckhohn, in Elting E. Morison (ed.), *The American Style* (New York, 1958), pp. 158–204.

open the possibility that new patterns of consumption and leisure actually are being assimilated to older values, e.g., "consumption" may be interpreted both as reward for achievement and as a kind of achievement itself; the use of "gadgets" may just confirm the value of instrumental activity; and recreation may be evaluated as a means for maintaining the capacity for work and achievement.[51] The conclusion that "material comfort" leads to loss of high evaluation of disciplined endeavor would be premature.

Equality

The avowal of "equality," and often its practice as well, has been a persistent theme through most of American history. Even modern economic organization, which in many ways epitomizes inequality,[52] has stressed "equality of opportunity." Yet few other value complexes are more subject to strain in modern times.

The United States began its independent political existence as a congeries of societies, which in the main had broken sharply with the traditions of social deference and with the hierarchical social structures that still characterized Britain and Europe. The generalization has its exceptions. New England had been ruled by an elite of the religiously elect. Remnants of feudal land customs had persisted for a time in various areas in such forms as quit-rents and primogeniture. Indentured servitude and imprisonment for debt had represented direct transmissions of neofeudal practices. But in general all individual arrangements embodying traditional social inequalities were dissolving.[53] In retrospect, as always, this result now seems to have been inevitable. Actually it was the consequence of a highly complex constellation of factors: laxity of political control by England partly as a result of the distance from Britain and Europe; only a small number of the colonists had been aristocrats, the majority was middle and lower class and many actively opposed some features of their parent society; mass accessibility to abundant resources, which made it possible for "anyone to become a king on his own" and thus helped to dissolve old hierarchies and social forms through movement, acquisition, independence, potential equality of all sorts and manners of men; the ideological forces; the deeply individualistic strain brought in through Protestantism, as well as philosophical and political ideas that worked in the same direction. (Locke and the French rationalists, for instance, affected not only the Founding Fathers but much wider circles of eighteenth century America.)

Other factors encouraging the emergence of equality as a value may be left

[51][Footnote 51 has been omitted.]

[52]Note how far the ideology of Soviet Russia is from indicating the actual hierarchy of industrial organization there.

[53]"Feudalism never got a real footing in America. . . . The most striking feature of the land system of the colonists generally was the departure from the English system of primogeniture." W. Paschal Larkin, *Property in the Eighteenth Century* (London, 1930), pp. 140–41.

aside for present purposes.[54] It will suffice here to see that this society in its formative periods was one that could, and wished to, break with its hierarchical tradition and that this result was favored by fundamental objective and ideological conditions. Thus, until the late nineteenth century, America was able to develop without having to face widespread conflict between the principle of equality and the principles of achievement or freedom. In this remarkable historical experience, through generation after generation the values of equality were crystallized and elaborated. People saw the disappearance of primogeniture, the abolition of indentured servitude, of imprisonment for debt, of slavery, of property qualifications for voting and public office; there was provision for the common man to acquire a stake in the land and to secure a free public education; women gained one legal right after another; and even discriminations against minorities were sharply challenged time after time.

However, as Tocqueville saw more than a century ago, America had to face sooner or later a conflict of values that he described as a contradiction between the principle of freedom and the principle of equality. For instance, the cumulative effect of freedom to pursue individual advantage, given the opportunities and institutional framework of nineteenth-century America, was to destroy equality of condition. The liberty of which Tocqueville spoke was a freedom from feudal or mercantilistic restraints on the economic individualism so congenial to the early American situation. But this freedom could only lead under the historical circumstances to the emergence of what he called a manufacturing aristocracy, an outcome far from the perfect commonwealth of equal citizens that some idealizers of a yeoman republic desired. Not only did the specific conditions of American life accentuate the tension of equality versus liberty, but also the very attempt to blend Locke and Rousseau was intrinsically difficult.[55] Both liberty and equality are authentic and historically inseparable parts of Western democratic tradition, but for all their affinity their union has often posed perplexing dilemmas.

Already it becomes plain that the meanings of equality are various and that it does not help us very much to characterize a society as simply equalitarian or the reverse. Modern America, of course, shows inequalities of wealth, power, and prestige; and there is far from being perfect equality of opportunity to acquire these things. As Myers has eloquently indicated, men are not in fact equal in any specific ability or capacity;[56] in a complex and heterogeneous society they are likely to have very unequal access to scarce goods. The extent

[54] For example, the influence of geographic mobility, mutual dependence under frontier conditions, the lack of a complex division of labor and highly developed urban life, etc.

[55] "From its very beginning the theory of democracy linked together the two ideals of liberty and equality, and quite early it became apparent that these two would not unite as easily as the democrats of Thomas Jefferson's generation had hoped." George H. Sabine, "The Two Democratic Traditions," *The Philosophical Review,* Vol. LXI, No. 4 (October 1952), pp. 451–52.

[56] Myers, *Are Men Equal?* The author, however, argues congently for intrinsic equality as a central element in the American ethos.

of the so-called objective or material inequalities, however, is itself in part a function of the basic value-system.[57]

If equality is a basic value in our society, it must meet our operational tests: (1) the individual must feel guilt, shame, or ego deflation when he acts in inequalitarian ways; and (2) there must be sanctions supported by the effective community for conformity or nonconformity. The extensiveness of these reactions must be weighed against parallel responses to any behavior manifesting hierarchical principles of human relations. Although no such quantitative assessment can be made from the available evidence, it is nevertheless reasonably clear that inequalities, hierarchical emphases, and various kinds of discriminations are common in American life. Taken as a whole America appears to present a highly confused situation in which conflicts and compromises are accompanied by myths, legends, and conventional fictions until the main value directions become difficult to trace. Much of the seeming complexity, however, does not really concern basic value-orientations, but rather represents either *deviance* or, at least equally important, different restrictions of the value in different *social roles and situations.* Certainly the relationship between a police officer and the automobile driver to whom he gives a traffic ticket is not "equalitarian." But this is a narrowly limited and defined relationship in a specific situation; the police officer has no generalized superiority over the hapless motorist in other roles and situations.

The problems can be grasped more readily if we differentiate among the several senses in which equality may be a value. It is useful to distinguish between intrinsic and extrinsic valuations. Extrinsic valuations are those judgments of value that depend upon generalized social categories and external symbols of status such as sex, age, nationality, occupation, rank, income, wealth, medals, race, authority. Intrinsic valuation has to do with the immediately personal qualities of the individual apart from any categorical social attributes, and its presence is demonstrated wherever one person feels an obligation to treat another person as—in any degree—an end in himself rather than purely as a means. To put it negatively, the person is given an intrinsic value when we feel guilt or shame if we do not act with some regard for his presumed human sensibilities, regardless of his categorical social status or group membership. Whenever such intrinsic valuation is at work, it constitutes a "floor" below which the person cannot be devalued or degraded—a guarantee of minimal equality. Extrinsic valuations focus upon what a person *has;* intrinsic valuation concerns what the person is *qua* individual. It is obvious that the two imputations of value often do not coincide, as when we say that a man "doesn't deserve his rank," or "he may have a million dollars but he isn't worth two cents as a man."

[57]When the modern proponents of "inevitable inequality" argue that greatly unequal rewards are *necessary* in order to get the most *important* social functions performed, it is seldom noticed that the question of necessity is being begged along with the question of importance.

At the level of explicit doctrine, intrinsic equality is widespread in American culture, both in the form of a specifically religious conception (the equality of souls before God, the divine nature within every person, and so on), and in the more secularized formulations that attribute an irreducible quantum of value to every person: "a man's a man for all that," "after all they are human beings," or the categorical imperative to "treat others as ends rather than means." At the level of overt interpersonal relations, adherence to a sense of intrinsic human value is discernible in a wide variety of specific behaviors—perhaps most obviously in "democratic manners." America has always impressed observers from more rigid and hierarchical societies as being marked by an extraordinary informality, directness, and lack of status consciousness in person-to-person contacts.[58] This general openness of social relations can only be maintained in a culture in which intrinsic personal value is a widespread and effective assumption.[59]

In more concrete terms, equality is exhibited in the way individuals actually *relate* to others in ordinary interpersonal activities. Are individuals in American culture typically related to others by superordination and subordination, or are interpersonal relations typically horizontal? The answer to so sweeping a question can be built up only by induction from the enormous variety of social rules actually existing in our society; a definitive analysis must wait upon a great amount of further systematic research. However, much of the evidence in the preceding chapters on the major institutions is relevant here: we have seen, for example, how the central family-type emphasizes equailty of in-law families, and how the relations of husband-wife, parent-child, and sibling-sibling tend to be nonauthoritarian and nonhierarchical modes. In examining educational organization, it was suggested that, in spite of definite hierarchical emphases, the teacher-student relation in America is less rigid, formal, and authoritarian than in analogous European situations. On the other hand, we have seen much evidence of strongly hierarchical and authoritarian emphases, especially in large-scale economic and political organizations. And, running through the whole society, is the salient thread of nonequalitarian beliefs and practices concerning interpersonal relations with persons of a different racial or ethnic grouping. Nevertheless, in our provisional appraisal equality rather than hierarchy seems on the whole characteristic of concrete social relations—although perhaps more clearly at the level of the *goals and standards* of conduct than in the uneven compromises of going practice. As Professor Sabine puts it: "The demand that men of differing position shall meet on terms of

[58]The references are numerous. See the works by Commager and by Parkes, already cited. Also Kurt Lewin, "Some Social-psychological Differences Between the United States and Germany," *Character and Personality,* Vol. IV (1936), pp. 265–93.

[59]Cf. H. D. Lasswell, *World Politics and Personal Insecurity* (New York, 1935), p. 229: "The democratization of manners resulted in those 'man to man' forms of social intercourse which are so potent in reducing hostility against anybody who gets rich and stays a 'good fellow.' This relative universalization of deference claims has tended to nullify the consequences of a steep pyramid of wealth distribution."

mutual respect and self-respect has been and will continue to be a recurring demand made in the name of democracy."[60] On this point, something approaching a crucial "experiment of nature" is available to us in the reactions of American soldiers to military life in the Second World War. Military organization is the example par excellence of hierarchy; in time of war its norms are supported by all the enormous social assent that war can generate. In the Second World War, the vast majority of American soldiers accepted the necessity of war and the legitimacy of military authority. Yet, as hundreds of specific studies showed, these same soldiers resented almost above all else the unequal privileges of officers and enlisted men and the insistence upon detailed observance of rituals of subordination and deference. It was clear also that one of the strongest forces that kept men working and fighting as organized groups was loyalty to their comrades and equals, that "team work" (the term is significant) rather than psychological dependence upon authority figures was the crux of the American version of military morale.[61]

A second major type of equality consists of specific formal rights and obligations. In the United States the strain toward equality of legal rights for all citizens or even residents has been strong and continuing. Formally equal civil rights—from military service to voting, from public education to taxation—represent not only freedom but also equality. In the sense of freedom these rights may be said to guarantee the individual a certain openness in his life-space; in the sense of equality, they nominally establish a minimum life-space for every one. It is in this equality of specified rights that the second major theme of American equality has developed, rather than in doctrines of equal individual potentialities, achievements, or rewards.

The third type of equality is substantive equality of social and, above all, economic rewards. Here it seems quite clear that the principles of economic freedom and individual achievement have strongly dominated principles of equality.[62] The reigning conception has been that of *equality of opportunity* rather than *equality of condition.* Concessions toward substantive equality of condition—for example, the income tax in so far as it is graduated—have not leveled differences in wealth, and the upper and middle classes of the society continually have insisted upon a moral claim to the existing differentials. It is quite striking that one of the earliest and most widespread reactions to Marxism, as popularly understood, was to select precisely the idea of "equal distribution of wealth" as the target of censure and moral outrage.

Every principle of equality is subject to its sharpest violation in the case of

---

[60]George H. Sabine, "The Two Democratic Traditions," p. 473.

[61]See the findings presented in Samuel A. Stouffer, *et al., The American Soldier,* Vols. I and II (Princeton, N.J., 1949), especially Chaps. 6, 8, 9, and 10 of Vol. I, and Chaps. 3, 6, and 7 of Vol. II.

[62]Lewin: "Some Social-psychological Differences Between the United States and Germany," p. 16: "In spite of the democratic idea of equality of men, proclaimed in the American Constitution as one of its basic principles, there are probably no other people as interested in *individual accomplishments* . . . as the Americans."

minority groups, especially the American Negro. Few other aspects of our society are so well documented as this one.

In widest perspective it appears that the inequalities that are felt in American culture to contravene equality values most severely are of two kinds: first, the denial of nominally universal rights of citizenship and violations of nominally universal rules of impersonal justice; second, the denial of opportunities for achievement in the formally open competitive order. It is certainly true that American culture has never found it overly difficult to tolerate great differences in certain types of individual privileges or rewards. Where rewards have been seen as consequences of achievement—including the successful acceptance of responsibility and exercise of authority—inequality of reward tends to be accepted as legitimate. Where control of facilities is regarded as necessary for performance of valued functions, as in the case of the capable business executive or military leader, resentment is minimized. The tautology that inequality is not resented unless considered to be undeserved takes on an important meaning as soon as we are able to specify what "undeserved" actually means. By and large in the United States, it has meant *categorical* privileges —rewards not earned by effort and achievement (including moral achievement) within the basic institutional rules for fair competition. Here is the core of "the American tradition" of equality. The dominant cultural value is not an undifferentiated and undiscriminating equalitarianism, but rather a two-sided emphasis upon basic social rights and upon equality of opportunity.

It is important to note the role of this value complex in the periodic resurgence of native, homespun "radicalism" in America. The historical record indicates that the demand for equality of traditional rights and equality of economic opportunity has not, in the main, grown out of imported ideologies, but has emerged from the received traditions. The long ground-swell of the Populist movement[63] in the late nineteenth century provides a good example of how American movements for economic reform, at least until the depression of the thirties, have been essentially the attempt of the "little man," and especially of the farming population, to check the power of "big business." These movements never really challenged in any thoroughgoing way the concepts of private (individual) property and free enterprise; rather, they represented the counterattack of the old-style private (individual and familial) property and the free (small, independent, competitive) enterprise against the emerging forces of large-scale, corporate property and monopolistic industrial, financial and commercial combinations.[64]

It has been part of the fundamental pathos of American culture to believe that virtue should and will be rewarded—and more particularly that such

[63]An excellent source on this important phase of American history is John D. Hicks, *The Populist Revolt* (Minneapolis, Minn., 1931).

[64]See the discussion in Henry Bamford Parkes, *The American Experience* (New York, 1947), Chap. 13. For example: "The antitrust laws were peculiarly American and were a product of the agrarian tradition; they had no parallel in Europe" (p. 292).

economic virtues as hard work, frugality, and prudence should receive a proportionate reward. The axiomatic value of this moral equation has been closely linked with the premise that everyone (at least, all in "one's own" group) has an equal right to fundamental opportunities. Without question, this whole principle is currently undergoing severe strain and extensive redefinition. The essential present point is that values of equality in the received American culture of the modern period have centered around the dual themes of civil rights and economic opportunity.

Freedom

We need no research to tell us that the verbal affirmation of the value of freedom is widespread and persistent.[65] The widespread positive reaction to the symbolic value of the word is illustrated in many ways. For example, public opinion polls show that freedom in general, or in some specific application, such as freedom of the press or of worship, is most often mentioned as the greatest advantage of the American form of government.[66]

That something real in actual social relations lies back of the word freedom cannot be doubted. Yet the reality is not in the unconditional listing of categorical freedoms, for it can quickly be shown that actual social life and "unconditional freedom" are contradictions in terms.[67] Furthermore, what are restraints from one point of view may be rights or "privileges" from another, as when a person wants "to do his duty" (and finds it to his advantage to do so).

American conceptions of freedom mainly stem from an orientation that characterized European thought for several centuries: freedom is compatible with causality and determinism; it does not mean uncaused behavior, but rather behavior that is not subject to restraints that are in some sense external and arbitrary. In this view, although behavior is always determined—that is, influenced, caused, or conditioned—it is nevertheless possible to give a definite meaning to the statement that it may also be "free." All life in society involves the limitation of behavior not only by the physical world, including the limitations of the human body and mind, but also by reciprocal rights and obligations among persons; every social group furthermore must cope with problems of authority and power. What, then, is to be said of the American emphasis on freedom?

The historical context of freedom as a value pattern in our culture begins with the centuries-long process whereby area after area of life was removed from the web of interlocking controls of feudal Europe. With the rise of

[65]Savelle's conclusion from his study of the eighteenth century is: "Thus the great common denominator of American social thinking was the ideal of social freedom—freedom to rise, that is—individualism, and social fluidity. If the Americans still believed in aristocracy, it was now, in theory at least, predominantly . . . based upon the ideal of an aristocracy of merit, of individual worth." *Seeds of Liberty* (New York, Alfred A. Knopf, Inc., 1948), p. 280.

[66]See *Opinion News,* Vol. VIII, No. 6 (March 18, 1947).

[67]Cf. Linton, *The Study of Man,* Chaps. 8 and 16.

nation-states and of urban life and with the expansion of industry and trade, the settled, hierarchical society of Europe moved into an unprecedented colonizing phase. The American colonies were one result, and in them the trend toward emancipation was intensified. At one point it might be a struggle against quit-rents; at another, restiveness under mercantilistic restraints; still elsewhere, a revolt against an established religious hierarchy. Always the demand was for freedom *from* some existing restraint. That the major American freedoms were in this sense negative does not mean, of course, that they were not also positive: they were rights to *do,* by the same token that they were rights to be protected from restraint. Nevertheless, the historical process left its mark in a culturally standardized way of thought and evaluation—a tendency to think of rights rather than duties, a suspicion of established (especially personal) authority, a distrust of central government, a deep aversion to acceptance of obviously coercive restraint through visible social organization. At the time in which the primary political and economic structure of the new society was laid down, the great threat to freedom was perceived as coming from the centralized, absolutistic state, and the obvious course seemed to be to erect every possible barrier to centralized governmental control; the main import of the doctrine of checks and balances was to prevent the central state as much as possible from undertaking any positive action beyond a very few carefully defined areas of authority. Such a view of government reflected a society in which the politically effective elements of the community wanted above all to have "room" to make their own decisions, to develop their own spheres of social power, to escape from the surveillance of kings and ministers of state. This particular sort of freedom was premised on a sweeping faith: the confidence of the individual in his own competence and mastery.

It is thus in the peculiar features of the concept of freedom to which value is attached in America that our present interest centers. We know, for instance, that, when American leaders and the leaders of the Soviet Union say they value "freedom," the words do not carry identical value loadings. The differences cannot be wholly explained either as special pleading or as simple ignorance, and examination of the variation between the two orientations may help to clarify the American case. Broadly speaking, the Soviet conception of freedom emphasizes security in the sense of rights to employment, medical care, economic support, education, and cultural participation *within* an accepted framework set by the neo-Marxist state. In this system many of the liberties prized in Anglo-American culture are regarded as irrelevant if not meaningless. On the other hand, American spokesmen emphasize freedom of speech and assembly, a multiparty, representative political system, "private enterprise," freedom to change residence and employment.

The above contrasts, stated in oversimplified form, serve to pose more sharply the problem of what "freedom" it is that is valued in American society. In the historically developed orientation—which may no longer exist in the same form—the central principles seem reasonably clear. A major implicit cultural premise in the dominant valuation of freedom has been *the equating of "freedom" with control by diffuse cultural structure rather than by a definite social organization.* Thus, it has seemed to make a great difference whether the individual receives a certain income or has a certain type of occupation as a result of an apparently impersonal, anonymous, diffuse competitive process, as against "being forced" to accept that employment or remuneration by law or by the command of a visible social authority. A foreclosed mortgage has been culturally defined in a radically different way from governmental confiscation of the same property. To be tied to a given locality by diffuse cultural pressure and lack of economic opportunity is regarded as a quite different kind of constraint from such controls as a police order or a governmental regulation.

Upon this kind of axiomatic base, American culture has tended to identify a very great variety of forms of personal dependence as not freedom. To "work under a boss" was not so long ago regarded as a loss of freedom. The widespread reluctance to take employment as a domestic servant and the low evaluation attached to this type of occupation appear to reflect in part the same complex. One of the earliest and most persistent criticisms of American society by aristocratically minded foreign observers has concerned the absence of a docile serving-class and the impertinence of the lower orders.[68]

The underlying psychological constellation in traditional American attitudes toward freedom thus seems to be a posture of self-confidence and expansiveness, coupled with a tendency to reject all absolute claims to personal authority. This syndrome permeates relations of parents and children, men and women, employers and employees, the citizen and *Monsieur le Bureau.* In this sense the American conception of freedom is clearly that of Locke rather than Rousseau, of the protection of particular liberties and the tolerance of dissent rather than the homogenization of private groups and individuals into an omnipotent General Will.[69] Not "plebiscite democracy" but "inalienable rights" reflects the central value.

Viewed in these terms, the theme of freedom is far broader than any particular institutional sector of the society. It rests in the last analysis upon an even more basic conception of the individual as an integral agent, relatively autonomous and morally responsible. (See the section on "Individual Personality" that follows.) Above all, a sociological analysis must make explicit the difference between *freedom as a value* and the *particular historic definitions of freedom in terms of special institutional forms.* Liberty in America began as a release from certain political restraints; the economic liberty thus secured was eventually accompanied in its turn by discords and dislocations in the social structure. In our day the greatest threats to freedom, conceived in liberal democratic terms, appear in economic dislocation and class conflict. The

[68]Beard and Beard, *The American Spirit,* p. 488.

[69]"The absolutely sovereign and omnicompetent state is the logical correlate of a society, which consists of atomic individuals." Sabine, "The Two Democratic Traditions," p. 467.

reaction to this situation has given us a "welfare state" in which freedom is no longer so clearly tied to a social system of private property and inactive government. The necessary implications for freedom as value are by no means wholly clear; it is patent, however, that the dated and localized definition of freedom as practically synonymous with eighteenth century economic philosophies is no longer accepted by the great majority of people in our society.

The core meaning of this shift can perhaps be illustrated by a glance at the so-called laissez faire economics, which was so much more than either laissez faire or economics; it constituted, in fact, a whole system of social philosophy, an elaborate and interconnected set of social values and beliefs. The conception of man around which the doctrine centered was that of the discrete human atom, calculating his economic self-interest and acting "rationally" in the unlimited pursuit of gain. The "perfect system of natural liberty," suitable to this concept, would guarantee the sanctity of contracts, the stability of media of exchange, and the rights of private property. In such a system, so its proponents believed, "when men are free from all governmental interference, virtue finds its tangible reward in wealth and vice its penalty in economic failure."[70] In this way religious axioms were assimilated to the theory of universal social good through economic competition. Support of such a system, under a political democracy, was sought through an additional doctrine, which in this case held that the economically successful are fittest because this very success attests to their moral superiority. Freedom then becomes the economic freedom of the entrepreneur, and democracy becomes a form of government giving maximum protection of property rights. Progress becomes technological advance and economic expansion. Individualism is equated with the right of the individual to use his property as he sees fit, within very broad limits, and to compete freely with others. Society is a neo-Darwinian jungle in which only the fittest *should* survive, and the fittest are those who can win out by intelligence, industry, or ruthlessness.

This "organic" cluster of doctrines has foundered against twentieth-century realities. Because the cultural definition of freedom has changed and because the threats to freedom are now apprehended in different quarters it is easy to assume that the emergence of the welfare state signalizes our departure on a "road to serfdom." We suggest that the status of freedom *as value* must not be prejudged because of changing social mechanisms. Freedom inheres in the *relationships* between an individual and other individuals and groups. It exists to the degree that individuals are enabled to make the choices they wish to make, with minimal use of coercion and minimal infringement of the "spontaneous" actions of others. So long as American society safeguards the right of the individual to a wide range of moral autonomy in decision making, so long as the representative character structure of the culture retains a conscience

[70]Myers, *Are Men Equal?*, p. 140. The passage cited is a paraphrase of the doctrines of Sumner, the Yale sociologist and economist, whose theories are a quintessence of social Darwinism.

that is more than simple group conformity—so long will freedom be a major value. Emphatically, institutional forms are not unimportant; but their significance must be found by specific analysis, not by uncritical prejudgment.

Recent changes in the direction of equality through governmental action have sometimes been interpreted as a reduction in freedom. Assuredly the balance between the two is debatable. But it is oversimplification to regard graduated income taxes, or increased equality of income, or legal bars to racial discrimination and segregation merely as restrictions upon the wealthy or the racially prejudiced. A certain equality of rights is essential to fair bargaining, workable compromises, and mutual respect—all vital ingredients of freedom. Equality and freedom are necessary the one to the other, and neither can be pressed to extremes without damage to the other. The give-and-take between these two emphases is an inherent part of the drama of a democratic society.

It remains to be said that freedom has not meant and does not now mean a wide latitude for idiosyncrasies of individual belief and behavior. Someone has said that "every Frenchman is different, and the more different he is the better he likes it." Regardless of the dubious accuracy of this formulation as applied to French culture (e.g. Norman peasants), it certainly could not be applied to describe the American situation. For an appraisal of the value of "external conformity" we turn to the next section.

External Conformity[71]

Even as early as the 1830's, Tocqueville commented on the necessity of safeguards against a possible "tyranny of the majority" in America and thought that public compulsion had already penetrated into private affairs in a censorious way not usual in the France of his day. Nearly a century later Siegfried, another and more critical Frenchman, visualized America as a land of vast uniformity in speech, manners, housing, dress, recreation, and politically expressed ideas. In 1948, Laski pointed to an "amazing uniformity" of values, thought that "business *mores*" had permeated the culture, and tried to show that "the American spirit required that the limits of uniformity be drawn with a certain tautness."[72] Many Europeans in the period prior to the Second World War had thought American conformity-behavior to have a certain harried, compulsive quality, and have referred to standardization, "flatness," and lack of individuality in comparison with the Continent. In the period between 1920 and the Second World War European observers seem to have been especially (and overly) impressed with conformity themes in America. Thus, Muller-

[71]A spate of concerns about conformity is indicated by the popularity of such works as: David Riesman, *et al., The Lonely Crowd* (New Haven, 1953); William H. Whyte, Jr., *The Organization Man* (New York, 1956); Vance Packard, *The Status Seekers* (New York, 1959). Numerous other writings, as well as the mass media, give attention to the topic. One even suspects that many Americans are trying to find out how much they ought to avoid conformity in order to conform with an acceptable norm of nonconformity.

[72]*The American Democracy,* pp. 49–51.

Freienfels, in a book published in 1929: "Distance, uniqueness, and originality are European values, which are foreign to the American. His values are the very reverse of these: adherence to type, agreement, similarity."[73]

These appraisals—which in fact have often been biased and exaggerated—come as something of a shock to a people that has made much of individual initiative, the rights of the individual, personal independence, "rugged individualism." Yet it should be no surprise that an intensely active, democratic society should define tolerance of individual nonconformity largely in terms of sanctioning technological and economic innovation. In the field of so-called personal morals, the culture is one in which there is a tendency to legislate conformity—a tendency acted out again and again, from the early "blue laws" to Prohibition and the Hays Office. In the field of intellectual heterodoxy, although the United States has produced its Thoreau, its Henry George, its free thinkers and dissenters, a considered judgment would be that really radical nonconformity in speculative thought has not been outstanding, at least in comparison with other countries of Western culture. American "individualism," taken in broadest terms, has consisted mainly of a rejection of the state and impatience with restraints upon economic activity; it has not tended to set the autonomous individual up in rebellion against his social group. In a nation of joiners, individualism tends to be a matter of "group individualism," of the particularized behavior of subcultures.

Men universally seek the approval of *some* of their fellows and therefore try to be "successful" by some shared standards of achievement or conformity. This characteristic is the outcome of universal requirements of group life and of the basic nature of the socialization process; otherwise stated, conformity and the desire for social approval are formal qualities that are part of the very definition of society. In this sense, conformity is not a *value* at all, but simply an end-product of other values and the necessary adjustments entailed by life in groups.

Our real interest is in knowing how rigid the conformity is and what specific content defines conformity or success in a particular group or culture. There are societies in which conformity may be a matter of proficiency in religious ritual, others in which it consists of exemplifying warrior virtues, others in which esthetic activities are the measure.[74] Similarly, in all societies men tend to conform to the groups with which they are most deeply identified, but both the degree of conformity and its kind differ greatly in various cultures. In

[73]Richard Muller-Freienfels, *Mysteries of the Soul,* trans. by Bernard Miall (London, 1929). This view has been common among those who feel that if industry turns out standardized goods for a mass market it follows that the whole culture is "standardized."

[74]"A few hundred years ago it seemed the most natural thing in the world to the ambitious among our ancestors, to sell off their property, raise a company and set off to the Holy Land to rescue it from the infidels. This is incomprehensible to us, but we see nothing strange in a man of ambition and imagination devoting a lifetime of strenuous endeavor to the making of tubs or the organized slaughter of hogs." Charles Horton Cooley, *Sociological Theory and Social Research* (New York, Henry Holt & Company, Inc., 1930), p. 225.

short, conformity can be treated as a value only in so far as *sheer adherence to group patterns* is actually divorced from the content and implications of those patterns. This is rare.[75] It is only among a people who have lost the capacity for autonomous value-decisions that the sheer conformity of a goose-step order can approach a terminal goal.

It is useful to examine American conformity emphases for the light they may throw upon other dimensions of the value system. Several general sociological hypotheses are relevant to this examination. We know that where a functioning group or society feels threatened from the outside, it tends to tighten social controls over behavior involving the group's solidarity and striking power. Wars supply the most dramatic examples, but the political "witch hunts" in periods of international tension are equally in point. We know further that a group ridden by internal insecurities and tensions will, under certain conditions that need not be specified here, tend to raise its threshold of toleration for non-conformity: "The looser the package, the tighter must be the string"—if the package is to hold together at all.[76]

Some preoccupation with external conformity is to be expected in a society in which upward social mobility is highly prized and frequently achieved. The competitive striving of an upwardly mobile group in a society organized around the economic enterprise requires stringent discipline over the expression of sexual and aggressive impulses, over patterns of consumption, over the uses of time and resources. In this aspect, conformity is derivative from equality of opportunity in conjunction with success-striving. Furthermore, an emphasis upon external conformity easily develops out of the premise of basic human equality: if all are equal, then all have an equal right to judge their fellows and to regulate their conduct accordingly to common accepted standards; some such cultural equation has been widely accepted in the broad middle classes of American society. The exceptions to the pattern occur in those classes and groups in which special license follows from exclusion of the group from the application of principles of equality (for example, the very rich, certain *declassé* strata, and so on).

Interestingly enough, the very heterogeneity of American culture tends to produce a stress upon external conformity. Given the varied cultural backgrounds of the population and the desire that the various groups should continue to live together in the same society, conformity in externals becomes a sort of "social currency" making it possible to continue the society in spite of

---

[75]Sabine goes so far as to say: "Every society depends upon and exacts some kind and degree of conformity, and different cultures support widely different systems of status, but no culture reduces its members to automata or fails to acknowledge that self-respect is both a genuine good and a powerful human motive." "The Two Democratic Traditions," p. 471.

[76]An alleged insecurity factor in American conformity has been often suggested. A representative statement is: "Today America shows perhaps more conformity in externals than any other country. . . . Americans had to establish a social tradition of their own to hold them together." H. M. Spitzer, "Presenting America in American Propaganda," *Public Opinion Quarterly,* Vol. IX (Summer 1947), p. 219.

many clashes of interests and basic values. If it is gradually learned that the exhibition of cultural differences—whether they be of dress, or language, or religious faith, or political philosophy—seems to lead to friction in interpersonal relationships or even to public disturbances, a whole series of complex adjustments are set in motion. Among the possible reponses to such a situation is the practice of withdrawing tension-producing items from general social circulation: for example, one finds popular maxims such as "never argue about religion or politics."[77] The individual comes to reserve controversial matters to an intimate social circle of like-minded persons; public discourse and behavior is correspondingly more highly standardized. An elaborate social currency develops; set conversation-pieces, clichés, and standardized public opinions that can be passed smoothly along the channels of social interaction almost as a counterpart to the flow of money in the exchange economy.

The economic system itself contributes to the conformity theme in two other main respects. First, the high degree of specialization of economic roles in a highly developed money economy means that much social interaction is functionally specific, impersonal, transitory, and frequently laden with clashes of immediate economic interests. These are precisely the kinds of conditions most likely to produce conventionalized or stereotyped behavior.[78] Second, the relations of individual economic dependence are often such as to permit stringent conformity demands.

Science and Secular Rationality

It has become a commonplace observation that the application of science and related secular rational approaches have transformed the external conditions of American culture—along with many other major cultures of the world.[79] Applied science is highly esteemed as a tool for controlling nature. Significant here is the interest in order, control, and calculability—the passion of an engineering civilization. This interest is congruent with the externalized orientation that we have already met in several previous guises; historically it is linked also to the fundamental assumption of an ordered universe in which rational human beings can continually improve their situation and themselves.[80]

---

[77]Obviously if people felt strongly enough about these difference-provoking symbols, this would not happen. The American situation implies that agreement on procedure has dominated over disagreement on other values.

[78]Cf. James W. Woodard: "The Role of Fictions in Cultural Life," in *Transactions of the New York Academy of Sciences* (1944).

[79]Compare the statement of a prominent physicist: "Our culture has the outstanding property of striving to convert all experience into rational scientific knowledge."—Henry Margenau, "Western Culture and Scientific Method," in Lyman Bryson, Louis Finkelstein, and Robert M. MacIver (eds.), *Conflicts of Power in Modern Culture,* Seventh Symposium of the Conference on Science, Philosophy and Religion (New York, 1948), p. 16.

[80]Clyde Kluckhohn and Florence R. Kluckhohn, "American Culture: Generalized Orientations and Class Patterns," in *ibid.,* p. 111: "Our glorification of 'science' and our faith in what can be accomplished through 'education,' are two striking aspects of our generalized conviction that secular, humanistic effort will improve the world in a series of changes, all or mainly for the better."

But the prime quality of "science" is not in its applications but in its basic method of approaching problems—a way of thought and a set of procedures for interpreting experience. We need only mention the long history of the "warfare of science and theology" in order to suggest the conflicts of belief and value that have accompanied the rise of science. However, it may be well to remember that the antievolution trials occurred only a few years ago, and that popular attitudes toward science still contain strong ambivalences. The caricature of the "diabolical scientist" co-exists with the stereotype of the benevolent laboratory magician. Faith in science is a faith; its continued existence is dependent upon other convictions, and these other convictions are interdependent with the real social structure. Science is a particular manifestation of the rational-theoretic theme, which Northrop among others regards as a distinguishing feature of our entire culture.[81] It is this ordering and stabilizing component that links science to the broader tendency in our culture to translate experience into systematic abstract concepts—to transform the fleeting, confused flow of immediate experience into standardized categories that permit, and in part create, prediction and control. Thus, science, socially considered, is above all a *discipline,* as Max Weber has so eloquently shown.[82] Our main interest here is accordingly to ask: a discipline for what?

Very broadly, emphasis upon science in America has reflected the values of the rationalistic-individualistic tradition. Science is disciplined, rational, functional, active; it requires systematic diligence and honesty; it is congruent with the "means" emphasis of the culture—the focus of interest upon pragmatism and efficiency and the tendency to minimize absolutes and ultimates. The applications of science profusely reward the strivings for self-externalizing mastery of the environment. We think it fair to say that science is at root fully compatible with a culture orientation that attempts to deny frustration and refuses to accept the idea of a fundamentally unreasonable and capricious world.

In recent years, certain social scientists have held that science is "morally neutral." If they mean merely that science cannot allow its findings to be distorted by value presuppositions extraneous to its accepted methods and models of proof, then these statements are acceptable. But it must be quite obvious that the findings of science will often have important value implications. It must be clear that the problems chosen for study are, or may be, selected in part on the basis of nonscientific values. Finally, the existence of basic theoretic science and the free exercise of scientific method presuppose a definite social structure and system of values.[83] Honesty and clarity are not just luxury virtues in science; on the contrary, they are essential defining charac-

---

[81]F. S. C. Northrop, *The Meeting of East and West* (New York, 1946).

[82]Especially in his *"Wissenschaft als Beruf,"* in H. H. Gerth and C. Wright Mills (trans. and eds.), *From Max Weber: Essays in Sociology* (New York, 1946).

[83]There are societies in which it has been held that biological theories must conform to political doctrines.

teristics.[84] The same can be said for the faith in the order of nature and the faith in human reason—these are elements of a definite credo, manifesting values that are widely assaulted in the contemporary world. Their preservation in America apparently depends upon the continued and adequate functioning of an orderly, pluralistic society.

Nationalism-Patriotism

In every society we find men participating in certain groups to which they feel they owe loyalty and with which they identify themselves—and we find other groups identified as outgroups toward which the individual feels estrangement, sense of difference, or enmity. This distinction, in small, localistic nonliterate societies, is often so sharp that others are not considered "men." Analogous situations exist in the so-called complex civilizations, perhaps most strikingly in the denial of a common humanity to the enemy in time of war. Such intergroup cleavages involve that scaling of values called ethnocentrism, that is, the diffuse value-attitude making one's own group the point of reference for judging all others. All known societies are to some extent ethnocentric; individuals everywhere tend to give a preferential value to their own culture. Strictly speaking, ethnocentrism applies to every distinctive group from the smallest clique to the largest civilization. Today, however, the sentiments attached to the nation-state have overwhelming importance, and nationalistic feelings seem the prime example of ethnocentric values. For this reason, it is particularly important to examine the place of nationalistic or patriotic evaluations in the social systems of America. As in the case of conformity, nationalism is not a single, clear value-orientation, used in making judgments of desirability, but rather a complex set of evaluations and beliefs. We are dealing here with a diffuse and extremely complex phenomenon, and can do no more than to suggest a few very elementary points.

First, we distinguish between two polar types of nationalistic values that are inextricably mingled in concrete situations. The first type may be described as undifferentiated or totalistic nationalism, demanding total and unquestioning allegiance to national symbols and slogans and tending to make "Americanism" a rigid orthodoxy. Criticisms of any features of American life are close to treason, and "un-American" is the epithet for any deviation from a rigid, although vaguely defined, cult of conformity. The quasi-religious character of this complex is manifest in its creedal emphasis, its concern with ritual and symbolism, its elaboration of dogma and its correlative "inquisitions." The contrasting ideal type of national-patriotic orientation tends to place less emphasis upon undifferentiated loyalty, rather conceiving of patriotism as loyalty to national institutions and symbols because and in so far as they *represent*

[84]A valuable analysis of the institutionalization of values in relation to the control of deviant behavior in scientific work is given in Robert K. Merton, "Priorites in Scientific Discovery: A Chapter in the Sociology of Science," *American Sociological Review,* Vol. 22, No. 6 (December 1957), pp. 635–59.

values that are the primary objects of allegiance. Thus, "America" may be felt as worthy of loyalty because it is considered to embody or to stand for political democracy, respect for individual personality, a high standard of living, freedom of worship, or any other important value. This pluralistic patriotism usually presupposes basic acceptance of the nation-state as a framework of allegiance, but it does not preclude critical appraisal of men, events or policies in value terms broader than those of in-group loyalty as such.

The possible tension between these contrasting orientations[85] is compactly summarized by the fact that a legislative group concerned with "un-American" activities can itself be condemned as un-American.

Nationalism in the modern sense is, of course, a relatively recent development in Western history. In the case of American nationalism, it is clear that the early colonists for a long time thought of themselves as Englishmen (or Germans, Swiss, etc.) rather than "Americans." Even after the establishment of the new nation it was not uncommon to find that "my country" might as well mean Dinwiddie county, Virginia, or the state of Vermont, as the nation taken as a whole.[86] It took the Civil War and a whole series of subsequent developments[87] to really displace provincial patriotism in favor of national feeling.

An important component of American nationalistic values is that a generalized sense of fulfilment and confident hope has been built into the culture for over two centuries, and even the shocks of recent depressions, wars, and other deep crises have not dissipated the widespread satisfaction of a people who feel that the country "has been good to them." Indeed, in some respects the Second World War and its aftermath seem to have reinforced the attitude by producing a vivid sense of social and economic conditions in other areas of the world. Bearing on this point, roughly comparable public opinion polls in a number of countries indicate that only in Australia (itself also a "colonial" nation) did so small a proportion of the people as in the United States in the immediate post-war years express any desire to live in another nation.[88]

This sense of satisfaction incorporates supposedly *universal* values. A purely

---

[85]Cf. Max Savelle, *Seeds of Liberty,* p. 568: "The split in nationalistic pride between those who glorify the melting-pot and those who fear the un-American activities of foreigners whose ideals do not exactly coincide with their own is no new thing: it has apparently been one of the dialectical strains within American nationalistic feeling almost from the beginning."

[86]Merle Curti, *The Roots of American Loyalty* (New York, 1946), Chap. I. Even in the Second World War, an appreciative chord was struck by the Secretary of the Navy when he told a Texas gathering that he had been assured that Texas would not make a separate peace.

[87]For example, modern methods of communication and transportation which break down the barriers between local communities. It may be added that the modern cult of nationalism has emerged concurrently with the dramatic weakening of family and other *gemeinschaftliche* structures, and there are apparently definite functional connections between these two developments.

[88]Surveys by International Gallup Polls, reported in *Opinion News* (June 15, 1948), National Opinion Research Center, University of Chicago.

tribal patriotism conceives of its cultures as having a unique destiny and does not think of extending its values to the rest of mankind. But American nationalism, like the religions that have contributed so heavily to the culture, involves the idea that the American way of life is so morally superior that it should be widely adopted elsewhere.[89] This secular counterpart of the missionary spirit is both an index of the strength of nationalistic feeling and a potent source of misunderstanding and resentment in international affairs. In peace as well as in war, the United States must appear to itself to have a mission as a crusader for righteousness.[90] Other peoples have not always regarded the matter in that light.

The universalistic elements in national feeling, however, have conflicted with certain kinds of expansionism, on the one hand, and tendencies toward isolationism and national autarchy on the other. American expansionism in its earliest phases was undertaken by the pioneer, the speculator, the trader, and the missionary, and aimed at the possession of the land, chiefly through purchase, rather than at the conquest and the rule of alien peoples. It was only toward the close of the nineteenth century when the economic exploration of our own backwoods was nearing completion that chauvinism of an expansionist turn became widespread.[91]

On the other hand, autarchic nationalism goes back to the very beginnings of the Republic. A sense of alienation from Europe, a "belief in the degradation of the Old World and the mounting fame of America . . ." (Curti), was common even before the Revolution. The entire socioeconomic situation of early America encouraged turning attention away from Europe and the past and toward the mastery of the new continent. Thanks in large part to geographic position—and the British Navy—nineteenth-century United States could with impunity make a slogan of the doctrine of no entangling alliances. The isolationism that began as a matter of necessity and historic accident became a positive virtue throughout a good part of the nineteenth century. Although the old-style isolationism has been rendered objectively impossible by the Second World War and its aftermath, some of the values it symbolized remain active in the current scene.

Perhaps the most important sociological generalization that can be invoked here is that intense nationalistic conflict will always have drastic consequences upon the value systems of a democratic society. In particular, it inevitably brings in its train a large military establishment—and a centralization of social power. The modern state in time of war must by its own terms of existence

---

[89]Concerning the very tangible influence of a moralistic orientation, with its attendant "sense of mission," upon America's role in world affairs, see Chap. 14 of Henry B. Parkes, *The American Experience.*

[90]This is abundantly documented in many studies. See for example Curti, *The Roots of American Loyalty,* pp. 48 ff.

[91]James Truslow Adams, *The American,* pp. 304 ff. and 346 ff.; Miriam Beard, *A Short History of the Businessman,* Chaps. 24 and 25; Curti, *The Roots of American Loyalty,* p. 6.

have centralized control of production; it must regulate consumption—there is actually no more infallible prescription for the destruction of laissez faire, the free market, and the individual entrepreneur.

Democracy

Like freedom or progress, democracy in American culture is a highly complex and derivative theme. The nation that fought a great war under the slogan of making the world safe for democracy lives under a Constitution that contains no direct reference to democracy; the democracy of the Founding Fathers is not that of twentieth-century industrial society; the meaning of democracy is one thing to the American Negro and another to the Ku Klux Klan. Here again the cultural meanings of a value theme and its actual role in social structure are full of complex variations, conflicts, and shadings through time and from one part of the society to another at a given time. Furthermore, the content of democracy is in considerable part subsumed under other value complexes discussed eleswhere in this chapter: for example, freedom, equality, humanitarianism; and, in any case, a reference to democracy does not denote a clear, unitary value but a multiple nexus of more specific beliefs and primary values.[92] Nevertheless, no matter how elaborately qualified, the sheer prevalence of culturally sanctioned attention to something called democracy[93] forces us to include it in our listing of major value-themes.

Along with majority rule, representative institutions, and the rejection of the monarchial and aristocratic principles under which the society began, early American democracy stressed the reservation of certain "inalienable rights" as unalterable by majority rule.[94] Basically this sort of democracy rested upon the implicit belief in natural law as opposed to personal rule, and in the moral autonomy of the individual. The actual shape of the democratic credo was a synthesis of clashing ideologies; but it was the insistence of the average citizen upon equality of political rights that actually forced the Bill of Rights into the Constitution. Major themes in the gradual crystallization of the main democratic creed thus included equality of certain formal rights and formal equality of opportunity, a faith in the rule of impersonal law, optimistic rationalism, and ethical individualism. What the Kluckhohns have called the cult of the common man[95] was a major expression of the democratic ethos that developed out of these definitions of man and society. As already suggested in the dis-

[92]Cf. Carl Becker's comment that democracy is a word "which has no 'referent'—there is no precise or palpable thing or object which we all think of when the word is pronounced." *Modern Democracy* (New Haven, Conn., 1941), p. 4.

[93]It is sufficient to note that Coleman ("What Is American?", p. 498) found that democracy is one of the few "national traits" mentioned by observers in all major historical periods.

[94]James Truslow Adams, *The American,* p. 258.

[95]Clyde Kluckhohn and Florence R. Kluckhohn, "American Culture: Generalized Orientations and Class Patterns," in Bryson, Finkelstein, and MacIver (eds.), *Conflicts of Power in Modern Culture,* pp. 106–28.

cussion of freedom, the theme of democracy was, concretely, an agreement upon *procedure* in distributing power and in settling conflicts. Liberal democracy, American model, arose in reaction to an epoch in which the great threats to security and freedom were seen in strong, autocratic central government. The new system was devised in such a way as to limit and check centralized governmental power and to establish an ordered pattern for agreeing to disagree. Such a pluralistic view of social power was clear and explicit on questions of procedure while it left the common ends of the society largely undefined.

In a culture which strongly emphasizes universalistic rules and an active, instrumental approach to life, the stress upon individual achievement, especially in business occupations, tends to direct attention and energy away from collective goals, as well as away from expressive and contemplative concerns. Although these emphases may be changing, they are still strong enough to lend a distinctive quality to this innovative, flexible, open-ended system.

As can be seen, the theme of democracy has converged with those of equality and freedom, and all three have been interpreted and reinterpreted along with the moralistic optimism of the doctrines of progress. Our previous surveys have shown some of the complicated deviations and conflicts within these orientations; the present section is briefly handled because of the overlapping of democracy with other themes. The cumulative review of major value-orientations seems more and more clearly to point to one central constellation that gives coherence to a wide range of others, including democracy. This nuclear or focal theme we shall call the value of individual personality. In one aspect, its relation to democracy has been given a classic statement by Carl Becker:

> Its [modern liberal democracy's] fundamental assumption is the worth and dignity and creative capacity of the individual, so that the chief aim of government is the maximum of individual self-direction, the chief means to that end the minimum of compulsion by the state. Ideally considered means and ends are conjoined in the concept of freedom: freedom of thought, so that the truth may prevail; freedom of occupation, so that careers may be open to talent; freedom of self-government, so that no one may be compelled against his will.[96]

Thus, insofar as majority rule and conditional and limited authority based upon uncoerced consensus are highly evaluated in the culture, the main American concepts of democracy are consistent with a particular set of value postulates concerning the nature and significance of the individual in society.

Individual Personality

Writing in 1897, Émile Durkheim incisively described a pattern of value in Western civilization that he called the cult of individual personality.[97] Basically this cult sets a high value on the development of individual personality and is

[96] Carl Becker, *Modern Democracy* (New Haven, Conn., Yale University Press, 1941), p. 27.

[97] *Le suicide* (Paris, 1897; new ed., 1930), Book III, Chap. I.

correspondingly averse to invasion of individual integrity; to be a person is to be independent, responsible, and self-respecting, and thereby to be worthy of concern and respect in one's own right. To be a person, in this sense, is to be an autonomous and responsible agent, not merely a reflection of external pressures, and to have an internal center of gravity, a set of standards and a conviction of personal worth. Above all, the individual is not considered to be released from all sociocultural controls. As Parsons has put it: "This is not a matter simply of freeing the individual from ethical restraints imposed by society, it is a matter of the imposition of a different *kind* of restraint. Individuality is a product of a certain social state. . . ."[98] Not the unrestrained biologic human being, but the ethical, decision-making, unitary social personality is the object of this cult of the individual. What is positively valued in the tradition now under examination, in other words, is not just any kind of personality whatsoever, but rather a certain kind of individual.

The personality that is the object of high value in this particular tradition is something of intrinsic worth, not valued simply as a member of a group nor as a means to some ulterior end. This orientation to the person, it must be repeated, is the product of a definite social situation. There is no real paradox in saying that individuality can be a social product and a common social value; the development of individual personality is a *shared value* rather than a *collective end* in a group or social system. The emergence and maintenance of this state, however, is intimately related to other aspects of the society. To maintain a high evaluation of individual personality in this peculiar sense is surely a difficult and precarious feat, for there are factors inherent in society that continually threaten the value. The crucial fact in this connection is that other persons are always potential tools or threats in relation to the attainment of any one individual's separate interests; control over others is always a potentially efficient means to securing one's individual desires. There is always some measure of this centrifugal bombardment of interest that creates pressures toward "using" other people in an essentially amoral utilitarian fashion. Under certain social conditions, the integrity of the individual *qua* personality, thus, may largely disappear. Slaves in the ancient world were not persons in the modern meaning. The fate of the laboring population during certain phases of the Industrial Revolution further illustrates how strong interests sometimes break through protective values centering around the person. A high valuation of the individual in the present sense is difficult to maintain under conditions of great social stress, crisis, and privation—in war, famine, natural disaster, revolution, plague, and the like. In general, whenever great urgency is felt for the accomplishment of a collective task, requiring co-ordination, speed, and great differentials of sacrifice, there is a tendency to regard individuals as tools rather than values in themselves. Militaristic societies often tend to exalt the collectivity over the indi-

[98]Parsons, *The Structure of Social Action*, pp. 333–34.

vidual, and for functionally understandable reasons.[99] Similarly, an overwhelming stress upon profit making in organized economic enterprises quite obviously would tend toward an impatience with individual scruples, needs, and peculiarities and toward a calculating, impersonal use of others solely as a means toward the dominant end. In our own society the pressures and ambivalences involved in the valuation of individual personality are highlighted by the specific case of respect for freedom of conscience in religious matters.

We have said that the value of individual personality has been important in the received tradition of America, but that it is subject to very powerful contravening influences. What evidences are there as to its actual place in the total culture? In the first place, we note a large number of important legal provisions that appear to have as *part* of their function the protection of personal freedom or the physical or social integrity of the person; to mention a few—illegality of slavery and peonage (note that a person cannot even voluntarily sell himself as a slave); illegality of imprisonment for debt, and provision for bankruptcy proceedings (in this context, also, a limitation on economic rights in the interests of personal freedom); prohibitions against personal defamation (libel and slander); prohibition of "improper search and seizure"; prohibition of "cruel and unusual punishment"; right of *habeas corpus,* and so on. Perhaps the most striking instance of the lengths to which the law has gone in the attempt to preserve the person from attack is found in the definition of suicide as a crime. The free individual in our society is not free to take his own life because of the axiomatic value which he is not presumed to have the right to destroy.[100] A number of facts, already cited in preceding pages also may be taken as evidence of the value attached to the integer-personality. So, for example, the presumed universal and impersonal system of legal justice not only reflects equality and democracy but also, at what is probably a still more basic level, the concept of an universal worth, a claim for consideration, simply because one is an individual. "Status-justice," graded according to external criteria of rank, birth, and so on, is in principle radically incompatible with this orientation. Similarly, humanitarian practices may be interpreted as partly expressive of concern for personality as a value—whatever *other* values and specific interests may be involved.[101] Still another, and crucially important, datum is found in the religious tradition of Western

[99]Cf. Hiller, *Social Relations and Structures,* p. 321.

[100]The contrast with the traditional Japanese *hara kari* or Hindu *sutee* is striking evidence of the basic nature of the value-belief complex we are examining.

[101]Again the general principle is illustrated that any concrete social behavior typically is multivalued; the referents of value can be disentangled only through painstaking analysis. Although the necessary research largely still remains to be done, sufficiently precise and comprehensive studies would probably show trace lines of this value in exceedingly diverse manifestations. To what extent is the practice of tipping resisted because of "degrading" implications? Is there repugnance to cremation of the dead because it is felt to be a symbolic dissolution of the concept of the individual? Is the value of individual personality an important factor in resistance to sterilization legislation—or to legalization of euthanasia?

society, where the value of individual personality has stood in close relation to the religious doctrine of the soil—that every human being has an immortal soul and is by the same token invested with the value imputed to the soul.

The reality of the value of individualism in our culture is observed not only in derivative forms such as manifest ideology, law, and formalized behavior patterns but also at the level of implicit assumptions and unconscious practices. For example; it is typical of the culture that the question as to whether there is actually such an entity as "the individual," "self," or "ego" is usually not even thought of, and, if raised, is greeted with surprise or shock. *Of course* individuals exist, of course they have separate individual needs and rights. As Dorothy Lee says:

> The value of individualism is axiomatically assumed. . . . A newborn infant must become individuated, must be taught physical and emotional self-dependence; we assume, in fact, that he has a separate identity which he must be helped to recognize. . . . The need for privacy is an imperative one in our society, recognized by official bodies such as state welfare groups and the Department of Labor. And it is part of a system which stems from and expresses our basic values.[102]

A society that draws up a Declaration of Rights for Children, that is revolted by a self-immolation of the individual for the group, that perceives groups as aggregates of co-operating but separate individuals—such a society incorporates the value of the individual at the deepest levels of its unconscious presuppositions. As a matter of fact the sociologically alert student is likely to guess at once that so pervasive a theme is maintained by quite special modes of child training and basic socialization; the hypothesis would be that this value complex is embedded in the central affective-cognitive structure of the representative personalities of the culture.

Racism and Related Group-superiority Themes

The commitment of large segments of American society to doctrines stressing the value and dignity of the individual has been real, deep, and widespread. The same can be said of the principles of equality, of humanitarian values, of political freedoms—and so on through the list of "publicly dominant" value patterns already listed. Once full weight has been given to all these "rational-humane" values in the received traditions of the society, it must be recognized at the same time that the values of the Creed have continually struggled against pervasive and powerful countercurrents of valuation. One of the chief conflicts, and in many ways the most important conflict, has

[102]Dorothy Lee: "Are Basic Needs Ultimate?" *Journal of Abnormal and Social Psychology,* Vol. XLIII, No. 3 (July 1948), pp. 393–94. But compare the following: "The right of privacy is among the most important of all rights, as it is the most neglected and the most attacked in our time." (Thomas I. Cook, "Individual Liberty Today: Challenge and Prospect," in Morroe Berger, Theodore Abel, Charles H. Page (eds.), *Freedom and Control in Modern Society* (New York, 1954), p. 190.

centered around those diverse patterns which have as their common element *the ascription of value and privilege to individuals on the basis of race or particularistic group membership* according to birth in a particular ethnic group, social class, or related social category.

Racialistic doctrines were first given widespread currency and intellectual elaboration in the slavery controversy during the decades immediately prior to the Civil War. The value anomalies into which the proslavery position led,[103] in a culture so strongly stressing an individualistic religion and a democratic political system gradually produced an explicit system of thought which relied upon assumptions of biological superiority to buttress the existing system of power and privilege.[104]

Space forbids anything like full documentation of the pervasiveness of organic, or more narrowly racist, orientations in our society. Adequate evidence is to be found in works already cited. It is enough to say that categorical discriminations are widespread in established practice, and are often crystallized into whole systems of legislation. It is not necessary here to explore the fears, vested interests, and multiple sociopsychological sources of the superiority-exclusiveness theme indexed by these legal acts. We must agree with Opler,[105] however, that these facts—only a tiny sample of other similar manifestations—reflect a view of society that in its extreme forms implicitly rejects "freedom" and individual ethical responsibility, certain conceptions of progress, and rational mastery of culture. Thus, the organic-racist view of man—insofar as its logical implications are actually worked out in human relations—stands in sharp opposition to most of the value orientations already reviewed. If a society begins with the premise that the human nature of individuals is biologically fixed and that different physical types or "races" are innately superior or inferior, then the unlimited development of this theme will make meaningless, or positively evil, the values of equality, democracy, freedom, rationality, progress (in the sense of human improvement through learning), humanitarianism, individual achievement linked with moral autonomy, and the central values of personality. The ultimate logical outgrowth of complete organicism is an exclusionistic society, rigidly organized in a static hierarchy.

It becomes apparent that a very important part of the conflict of value systems in the United States can be economically summarized in terms of tension between *values centering around the concept of the responsible individual personality versus values organized around categorical organic conceptions.*

Without doubt, group discrimination and racism are deviant themes, con-

[103] Wilbert E. Moore and Robin M. Williams, Jr., "Stratification in the Ante-Bellum South," *American Sociological Review,* Vol. VII, No. 3 (June 1942), pp. 343–51.

[104] "The race dogma is nearly the only way out for a people so moralistically equalitarian, if it is not prepared to live up to its faith." Myrdal, *et al., An American Dilemma,* Vol. I, p. 89.

[105] Morris E. Opler, "Cultural and Organic Conceptions in Contemporary World History," *American Anthropologist,* Vol. XLVI, No. 4 (October–December 1944), pp. 448–49.

trary to the main thrust of American society. But the sharp conflicts and agonizing dilemmas they occasion require us to make explicit the bases of the ideological conflict.

CONCLUSION

This rather lengthy and schematic review has not done justice to any one theme, but perhaps it has at least placed before us a range of important value-positions current in our society, and hinted at their complex interrelations. It must be always kept in mind that these themes, values, and systems of belief *do not operate as single and separate units* but *are in continually shifting and recombining configurations* marked by very complex interpenetration, conflct, and reformation. Furthermore, our descriptive scheme that necessitated separate isolation and labeling of themes must not be allowed to leave the impression—to repeat an earlier caution—that values are disembodied elements which somehow function apart from concrete social relations and personalities. Although values *are* abstractions, everything described in this chapter must be capable of observation, in some sense, in the behavior of real personalities and in actual social structures, or else we have mistaken fancy for fact.

Perhaps the total picture may be clarified by a summary classification. In the first place, there are the quasi-values or *gratifications,* taken at a hedonic or physiological level, implicit in the entire analysis, and especially important in the section on "material comfort." Second, we may identify the *instrumental interests* or means-values, for example, wealth, power, work, efficiency. Although these interests may become values in themselves, it is convenient to consider them primarily as instrumental to the achievement of other values. Third, we have the *formal-universalistic values of Western tradition:* rationalism, impersonal justice and universalistic ethics, achievement, democracy, equality, freedom, certain religious values, value of individual personality. Fourth, there is a class of *particularistic, segmental, or localistic evaluations* that are best exemplified in racist-ethnic superiority doctrines and in certain aspects of nationalism.

Running through these patterns of interests and values are certain still more general "dimensions" or "orientations" that are not typically explicit but must be identified by highly abstract inference. Because of this abstract quality, the inadequacy of the data, and the removal from observed phenomena by several stages of inference, the statement of such basic dimensions is a difficult undertaking and the following propositions must be taken as suggestive rather than definitive.[106]

1. American culture is organized around the attempt at *active mastery* rather than *passive acceptance*. Into this dimension falls the low tolerance of

[106]In the nature of the case, anyone—including the author—can think of numerous exceptions to each of these generalized formulations, as well as widespread *alternative* themes.

frustration; the refusal to accept ascetic renunciation; the positive encouragement of desire; the stress on power; the approval of ego-assertion, and so on.

2. It tends to be interested in the *external world* of things and events, of the palpable and immediate, rather than in the inner experience of meaning and affect. Its genius is manipulative rather than contemplative.

3. Its world-view tends to be *open* rather than closed: it emphasizes change, flux, movement; its central personality types are adaptive, accessible, outgoing and assimilative.

4. In wide historical and comparative perspective, the culture places its primary faith in *rationalism* as opposed to *traditionalism;* it de-emphasizes the past, orients strongly to the future, does not accept things just because they have been done before.

5. Closely related to the above, is the dimension of *orderliness* rather than unsystematic *ad hoc* acceptance of transitory experience. (This emphasis is most marked in the urban middle classes.)

6. With conspicuous deviations, a main theme is a *universalistic* rather than a *particularistic* ethic.

7. In interpersonal relations, the weight of the value system is on the side of *"horizontal"* rather than "vertical" emphases: peer-relations, not superordinate-subordinate relations; equality rather than hierarchy.

8. Subject to increased strains and modifications, the received culture emphasizes *individual personality* rather than group identity and responsibility.

In broadest outline, then, American society is characterized by a basic moral orientation, involving emphases on active, instrumental mastery of the world in accordance with universalistic standards of performance. It is a pluralistic system in which it is not easy to secure unitary commitment to collective goals. It permits a wide range of goals for achievement.

JOHN GILLIN

National and Regional Values

The following partial list of values is offered as being dominant in United States culture as a whole. Space is lacking for documentation or discussion of numerous corollaries and variations.

1. Personal output of energy is regarded as a good thing in its own right, whether in earning a living, in recreation, or in other endeavors. It does not necessarily mean "manual labor," but does imply "keeping busy" and "hard work." Personal effort is necessary to the solution of all problems. "Laziness" is bad.

2. Pragmatic ingenuity is valued and is expected to be applied not only to materialistic problems, but to all problems, including social and personal maladjustment. Conversely, low rating is given to the passive contemplation of "unsolved mysteries" for sheer aesthetic or other "impractical" reasons. It should be noted that *thrift* is a value probably to be included under this heading.

3. Mechanistic world view: the universe and any discrete aspect of it are wholes consisting of parts that work together, well or badly, as the case may be, and this image is of course, valued as the correct one. Through pragmatic ingenuity and energy man may discover and manipulate these mechanical relations. (a) Practically all features of life experience are seen in the image of material things, which are regarded either as parts or as mechanically interrelated mechanisms; this concept includes time as a thing, also "personality," "group relations," etc. (b) Precise measurement is highly valued, not only for material objects, but also for time, "intelligence" of the individual, interpersonal interactions, etc. The idea is that in a mechanistic scheme the component parts must "fit" and therefore must be of exactly the correct size. "Adjustment" in this sense means essentially the same thing. Great value is placed upon money, not only as an economic instrument, but also because of its usefulness in "measuring" many intangibles, such as social status, in-

---

Reproduced by permission of The University of North Carolina Press from John Gillin, "National and Regional Cultural Values in the United States," *Social Forces,* XXXIV (December, 1955), pp. 107–13.

fluence, etc. (c) Cleanliness and orderliness may also be seen as subsidiary values of a mechanistic world view. Machines do not work well if dirty and if the parts are out of place; neither do individuals or social groups. (d) Science is appreciated so long as it is applied in such a way as to "make things work better." Pure science or curiosity for its own sake is each regarded as dubious in the general culture.

4. Mobility of the person, whether with respect to physical or social position, rates high. One is reminded of the mechanical interchangeability of adjustment of parts, because whether one moves to a strange locality or to a higher social stratum great emphasis is put upon "fitting into" the new situation, unless one goes outside the boundaries of the nation.

5. Change and novelty are values in themselves within a restricted area of the culture, such as styles of consumer goods, amusements, and vacations. Such things are supposed to give the average American a "thrill," i.e., relief from the ennui of routine. Changes in basic social institutions or in the general value system, however, are usually viewed as "radical" when first proposed.

6. Optimism, as contrasted with fatalism or melancholy, is valued. Any problem can be solved if suitable energy and ingenuity are applied to it. Furthermore, God, insofar as he represents a general cultural formulation, will help, because he approves of these methods. When God is looking the other way, about the only thing that can block success is bad luck. But if one keeps at the job and uses his head, the "breaks are bound to come his way."

7. Individualism, always highly praised, has some aspects more or less peculiar to the American system. Among them are the following. (a) Ideally each person should have an equal opportunity economically, socially, and politically at the start of his adult life. Officially this is supposed to be guaranteed by the refusal to recognize hereditary economic and social classes, by universal free education, by universal adult suffrage, and the right to hold public office open to all native-born citizens. These rights are supposed to be upheld regardless of race, creed, or color. Given such equal opportunity the individual's success in winning the rewards provided by the culture depends upon his following or applying the appropriate values of the system, especially energy and ingenuity. (b) Freedom or liberty for the individual is prized and is formally guaranteed by such legal formulations as the Bill of Rights. Liberty is regarded as freedom from unnecessary frustrations and interferences, many of which are explicitly spelled out. What freedom is *for,* on the other hand, is much less clear. Officially, it is described as "the pursuit of happiness," but the system of values contains neither a general nor a specific definition of "happiness" as a state of affairs. (c) Self-reliance and initiative are expected of individuals; Americans are supposed to be "self-starting." Courage in the face of obstacles is also involved, and the individual is borne up by adherence to the general value of optimism. (d) Status achieved "through one's own efforts" is valued. Although high status carries with it many perquisites, it does not, according to the pattern, confer the right to treat persons of lower

status openly as "inferiors," implying that their less fortunate position is due to failure to apply the values of the system. Other persons may make such comparisons, but not the occupant of high status. (e) Achievement requires a certain competitiveness in the individual, and competitiveness is also a general value of the culture, expected not only of individuals but also of groups.

The individualistic values are tempered by the worth placed on (f) generosity and (g) social conformity. The ideal individual is generous and takes an interest in other members of his group or society, in the weak, the unfortunate, the underdogs. In modern America, acting, at least, in conformity with this value wins more rewards than crass "selfishness." Outward conformity to the opinions of others has a certain value in relation to the individual. Although some observers hold that conformity in thoughts and "feelings" is also a part of the value system, this writer postulates that it is not—yet. (h) However, individuals are expected to have consciences; that is, the values of the cultural system are supposed to be internalized in persons and the internal punishment of guilt sanctions deviations from them. In common parlance an individual with a well developed conscience or super-ego who acts in accordance is a man or woman of "character."

8. Competitiveness has already been mentioned in connection with individualism. Most observers, as well as native defenders, of the system hold that it is a general value permeating almost all parts of the culture. It is institutionalized among business organizations, but also appears among religious sects, certain social classes, groups of scholars, and so on. Conversely anything which tends to stifle competition, such as economic monopoly or inherited perquisites, is regarded unfavorably.

9. In the American system competitiveness is tempered by the value of "fair play," probably borrowed from British culture.

10. Cooperation in the common welfare is another value that mitigates competitiveness. It is manifested by a great variety of voluntaristic groups and organizations, all of which are oriented at least toward the common welfare of their members and often toward that of the whole society. Voluntary charitable contributions in which all are expected to participate, controlled neither by church nor state, are characteristic of the society.

11. Honesty or frankness in human relations has high value ideally, while dissimulation is "bad."

12. Prestige as manifested in respect or deference given by others is highly valued. No space is available to discuss the numerous forms of prestige, but it should be remarked that, contrary to some superficial observations, it is not exclusively a matter of high social position or large financial resources. It is held in the system that prestige and respect *can* be achieved by any member of the society, and that, strictly speaking, all prestige *must* be achieved or "earned."

13. Power or the ability, by some means or other, (a) to influence or control other persons or groups is an American value. In the system, however,

power exerted over other persons through force is given a low rating. The ideally "best" type of power is that achieved and maintained by "moral" suasion and influence. (b) Power over material things, including other animals, and over the forces of nature, is a basic value and is sought without limit.

14. Recreation is a "right" for Americans, but from the ideal point of view, is defined somewhat literally. This is to say that, although recreation is doing something one is not required to do (in distinction to "work"), whatever is done should recreate one, it should "be good for you." Thus recreation is to be distinguished from mere pleasure; only certain pleasures are also recreational. Activities that run counter to the major values are bad, regardless of how pleasurable they may be. Needless to say numerous members of the society do not behave entirely consistently with this value pair.

15. Efficiency is another ideal value sometimes, of course, not followed. In line with the mechanistic world view it is held that all things should operate to the full extent of their inherent capacities and at the lowest cost in whatever terms. This applies not only to machines, but also to social organizations and personalities. One of the virtues of pragmatic ingenuity is that by its application the efficiency of anything can be increased. With respect to the population as a whole, as well as the individual organism, good health, both physical and mental, is valued, not only because it is pleasant but also because it is efficient.

16. Love is a state of interpersonal relations that practically all Americans cherish. It is generally regarded as a satisfying feeling state which may be enjoyed by the individual either actively or passively. The "best" kind of love, however, is reciprocal. Although one hears most about love of the romantic kind, nevertheless the non-sexual love of the family and friendship types is highly prized. Whether between the sexes, in the family or in friendship, love means essentially a sort of intimate relationship in which most thoughts or feelings of individual advantage are submerged in one's regard for the loved person or persons.

17. Inner-regulated morality is believed to be one of the virtues of the system. In the general culture it is thought that all individuals should have a "conscience" and should "feel guilty" when doing "wrong." In other words, the value system is supposed to be supported and maintained in conduct by an inner mechanism in each individual whose sanctions are internal rather than external. This is believed by many to be one of the bases of the American type of democracy. As American society has grown in size and complexity, doubts have arisen as to the effectiveness of this mechanism, supported by evidence of crime, delinquency, and other forms of "social disorganization." And there is, as Riesman has pointed out, some reason to question whether inner-regulated morality can still be regarded as a basic value of the system.

It will be noticed that no place is given in the above list to values of a "spiritual" or transcendental type. Foreign observers frequently ask: Is there nothing Americans value beyond these? What are the ultimate goals of existence? Does not life and the universe have some "higher" meaning? And so on. With the decline in this century of general acceptance in America of the traditional theological answers to such questions, the average person as well as those who speak for the nation find it difficult to provide positive formulations that have meaning to others not reared in the United States value system. This writer believes that convincing evidence can be produced that, buried in the American culture, certain values of a spiritual and transcendental nature do exist, of which few Americans are consciously aware and which, therefore, they are unable to make explicit. This is not the place to attempt a demonstration and formulation. It does seem to be true that the culture has so developed during the past fifty years as to set up defenses, one might say, against overt consideration of the "soul," "the absolute," and the like. Not the least of such defenses is American humor, which in addition to serving as a social sanction and tension-reducer, also acts as a deflector of serious attempts to discuss submerged values that have become unfashionable.

Since any culture is in part a set of customary adaptations to natural environment and resources, it is to be expected in a territory of the size and geographical diversity of the continental United States that a considerable variation in adaptive and exploitative aspects of culture will occur. Despite the efficiency of transportation and communication which has made the United States the most culturally homogeneous nation of its size in history, there is every reason to expect some continued diversity in the cultural aspects of materialistic adaptation and exploitation of natural resources. These diversities will not be listed here, nor can we discuss the values attached to them. Whether such factors, together with variety in historical backgrounds, will continue to have a controlling effect on basic regional value systems is a matter for further investigation.

Here I shall venture to set down only a tentative check list of regional cultural values that may serve to stimulate further research. Perhaps it is necessary to emphasize that no judgment of relative worth of the various regional values is made or implied. Where nothing is said about a certain value of the national culture it will be assumed that the regional culture conforms to the national standard.

1. NORTHEAST. (a) *Special emphases.* Hard work and thrift are still given special emphasis in rural subcultures. Hereditary status is more firmly established than in the country as a whole. Power over persons and groups, including those in other parts of the nation is emphasized, and is more explicitly justified, especially in cosmopolitan centers like Boston and New York. Change and novelty are played down in rural areas, rated high in New York metropolitan area. Very strong differences are shown between metropolitan and rural values in general. (b) *Special values.* Seaboard cities tend to be internationally "minded" and to blend European values into the system rather than rejecting them outright.

2. SOUTHEAST. (a) *Special emphases.* Protestant morality is especially strong. Non-commercial recreations of the "folk" type are well developed. Family relations are strong and include extended kin group. Status and power tend to be based on kinship connections more than in any other region with the exception of Back Bay Boston. Hard work is necessary for most, but little valued as a good in itself. Pragmatic ingenuity, and the corollaries of the mechanistic world view, especially cleanliness and orderliness, are rated lower than in the country as a whole. Mobility of the person is a necessary evil rather than a positive good. Change and optimism for their own sakes rate low. Freedom for the individual from outside (non-Southern) interference is highest of the individualistic values. General competitiveness is restrained by the power and kinship systems. (b) *Special values.* Doctrine of white supremacy and resulting race-castes. Idealization of women in the image of the "lady." Violence as a solution of interpersonal and intergroup problems. Regional cultural chauvinism resulting in attitude that the Southeast can solve its problems if outsiders will not interfere, that it is a special region with a culture uniquely fitted to it, and that "the rest of the country is against us."

3. MIDDLE STATES. This region is often described as the "most typical" of the United States. (a) *Special emphases.* Outward symbols of prestige and power are devalued and emphasis is placed on "democratic leveling." Much of Middle Western suspicion of "Easterners" and "foreigners" may be connected with the notion that money is supposed to be an instrument for work but not for the gaining of (financial) power. Optimism is strong, especially in the form of community "boosting." Conformity to community norms is rated high by various observers. Honesty and outspokenness are especially valued and the notion is often expressed that "Easterners are crooks," and "foreigners, frankly, are inferior." All the other national values are, in general, strongly held. (b) *Special values.* "Isolationism," if it may be called a value, is the feature of the Middle States most often cited. The basic notion seems to be that the United States is quite capable of "going it alone" without becoming entangled in international affairs.

4. SOUTHWEST. This region, lying along the border with Mexico was, of course, formerly a part of that country. It also contains a large area originally settled by the Mormons, as well as other areas (mostly in eastern Texas) settled from the Southeast. (a) *Special emphases.* Although the personal application of energy is highly regarded, manual labor, such as work in the fields, is denigrated for Americans and often considered to be the proper function of Mexicans and Negroes. Whether this is a heritage from Mexico or is connected with the fact that much of the region was originally exploited by cattle and sheep raising on the open range (a type of work that does not require "manual labor") remains to be determined. The original distinction between the horseman and the field worker has led to a degree of classification of the population, although the value of equality of opportunity is strongly held, at least for white "Americans." If we are to believe the publicity, the recent oil millionaires have

substituted the Cadillac for the horse as a symbol of status. Physical mobility, whether by horse or mechanical means, has always been highly valued. Optimism is high and perhaps "luck" and "taking a chance" are valued more than in the country as a whole. With respect to measurement, bigness seems to have a certain value in its own right, often said to be associated with a world view conditioned by "wide open spaces." (b) *Special values.* A certain romantic and nostalgic value is given to Spanish-Mexican culture, as evidenced to some extent in architecture, costume, Catholic fiestas, and popular music. Otherwise it is difficult to find much Mexican influence in the value system of the culture. Likewise a sentimental value is given to the image of the old days of the "open range," celebrated in roundups, rodeos, and "covered wagon days" of ceremonial significance. Of course, the cult of the "Old Southwest" has been spread nationally through the mass media of communication mainly for the consumption of moppets of the male sex.

5. NORTHWEST. (a) *Special emphases.* Although originally settled by a fairly homogeneous North European Protestant stock from the Southeast and New England, the region has lately received large increments of newcomers with Catholic European backgrounds. Frugality and hard work have been traditionally highly valued in this region, and optimism would probably be rated lower than the national level, partly because of the comparative harshness of nature. In fact, during ruinous periods of drouth in the Dakotas, for instance, it has seemed that the regional culture contained a certain fatalism. The former open range country culture shares some of the "horse culture" values of the Southwest.

6. FAR WEST. (a) *Special emphases.* Outstanding, perhaps, is optimism. This is the region of "progress unlimited." As someone has said, the Far West is the melting pot of elements from all over the United States, rather than from the Old World. Consequently family ties count for comparatively little, and the emphasis on social and physical mobility is strong. Conformity for the individual probably is lowest of any region, and is reflected in great freedom and informality in dress and interpersonal relations. Recreation in the form of "outdoor living" receives special emphasis and there is a more conscious attempt to blur the line between work and play than elsewhere. The Far West has a special focus on cooperation for the public welfare in the unusually high emphasis placed on development of water and other natural resources. As a whole Far Westerners are perhaps less bound by Puritan consciences than residents of other regions. There is high tolerance for eccentricity and flamboyant expressions of individualism. Change and novelty are valued in many ways for themselves. It is difficult to say that the Far West has developed special values, but, as indicated, its regional subculture has given a special "twist" to many of the universal American values.

CORA DU BOIS

The Dominant Value Profile of American Culture

This paper is an attempt to synthesize and systematize the relevant insights on American values advanced by a diverse group of writers from De Tocqueville through Myrdal to the authors of the polemic or conversational pieces that have been so numerous in the last decade. It will be addressed to the dominant value system of middle-class Americans. This system is rooted in the Protestant ethic and eighteenth-century rationalism. Many of its specific values are shared with other societies, but its configuration has come to be considered peculiarly American.

Since the allotted space is limited, what is said here must be condensed, schematic, and highly selective. There is no attempt to give a new definition of value or to adhere rigidly to existing ones. Distinctions between value and related concepts like themes, configurations, etc., will not be argued. Furthermore, the comments made here do not stem from scientific investigations. . . .

THE OPPOSITIONAL MODE

Oppositional propositions are a consistent aspect of Western European culture. They represent recurrent dilemmas in logic and ethics. They are reflected in, and fostered by, the structure of Indo-European languages. They have permeated sociological and psychological conceptualization. A wide range of oppositional propositions can be offered as illustrations: thesis–antithesis; good–evil; subject–predicate; folk–urban; aggression–submission; superordinate–subordinate; mind–body. Of these oppositional propositions some may be genuine in the sense that they are, logically speaking, contraries. But it seems probable that most oppositional propositions current in Western culture are preponderantly spurious in the sense that they are poorly conceived contradictories.

Reprinted by permission of Cora Du Bois and *American Anthropologist* from Cora Du Bois, "The Dominant Value Profile of American Culture," *American Anthropologist,* LVII (December, 1955), pp. 1232–39.

The assumption is made here that no system of values can encompass genuine contraries and therefore that the oppositional propositions in any value system are spurious. The further assumption is made that in any value system where such spurious oppositions exist there will be a strain for consistency.

The implication of these assumptions for the processes of value change are clear. Analytically, any attempt to present a value system should avoid the formulation of new and spurious oppositions. The avoidance of analytic oppositions may help to reveal those already extant in the existing value system, and the associated strains for consistency may emerge more clearly.

The strain for consistency in the American value system may be one of the forces accounting for changes in its configuration over the last three hundred years. Whether that strain is more intense in the American value system than in others it is impossible to estimate here. However, that the strain exists has been manifest in two major directions: (1) the prizing of change itself, usually expressed as effort, struggle, and progress, which will be discussed again in connection with the focal value called "effort-optimism"; and (2) compromise, which is not exclusively American but has received characteristic expression in the phrase "splitting the difference." This phrase reveals particularly an appreciation of the spurious quality of the oppositions, since it implies that neither oppositional term represents "truth" and that by retreating from false dichotomies a valid equilibrium may be achieved.

FOUR BASIC PREMISES

For our purposes the value premises of any culture can be considered to rest upon the assumptions made concerning man's cognitive view of the universe, man's relation to it, and man's relation to other men. For the American middle class it is postulated that: (1) the universe is mechanistically conceived, (2) man is its master, (3) men are equal, and (4) men are perfectible. From these four basic premises alone many of the focal and specific values, as well as the directives, of the American value system can be derived. In the context of the last three hundred years of American history these assumptions have proved valid both experientially and integratively (i.e., in a self-reinforcing sense) for the United States as a whole and, more specifically, for the American middle class. Despite changed situations and therefore the potential loss of experiential and integrative validation, we may nevertheless expect these assumptions to persist for a considerable period of time. There may be lags in a value system as there are in other aspects of culture.

FOCAL VALUES AND THEIR DIRECTIVES

[Ethel M.] Albert uses the term "focal" to designate a value about which numerous specific values cluster. Directives are used to designate the do's and dont's inherent in specific as well as in focal values.

The four premises given above yield at least three major focal values: material well-being that derives from the premise that man is master of a mechanistic universe; conformity that derives from the premise of man's equality; effort-optimism that derives from the premise of man's perfectibility. (The fortunate term "effort-optimism" was coined by the Kluckhohns.)

The nexus of specific values and directives clustering around each of these focal values can now be considered. Simultaneously the mutual reinforcement that occurs between the basic premises and their focal values, as well as the constant effort to resolve spurious oppositions through change, can be underlined. The inner consistency of the value system here presented accounts for much of the traditional vigor of "the American way of life" in the past. However, such vigor could not have existed without the reinforcement provided by the geographic setting of the American nation and the historic forces operative in the broader setting of Western European commercial, industrial, technical, and scientific growth in which the American nation shared.

1. Effort-Optimism

Work is a specific value in American society. It is not so much a necessary condition of existence as a positive good. It is a specific instrumental value through which man strives to reach not only the goal of his own perfectibility but also the goal of mastering a mechanistically conceived universe. But in values Vaihinger's "law of the preponderance of the means over the ends" is frequently operative. Thus work becomes a goal in itself and in the process may acquire the quality of activity for its own sake. Thus recreation, although theoretically the antithesis of work, nevertheless in its activism shows many of the aspects of work. "Fun" is something that most Americans work hard for and at, so that they must be warned at forty to give up tennis for golf, or hunting trips for painting. Touring, whether at home or abroad, acquires the quality of a marathon. And this in turn is closely associated with another specific value linked with the effort-optimism syndrome, the importance placed on education. However, as we shall see later, the educational effort acquires a particularly American cast when taken in conjunction with the other two focal values, material well-being and conformity. In sum, as many foreigners have observed, American life gives the impression of activism. The directives, as well as the virtues and vices, associated with this optimistic activism are numerous: "If at first you don't succeed, try, try again"; or, in the more contemporary idiom, "Let's get this show on the road." The optimistic quality that pervades the American mood is clearly conveyed by the "bigger ergo better" mentality; the "never say die"; the "up and at 'em."

Vigor, at least as motility, connotes biologic youth. The cult of youthfulness in this society is again a specific value frequently commented upon by foreign observers. This observation is borne out by the popularity of the heroes manufactured in Hollywood and in the world of sports, by the advertisements of styles and cosmetics. As the average age of the population increases, this value is already showing signs of being given new interpretations in terms of geriatrics, etc. This will be alluded to again in following paragraphs.

2. *Material Well-Being*

If indeed effort is optimistically viewed in a material universe that man can master, then material well-being is a consistent concomitant value. Not only is it consistent within the value system, but it has been amply demonstrated in our national experience. It has been manifest in the American standard of living. The nation's geographic frontier and its natural resources, combined with an era of invention, have convinced most Americans of the validity of such a proposition. In the American scene progress and prosperity have come to have almost identical meaning. So deeply convinced are most Americans of what is generally called "prosperity" that material well-being is close to being considered a "right" due to those who have conscientiously practiced the specific value of work. The congruence of this view with the new science of geriatrics, social insurance, and the growth of investment trusts is obvious. It represents a consistent adjustment of specific values to a changing situation. However, as the situational context changes it may weaken the present linkage between effort and optimism with the resulting devaluation of both and thereby set up a new strain for consistency that may alter the present configuration of the American value system.

One of the most common stereotypes about the United States is its materialism. Viewed in the context of the value system presented here, materialism is less a value *per se* than an optimistic assertion of two value premises (mastery over material nature and the perfectibility of man) that have operated in a favorable environment. What foreign observers may call materialism, with derogatory or envious innuendos, is to the American a success that carries the moral connotation of "rightness"—of a system that proves itself or, as Americans would say with complete consistency, that "works." Within the frame of American value premises, success phrased as material well-being resolves the material-spiritual opposition and becomes a proof of right-mindedness. "Hard work pays off." The old and widely known proverb that "Virtue is its own reward" has a particularly American slant, meaning not that virtue is in itself a reward but rather that virtue is rewarded.

If hard work is a "good thing" in a material universe and since it has been rewarded by material well-being, consistency requires that manual labor should be accorded dignity or, at least, should not be considered undignified. Furthermore, manual labor is an unambiguous manifestation of that activism alluded to earlier.

The salience of material well-being as a focal value in American life leads into many by-ways, some of which confuse and confound members of societies founded on a different value configuration. In military terms, for example, Americans are so profoundly convinced of the correctness of the material well-being formula that logistics forms our basic strategy. Personal heroism, though it may amply exist, is not assumed to be the fundamental requisite for victory, as it is in France. In American terms, victory is won by the sheet of matériel laid down in front of advancing infantry and by the lines of supply that must be built up to provide such a barrier between hand-to-hand combat.

In the same vein, there is little room in the American middle-class value system for the realities of physical pain, brutality, and death. Since they are nonetheless natural and undeniable, they are given a highly stylized treatment in detective fiction, newspapers, and movies that provide an acceptable discharge of tension created by the discrepancy between values and reality. Many Americans are alienated and morally repelled when they encounter the poverty and misery prevalent in certain lands. They manage to go through life untouched experientially even by those in our own population who have not succeeded—those who exist hopelessly in rural or urban slums or those who are victims of physical or psychic disasters. We have provided for the latter so effectively that they are whisked away into institutions that our national surpluses permit us to provide comparatively lavishly. Death itself has been surrounded with appurtenances of asepsis. Evelyn Waugh's *The Loved One* could never have been written with India as a setting. The compelling quality of this value emerges when we consider world statistics on human welfare facilities. In this respect, the United States is consistently in the lead. Yet, if we compare these statistics with the outbursts of compassion that a newspaper account of a "blue baby" will elicit, we become aware not only of the power of this focal value but also the resultant constellation that might be summarized as compulsive compassionate activism.

3. Conformity

Viewed historically it seems probable that conformity is a more recent focal value in American culture than effort-optimism and material well-being. It may represent one of the valuational changes induced by the strain for consistency assumed earlier in the paper to be one of the forces that alter value systems. Over a century ago De Tocqueville saw with singular clarity the potential threat to national solidarity inherent in the values of individual liberty, on the one hand, and of the sovereignty of enfranchised masses, on the other hand. In the contemporary American value system, conformity represents an attempt to resolve this dilemma. The France of today, with a comparable dilemma, has still to find a resolution.

If the premises of perfectibility and equality are linked with the focal value labeled effort-optimism, then each middle-class American may legitimately aspire to maximal self-realization. But, if man is to master through his efforts a mechanistic universe, he must co-operate with his fellow-men, since no single man can master the universal machine. In other words, people are individuated and prized, but if they are to co-operate with their fellow-men for mastery of the universe or, in more modest terms, of the immediate physical and sociopolitical environment, too great a degree of individualization would be an impediment. Also since the American value premises—in contradistinction to much of the rest of the world—include equality, the realization of the self in such a context would not necessarily imply the development of highly personalized and idiosyncratic but rather of egalitarian traits. Self-cultivation in America has as its goal less the achievement of uniqueness and more the achievement of similarity. This is a proposition many Frenchmen, for example, find difficult to grasp. The Japanese, with their stress upon self-cultivation in order more perfectly to discharge the obligations they owe their family and society, might come closer to understanding this American formulation.

The assimilation of diverse immigrant groups to middle-class American values has been one of the remarkable sociopolitical achievements of the nation and testifies to the compelling vigor of its value system. As resources and space were more fully manned, the very lack of tolerance for differences that facilitated assimilation was finally to curtail the admission to this country of those who presented such differences.

Earlier in our history self-reliance and initiative were specific values attached to the focal value of liberty. Today these specific values have a new focus. Individual self-reliance and initiative are attached to the promotion of the commonweal and to the progress of society. Conformity has replaced liberty as a focal value to which these specific traits are attached. Co-operation has been added as a specific value that has facilitated the shift-over. The present American value system manifests a highly effective integration of the individual to society.

The ramification of this nexus into the sphere of education has been alluded to already. Education is envisaged as a means by which all men through effort can realize themselves. But since co-operativeness is a specific value also asserted into this equation, education comes to be envisaged as a means to make more men more effective workers and better citizens. The land-grant colleges, the vast network of public schools, and the system of free and compulsory education with its stress on education for citizenship and on technical skills have set the American educational system apart from that of many other countries. In the American context the linkage between conformity, effort-optimism, and material well-being leads inevitably to mass education with the emphasis on the common man rather than the uncommon man, to its technical and practical cast, to what seems to many observers its low standards. Simultaneously, to many Americans schooling has acquired the weight of a goal rather than a means. A college degree is a "good thing" in itself, whether or not the education entailed is prized. This concatenation does not lead one to expect perfection as a directive for performance in American life.

In a society where co-operation and good citizenship are valued and where the commonweal is served by having each man develop himself through his own efforts, a generous friendliness, openness, and relaxation of interpersonal relations are not only possible but desirable so long as the associated expanding economy furnishes the situational possibilities. Rigid class structures and protective privacies are inconsistent with the values here enumerated. Doors need not be closed to rooms; fences need not be built around properties. The tall hedges of England and the enclosing walls of France are not appropriate to the American scene, where life faces outward rather than inward. If every individual is as "good as" the next and all are good citizens—what is there to hide? The open front yards, the porches, or more recently the picture windows that leave the home open to everyone's view, the figurative and literal klieg lights under which our public figures live are all evidence of the value placed in American life on likeness and the pressure exerted for conformity. This is very different from saying that American middle-class individuals are in fact all alike. It means merely that likeness is valued.

The American hostility to figures in authority has been frequently noted, and in this connection the almost placatory informality and familiarity of American manners that serve to play down status differences have been pointed out. The apparent contradiction between the striving for upward mobility and the distrust of those who achieve pre-eminent positions can now be seen in more balanced terms. If the argument advanced here is correct, upward mobility is valued as successful activity, but when it reaches a point where it outstrips the premise of equality and the focal value of conformity it borders on *hubris.*

In this connection then the relaxed, friendly manner of American life so frequently commented upon by foreign observers can be gauged in the broader context of an adjustment to incompatible values. The search for popularity, the desire to be liked, the wish to be considered a "good fellow," are searches for reassurance that, in striving to achieve all the ends implied by the focal value of effort-optimism, one has not exceeded the bounds set by the other focal value of conformity. That this process can operate at any level of actual achievement, from the presidency of the United States to chairmanship of an Elks Club committee, need not be stressed. It is the boss, the politician, the teacher, the "big shots" who are disvalued figures to the extent that their superordinate position implies authority. It is the movie star and the baseball hero who are valued figures since their pre-eminence connotes no authority but at the same time dramatizes the meteoric rise to fame and popularity through hard work and youthful striving.

Another aspect of American social life is thrown into relief in the effort to balance effort-optimism, material well-being, and conformity and their linked specific values. In the business and financial world, despite conservative tendencies, there has been a steady trend toward consolidation and standardization. Although the familiar and now perhaps inappropriate hue and cry is still raised about monopoly and big business, the latter, at least, serves the greater material well-being of the American mass consumer, whose values are geared to conformity. "Big business" is consonant with the American value system here portrayed so long as the owners of such enterprises are pictured as the American middle class, so long as savings are invested in the stocks and bonds of these enterprises so that the middle class shares "equally" in its successes, and so long as the authorities in such enterprises are presented as servants of the people. In these terms the American value system is served. The dangers of a too extreme individualistic power-centered authority are thus allayed, and competitive rivalry is brought under control.

SUMMARY AND CONCLUSIONS

Two basic assumptions were made: (1) that no viable value system *qua* system can entertain logical contraries, and (2) that there is a strain for consistency among the spurious contradictions that may be inherent in any value system. Four major premises were assumed to underlie the American middle-class value system: (1) a mechanistically conceived universe, (2) man's mastery over that universe, (3) the equality of men, and (4) man's perfectibility. From these four premises three focal values were suggested: (1) effort-optimism, (2) material well-being, and (3) conformity. Each of these focal values is envisaged as being more or less directly derived from each of the premises. Each in turn constitutes a series (here not fully explored) of specific values and directives. Each of the three focal and their constituent specific values are more or less consistently interlocked. But the viability of a value system does not rest exclusively on its internal coherence. It must also manifest a considerable degree of congruence with the situational context within which it exists. Changes in value systems will result, therefore, from a strain for consistency not only within the value system but also between values and situational factors.

DAVID M. POTTER

Individuality and Conformity

Unlike most nationality groups in the world today, the people of the United States are not ethnically rooted in the land where they live. The French have remote Gallic antecedents; the Germans, Teutonic; the English, Anglo-Saxon; the Italians, Roman; the Irish, Celtic; but the only people in America who can claim ancient American origins are a remnant of Red Indians. In any deep dimension of time, all other Americans are immigrants. They began as Europeans (or in the case of 10 per cent of the population, as Africans), and if they became Americans it was only, somehow, after a relatively recent passage westbound across the Atlantic.

It is, perhaps, this recency of arrival which has given to Americans a somewhat compulsive preoccupation with the question of their Americanism. No people can really qualify as a nation in the true sense unless they are united by important qualities or values in common. If they share the same ethnic, or linguistic, or religious, or political heritage, the foundations of nationality can hardly be questioned. But when their ethnic, religious, linguistic, and political heritage is mixed, as in the case of the American people, nationality can hardly exist at all unless it takes the form of a common adjustment to conditions of a new land, a common commitment to shared values, a common esteem for certain qualities of character, or a common set of adaptive traits and attitudes. It is partly for this reason that Americans, although committed to the principle of freedom of thought, have nevertheless placed such heavy emphasis upon the obligation to accept certain undefined tenets of 'Americanism.' It is for this same reason, also, that Americans have insisted upon their distinctiveness from the Old World from which they are derived. More than two centuries ago Hector St John de Crèvecoeur asked a famous question, 'What then is the American, this new man?' He simply assumed, without arguing the point, that the American is a new man, and he only inquired wherein the American is different. A countless array of writers, including not only careful historians and social scientists but also professional patriots, hit-and-run travellers, itinerant lecturers, intuitive-minded amateurs of all sorts, have been repeating Crèvecoeur's question and seeking to answer it ever since.

From "The Quest for the National Character" by David M. Potter. Reprinted by permission of Harper & Row, Publishers, from John Higham (ed.), *The Reconstruction of American History,* copyright 1962.

A thick volume would hardly suffice even to summarize the diverse interpretations which these various writers have advanced in describing or explaining the American character. Almost every trait, good or bad, has been attributed to the American people by someone,[1] and almost every explanation, from Darwinian selection to toilet-training, has been advanced to account for the attributed qualities. But it is probably safe to say that at bottom there have been only two primary ways of explaining the American, and that almost all of the innumerable interpretations which have been formulated can be grouped around or at least oriented to these two basic explanations, which serve as polar points for all the literature.

The most disconcerting fact about these two composite images of the American is that they are strikingly dissimilar and seemingly about as inconsistent with one another as two interpretations of the same phenomenon could possibly be. One depicts the American primarily as an individualist and an idealist, while the other makes him out as a conformist and a materialist. Both images have been developed with great detail and elaborate explanation in extensive bodies of literature, and both are worth a close scrutiny.

For those who have seen the American primarily as an individualist, the story of his evolution as a distinctive type dates back possibly to the actual moment of his decision to migrate from Europe to the New World, for this was a process in which the daring and venturesome were more prone to risk life in a new country while the timid and the conventional were more disposed to remain at home. If the selective factors in the migration had the effect of screening out men of low initiative, the conditions of life in the North American wilderness, it is argued, must have further heightened the exercise of individual resourcefulness, for they constantly confronted the settler with circumstances in which he could rely upon no one but himself, and where the capacity to improvise a solution for a problem was not infrequently necessary to survival.

In many ways the colonial American exemplified attitudes that were individualistic. Although he made his first settlements by the removal of whole communities which were transplanted bodily—complete with all their ecclesiastical and legal institutions—he turned increasingly, in the later process of settlement, to a more and more individualistic mode of pioneering, in which one separate family would take up title to a separate, perhaps an isolated, tract of land, and would move to this land long in advance of any general settlement, leaving churches and courts and schools far behind. His religion, whether Calvinistic Puritanism or emotional revivalism, made him individually responsible for his own salvation, without the intervention of ecclesiastical intermediaries between himself and his God. His economy, which was based very heavily upon subsistence farming, with very little division of labor, also impelled him to cope with a diversity of problems and to depend upon no one but himself.

[1]Lee Coleman, 'What is American: a Study of Alleged American Traits,' in *Social Forces,* XIX (1941), surveyed a large body of the literature on the American character and concluded that 'almost every conceivable value or trait has at one time or another been imputed to American culture by authoritative observers.'

With all of these conditions at work, the tendency to place a premium upon individual self-reliance was no doubt well developed long before the cult of the American as an individualist crystallized in a conceptual form. But it did crystallize, and it took on almost its classic formulation in the thought of Thomas Jefferson.

It may seem paradoxical to regard Jefferson as a delineator of American national character, for in direct terms he did not attempt to describe the American character at all. But he did conceive that one particular kind of society was necessary to the fulfillment of American ideals, and further that one particular kind of person, namely the independent farmer, was a necessary component in the optimum society. He believed that the principles of liberty and equality, which he cherished so deeply, could not exist in a hierarchical society, such as that of Europe, nor, indeed, in any society where economic and social circumstances enabled one set of men to dominate and exploit the rest. An urban society or a commercial society, with its concentration of financial power into a few hands and its imposition of dependence through a wage system, scarcely lent itself better than an aristocracy to his basic values. In fact, only a society of small husbandmen who tilled their own soil and found sustenance in their own produce could achieve the combination of independence and equalitarianism which he envisioned for the ideal society. Thus, although Jefferson did not write a description of the national character, he erected a model for it, and the model ultimately had more influence than a description could ever have exercised. The model American was a plain, straightforward agrarian democrat, an individualist in his desire for freedom for himself, and an idealist in his desire for equality for all men.

Jefferson's image of the American as a man of independence, both in his values and in his mode of life, has had immense appeal to Americans ever since. They found this image best exemplified in the man of the frontier, for he, as a pioneer, seemed to illustrate the qualities of independence and self-reliance in their most pronounced and most dramatic form. Thus in a tradition of something like folklore, half-legendary figures like Davy Crockett have symbolized America as well as symbolizing the frontier. In literature, ever since J. Fenimore Cooper's Leatherstocking tales, the frontier scout, at home under the open sky, free from the trammels of an organized and stratified society, has been cherished as an incarnation of American qualities.[2] In American politics the voters showed such a marked preference for men who had been born in log cabins that many an ambitious candidate pretended to pioneer origins which were in fact fictitious.

The pioneer is, of course, not necessarily an agrarian (he may be a hunter, a trapper, a cowboy, a prospector for gold), and the agrarian is not necessarily a pioneer (he may be a European peasant tilling his ancestral acres), but the American frontier was basically an agricultural frontier, and the pioneer was

[2]Henry Nash Smith, *Virgin Land: The American West as Symbol and Myth* (1950), brilliantly analyzes the power which the image of the Western pioneer has had upon the American imagination.

usually a farmer. Thus it was possible to make an equation between the pioneer and the agrarian, and since the pioneer evinced the agrarian traits in their most picturesque and most appealing form there was a strong psychological impulse to concentrate the diffused agrarian ideal into a sharp frontier focus. This is, in part, what Frederick Jackson Turner did in 1893 when he wrote *The Significance of the Frontier in American History.* In this famous essay Turner offered an explanation of what has been distinctive in American history, but it is not as widely realized as it might be that he also penned a major contribution to the literature of national character. Thus Turner affirmed categorically that 'The American intellect owes its striking characteristics to the frontier. That coarseness and strength, combined with acuteness and acquisitiveness; that practical inventive turn of mind, quick to find expedients; that masterful grasp of material things, lacking in the artistic but powerful to effect great ends; that restless, nervous energy; that dominant individualism, working for good and for evil; and withal, that buoyancy and exuberance which comes with freedom—these are traits of the frontier, or traits called out elsewhere because of the existence of the frontier.'[3]

A significant but somewhat unnoticed aspect of Turner's treatment is the fact that, in his quest to discover the traits of the American character, he relied for proof not upon descriptive evidence that given traits actually prevailed, but upon the argument that given conditions in the environment would necessarily cause the development of certain traits. Thus the cheapness of land on the frontier would make for universal land-holding which in turn would make for equalitarianism in the society. The absence of division of labor on the frontier would force each man to do most things for himself, and this would breed self-reliance. The pitting of the individual man against the elemental forces of the wilderness and of nature would further reinforce this self-reliance. Similarly, the fact that a man had moved out in advance of society's institutions and its stratified structure would mean that he could find independence, without being overshadowed by the institutions, and could enjoy an equality unknown to stratified society. All of this argument was made without any sustained effort to measure exactly how much recognizable equalitarianism and individualism and self-reliance actually were in evidence either on the American frontier or in American society. There is little reason to doubt that most of his arguments were valid or that most of the traits which he emphasized did actually prevail, but it is nevertheless ironical that Turner's interpretation, which exercised such vast influence upon historians, was not based upon the historian's kind of proof, which is from evidence, but upon an argument from logic which so often fails to work out in historical experience.

But no matter how he arrived at it, Turner's picture reaffirmed some by-now-familiar beliefs about the American character. The American was equalitarian, stoutly maintaining the practices of both social and political democracy; he had a spirit of freedom reflected in his buoyance and exuberance; he was

[3]Frederick J. Turner, *The Frontier in American History* (Henry Holt and Co., 1920), p. 37.

individualistic—hence 'practical and inventive,' 'quick to find expedients,' 'restless, nervous, acquisitive.' Turner was too much a scholar to let his evident fondness for the frontiersman run away with him entirely, and he took pains to point out that this development was not without its sordid aspects. There was a marked primitivism about the frontier, and with it, to some extent, a regression from civilized standards. The buoyant and exuberant frontiersman sometimes emulated his Indian neighbors in taking the scalps of his adversaries. Coarse qualities sometimes proved to have more survival value than gentle ones. But on the whole this regression was brief, and certainly a rough-and-ready society had its compensating advantages. Turner admired his frontiersman, and thus Turner's American, like Jefferson's American, was partly a realistic portrait from life and partly an idealized model from social philosophy. Also, though one of these figures was an agrarian and the other was a frontiersman, both were very much the same man—democratic, freedom-loving, self-reliant, and individualistic.

An essay like this is hardly the place to prove either the validity or the invalidity of the Jeffersonian and Turnerian conception of the American character. The attempt to do so would involve a review of the entire range of American historical experience, and in the course of such a review the proponents of this conception could point to a vast body of evidence in support of their interpretation. They could argue, with much force, that Americans have consistently been zealous to defend individualism by defending the rights and the welfare of the individual, and that our whole history is a protracted record of our government's recognizing its responsibility to an ever broader range of people—to men without property, to men held in slavery, to women, to small enterprises threatened by monopoly, to children laboring in factories, to industrial workers, to the ill, to the elderly, and to the unemployed. This record, it can further be argued, is also a record of the practical idealism of the American people, unceasingly at work.

But without attempting a verdict on the historical validity of this image of the American as individualist and idealist, it is important to bear in mind that this image has been partly a portrait, but also partly a model. In so far as it is a portrait—a likeness by an observer reporting on Americans whom he knew—it can be regarded as authentic testimony on the American character. But in so far as it is a model—an idealization of what is best in Americanism, and of what Americans should strive to be, it will only be misleading if used as evidence of what ordinary Americans are like in their everyday lives. It is also important to recognize that the Jefferson-Turner image posited several traits as distinctively American, and that they are not all necessarily of equal validity. Particularly, Jefferson and Turner both believed that love of equality and love of liberty go together. For Jefferson the very fact, stated in the Declaration of Independence, that 'all men are created equal,' carried with it the corollary that they are all therefore 'entitled to [and would be eager for] life, liberty, and the pursuit of happiness.' From this premise it is easy to slide imperceptibly into the position of holding that equalitarianism and individualism are inseparably linked, or even that they are somehow the same thing. This is, indeed, almost an officially sanctioned ambiguity in the American creed. But it requires only a little thoughtful reflection to recognize that equalitarianism and individualism do not necessarily go together. Alexis de Tocqueville understood this fact more than a century ago, and out of his recognition he framed an analysis which is not only the most brilliant single account of the American character, but is also the only major alternative to the Jefferson-Turner image.

After travelling the length and breadth of the United States for ten months at the height of Andrew Jackson's ascendency, Tocqueville felt no doubt of the depth of the commitment of Americans to democracy. Throughout two volumes which ranged over every aspect of American life, he consistently emphasized democracy as a pervasive factor. But the democracy which he wrote about was far removed from Thomas Jefferson's dream. . . . [*Professor Potter's discussion of Tocqueville's main theses is omitted. The reader may wish to review the relevant portions of the selection from Tocqueville's* Democracy in America *in this volume*—Ed.]

For more than a century we have lived with the contrasting images of the American character which Thomas Jefferson and Alexis de Tocqueville visualized. Both of these images presented the American as an equalitarian and therefore as a democrat, but one was an agrarian democrat while the other was a majoritarian democrat; one an independent individualist, the other a mass-dominated conformist; one an idealist, the other a materialist. Through many decades of self-scrutiny Americans have been seeing one or the other of these images whenever they looked into the mirror of self-analysis.

The discrepancy between the two images is so great that it must bring the searcher for the American character up with a jerk, and must force him to grapple with the question whether these seemingly antithetical versions of the American can be reconciled in any way. . . .

. . . confronted with the conflicting images of the agrarian democrat and the majoritarian democrat, the investigator might avoid an outright rejection of either by taking the position that the American character has changed, and that each of these images was at one time valid and realistic, but that in the twentieth century the qualities of conformity and materialism have grown increasingly prominent, while the qualities of individualism and idealism have diminished. This interpretation of a changing American character has had a number of adherents in the last two decades, for it accords well with the observation that the conditions of the American culture have changed. As they do so, of course the qualities of a character that is derived from the culture might be expected to change correspondingly. Thus, Henry S. Commager, in his *The American Mind* (1950), portrayed in two contrasting chapters 'the nineteenth-century American' and 'the twentieth-century American.' Similarly, David Riesman, in *The Lonely Crowd* (1950), significantly sub-titled *A Study of the Changing American Character,* pictured two types of Americans, first an 'inner-directed man,' whose values were deeply internalized and who adhered to these values tenaciously, regardless of the opinions of his peers (clearly an individualist), and second an 'other-directed man,' who subordinated his own internal values to the changing expectations directed toward him by changing peer groups (in short, a conformist).

Although he viewed his inner-directed man as having been superseded historically by his other-directed man, Riesman did not attempt to explain in historical terms the reason for the change. He made a rather limited effort to relate his stages of character formation to stages of population growth, but he has since then not used population phase as a key. Meanwhile, it is fairly clear, from Riesman's own context, as well as from history in general, that there were changes in the culture which would have accounted for the transition in character. Most nineteenth-century Americans were self-employed; most were engaged in agriculture; most produced a part of their own food and clothing. These facts meant that their well-being did not depend on the goodwill or the services of their associates, but upon their resourcefulness in wrestling with the elemental forces of Nature. Even their physical isolation from their fellows added something to the independence of their natures. But most twentieth-century Americans work for wages or salaries, many of them in very large employee groups; most are engaged in office or factory work; most are highly specialized, and are reliant upon many others to supply their needs in an economy with an advanced division of labor. Men now do depend upon the goodwill and the services of their fellows. This means that what they achieve depends less upon stamina and hardihood than upon their capacity to get along with other people and to fit smoothly into a co-operative relationship. In short the culture now places a premium upon the qualities which will enable the individual to function effectively as a member of a large organizational group. The strategic importance of this institutional factor has been well recognized by William H. Whyte, Jr., in his significantly titled book *The Organization Man* (1956)—for the conformity of Whyte's bureaucratized individual results from the fact that he lives under an imperative to succeed in a situation where promotion and even survival depend upon effective interaction with others in an hierarchical structure.

Thus, by an argument from logic (always a treacherous substitute for direct observation in historical study), one can make a strong case that the nineteenth-century American should have been (and therefore must have been) an individualist, while the twentieth-century American should be (and therefore is) a conformist. But this formula crashes headlong into the obdurate fact that no Americans have ever been more classically conformist than Tocqueville's Jacksonian democrats—hardy specimens of the frontier breed, far back in the nineteenth century, long before the age of corporate images, peer groups, marginal differentiation, and status frustration. In short, Tocqueville's nineteenth-century American, whether frontiersman or no, was to some extent an other-directed man. Carl N. Degler has pointed out this identity in a very cogent paper not yet published, in which he demonstrates very forcibly that most of our easy assumptions about the immense contrast between the nineteenth-century American and twentieth-century American are vulnerable indeed.[4]

This conclusion should, perhaps, have been evident from the outset, in view of the fact that it was Tocqueville who, in the nineteenth century, gave us the image which we now frequently identify as the twentieth-century American. But in any case, the fact that he did so means that we can hardly resolve the dilemma of our individualist democrat and our majoritarian democrat by assuming that both are historically valid but that one replaced the other. The problem of determining what use we can make of either of these images, in view of the fact that each casts doubt upon the other, still remains. Is it possible to uncover common factors in these apparently contradictory images, and thus to make use of them both in our quest for a definition of the national character? For no matter whether either of these versions of the American is realistic as a type or image, there is no doubt that both of them reflect fundamental aspects of the American experience.

There is no purpose, at this point in this essay, to execute a neat, prearranged sleight-of-hand by which the individualist democrat and the conformist democrat will cast off their disguises and will reveal themselves as identical twin Yankee Doodle Dandies, both born on the fourth of July. On the contrary, intractable, irresolvable discrepancies exist between the two figures, and it will probably never be possible to go very far in the direction of accepting the one without treating the other as a fictitious image, to be rejected as reflecting an anti-democratic bias and as at odds with the evidence from actual observation of the behavior of *Homo americanus* in his native haunts. At the same time, however, it is both necessary to probe for the common factors, and legitimate to observe that there is one common factor conspicuous in the extreme—namely the emphasis on equality, so dear both to Jefferson's American and to Tocqueville's. One of these figures, it will be recalled, has held no truth to be more self-evident than that all men are created equal, while the other has made equality his 'idol,' far more jealously guarded than his liberty.

If the commitment to equality is so dominant a feature in both of these representations of the American, it will perhaps serve as a key to various facets of the national character, even to contradictory aspects of this character. In a society as complex as that of the United States, in fact, it may be that the common factors underlying the various manifestations are all that our quest

[4]Delivered on 30 December 1960, at the annual meeting of the American Historical Association in New York. [*A revision of Professor Degler's paper, "The Sociologist as Historian: Riesman's* The Lonely Crowd," *has since been published in* American Quarterly, *Vol. XV (Winter, 1963), pp. 483–97*—Ed.]

should seek. For it is evident that American life and American energy have expressed themselves in a great diversity of ways, and any effort to define the American as if nearly two hundred million persons all corresponded to a single type would certainly reduce complex data to a blunt, crude, and oversimplified form. To detect what qualities Americans share in their diversity may be far more revealing than to superimpose the stereotype of a fictitious uniformity. If this is true, it means that our quest must be to discover the varied and dissimilar ways in which the commitment to equality expresses itself—the different forms which it takes in different individuals—rather than to regard it as an undifferentiated component which shows in all individuals in the same way. Figuratively, one might say that in seeking for what is common, one should think of the metal from which Americans are forged, no matter into how many shapes this metal may be cast, rather than thinking of a die with which they all are stamped into an identical shape. If the problem is viewed in this way, it will be readily apparent that Tocqueville made a pregnant statement when he observed that the ideal of equality was 'the fundamental fact from which all others seem to be derived.'

The term 'equality' is a loose-fitting garment and it has meant very different things at very different times. It is very frequently used to imply parity or uniformity. The grenadiers in the King of Prussia's guard were equal in that they were all, uniformly, over six feet six inches tall. Particularly, it can mean, and often does mean in some social philosophies, uniformity of material welfare—of income, of medical care, etc. But people are clearly not uniform in strength or intelligence or beauty, and one must ask, therefore, what kind of uniformity Americans believed in. Did they believe in an equal sharing of goods? Tocqueville himself answered this question when he said, 'I know of no country . . . where a profounder contempt is expressed for the theory of the permanent equality of property.'[5]

At this point in the discussion of equality, someone, and very likely a business man, is always likely to break in with the proposition that Americans believe in equality of opportunity—in giving everyone what is called an equal start, and in removing all handicaps such as illiteracy and all privileges such as monopoly or special priority, which will tend to give one person an advantage over another. But if a person gains the advantage without having society give it to him, by being more clever or more enterprising or even just by being stronger than someone else, he is entitled to enjoy the benefits that accrue from these qualities, particularly in terms of possessing more property or wealth than others.

Historically, equality of opportunity was a particularly apt form of equalitarianism for a new, undeveloped frontier country. In the early stages of American history, the developed resources of the country were so few that an equality in the division of these assets would only have meant an insufficiency for everyone. The best economic benefit which the government could give was

[5]Tocqueville, *Democracy in America,* I, 57–58.

to offer a person free access in developing undeveloped resources for his own profit, and this is what America did offer. It was an ideal formula for everyone: for the individual it meant a very real chance to gain more wealth than he would have secured by receiving an equal share of the existing wealth. For the community, it meant that no one could prosper appreciably without activities which would develop undeveloped resources, at a time when society desperately needed rapid economic development. For these reasons, equality of opportunity did become the most highly sanctioned form of equalitarianism in the United States.

Because of this sanction, Americans have indeed been tolerant of great discrepancies in wealth. They have approved of wealth much more readily when they believed that it had been earned—as in the case, for instance, of Henry Ford—than when they thought it had been acquired by some special privilege or monopoly. In general, however, they have not merely condoned great wealth; they have admired it. But to say that the ideal of equality means only equality of opportunity is hardly to tell the whole story. The American faith has also held, with intense conviction, the belief that all men are equal in the sense that they share a common humanity—that all are alike in the eyes of God—and that every person has a certain dignity, no matter how low his circumstances, which no one else, no matter how high *his* circumstances, is entitled to disregard. When this concept of the nature of man was translated into a system of social arrangements, the crucial point on which it came to focus was the question of rank. For the concept of rank essentially denies that all men are equally worthy and argues that some are better than others—that some are born to serve and others born to command. The American creed not only denied this view, but even condemned it and placed a taboo upon it. Some people, according to the American creed, might be more fortunate than others, but they must never regard themselves as better than others. Pulling one's rank has therefore been the unforgivable sin against American democracy, and the American people have, accordingly, reserved their heartiest dislike for the officer class in the military, for people with upstage or condescending manners, and for anyone who tries to convert power or wealth (which are not resented) into overt rank or privilege (which are). Thus it is permissible for an American to have servants (which is a matter of function), but he must not put them in livery (which is a matter of rank); permissible to attend expensive schools, but not to speak with a cultivated accent; permissible to rise in the world, but never to repudiate the origins from which he rose. The most palpable and overt possible claim of rank is, of course, the effort of one individual to assert authority, in a personal sense, over others, and accordingly the rejection of authority is the most pronounced of all the concrete expressions of American beliefs in equality.

In almost any enterprise which involves numbers of people working in conjunction, it is necessary for some people to tell other people what to do. This function cannot be wholly abdicated without causing a breakdown, and in America it cannot be exercised overtly without violating the taboos against authority. The result is that the American people have developed an arrangement which skillfully combines truth and fiction, and maintains that the top man does not rule, but leads; and does not give orders, but calls signals; while the men in the lower echelons are not underlings, but members of the team. This view of the relationship is truthful in the sense that the man in charge does depend upon his capacity to elicit the voluntary or spontaneous co-operation of the members of his organization, and he regards the naked use of authority to secure compliance as an evidence of failure; also, in many organizations, the members lend their support willingly, and contribute much more on a voluntary basis than authority could ever exact from them. But the element of fiction sometimes enters, in terms of the fact that both sides understand that in many situations authority would have to be invoked if voluntary compliance were not forthcoming. This would be humiliating to all parties—to the top man because it would expose his failure as a leader and to the others because it would force them to recognize the carefully concealed fact that in an ultimate sense they are subject to coercion. To avoid this mutually undesirable exploration of the ultimate implications, both sides recognize that even when an order has to be given, it is better for it to be expressed in the form of a request or a proposal, and when compliance is mandatory, it should be rendered with an appearance of consent.

It is in this way that the anti-authoritarian aspect of the creed of equality leads to the extraordinarily strong emphasis upon permissiveness, either as a reality or as a mere convention in American life. So strong is the taboo against authority that the father, once a paternal authority, is now expected to be a pal to his children, and to persuade rather than to command. The husband, once a lord and master, to be obeyed under the vows of matrimony, is now a partner. And if, perchance, an adult male in command of the family income uses his control to bully his wife and children, he does not avow his desire to make them obey, but insists that he only wants them to be co-operative. The unlimited American faith in the efficacy of discussion as a means of finding solutions for controversies reflects less a faith in the powers of rational persuasion than a supreme reluctance to let anything reach a point where authority will have to be invoked. If hypocrisy is the tribute that vice pays to virtue, permissiveness is, to some extent, the tribute that authority pays to the principle of equality.

When one recognizes some of these varied strands in the fabric of equalitarianism it becomes easier to see how the concept has contributed to the making, both of the Jeffersonian American and the Tocquevillian American. For as one picks at the strands they ravel out in quite dissimilar directions. The strand of equality of opportunity, for instance, if followed out, leads to the theme of individualism. It challenged each individual to pit his skill and talents in a competition against the skill and talents of others and to earn the individual rewards which talent and effort might bring. Even more, the imperatives of the competitive race were so compelling that the belief grew up that everyone had a kind of obligation to enter his talents in this competition and to 'succeed.' It was but a step from the belief that ability and virtue would produce success to the belief that success was produced by—and was therefore an evidence of—ability and virtue. In short, money not only represented power, it also was a sign of the presence of admirable qualities in the man who attained it. Here, certainly, an equalitarian doctrine fostered materialism, and if aggressiveness and competitiveness are individualistic qualities, then it fostered individualism also.

Of course, neither American individualism nor American materialism can be explained entirely in these terms. Individualism must have derived great strength, for instance, from the reflection that if all men are equal, a man might as well form his own convictions as accept the convictions of someone else no better than himself. It must also have been reinforced by the frontier experience, which certainly compelled every man to rely upon himself. But this kind of individualism is not the quality of independent-mindedness, and it is not the quality which Tocqueville was denying when he said that Americans were conformists. A great deal of confusion has resulted, in the discussion of the American character, from the fact that the term individualism is sometimes used (as by Tocqueville) to mean willingness to think and act separately from the majority, and sometimes (as by Turner) to mean capacity to get along without help. It might be supposed that the two would converge, on the theory that a man who can get along by himself without help will soon recognize that he may as well also think for himself without help. But in actuality, this did not necessarily happen. Self-reliance on the frontier was more a matter of courage and of staying power than of intellectual resourcefulness, for the struggle with the wilderness challenged the body rather than the mind, and a man might be supremely effective in fending for himself, and at the same time supremely conventional in his ideas. In this sense, Turner's individualist is not really an antithesis of Tocqueville's conformist at all.

Still, it remains true that Jefferson's idealist and Tocqueville's conformist both require explanation, and that neither can be accounted for in the terms which make Jefferson's individualist and Tocqueville's materialist understandable. As an explanation of these facets of the American character, it would seem that the strand of equalitarianism which stresses the universal dignity of all men, and which hates rank as a violation of dignity, might be found quite pertinent. For it is the concept of the worth of every man which has stimulated a century and a half of reform, designed at every step to realize in practice the ideal that every human possesses potentialities which he should have a chance to fulfill. Whatever has impeded this fulfillment, whether it be lack of education, chattel slavery, the exploitation of the labor of unorganized workers, the hazards of unemployment, or the handicaps of age and infirmity, has been the object, at one time or another, of a major reforming crusade.

The whole American commitment to progress would be impossible without a prior belief in the perfectibility of man and in the practicability of steps to bring perfection nearer. In this sense, the American character has been idealistic. And yet its idealism is not entirely irreconcilable with its materialism, for American idealism has often framed its most altruistic goals in materialistic terms—for instance of raising the standard of living as a means to a better life. Moreover, Americans are committed to the view that materialistic means are necessary to idealistic ends. Franklin defined what is necessary to a virtuous life by saying 'an empty sack cannot stand upright,' and Americans have believed that spiritual and humanitarian goals are best achieved by instrumentalities such as universities and hospitals which carry expensive price tags.

If the belief that all men are of equal worth has contributed to a feature of American life so much cherished as our tradition of humanitarian reform, how could it at the same time have contributed to a feature so much deplored as American conformity? Yet it has done both, for the same respect of the American for his fellow men, which has made many a reformer think that his fellow citizens are worth helping, has also made many another American think that he has no business to question the opinions that his neighbors have sanctioned. True, he says, if all men are equal, each ought to think for himself, but on the other hand, no man should consider himself better than his neighbors, and if the majority have adopted an opinion on a matter, how can one man question their opinion, without setting himself up as being better than they. Moreover, it is understood that the majority are pledged not to force him to adopt their opinion. But it is also understood that in return for this immunity he will voluntarily accept the will of the majority in most things. The absence of a formal compulsion to conform seemingly increases the obligation to conform voluntarily. Thus, the other-directed man is seen to be derived as much from the American tradition of equalitarianism as the rugged individualist, and the compulsive seeker of an unequally large share of wealth as much as the humanitarian reformer striving for the fulfillment of democratic ideals.

To say that they are all derived from the same tradition is by no means to say that they are, in some larger, mystic sense, all the same. They are not, even though the idealism of the reformer may seek materialistic goals, and though men who are individualists in their physical lives may be conformists in their ideas. But all of them, it may be argued, do reflect circumstances which are distinctively American, and all present manifestations of a character which is more convincingly American because of its diversity than any wholly uniform character could possibly be. If Americans have never reached the end of their quest for an image that would represent the American character, it may be not because they failed to find one image but because they failed to recognize the futility of attempting to settle upon one, and the necessity of accepting several.

CHANGE AND CONTINUITY

VI

INTRODUCTION VI

Either directly or obliquely, virtually every reading in this collection speaks to the large and challenging questions that are connected with the appraisal of change and continuity in the character of Americans. Historians have chronicled the transformation of the United States from a nation composed predominantly of small yeoman farmers into an urban-industrial Gargantua characterized by metropolitan clusters of population, an advanced technology administered by corporate and political bureaucracies, an elevated average standard of living, and a high degree of social and economic interdependence. How has the national character been affected by such immense changes in the scale, quality, and complexity of American life? In what ways, to what ends, and with what effect have these changes been directed or influenced by the national character itself? These conjoined questions demand bold, imaginative, and rigorous treatment by behavioral scientists and historians working in tandem.

It is both possible and permissible to describe the American as he is, in present tense, without express regard to what he was or how he came to be what he now is, as though he were a man without a past. Such unidimensional writings furnish useful checkpoints for the analysis of the national character over time. Most scholars, however, have not been satisfied with a narrowly contemporaneous taxonomy, lacking historical perspective. To grasp the shape of the national character, it is necessary to know a good deal about its shaping; to apprehend its form, the student needs to examine its formation. Thus whenever a social scientist undertakes to *explain,* rather than merely *describe,* the American character—whether he studies the processes of personality formation, or the evolution of the value system, or the acculturation of the sons and grandsons of immigrants, or the institutional determinants and expressions of character—he enters into historical discourse and encounters the problem of change and continuity.

The most influential recent investigation of these matters is *The Lonely Crowd: A Study of the Changing American Character* by David Riesman, professor of social relations at Harvard University, in collaboration with Nathan Glazer and Reuel Denney. Published in 1950 and reissued in two paperback abridgments, Riesman's seminal work is concerned with the major themes of individuality, conformity, and autonomy. Its central thesis, broadly stated, is that a momentous change has occurred and is still occurring in the character of Americans, specifically in the normative character type of urban upper-middle-class Americans. Using the conceptual apparatus of "ideal-types," Riesman describes a shift from "inner-direction" to "other-direction"—terms which have now entered the working vocabulary of social analysis and criticism. These categories are defined, and Riesman's principal contentions are summarized with particular reference to political styles, in the first selection in Part VI, taken from a lecture at the Washington School of Psychiatry in 1950. Riesman's main positions are illustrated in the second selection, "The Found Generation" (1956), in which the goals and values of college students, vintage 1955, are contrasted with those of the author's own college generation of 1931.

A parallel evaluation of contemporary trends comes from the pen of William H. Whyte, Jr., free-lance journalist, social critic, and former editor of *Fortune Magazine,* whose book, *The Organization Man* (1956), has enjoyed a remarkable vogue. The "organization men" occupy the lower and middle echelons of corporate management; they are, in Whyte's judgment, "the dominant members of our society" whose "values . . . will set the American temper."[1] The scheme of Whyte's study is historical: he detects a movement away from the Protestant Ethic of hard work, self-reliance, thrift, and individual risk taking, toward what he calls the "Social Ethic," defined as "that contemporary body of thought which makes morally legitimate the pressures of society against the individual." The Social Ethic embodies three principal propositions: "a belief in the group as the source of creativity; a belief in 'belongingness' as the ultimate need of the individual; and a belief in the application of science to achieve the belongingness."[2] These articles of faith compose the basic ideology of the well-adjusted organization man. Two of them are examined by Whyte in the essays on "Groupthink" and "The Outgoing Life" which are reproduced from *Fortune.* Published respectively in 1952 and 1953, these pieces were later revised for inclusion in *The Organization Man.*

Though the fit is not exact, Whyte's Social Ethic may be regarded as the ideology of Riesman's other-directed character type, just as the Protestant Ethic articulates the values of the inner-directed man. There is, however, a more fundamental consonance between the two analyses. Each employs what Seymour Martin Lipset, professor of sociology at the University of California at Berkeley, calls a "materialistic interpretation" of the change in values and character. Each examines, in Riesman's words, "the way in which society ensures some degree of conformity from the individuals who make it up," and each emphasizes the molding forces of technological development and economic organization. To Riesman, both inner- and other-direction are "modes of conformity," and the term, "mode of conformity," is used interchangeably in *The Lonely Crowd* with the term "social character."[3] By the same token, the character of the organization man is shaped by the bureaucratic structure and pressures of the large organization.

These deterministic assumptions, as Lipset observes, are probably valid;

[1] *The Organization Man* (Garden City, N.Y.: Doubleday Anchor Books, 1957), p. 3.
[2] *Ibid.*, p. 7.
[3] *The Lonely Crowd* (New Haven: Yale University Press, 1961), pp. 5–6.

there may be reason, however, to query their adequacy as an explanation of character change. Riesman's historical thesis is also open to challenge in the light of numerous observations by foreign visitors which point to the prevalence of other-direction, or something strikingly similar to it, among Americans of the nineteenth century. These objections are strongly urged by Lipset in his essay, "A Changing American Character?" published in 1961.[4] Lipset contends that the persistent values of equality and individual achievement have played, and continue to play, a vital role in the determination of social character through their influence on technological and economic change. Other-direction, in this view, is "an expected consequence of a social system founded upon the values of equality and achievement." While the traits of other-direction may be exhibited more patently by the middle-class urban American today than by his ancestors of a century ago, the difference is one of degree rather than one of kind. Lipset's essay is not only an illuminating critique of Riesman's ideas but a valuable contribution in its own right to the literature of American character.

Though Lipset introduces nonmaterial factors into the explanation of the national character, the presuppositions of his position are no less deterministic than those of Riesman and Whyte. Determinism itself is fiercely assailed in the next selection by Harold Rosenberg, essayist and social critic, as a species of fatalism which precludes a "radical and realistic" attack on the problems of American society. Expressing alarm at what he takes to be the acquiescent attitude of the "new sociology" and its failure to prescribe effectively for the ills of modern culture, Rosenberg rejects Whyte's injunctions to "pull down the blind" on the picture window and to cheat on the corporation's personality tests. These are counsels of despair: not only are they inadequate as tactics of individuality, but, more consequentially, they give over the quest for the radical reform of institutions which is essential to the preservation of individuality. Thus Rosenberg concludes that "Neither Whyte nor Riesman indicates any direction in which the American person can realize himself in the actual world." He contends further that the world they depict is not, in fact, the "actual world." Out of nostalgia for a presumptive golden age of individualism, according to Rosenberg, the practitioners of the "new sociology" project a "morbid" and distorted image of America. Arguing *ad hominem,* Rosenberg attributes that distortion to the other-directed malaise of social scientists and journalists whose picture of the outer world is actually an expression, writ large, of their own personal discontents.

The penultimate selection, excerpted from Riesman's essay on "The Saving Remnant," spells out the ethical imperative in Riesman's characterology and enables the reader to gauge the relevance of Rosenberg's indictment. Riesman is by no means unconcerned with institutional and structural reform: "I have always felt it important," he wrote in the preface to the most recent edition

[4]A revision of this essay appears in Lipset's *The First New Nation: The United States in Historical and Comparative Perspective* (New York: Basic Books, Inc., 1963), chap. 3.

of *The Lonely Crowd,* "to think on two levels simultaneously: a middle-level area of reformist concerns and possibilities where one works within the given system, and a more long-run Utopian concern with fundamental transformations."[5] Reform at either level can be accomplished only by the action of "the saving remnant"—that small minority of autonomous or self-directed persons who are not implacably driven by compulsive conformity to the dictates and expectations of others. Such persons are psychologically "capable of freedom": they can determine, within limits, the extent of their conformity. Because, moreover, the essence of autonomy is "heightened self-consciousness," the other-directed society may be a singularly congenial milieu for its development. Finally, autonomy presupposes an enlightened understanding of the conditions of social life as they actually are. To advance that requisite knowledge is the entire point of Riesman's analysis of the character of Americans.[6]

The study of change and continuity in the national character is not merely retrospective, nor is it the concern solely of Americans themselves. It is therefore fitting for a foreign observer to have the last word in this volume, and for that observer to reflect upon the prospects for America. In "Adieu to America" the French writer and critic Simone de Beauvoir takes leave of the United States after a four-months' visit with some astringent and provocative remarks on the problems and promise of the New World nation. To Mlle. de Beauvoir, as to her countrymen Crèvecoeur and Tocqueville, the destinies of mankind are foreshadowed in America: "the future of man is at stake here." To that future, full of opportunities and perils, and to the Americans who will live in it, this collection of readings is hopefully and soberly addressed.

---

[5]Riesman, *op. cit.,* p. xxxiii.

[6]See *ibid.,* Part III, for a discussion of the opportunities for, and obstacles to, autonomy in contemporary America.

DAVID RIESMAN

From Morality to Morale

It is a difficult problem to attempt as in this series of lectures to link the psychological understanding of people to specific political and other social phenomena. In his paper Professor Parsons tried to show how individuals play roles in a society and how these roles within a social system may harness various types of personalities. To put it more specifically, you can get the same kind of political behavior, for instance, out of quite different human types. Although the behavior has different meanings for these people, the understanding of their differences and those different meanings may be quite irrelevant to their political and public role.

Nevertheless, and this is the topic of my discourse, it seems to me that personality does influence political behavior if we look at it in a sufficiently long-run historical view. Its influence is felt not in terms of specific behavior—in terms of explaining why somebody votes for Truman or Dewey or Wallace—but only in terms of what I like to call political style, the kind of attitude a person has towards the political cosmos: how he reacts to it, how he feels it reacting to him. If one is to speak as more than a spot-news analyst of political crisis, then he must be concerned with these long-run developments both in politics and personality.[1]

In fact, I think there is a danger for the social scientist if he allows such a phrase as political crisis to make him try to be particularly relevant in talking about spot news, the atom bomb, or what not. Because curiously enough if the social scientist is any good he can't help being relevant. He lives in our society as a participant-observer and it is no problem for him to be relevant—he can't help it. If he isn't any good, and hence irrelevant, he is sometimes likely to compensate by grandiose ambitions; and when he tries to communicate about politics—to solve present crises—he is likely to say more about his own personality than he says about politics, ironically just because he is trying too hard to talk about politics.

Reprinted with permission of the publisher from *Personality and Political Crisis* edited by Alfred H. Stanton and Stewart E. Perry. Copyright 1951 by The Free Press, A Corporation.

[1]This topic is treated more fully in *The Lonely Crowd,* by David Riesman (with the collaboration of Reuel Denney and Nathan Glazer) ; New Haven, Yale University Press, 1950 ; chapters 8–12.

That is at least my prologue for taking an excursion in this paper which will go back 100 years in American history. In this way we can take a look at the changes in American character and American political style as developing from the nineteenth century to the present. I know what I have to say is difficult, and I hope that in the discussion period the unanswered ambiguities in what I say can be brought up and threshed out.

Let me first present my dramatis personae. There are two types of character in the cast: one I call the inner-directed type and the other I call the other-directed type. And they orient themselves to the world in two political styles. I call the first, the style of the moralizers, and the second, the style of the inside-dopesters. And the scene on which these moralizers and inside-dopesters play their parts is in the changing power configurations of this country in the last decades. Naturally, the broad outlines of such a drama as this must be tentative, must be experimental.

Let me begin by describing what kind of people the inner-directeds are. In framing my character types, in trying to work with character types which have psychoanalytic depth and also historical relevance, I have focused on the problem of how conformity is assured; what these people conform to; what their society or their group in society expects of them. This, it seems to me, changes over historical time. In the nineteenth century—and still to a great extent in this century—it seems to me that conformity was assured by a mechanism which I call inner-direction, in which a person was socialized in an authoritative family group by impressive and often oppressive parents and in which he internalized his image of these parents. Freud's picture of the superego is a magnificent picture of this type. This was the typical American of the middle class of the last century, the parents and grandparents of most of us today. Some of us could still be called inner-directed.

Now, the inner-directed person is oriented early in childhood towards very clear goals in life. It may be money, fame, power, goodness, or any blend of these. And he is headed for these by the kind of intimate family socialization characteristic of his age. I like to use a metaphor to describe this mechanism. I speak of these people as gyroscopically-steered. The parents install a gyroscope in them and it stabilizes them all their life. They are less independent than they seem because the gyroscope keeps them on the course for which their parents headed them.

What is the kind of society in which such types will live and work? Theirs is a world in which the opening frontiers are the frontiers of production, discovery, science. We might call it the job-minded society—a society in which people are very much aware and interested in the malleability of the physical environment, the organizational environment, and in their social mobility, their ambitions. Their preoccupation is to harness themselves to fulfilling the tasks of the expanding society which needs a large physical plant, extensive social organization, extensive military preparation. In this kind of a job-minded society people are protected from too close resonance with each other by their concentration on these necessary and rewarding tasks.

It does not follow from this that the inner-directed man, concentrated on these tasks, is not concerned with people. People may be means to the ends of his gyroscopically-installed goal—people as voters, workers, soldiers. And he may be a pretty good manipulator of them for these ends. The point that is decisive in distinguishing him from the other-directed man is that he does not need anything from these peoples as ends in themselves. He does not look to them for approval. He does not look to them for warmth. He looks to them for usefulness and in other more specific and more tangible ways.

Obviously I am speaking in terms of contrast, and in order to do so I create what those who have sociological training would recognize as an ideal type—ideal not in the sense of noble, but ideal in the sense of abstract. There is no pure inner-directed man. Most of us are blends. We can make a judgment of the emphasis of these tendencies within given individuals or given social epochs.

In this job-minded society in which people oriented themselves early towards clearly defined goals, young people had clear models to follow. They might be very ambitious and hitch themselves to some star in the ancestral firmament. If they were going to be scientists, they might want to imitate Pasteur; or if painters, they might want to imitate Renoir. They thought in terms of great men. Maybe they thought their parents were great men; and they headed for that. They modeled themselves on these people. This was possible because the personal star developed in this way did not become obsolete but was good for a lifetime. In the case of the personality market, the market on which people sell themselves, there was a fair amount of stability so that a person who decided, when he was very young, that he wanted to be like, let us say, Henry Ford or Abraham Lincoln was not likely to find people calling him quaint by the time he was fifty—because others had gyroscopes too, spinning at about the same pace, moving in the same direction. People who had this type of character found themselves on the whole rewarded, found their lives unproblematical in the sense of concern with whether they fitted or not. To put the matter more generally, there was a certain fit between social structure and character structure.

Having said this, I think I have to stop at once and suggest that one should not get nostalgic about "life with father." As a play it may be amusing; but if he is your father, if he has hurt you, that may be a different matter. I think this nostalgia is actually an important social and political force in our time, and I want to come back to it later on.

Let me now introduce the next person in the dramatis personae, the other-directed. A new source of conformity is required, it seems to me, for the urban upper middle class in our big cities, a conformity for which gyroscopic adaption is not sufficiently flexible, not sufficiently resonant with other people. And for this new source of conformity I like to use the metaphor of the radar set. The other-directed child has a radar set installed, by which he can understand the interpersonal environment and see its signals around him. He is oriented very early in life, not to his ancestors, not to his parents or to his image of their exalted selves, but to his peers; that is, the other kids on the block, the other kids at school, the people who will do a great deal of the job of socializing him. In fact, those who are familiar with the work of Harry Stack Sullivan can see that he has become in a sense the analyst of this age because he was the person above all others who called attention to the importance of the peer group in the process of socialization.

One can see that the parents play a hand in this by their concern with whether the child is popular, how he is getting along with the other kids. One can see that the school also is concerned today more with morale than with morality—concerned with the social atmosphere. I speak now obviously of the progressive schools in the suburban and urban areas where the other-directed as a character type is emerging. The school puts a youngster in with the five-year-olds to see if he fits with the five-year-olds, not in terms of how much he knows, but in terms of how he gets along. And the parents are anxious and judge their success with their children by how the children get along, how popular they are; the parents act as chauffeurs and managers for the continuous stage performance of their children in the peer group.

It is important to see what the radar brings to the other-directed child. It brings direction; it brings a sense of what is worth having in life, what is worth experiencing, what is worth talking about, thinking about. And the goals obviously change with what the radar senses rather than being set for a lifetime as in the earlier epoch. Obviously I don't mean to imply that parents set about consciously to create little paragons who will fit into the society of 1950 or 1960 or 1970. They aren't that calculating, even if they would like to be. It is a long and complicated story and one, I am sure, many social investigators have worked on and thought about: how it happens that the parents, without actually being consciously aware of their role in this process, produce the children whom the next society makes use of. It is a story I cannot go into here. But I want to remark on just one of the changes from inner-direction to other-direction which might be called the change from bringing up children to bringing up father, for children may bring up parents in the other-directed society.

I think one might recognize, if he is interested in historical questions, that this does not sound so new. Perhaps the other-directed American is in a way the American as he appeared to the eyes of 150 years of European observation. The European always thought that the American was a person who cared more for what his fellows thought than anything else, that the American was more concerned with indiscriminate approval and with warmth, more dependent on his neighbors than the European was—or at least more than the European who came to America to look around. And certainly there is very much in the way of social change and so on which helps to explain why it is we have a comic strip called "Bringing Up Father" in which the daughter as well as the mother cooperates.

Now, what is the kind of society in which the other-directed person moves?

For him the frontiers are not the frontiers of production but the frontiers of consumption, the frontiers of much more abundant leisure and consumer goods. He moves in a society where—at least in his picture of it—the main productive job is done. The steel mills are built, the railroads are built, the mines are dug, the government organizations are set up. And his concern is to live as a consumer. Those who may be economists can recognize the touch of Keynesian economics in that. But I want to make clear that I am not talking about conspicuous consumption—I am not talking about keeping up with the Joneses. That is an older, perhaps a traditional pattern. As long as one is concerned only with what goods he is getting out of society, out of its physical productiveness, he is still inner-directed. A person is other-directed only when his interest is not in the goods—he takes those for granted. After all, the middle-class family can have a car, a mink coat, good food, and so on. Consumption itself is no issue for most of these people. The problem for the other-directed person is not the goods themselves, but the right attitudes about the goods. Is he having the right experiences vis-à-vis the wine he drinks, the car he drives, the girl he sleeps with, and so on? That is the problem. And he looks to others for guidance as to whether he is experiencing the right experiences on the frontiers of consumption. He takes more or less for granted that he has the wherewithal, the ability to pay unremittingly to provide himself with the goods themselves.

This is another way of saying that in America we have moved from a job-minded society to a people-minded society in which one's concern is no longer with the malleability of the material but with the malleability of the personnel. It is a society in which people are no longer protected from each other by the objectivity of their workaday tasks and in which response from others becomes an end in life as well as a means.

In fact, I think it is quite interesting to look at specific individuals and see to what extent they may rationalize their need for warmth, their need for approval from others, in terms of, let us say, some sensible and easily rationalized goal such as money or security.

Think of Willy Loman, in the play, *Death of a Salesman,* as a man who looked to selling, not primarily for money—that too—but as a source of affection, a means of justifying himself, a *Weltanschauung*—all these things wrapped up in the job of the salesman. Incidentally, the play seemed quite incomprehensible to Londoners. They couldn't understand why anybody was that interested in selling and why people responded in terms other than cash. The English response showed that they didn't understand Americans. Obviously in such a society the old clear goals of ambition, the old stars of the heavenly firmament by which the inner-directed man guided himself no longer guide people.

Let me give an illustration. There was an interview with a thirteen-year-old girl about her comic-reading habits.[2] She was asked what comics she preferred

[2]The interview is reported by Katherine M. Wolf and Marjorie Fiske, "The Children Talk About Comics"; in *Communications Research 1948–1949,* edited by Lazarsfeld and Stanton; New York, Harper, 1949; pp. 26–27.

and she said Superman. Then she was asked why. "Oh, Superman can fly," she said, "and flying is very important." "Would you like to be able to fly?" the interviewer asked. "Oh, no, that would be kind of conspicuous," the girl said. Here one sees the fear of being conspicuous, the fear of being too ambitious, the fear somebody might say, "So you think you're big—so you think you're something." These are the fears which make it hard for people brought up in other-directed circles to have the same kind of sometimes fanatical and crushing ambition which was a characteristic of the middle-class man of an earlier epoch, a characteristic which still hangs on in this country because—obviously I am talking about trends—there are still men like Henry Ford.

I am talking about something that the investigator finds more among the young than the old, more in the upper middle class in the very large metropolitan areas than in the smaller cities and smaller towns. And this seems to me to be connected in subtle ways with the alteration of mobility channels. One no longer gets ahead in the society by making a better mousetrap but by packaging an old mousetrap in a new way and selling it by selling one's self first.

Those who know Erich Fromm's book *Man for Himself*[3] will recognize the similarity of his marketing orientation to what I call the other-directed man. The man of the marketing orientation is concerned with how he is doing on the personality market of the large corporate enterprises, private, public, academic, and what not, of our society. And in order to succeed on the personality market he must be different but not too different; as different as Ford from Chevrolet—maybe as far different as Studebaker from Ford. And so he must always use his radar to find out: "Am I different enough to be recognized—to have a brand name, so to speak, for my personality—but not so different that I will be priced out of the market as an eccentric?" But even eccentricity can be made to pay in the right professions. Success comes in our society increasingly, it seems to me, through a person's ability to be malleable enough to fit into a cooperative network.

Adam Smith used the phrase "the invisible hand" to describe the economic organization of the free market. I think we have moved from the invisible hand to the glad hand and that today people in industry and the professions—particularly in medicine—are engaged in a cooperative network in which the esteem of colleagues is decisive for one's fate and in which to be known as a rate-buster would exclude one from the system. To be sure, there are survivals of the older age, but I am talking of the social character that seems to me to be emerging.

Let me now turn to the question of the political styles which seem to me in a rather indeterminate way to spring from these respective types of character. Yet first of all it must be recognized that the majority of Americans have no distinctive political style at all. There is very little traceable connection, it seems to me, between their character and their politics. Their politics depends

[3] New York, Rinehart and Company, 1947.

on their situation, as I said at the outset, and not on their personality. Let me give an illustration.

If one takes a look at the book called *Southern Politics,*[4] he will see that Professor Key interprets southern politics in America today as being dominated by what he calls the black-belt whites, the whites who live in the counties of large Negro predominance, and that their influence is, to a degree, based on the southern electoral systems as these have been inherited in several southern states. Now here is a situation in which—in order to understand this kind of southern politics—it would do very little good to interpret in idiosyncratic terms the character structure of the black-belt whites. To be sure, the fact that they are black-belt whites will reveal something about their character structure. But the situation and the electoral machinery in which the populace is caught matters much more than their character. Consequently, when I speak of style, I speak here only of those people in whom one can trace a connection between politics and character, and this limits me to those who are politically active either as political leaders and operators or as avid consumers of the political news of the day.

The first style I shall describe is the style of the moralizer—the political manifestation of inner-direction. However, not all inner-directed people are involved in politics; and they are not inevitably moralizers. Rather, this is the style which is politically compatible with their character. Their character gives them a slight push in the direction of being moralizers.

The moralizer is a person who views politics as a field of work and not primarily as a field of entertainment or consumption. To be sure, in the nineteenth century when the moralizer was in his heyday, there were torchlight parades, and politics was not entirely unamusing and unsportive. But on the whole politics was a field of work or, as many businessmen thought, interference with work. It was judged from the standpoint of work, from the standpoint of the harnessing of the resources of the society. The moralizer would never have attended a lecture with a title of *Personality and Political Crisis.* He would not have known what it meant, because for him politics stayed in its limited place. He thought of it in terms of government institutions, electoral machinery, and so on. Because he defined politics in a limited way, it helped him to view politics as a manageable domain—small, encompassable, not too complicated. He defined it in such a way as to leave it relatively uncomplicated. And correlatively his own relation to it was uncomplicated because he knew what he wanted. Because his goals were clear, he could decide where in politics his interests lay, either in terms of self-interest, or the interest of his group, his nation, or his god. The moralizer, by defining politics in a limited way, by defining his relationship to it in terms of a clear picture of his self-interest—often mistaken, but clear—did not feel overwhelmed. So many people today feel overwhelmed by politics, but to the moralizer, politics was masterable, was graspable. One had a vision—if one were inner-directed and a moralizer—of what was good work, what was a good political performance, and what was

[4]V. O. Key, *Southern Politics in State and Nation;* New York, Knopf, 1949.

a bad political performance; and one could relate politics to these definitions.

The term moralizer is a little misleading in this connection. I don't mean that the moralizer was necessarily a moral man in the sense of having high morality or ethics. Rather, he was a person who clearly defined his relation to the political world, and since the discourse in this country in the nineteenth century was largely moralistic, he didn't have too much trouble in defending, let us say, a log-rolling job in moral terms.

But we must also think of the nineteenth century as a period in which enormous moralizing energies were harnessed in the political scene. To expand the school system, to do something about prisons and the insane, to free the slaves—all these issues provided a moralistic frame of reference in which people could take clear positions and feel relatively unfloundering in a narrowly-defined political ocean.

But this statement is an oversimplification of the nineteenth century. How much of an oversimplification? We can remind ourselves if we take a look at a very, as I think, exciting passage from Tocqueville who came over and took an unequalled brilliant look at this country in the 1830's. He wrote:

> It is difficult to say what place is taken up in the life of an inhabitant of the United States by his concern for politics. To take a hand in the regulation of society and to discuss it is his biggest concern and, so to speak, the only pleasure an American knows. In some countries the inhabitants seem unwilling to avail themselves of the political privileges which the law gives them. It would seem that they set too high a value on their time to spend it on the interests of the community. But if an American were condemned to confine his activities to his own affairs, he would be robbed of one half of his existence. He would feel an immense void in the life he is accustomed to lead. His wretchedness would be unbearable.[5]

One can see by this quotation some of the ambiguities of the use of politics as an agenda, as a way to get through the day, as a way to harness one's self in the nineteenth century.

It is awfully hard to say where the nineteenth-century American stood. Think of the people up in the State of Vermont who thought the country was engulfed in a masonic conspiracy. Think of the people who thought that Phi Beta Kappa was a subversive organization. But on the whole the moralizer's picture of the world was a pretty clear picture, and the Know-Nothing and so on of that day was rather the forerunner of what I like to call the bewildered moralizer of today—the person whose world has vanished and who turns into a curdled indignant when he contemplates the political scene. He no longer understands it—politics refuses to fit into its narrow compartments. Much of the outcry against the welfare state and so on comes from people who say, "Politics ought to stay where I put it." And it won't stay. Then the self-interest of a person no longer seems clear.

What way does self-interest lie today in politics? What way does morality lie?

While the conflict between public and private moralities is an old one, the network of publics to be considered makes the discussion of moral issues today

[5]Alexis de Tocqueville, *Democracy in America;* New York, Knopf, 1945.

ever more complicated, ambiguous, and equivocal. The bewildered moralizer, the curdled indignant, reacts negatively to this. The world doesn't make sense to him. And one thing that facilitates this development is the fact that he lives in a society increasingly other-directed, in which the mass media of communication bombard him with messages which he can't understand.

What is the small-town curdled indignant to make of Billy Rose's accounts of love and life at Lindy's? What is he to do about network radio, about the sophisticated pace of A-budget movies? He can't follow them. But there is one place where he can follow. He can follow politics because he can make politics obey him. The editorial writer, the political campaigner appeal to the curdled indignant with an old familiar tune. They tell him that after all his world would make sense if only a few bad people, these smooth city slickers, these other-directed men, were to be thrown out. Then the world would go back to where it could be run by the invisible hand.

This brings me to the inside-dopester, the political manifestation of the other-directed. He is socialized in a setting where he can't be too conspicuous, where he learns to hold his emotional fire, and where he learns to bring certain skills to bear which are chiefly skills of consumption, skills of the consumer.

A short time ago I was talking with some friends of mine who have two children, aged four and five. They told me the children could look at the cars in the street and tell which is a '50 Pontiac and which is a '49 Oldsmobile. As very young children they have become members of the consumers' union. And when they become a little bit older, they bring this consumers'-union skill to bear on politics. They may bring it to bear in one of two ways. First, the inside-dopester may try to manipulate others, in which case he will interpret politics as a problem of being able to get the right man on the telephone. But if he is less close to the switchboard, if he is less close to the politically-operative group, then he is likely not to be able to manipulate others. In this case he will choose the second way: he will harness his manipulative energies solely to himself, in order to make sure that he has the right reactions to the political news.

Many people have doubtless observed, if they have been in government service—or indeed anywhere—that politics is a form of office gossip in which to have the right reaction is all that is required of one. The goal of the inside-dopester is never to be taken in by any person, cause, or event; that is, to be a sharp member of the consumers' union. It is interesting to trace these developments, even in radical left-wing politics. A generation ago the young Communist, for instance, had to have a working knowledge of Marxism, had to be able to handle the dialectic, had to make noises like a Marxist. Today all he has to do is know how to get Marcantonio elected. It is no longer necessary for him to be able to have a stance on principle, at least in the political scene.

I think one can say in general that the inside-dopester sees politics as a field of mood engineering. Sometimes the only moods he can engineer are his own and those of his small peerage. At other times he can try to engineer the mood of a nation. This is his way of coping with the growing complexity of politics, the complexity which no longer submits to the simplifications of the moralizer.

One other way of tracing this development is to ask one's self: In any social setting, who are the people who make a living by scaring businessmen or government officials? In the nineteenth century the people who made the best living in this way were lawyers, and they frightened businessmen and government officials about their standing with two very limited publics—judges and legislators. The scare was not great because often the judges and legislators could be managed for cash on the barrelhead. In this rather simple picture the businessman might be a little frightened by the pictures his lawyer drew for him, but after all he knew what the lawyer was describing; and the lawyer himself was a fellow who knew the institutional structure, knew how to talk to judges and legislators.

Today it is my impression that the dependence on the lawyer has lessened and it is the contact man who frightens businessmen and government officials about a whole range of publics which are as likely to disappear on inspection as did the Cheshire cat. These are all those publics who may say nasty things about the businessman, if, for instance, he does not do the right thing or make the right public-relations move. In this amorphous sea of contacts the businessman no longer knows what his interests are and he has to ask his public-relations advisor not only what publics to propitiate but what interest he has in propitiating them. Of course, this work may still be done by lawyers —that is, members of the bar who have not had this attitude trained out of them by their education.

It may be said, in fact, that whereas the moralizer's gullibility about politics was often based on limiting his definition of politics, the inside-dopester's gullibility about politics is often based on the delusion, basic to his whole character and basic to his attitude, that there is somebody somewhere—maybe Kiplinger, maybe the people who write the *Newsweek* "Periscope," maybe a private eye of some sort—who sees all and knows all. But actually—and this is part of the ambiguous development of our society—the inside-dopester *does* know more than the moralizer. He is better informed; his range is wider; he is able to see both sides. There are very few innocents left to go fight city hall.

Another facet in this development which has moved us from morality to morale is the necessity of the political consumer today to be ready for rapid changes of line. His political attitude, his political style might be obsolete in a moment if he did not have his radar set in good working order. And this is part of the increasingly fast pace with which our society makes obsolete automobiles, people, and ideas. One interesting way of tracing this empirically—of course in a very tentative way—is to study public opinion polls. And there we see, interestingly enough, that the middle class—that is, the group in which these tendencies are far more manifest than in the working class—shifts its political attitudes much more rapidly and readily. It is true about their opinion on the last war and on Russia.

I have been struck by Machiavelli's observation—contrary to all the political observers of his day and many since—that the masses are far less fickle than the rulers. And I think public opinion polls show this to be true. "Fickle" may be the wrong word, too biased a word, because the readiness of the middle class for rapid changes of line is connected with the actual changes in the situation; with the greater reality-orientation vis-à-vis politics which many inside-dopesters have.

The problem is that the inside-dopester's motive for political consumption, for political operation, is not to secure a reality-orientation. For him politics is a means of group conformity, if he lives in a group where it is fashionable to be up on the political news of the day. In other groups (and, to a degree, in the same group) one might be up on the sporting news.

These are the compelling motivations that keep the inside-dopester political in spite of the evaporation of his political emotions. It is an interesting problem: the inside-dopester is a person who is not committed, who does not bring to politics a clear notion of his own self-interest or clear principles—yet he follows politics. I think he follows politics because he lives in a group which follows politics. Then one might ask, why does the group follow politics? This is a question that I cannot get into here. I would just mention one paradox. Where the group to which the inside-dopester belongs is a moralizing group, he will look like a moralizer, sound like a moralizer, feel himself to be a moralizer.

I want to get into a more fundamental paradox; namely, the fact that the word "morale" conceals a moral judgment. I think we in the Western society have changed our style in hypocrisy. The Victorian hypocrite was a person who concealed bad actions under the high-sounding cloak of good ones. But ever since Freud and a number of other people, the hypocrite has concealed his good actions under the cloak of solid self-interest. This hypocrisy makes it possible to disguise, under such a term as morale, one's morality.

A student working with me has been doing a number of interviews in the community outside Chicago called Park Forest, a newly-developing suburb which has been built by the American Community Builders, a large real estate operation. This student went out there in the early days of this development and he asked people what they thought about the American Community Builders, what they thought about their community, and what their political attitudes were. Many had grievances about their homes, lawns, roads, and so on. But from many of those people with grievances he got this answer: "The American Community Builders has bad public relations." They emphasized no grievance as much as that. What does that mean if you try to analyze it for latent meaning? The respondent seems to be saying: "The trouble with the stupid people who run this town is that they haven't made me like it." Or he might not even be saying that. He may be saying: "They haven't made those other fellows like it." He conceals any judgment based on principle, on his own experience, on his own life, under the cover of the bad mechanics, the poor mood engineering on the part of the operators.

I will cite another illustration. Some of my associates and I did some interviews before the last election. We asked people about the candidates. And we found many people who said, "Well, Truman is sincere and Dewey is insincere." We tried to think what that meant. Why did they use this word? And I was reminded of the fact that in doing interviews on popular music a student came across the same expression. He played a record for people and then asked, "Well, did you like the record?" "Oh, yes, I like Dinah Shore. She's so sincere." Or, "I like Frank Sinatra. He's so sincere." What does this judgment mean? I don't know all the answers to that question. I think we would understand a lot if we knew. I have some hunches about it. I think for one thing this judgment on the basis of sincerity is a moral judgment; that is, "This man can manipulate me because he involves himself in his performance. He sends me. And I allow him to send me because he is sending himself too." But there is more to it than that. This is a judgment in terms of personality—at least in the field of politics and I think also in the field of popular music—and it is not one of personality only. Using the criterion of sincerity may be an avoidance of the judgment of performance. Is Dinah Shore a good singer? Has she got the right vocal equipment? Is the political candidate able to deliver? Judgment on the basis of answers to these questions is ducked by focusing on an issue of mood which in many political situations is of little importance. If the moralizer thought that he wanted a government of laws and not of men, the inside-dopester thinks he wants a government of men and not of laws. Both have unattainable ideals.

I have said that there were concealed moral judgments—repressed morality—in the reaction of the inside-dopester. The psychiatrist knows, I think, that people often end up being what they play at being. And since the inside-dopester has given up trying to find out what he wants in politics, he is more and more apt to tolerate what is wanted of him, provided it is put in a nice way.

I want to turn now to the stage on which these characters play, and ask what are the changes in the political configuration of this country that may evoke and reward either inner-directed or other-directed tendencies within people—thus, in turn, encouraging or repressing one or another political style. In my opinion it is of decisive importance both for political style and for character that we no longer have a clear social-class hierarchy in America.

Let me put the problem this way. Who runs the country? This was a relatively easy question to answer in 1896. The people like Morgan were at the top of the prestige ladder; they were models for ambitious youth, whether in the Horatio Alger stories or in the *Saturday Evening Post*. They were the focus of attention. These were the captains of industry, and they dominated the country fifty years ago.

Who runs the country today? It's a hard question. Who ranks whom at a dinner party? Is an Army colonel superior to a doctor at the Washington School of Psychiatry? How about a college professor, the head of an oil company, the head of a big advertising agency, Jack Benny? Which way is up? Who are the models for youth? The answer to these questions as stated in the mass media—see the brilliant study made by Leo Lowenthal of the popular magazines, *Saturday Evening Post* and *Colliers*[6]—is that the focus of attention is no longer on the captains of industry but on what I like to call the captains of nonindustry: a Hollywood star, a golf pro, a cafe-society boy. Take a look at the men-of-distinction ads and tell me who runs the country!

It seems to me that what we have today is a situation in which the older hierarchy has crumbled and has been replaced by a lot of smaller hierarchies which I like to call the veto groups; that is, the lobbies. And whereas the political leader in 1896 had a clear relationship to his public, the political leader today is found within the lobby, within the Farm Bureau, the trade associations, the American Jewish Congress, the American Medical Association, and so on, endlessly. They are veto groups because they have a much better opportunity to stop action than to start it. Their concern is chiefly with prevention. But with this change in hierarchy comes a change in the type of attitude one has to have to operate in politics and understand politics. The lobbyist within one of these veto groups is concerned with the veto subgroups within his own group down to the last veto group of one. It may be a recalcitrant farmer who will not conform with the Farm Bureau's policies. It may be a recalcitrant who holds out on the union leader. And when the lobbyist is operating with other co-equals who are heads of other veto groups his concern is that each of them has a "reasonable" and just slightly expanding cut of the political pie. In today's politics there are a great many ins and very few outs. And the leader, therefore, in the older sense is virtually disappearing. What we see instead as the so-called leader is either the man who can placate the veto groups and operate within this framework of coalitions—as Roosevelt did so capably—or the man who tries to deal with the few unorganized wretches who have not yet invented their group. But obviously this leads to a situation in which there is a constant elaboration of the publics with which leaders are concerned. The need to see and propitiate these publics can be rationalized in terms of public relations.

One sees a very interesting thing in the discussion of the atom bomb and the hydrogen bomb today which I might put in terms of the old cartoon "Who's excited?" Everybody is concerned with everybody else's mood and asking that question in regard to all these various publics, whether or not these publics have any actual power to affect the course of events. In fact, actual ignorance of who has power is in some ways an asset if one is to be a veto-group leader because it permits one to propitiate still other publics in terms of the fact that they might have power. Let me give an illustration: If a college professor writes a book attacking business, he makes a lot of jobs for his students in the business world, for business must answer him. The businessmen want to be told that there are some people who don't like them and whom they

[6]Leo Lowenthal, "Biographies in Popular Magazines," in *Radio Research 1942–43,* edited by Lazarsfeld and Stanton (New York, Duell, Sloan & Pearce, 1944), p. 507.

need to propitiate, whether or not the professor's book sells any copies or has any weight.

In this situation of complex and tenuous interpersonal webs within the lobbies and among the lobbies, obviously it takes a man with the gifts and the social skills more nearly like those of the inside-dopester to get along rather than those skills associated with the moralizer. Thus the skills of the inside-dopester are in demand.

Of course, many people still assume we have a ruling class in this country. But I think one of the reasons they assume this is that they need to justify their own propitiation. They can't tell themselves that they need to be liked; therefore they have to assume somebody has power. I think another reason, perhaps more basic, is the feeling of discomfort if there is nobody in charge. Everyone likes to think that there is someone in charge, even if the person in charge does not represent him.

Plainly, these emotional ideas of the inside-dopester are not the only ones current in politics. I have left aside for a moment the curdled indignant—the bewildered moralizer who feels that the world doesn't make sense to him. Mood engineering on the part of the inside-dopester is a red flag to the curdled indignant. What the latter responds to is the appearance of impiety, violence, on the part of a Pegler or the *New York Daily News* or Branch Rickey; that is, the very mood engineering which the inside-dopester attempts as a way of propitiating publics may be just the thing which makes the curdled indignant feel most bewildered and most angry. So he falls back, as I indicated earlier, to a more familiar style, a style of the *political* indignant, of the leader who is able to say: "There are a few bad men around and all we have to do is get rid of them." But even the other-directed man, just because he doesn't know what he wants, just because of his concern with the plethora of publics, has a tendency to call on older types when the going gets rough. When the glad hand is rebuffed, the inside-dopester may even wish *not* to reach an agreement, whereas earlier he would have given anything for someone to say: "Let's agree to disagree." So it is that the inside-dopester is in some ways unfit for conflict. In fact, "conflict" is a word he avoids. He prefers the words "tension," "low morale," or "poor communications."

All this may delay the triumph of morale over morality. But little hope lies in that delay. I think it should be clear, from what I have said, that neither the style of the moralizer nor the style of the inside-dopester is adequate to politics. The former sees politics in too limited a context. And the latter fails to bring to politics the very humanity which would let him react as a human being; as a result, he often fails to see the potentialities which lie underneath the "reality" to which he is so passionately attached.

Now we might ask, What changes in American political structure and what changes in American character structure might bring new motives into play in the political arena and thus reward the development of a more mature political style?

People today are asked to participate and involve themselves in politics for motives that seem to me inadequate. They are asked to involve themselves by appeals to self-interest—as if we were still living in the days of the moralizers when everyone knew what his interests were. They are asked to involve themselves by appeals to group conformity—often snob appeals to be active politically and belong to the PTA or the DAR or what not. Or they are appealed to on behalf of a Sincere Candidate who will decide all the questions for them.

It is probably not possible to decide how to appeal to other motivations and get results. But at least it is necessary to raise the question of whether the trouble lies always with the people, or whether it might not be found in the politics. Is the American political scene so dull or uninteresting that there is no reason why people should be interested for good motives? Might it not make more sense to improve the political wares that are offered to the American people, rather than to spend energy on asking Americans to participate in, to be concerned about, to be less apathetic about politics? Are there not other political packages that Americans can buy?

I think that a beginning can be made on this problem by concentrating on evoking more political imagination. Why not indicate more alternatives to the American people, especially in the domestic scene? For instance, it might be pointed out that there is a wider range of choice in the kinds of lives people might lead, if they wished. But this is only possible if in such an attempt a more experimental attitude is assumed: Americans need not always be satisfied with denouncing the political show, as curled indignants; or with trying to alter the mood of the show or their own mood towards it, as inside-dopesters.

DAVID RIESMAN

The Found Generation

It is not easy to say when one generation ends and another begins (as Karl Mannheim noted in his essay on "The Problem of the Generations"), for people are not produced in batches, as are pancakes, but are born continuously. And it is only in certain countries and in certain epochs that historical events, as unconsciously transmitted through parents to their children, lead to a generational gap rather than a smooth and silent succession—a gap across which the young cannot easily talk to the old who grew up in a different world. Obviously, moreover, even the most drastic changes fail to break the continuity in every family, and there will always be members of any current generation who resemble their ancestors more than they resemble their peers.

Still, we have certain conventions, as illustrated in silver weddings, twenty-fifth reunions—and twenty-fifth anniversaries of magazines, colleges and corporations; these make sure that people with a normal life span will have some occasions for an intellectual sabbatical or day of reflection. What for others, however, is a sabbatical occasion is for me, as a social scientist, a regular preoccupation with discontinuities in attitudes and values, both between "my" generation and its predecessors and successors. I have become a reader of college class-reports, which permit the comparison at least of college "generations" with their rapid turnover, as well as make it possible to follow shifts in the attitudes and career patterns of the same generation at five-year or ten-year intervals.

To be sure, there are flaws in such a procedure, among them the fact that the regional and social-class base of a college does not remain constant: one might find great changes which said more about the "career" of the college—for instance, its loss of religious tone, or its wider geographic base—than about changes in the values of comparable individuals. We know, moreover, that not everyone responds to the appeals of the class secretary to get his report in; and if he does, he may respond in a very perfunctory way with little more data than "name, rank, and serial number"; the nonrespondents are very likely the less successful, but they may also include those who despise old-grad nostalgia and ceremonies.

If I put aside such misgivings, I can find a certain coherence of values uniting those who were graduated from the major Ivy League colleges between, say, 1920 and 1946. (I shall touch later upon certain differences.) Thus, in the Yale 1946 report, *Decade of Decision,* which has just appeared, one gets an impression of men who remember the Great Depression, who attended college in a wartime era of transition, and whose impetus and drive reflect these origins. In contrast with this, however, it is at least arguable that the men just graduating, whose parents experienced the Depression but who were themselves growing up as the economy improved—men, moreover, many of whose parents, rigidly raised, shifted to a more permissive child-rearing—that these men would belong to a different psychological generation from any comparably large body of previous college graduates. While as a teacher I have had some impression that this may be the case, I have hesitated to trust my impression, since I know I am getting older while my students are not, and that I may not be free of old-grad nostalgia myself.

Thus, I was delighted when recently given the opportunity to study 183 *Time*-commissioned interviews of seniors in last year's graduating class—interviews asking the student respondent what he expected his life to be like in fifteen years, i.e., 1970. Perhaps since so much of that life seemed to be concerned with hunting and fishing, golf, boating and puttering, *Time* turned the interviews over to our Center for the Study of Leisure at the University of Chicago. Our first reaction to the material—I speak here for myself and for Robin Jackson, who independently studied the interviews—was that it was too unreliable to take seriously. Nevertheless, a picture of the Class of 1955 emerged which was congruent with other data—a picture which contrasts sharply, I believe, with what would have been obtained from seniors in the same colleges twenty-five years ago.

Twenty-five years ago, of course, the Great Depression had been under way for two years, forcing many who were graduated then to drop plans for further training, others to take refuge in graduate school against the uninviting job-market. But it was not only the Depression that made students of the Class of 1931 feel uncertain about the future (in contrast to the relative certainty felt by college graduates today) ; it was ambition also. Many of us wanted to make our mark, and were not sure how high we would get. Our class had no floor under it, and by and large did not want a ceiling—indeed, in our generation a number of wellborn men whose floor seemed all too solid chose, in many different ways, to test their ability to live without a floor: they beachcombed (although not so drastically as George Orwell in *Down and Out in Paris and London*) ; or they became anthropologists, labor organizers or cold-water-flat artists and poets; and a number became that bright combination of adventure and responsibility, the foreign correspondent. Such men often wanted to lose the self they had inherited and, romantically, to create a new one out of whole cloth.

Most aspirations pursued by our class, and by classes of the same era at Princeton, Yale, Dartmouth and other colleges concerning which I have scraps of evidence, were more conventional: to make much money, to rise high in the government, to become a doctor, lawyer, merchant or chief. Since the first jobs we got were often makeshifts or didn't appear to lead anywhere, we changed jobs frequently. In a rough estimate, I would say that at least 40 per cent of us in the Class of 1931 have actually changed occupations at least once, not counting war service. There are, naturally, a great many exceptions: men who went into medicine were captured in all but a few cases by the severe system of rehazing and resocializing the student in the medical apprenticeship (but we should recognize that a man who has shifted from internal medicine and private practice to epidemiology and the Public Health Service has actually made a drastic shift of self-definition); men who went into their fathers' business and stayed there; men who are teaching school or practicing law or architecture without infidelity to their first love.

One reason so many of us shifted jobs was that we didn't know ourselves very well, and we knew the world even less well. As Charles McArthur of the Harvard Psychological Clinic has observed, many of the upper-middle-class boys at Harvard in the late 1930's did not know what they wanted to become but only where they wanted to land—up. The route had to be surveyed as they proceeded. Upper-class boys, in contrast, knew what they were expected to become—lawyers, bankers, trustees—but may have tired later of that inherited role and switched into something closer to their repressed desires. In line with these findings, a number of us became critical of our values as we went along. I recall two friends who left Wall Street, where they were doing nicely, one to run a mattress factory for the unemployed, and the other to develop a ranch in the West and get into local politics. Quite apart from depression and taxes—though as part of the same world that brought the latter as a homeopathic remedy for the former—some of our generation concluded that money isn't everything. I remember in college snorting a bit sarcastically at those of my classmates who said that they were going to make a million before they were forty and then retire and "live." But the astonishing thing is how many did something not so dissimilar: they left a profitable job in New York—the mecca for so many then at Harvard and other New England colleges—to find "the good life" in some other work and some other part of the forest. We shall see in contrast to this that hardly any of the Class of 1955 would ever want to live in New York in order to make a million, or in any other big city. "No life in the ulcer belt for me," as one of them says, explaining why: although he plans to enter advertising, he will stay away from New York despite his realization that most big firms have their head offices there.

The same uncertainties that led to changes in occupation and aspiration also seem to me to have been a factor, along with the obvious economic hazard, in the relatively late marriages of so many of our generation. Many of us were searchers, not sure of the type of family life we wanted. Many did not want to be tied down. Nor would it have occurred to us to have our wives support us through graduate school, as is so common today among the young. And,

Skidmore, we realize that these young women were often ambitious, too: indeed, if we think of the Class of 1931 at Radcliffe or Smith, Bryn Mawr or they wanted careers, and not simply an intermittent series of low-level jobs that would help support four or five children and the suburban life the children "deserved." Those of us who did marry before or soon after graduation were often the well-to-do boys who seemed clearly headed down the ancestral occupational paths; and not a few changed wives as well as jobs—perhaps marrying the Mary Monahans that the George Apley family tradition had first forbidden.

World War II served some in these uncommitted groups as a punch bowl serves at a cocktail party—as a switching point allowing the formation of new affiliations. Coming after ten years of doubt or underemployment, it permitted us to discover the potentialities we were often unaware of, to find new confidence and see new parts of the country. It served, of course, for many noncollege men in the same way, and California—the great American suburb, which many saw for the first time during the War—still gains light industry and population as a result. Others, obviously, were affected in other ways: some became better at what they already were—notably so, the doctors, who beefed if the War wasn't arranged for their postgraduate benefit; or, sadly, still others were cut off or, though still living, remained lost. Coming back from the War into an expanding economy (so different from some of the post-World War I economies) we were able to confirm experiences which had only been potential; age might, with equal prosperity, have brought much of this, but the War speeded up things and gave us, I think, more differentiated fates.

Going over our class reports, that recount this at five-year intervals, I have detected a tendency to emphasize increasingly the nonvocational aspects of our lives: the family and hobbies and, markedly, the fabulous array of philanthropic and civic activities into which we have been drawn. It is hard to think of a disease or a civic bane that one of us hasn't "taken" and become a vice-president of! Many of us have, we report, moved to the suburbs for the benefit of the children, or even become exurbanites for the sake of a better family life. Still, we bring these things up because we have done well enough vocationally to "afford" these concessions to the rest of life. Were we without drive, men without readiness to sacrifice the nonwork sides of life, we would not seek the high and demanding posts in business, government and the arts which so many of our class and neighboring classes do hold in far above average trajectories of energetic mobility (even taking account of our inheritances of opportunity). In reading the reports, moreover, I get the impression that our class, though it may no longer have as many Frank Merriwell ambitions, is by no means ready to retire, even if it could financially afford it. (Some of the Class of 1955 talk in the *Time* interviews of the retirement plans in the companies they are going to enter.) Our class still has wants which are unfulfilled, not for things—which it owns in a measure to gladden

New Yorker advertisers of gifts for the man who has everything—but rather for meaning and purpose. George Weller defined us, in his novel of Harvard, as coming to college "not to eat, not for love, but only gliding" (an observation Emerson once made of snakes in Concord) ; we have done a lot of gliding but, unlike snakes, we want to understand what we have endured.

If, then, in this perspective upon ourselves (a perspective which may be too "projective"), we look at the *Time* interviews, we are struck by the knowingness of the present college generation: they come to college to eat, to love (and often to get married), but certainly not to glide. Although they enter a far more prosperous and secure world in economic terms, they appear in more of a hurry—not from a driving ambition which, as we shall see, not many have, but because they have already made up their minds as to exactly who they are and exactly where they want to go on the superhighway of their chosen corporation or profession.

Each knows, understandably enough, the branch of military service he is entering. (At Michigan, for example, the students speak of the "deal" they have in the guided missiles branch of the Army or the personnel section of the Marines or a reserve branch.) No one voices objection to service on political grounds or as a pacifist; and only two complain of the interruption to their careers; a great many see the period of military service as a kind of postgraduate training, helpful to their careers. In any case, such service is a fact of life to be casually accepted and gotten over with. War as a possible interference is scarcely contemplated by these rather optimistic men, and not anticipated by any but a few—largely Catholics for whom world communism is more of an omnipresent menace than it is for most of the respondents. Nor is there anything opaque for the majority about their careers: they know the type of professional office or large corporation they want; and most who are going into business (which includes many who have majored in engineering or chemistry and are going to business school after that) prefer the salaried life of the large corporation. As one Princeton senior says:

> Let's face it, I'll be on salary, not making capital gains, even at 36. . . . Why struggle on my own, when I can enjoy the big psychological income of being a member of a big outfit?

And he points out that he doesn't have the brass his father had to be a lone wolf—a comparison a number of them make, in almost every case with detached admiration for the old man's toughness, but with hardly any despondency for not living up to him as a model.

As another young man says, speaking of the large corporations in general:

> They try to do what's best for you and best for them—if they see you'd do better in one department than in another, they transfer you. . . . There's no back-stabbing and politics like there is in a small firm. Your worth is recognized.

The notion that the company might also recognize negative worth, failure, just doesn't come up; it is the company's role to develop and train, never to threaten or fire. This, indeed, is part of the benevolent world these men foresee and will perhaps help create as a self-confirming prophecy. As one of them remarks:

> I've always believed that if you are honest and sincere and can convince other people that you are, you'll get ahead, and I don't think I'll find out that I am wrong when I get out in the business world.

This is an understandable outlook, especially in view of the experience these men have had of being courted by large corporations. One Michigan senior tells the interviewer:

> One nice thing about it is you don't really have to go out looking for a job—they come around looking for you!

In Stephen Potter's handbook of gamesmanship, he has a ploy to floor any generalizer, namely, "What of the South?"—a question you can ask in any country, for whether in Italy or France, China or the United States, the South is always another country, sometimes another colony. So it is that in these interviews, some of the Southerners, including Texans, seem more eager for the big money, and more willing even to desert the big corporation and the suburb in its pursuit. One senior at Georgia Tech tells the interviewer:

> Fifteen years from now—well, I'm pretty ambitious and I think that I'll be with a progressive company at Burlington. Maybe I'll be a division director making—say—$25,000 a year.

This is a modest aim enough, in all reality, but large in comparison with the others who expect to be making $15,000 or $18,000 at most to support the four children and the two cars, the club dues and church contributions, the vacations in Europe and Bermuda, and the small boat on the lake. He continues:

> And I'll probably be working in the Southeastern states since the trend is definitely toward the elimination of the Eastern mills. But South and Central America are going to move up as textile areas . . . if I do get overseas I think I would enjoy it.

Another Georgia Tech student wants both to write a big novel about the Civil War—he says he thinks there's still a big market for all the magnolia stuff—and to make a lot of money on his father's Mississippi Delta farm. A Texas boy at Princeton is going into the oil and gas business with his father. To this group I should add a Notre Dame boy from Pittsburgh who expects to make big money practicing law, in part because he can count on the influence of his father, a probate judge; and another Catholic, son of an oil and gas producer, a Harvard senior, who says, "Christ, I'd live in Nome, Alaska, if there was money there."

These are the exceptions, however, the immoderates, who want neither the fringe benefit nor the fringe suburb. Their idiosyncracy is evident in the fact that they say more about their careers and less about their prospective wives and families than most. Rather than looking to a large corporation to advance them if they deserve it, they want to find a situation to which *they* make a difference—a situation small enough for them to make an impact on it. They want a ladder, not an escalator.

Most of them, however, as I've indicated, think of themselves as too mature —and perhaps of the economy as too mature as well—to be that interested in self-advancement. The career they want is to find the good life, for which their corporation or profession serves as the good provider. These men already know they won't be president—the wouldn't want the job with its unpredictable demands, its presumptive big city locale, its disruption of family and recreational life. This is all the more striking since it is my impression that the interviewers tried to get "representative men," who were often big men on campus (a strategy which seems to have totally failed at Harvard, where the respondents—some of them prospective doctors—include neither the intellectual nor the social elite who would, I suspect, have avoided or kidded the whole "deal").[1]

This relative subordination of career ambition goes together with the fact that for most of the respondents the girl they are to marry is already picked out in fact or fancy, and the style of life the family will lead is foreshadowed with equal clarity. Some sound rather psychological about it (like a Harvard man, already engaged, who declares: "Well, it's supposed to be psychologically bad for the middle child if you have three, so I suppose we'll have four"). Others are as uncomplex as the Michigan engineering student who says that he and his girl have "talked some about a family, and we're agreed that we'd like a pretty fair-sized one—maybe four or five kids. We're both fairly easy-going and a lot of noise wouldn't bother us."

One Princeton senior is so very explicit that I first thought he must be pulling the interviewer's leg, but that was because I happened to read his interview first and didn't realize that it only highlighted a norm. He is going into law, and he declares:

[1]At the University of Denver, the interviewer got a more Bohemian and unconventional range of respondents. They include an actor, aggressively individualistic, who says he's willing to live in "a room which is yours and nobody else's" ; a man who wants to produce plays (but not live in New York) ; a self-proclaimed Taft Republican, who's going into nuclear engineering because that's the future ; and a girl who wants to become a missionary. Oberlin also presents a contrast, with one man who wants to be a foreign correspondent ; another who plans to become an agronomist for missions to underdeveloped lands ; one wants to be a philosopher ; and several are going into psychology (one of whom aims at becoming a dean of students). In general, the Oberlin seniors are quite outspokenly idealistic and prepared to accept modest incomes.

Nevertheless, taking the interviews as a whole, it seems probable that many of the more interesting students were either left out or sounded more "normal" in their interviews than they might under less stilted conditions. But three woman got into this jumbled sample: the comments of one form a curious obbligato to the image the men have of the kind of wife they want. She is a Wisconsin senior who says that she's afraid of "that nice little pattern that everyone wants to fit into ; the cheery little marriage and the husband working to get ahead in his job, the wife being a clubwoman and helping her husband to advance. . . . Beating the pattern is the hardest thing of all, and I'm not much for fighting. It would be a lot easier just to go off to Africa or somewhere and live there. . . . It isn't that I want to be an odd-ball. I like odd-balls but I wouldn't want to be one."

I'll belong to all the associations you can think of—Elks, V.F.W.'s, Boy Scouts and Boys' Clubs, Y.M.C.A., American Legion, etc. It will keep me away from home a lot. But my wife [a purely hypothetical wife, remember] won't mind. She'll be vivacious and easy with people. And she will belong to everything in sight too—especially the League of Women Voters. I won't marry her until I'm twenty-eight, and so when I'm thirty-six we will have only two of the four children I hope for eventually. We'll be living in an upper-middle-class home costing about $20,000 by then, in a suburban fringe. . . . We'll have two Fords or Chevvies when I'm thirty-six, so we can both keep up the busy schedule we'll have. But in addition to this public social life, we'll have private friends who don't even live around Toledo—friends with whom we can be completely natural and relaxed. That's where Princeton friends will be very important.

To members of an older generation, this may sound like a young man on the make who wants contacts. But that is only a small part of it: the civic-minded life, the gregarious life, is at once felt as an obligation, seen as professionally useful, and anticipated as a pleasure and an end in itself. The wife is an indispensable auxiliary to this life which, even if it is a very outgoing, two-car life, is still centered in the backyard bosom of the family. This is an element in the resentment which appears again and again in the interviews toward the (almost purely hypothetical) career girl. One Harvard man says about the sort of girl he wants to marry:

She shouldn't be submissive, she can be independent on little things, but the big decisions will have to go my way . . . the marriage must be the most important thing that ever happened to her.

Another says what many feel:

My wife can work if she wants when we are first married, but she shouldn't work when we have children.

At the same time, they don't want a stay-at-home wife; they want a presentable date who, as we have seen, will be active in community affairs; she must be college-bred, she must understand her husband and know how to bring up children. There are contradictions lurking here; as one Harvard man says:

I want someone who would stay home and take care of the children, but on the other hand I want someone who can stimulate me intellectually, and I don't know if those things are compatible . . . if a woman goes to Radcliffe and takes up economics, she isn't learning how to bring up children.

In order to see what kind of mother their girl will make, a number of men say they will take a hard look at the girl's mother, to see what kind of a model mother she is—a rather awesome theme for those of us in the Class of 1931 who have eligible daughters and hopelessly impractical wives.

One Princeton senior is more graphic than most about all this. He says:

Life will not be a burden for me at thirty-five [How old and tired he makes that august age sound!] because I will be securely anchored in my family. My main emotional ties will center in my wife and family—remember, I hope for five children. Yes, I can describe my wife [again, quite a hypothetical person]. She will be the Grace Kelly, camel's-hair-coat type. Feet on the ground, and not an empty shell or a fake. Although an Ivy League type, she will also be centered in the home, a housewife. Perhaps at forty-five, with the children grown up, she will go in for hospital work and so on.... And improving herself culturally and thus bringing a deeper sense of culture into our home will be one of her main interests in fifteen years.

And then he concludes: "... in fifteen years I look forward to a constant level of happiness."

It is this vision of life on a plateau that perhaps most distinguishes the Class of 1955 from that of 1931. We who were graduated twenty-five years ago found our way by trial and error—and I emphasize the error as well as the trial—to many of the values and styles of life the Class of 1955 already begins with. We were, as I've suggested, more immature in many ways, and by the same token we expected to change and to be changed by our work and our experiences. The Class of 1955, judging by these interviews and forgetting their unreliability, would appear to expect to go on successfully adapting as they've already done, but not to change in any fundamental way, save that the family will take the place of the fraternity. The girls in question, however, may find it harder to stay on the plateau—or if they're *that* good, they may not want these boys;[2] after all, Grace Kelly has had a career and has married a prince.

But there is very little evidence in the interviews that the respondents have had to struggle for anything they want—or have wanted anything that would cost them a struggle. Some of the things they have surrendered are surely baubles. Thus, I have the impression that hardly anybody seeks swank or social distinction, and this seems not merely an artifact of the interview but an expression of the prevailing democratic ethos. A number who themselves went to prep school say they will send their children to public school. The suburb they aim for is regarded as the scenic backdrop for the happy family, not the locale of mobility as in *Point of No Return.* As I have implied, they have very few dreams, these young men; they dream of neither conventional prestige and social éclat nor, in general, of unconventional accomplishments. A fortune which can be passed on to children would be one sort of accomplishment, but very few of these seniors look for even modest capital accumulation; the capital is, as it were, society's, built into the schools and suburban developments and Blue Cross plans and corporate reserves. A floor is under these men, a low ceiling over them (analogous to the ranch-type houses in which they will live, in contrast to the high-ceilinged Victorian home), and these provide a narrow and "constant level of happiness." As one Harvard senior declares,

[2]In 1954, *Mademoiselle* magazine sent out questionnaires to women undergraduates at a number of colleges, and also to a few graduates. I had an opportunity to examine these, and the picture they present is not different from that presented by the men: they, too, want the well-rounded life, suburban and family-centered (but, like the men in the *Time* interviews, near enough to a big city for cultural advantages—it isn't clear who will populate the city), and fear ambition in themselves and their prospective spouses. Russell Lynes, in "What Has Succeeded Success?" (*Mademoiselle,* September, 1954), discusses these interviews perceptively, pointing out how demanding and strenuous the goals of well-roundedness and contentment can become, and what effort it takes to be "cool."

explaining why he had dropped his plan to enter the strenuousness of a medical career: "I think contentment is the main thing."

Do they see the political future as a possible interference with having all utilities "laid on," as the British would say? They were all asked about the political future—a boring topic for most of them. I am sure few know or care who is our Ambassador to France, and, save for a few Catholic nationalists already referred to, they expect peace within the country and with the Soviet powers. Their political views are decent and, in a nonpolitical sense, liberal; the Southerners are generally opposed to segregation, and are optimistic that it will cease to be a problem as the older generation dies out. They like Ike; and in a certain complacency, a fondness for golf (which many in our generation thought an old man's game) and the outdoors, they are like Ike. For most of them, save for a few who are going into law and want to dabble in politics, the national and international political scene holds neither fear nor fascination.[3]

This doesn't mean they aren't civic-minded; they are very much so. Whereas quite a few of our generation moved to the suburbs, at least allegedly on the children's account, while resenting the life of a commuter, the Class of 1955 has an emotional attachment to the suburb and sees it as far more than a spawning bed. As one Michigan student says:

> I'm definitely interested in community activities. More than anything, I'd like to work with the youth of the community, especially in athletics. . . . When I say I'm interested in community activities, that doesn't mean politics. I'm not interested in politics whatsoever, and I never will be! I hate to say anything against politicians, but they just waste too much time. . . . I want to live my own life, not a public life.

The suburb appears to be an extension of private life: its P.T.A.'s, its Little League baseball, and in some cases its general cultural level—these the Class of 1955 wants to take on as its proper responsibilities. This goes for religion, too; as one civic-minded Cal Tech senior says:

> I think that I will be going to church. . . . It is good for a whole family to do things together; more or less builds unity.

Indeed, it would perhaps be as correct to say that private life is the domestic intensification of the suburb, as we can see in the remarks of a Harvard senior:

> I'd like six kids. I don't know why I say that—it just seems like a minimum production goal. I like kids and I've done a lot of work with them. . . . I like group life and family life and I want to have a home filled with inner richness. Nothing is as human as a child.

A world populated by the men who appear in these interviews, and by the girls they almost without exception have in mind—the bachelor's freedom is a vanishing theme—would be a decent world; nobody in it would blow up or

[3]One Harvard man of top academic standing, who is going into law, says: "I suppose as I become more allied with the business world and with business associates I'll tend to shed my Democratic preferences." This is not said cynically or bitterly, but as part of an image of a relaxed, suburban future.

blow it up. If we ourselves manage to live the next fifteen years in such a world, we may count our bland blessings, though some of us of 1931 may not regret that we lived for our first fifteen years after graduation in a world of passion and turmoil which many of us experienced as such, whether it touched us closely or at one remove.

Afterthought: When I presented the foregoing observations to the Class of 1931 and to their wives and college-age children, I set going something of a cross-generational argument in which the "younger generation" felt a need to explain their apparent security-proneness and members of my own generation to berate them for it; to berate them even for not revolting against us—and then to berate ourselves for being so mild and nice as not to produce revolt. Indeed, as I have indicated, the Class of 1955 is at peace with its parents in so far as the *Time* interviews shed light on the matter. They may regard their fathers as tougher men than they (perhaps we are not as tough as we appear), but they do not regard them as Philistines to be overcome by fight or flight, but rather as helpful and even exemplary older siblings. On the other hand, judging from our discussions in Cambridge, parents worry that life has been made too easy for their children, that they do not crave eminence or seek excellence, that they are almost too well rounded. In this particular sequence of the generations, as so often in the history of this country, the self-made person finds that—at least in the absence of powerful Puritan traditions—he cannot reproduce his kind.

But it is, of course, much too early to predict to what degree the Class of 1955, with all its considerable realism, will succeed in finding the good life so many now look forward to. Perhaps unjustifiably extrapolating from the interviews, they appear to have encountered few moral and psychological hardships; school and college have been for many an extension of the nest rather than a traumatic initiation outside its protections. Military service still lies ahead of most of them, and after that the suburb with (as William Whyte of *Fortune* has indicated in many articles[4]) its subtle pressures for smooth performance in personal relations. Moreover, the job may not turn out as promised, either in terms of what it will buy or of what strains in family life it may involve. Just as many of us in the Class of 1931 could not tell what we were like until war experience revealed us to ourselves, so obviously we cannot know in advance what demands will be made on our children or how in the light of their experience they will interpret them. Conceivably, they will have to face an existence which at forty-five, with the children grown and flown, the job

[4] I have learned much from his forthcoming book, *The Organization Man,* describing the junior executive life on and off the job; see, also, his *Fortune* article on "The Class of '49," June, 1949, the argument of which is largely congruent with my own. Whyte (in corspondence) observes one interesting difference between the Class of 1949 and that of 1955, namely that the former chose the big corporation reluctantly, out of a Depression-bred insecurity, and fearing for their individuality, whereas the Class of 1955 does not, for the most part, feel the need to make a choice.

ceilinged and routine, the hobbies long since explored, will bring a quiet crisis of meaning—somewhat like that of some members of an older generation who cannot, being work-driven, face retiring at sixty-five or seventy. But such a notion is probably ethnocentric to our generation, as it stares into the opaqueness of another age-culture; and I guess our curiosity will have to wait until the Class of 1955 tells us, in more artistic and dramatic ways than through brief interviews, what it feels like to belong, by birth rather than individual effort, to an economy (though it be a war economy) of abundance.

WILLIAM H. WHYTE, JR.

Groupthink

A very curious thing has been taking place in this country—and almost without our knowing it. In a country where "individualism"—independence and self-reliance—was the watchword for three centuries, the view is now coming to be accepted that the individual himself has no meaning—except, that is, as a member of a group. "Group integration," "group equilibrium," "interpersonal relations," "training for group living," "group dynamics," "social interaction," "social physics"; more and more the notes are sounded—each innocuous or legitimate in itself, but together a theme that has become unmistakable.

In a sense, this emphasis is a measure of success. We have *had* to learn how to get along in groups. With the evolution of today's giant organizations—in business, in government, in labor, in education, in big cities—we have created a whole new social structure for ourselves, and one so complex that we're still trying to figure out just what happened. But the American genius for co-operative action has served us well. "Human relations" may not be an American invention, but in no country have people turned so wholeheartedly to the job of mastering the group skills on which our industrial society places such a premium.

But the pendulum has swung too far. Take, for example, the growing popularity of "social engineering" (*Fortune,* January, 1952) with its emphasis on the planned manipulation of the individual into the group role. Or, even more striking, the extraordinary efforts of some corporations to encompass the executive's wife in the organization—often with the willing acquiescence of the wife in the merger (*Fortune,* October, 1951). And these, as we hope to demonstrate, are no isolated phenomena; recent public-opinion polls, slick-magazine fiction, current best-sellers, all document the same trend. Groupthink is becoming a national philosophy.

Groupthink being a coinage—and, admittedly, a loaded one—a working definition is in order. We are not talking about mere instinctive conformity—it is, after all, a perennial failing of mankind. What we are talking about is a *rationalized* conformity—an open, articulate philosophy which holds that

---

group values are not only expedient but right and good as well. Three mutually supporting ideas form the underpinning: (1) that moral values and ethics are relative; (2) that what is important is the kind of behavior and attitudes that makes for the harmonious functioning of the group; (3) that the best way to achieve this is through the application of "scientific" techniques.

Once grasped, as the work of the social engineers makes clear, these principles lead us to an entirely new view of man. And what a dismal fellow he is! For the man we are now presented with is Social Man—completely a creature of his environment, guided almost totally by the whims and prejudices of the group, and incapable of any real self-determination of his destiny. Only through social engineering—i.e., applied groupthink—can he be saved. The path to salvation, social engineers explain, lies in a trained elite that will benevolently manipulate us into group harmony. And who's to be the elite? Social engineers modestly clear their throats.

The Vanishing Layman

This vision of a new elite guiding us to the integrated life has inspired some interesting speculations (e.g., Aldous Huxley's *Brave New World,* George Orwell's *Nineteen Eighty-Four*). The real danger, however, is something else again. It is not that the layman will be pushed around by the social engineers: it is that *he will become one himself*. Rather than the pawn of the experts, he will be the willing apprentice—and embrace groupthink as the road to security.

Is this coming to pass? Let's look for a moment at the direction American values are taking among the oncoming generations. There has been a rather disturbing amount of evidence that they are changing rapidly—and in a way that must warm social engineers' hearts. Every study made of the younger generation, every portrayal they make of themselves—from their dating habits to their artistic inclinations—uncovers one clear fact: our youth is the most group-minded we have ever had. Gregariousness, *Time*'s recent study indicated (November 5, 1951), has become a necessity. "They are parts of groups," one girl shrewdly appraises her contemporaries. "When they are alone they are bored with themselves."

While youngsters are not inclined to philosophize, their attitude toward life adds up to a fairly discernible set of values. It could be described as a "practical" relativism. The old absolute moral values are disappearing. There is still black and white, to be sure, but it is no longer determined by fixed precepts; it is determined rather by what the group thinks is black and white—and if someone does things the way his group does, well, who is to censure him for his loyalty?

The colleges furnish documentation of the drift. If recent surveys are any indication (*Fortune,* June, 1949), a startling swing has taken place among students to the twin ideals of group harmony and expertism. "These men," one of their mentors says in praise, "don't question the system. Their main aim is to make it work better—to get in there and lubricate the machinery. They're not rebels; they'll be social technicians for a better society."

The registrar's records bear him out. Along with a concurrent drift from the humanities, there has been a tremendous increase in specialized courses —and of specialization within specialties. Significantly, the courses that enjoyed the most phenomenal popularity among postwar classes were those connected with personnel work. "I like people" became a universal cry, and in droves students aiming for business turned thumbs down on the idea of general, executive apprenticeship in favor of personnel work; here, with stop watch and slip stick in hand, they could measure away, safe from the doubts and intangibles of the world without. The picture was a mirage, of course, but it was only by the most strenuous efforts of placement officers and corporation personnel people that students gave it up.

Does entry into business life transform these values? Apparently not. Talk with members of the younger generation of management—and we speak not of the disaffected but of the successful—and one is struck by a curious strain of resignation that often runs through their discussion. Like the heroes of J. P. Marquand's perceptive novels, they are disturbed by a sense of individual impotence. Dispassionately, they describe themselves primarily as members of their environment—men more acted upon than acting. They are neither angry nor cynical about it; they are caught on a "treadmill" from which they will never escape, perhaps—but the treadmill is pleasant enough, they explain, and in the group role they find the emotional security they want so very badly.

So with their wives (*Fortune,* October and November, 1951). No matter what problem they are discussing—from the possibility of advancement to the style of their living—they instinctively phrase their problems in terms of their relations with the group. The relations, they concede, are not simple—there are the girls, the gang on Ferncrest Road, Charlie's people at the office, and a host of lesser constellations to conjure with. Tough as the job may be, however, it is a job to which they have dedicated themselves.

The System Lovers

Turn to the image of the good life in popular cultures and you find the same phenomenon at work. Slick-magazine fiction tells the story. It has never, of course, exactly called for a rebellion against the status quo, but back in the thirties it did present heroes and heroines who engaged in some kind of mild strife with their environment, told the boss off, or did something equally contentious. No longer. A *Fortune* analysis of 1935–36 plots and 1950–51 plots indicates that heroes and heroines have been growing remarkably submissive. Not only is the system they abide by—be it an Army camp, a business office, or a small-town environment—shown as more benevolent; in some cases the system itself becomes the *deus ex machina* that solves the problem.

So in serious fiction. More and more, writers are concerning themselves with the relationship of the individual to the group, and more and more resolving it in favor of the latter. The system—and they don't mean God or the universe—is eventually revealed to the hero as bigger than any of us, and thus it is not only foolish but wrong for him not to reconcile himself to it. From the extreme of the angry, to-hell-with-the-whole-lousy-setup tracts of the 1930's we seem to be going whole hog in the opposite direction.

Let us have a look at the current best-seller, Herman Wouk's *The Caine Mutiny*. Since it is about the Navy, the system shown has some aspects peculiar to service life. The basic question posed, however—the individual's place in the system—has great universality, and in an excitingly told tale Wouk sketches one point of view with such striking overtones that the book could almost go down as a landmark in the shift of American values.

The story tells of the terrible dilemma facing the officers of a mine sweeper; their captain, one Queeg, is a neurotic, cowardly incompetent. A typhoon brings the problem to the breaking point. Through hysteria and cowardice, Queeg is about to sink the ship. In vain, Maryk, the stolid, conventional executive officer, tries to get him to keep the ship headed into the wind. Queeg refuses. In the nick of time, Maryk makes his decision. Under Article 184 of Navy Regulations, he relieves Queeg of his command. The ship is saved.

What is the moral? Maryk, we find, shouldn't have done it. Says the author's protagonist, Lieutenant Willy Keith, in a letter to his girl (p. 463): "... I see that we were in the wrong ... The idea is, once you get an incompetent ass of a skipper—and it's a chance of war—there's nothing to do but serve him as though he were the wisest and the best, cover his mistakes, keep the ship going, and bear up. So I have gone all the way around Robin Hood's barn to arrive at the old platitudes, which I guess is the process of growing up."

In other times, perhaps, this definition of maturity might have been regarded as downright parody. Obedience and discipline few could have caviled at. But would they have applauded the counseling of an obedience, so abject, so *unquestioning,* that we are asked, in effect, not only to put up with the evils of a system but to regard them as right—to reach out, as Norbert Weiner's phrase goes, and kiss the whip that lashes us? Would they have joined in censuring an act to which the only logical alternative is the passive sacrifice of several hundred lives? Hardly. The executive officer's action might well have been seen as an act of great moral courage—and one, furthermore, in true allegiance to the service; it did, after all, save the ship. The other byproduct, the withdrawal of Queeg from line command, might also have been interpreted as something less than a disaster to the system.

Not so A.D. 1952. The moral, to judge from what critics and readers have been saying about it, has struck exactly the right chord. The exec, as the dust jacket has it, was merely a well-meaning man "beyond his depth," and more to be pitied than censured. It is not for the individual to question the competence of the Queegs a system may contain. Queeg was a teacher. Queegs are necessary. We needed Queegs to win the war. So goes the assent. "It is about time that more books of this sort were written," says J. P. Marquand. "The lesson the newcomer must learn is in many ways the antithesis of democracy. It is essentially a final acceptance of the doctrine that full and unquestioning obedience must be accorded a superior officer, no matter how personally odious or stupid this individual may be—and that without this individual surrender we can never win a war."

Love that system.

The Permissive Way

What makes this wave of the present particularly unsettling is the surprising fact that it is in rhythm with one of the dominating currents in contemporary American academic thought. It would be a mistake, of course, to treat the connection as cause and effect; groupthink's roots go too deep to be so summarily explained. But it would be just as much of an error to dismiss the academic underpinnings, as the layman is so tempted to do, as mere ivory-tower mumbo jumbo. The ideology of groupthink is often incomprehensible to the uninitiated, but it is of great power nonetheless. Translated by its disciples in hundreds of lecture halls and papers, and by their disciples in turn, it has given a purpose and direction to the groupthink movement that it would otherwise lack.

The movement, in a sense, is an offshoot of the great academic revolt at the turn of the century against formalism. To Young Turks of the day the individualistic tradition of American thought needed re-definition. Too much attention, they felt, had been concentrated on the lone individual; as a consequence, the rigid values built up for his protection were inapplicable to the great social upheavals that were taking place. What was needed was a social view of man—man as a unit of the group—and a willingness to adapt society to his needs.

Most of the credit generally goes to John Dewey, who, with William Kilpatrick, gave "progressive" education its impetus. But there were many others —Veblen in economics, for example, and Roscoe Pound in the law ("The law is social engineering"). Like a fresh breeze, through almost every field of American thought, the new concepts swept, as converts enthusiastically fell to whacking away at the restrictions of the old absolutes. Social Man was coming of age.

When the cultural anthropologists got to work on him, his final link to the old moral absolutes was severed. From their comparisons of primitive cultures, and, later, our own, many anthropologists came to the view that the ethics of a people are relative. By this they do not mean that ethics are unimportant, but rather that they are not to be judged by any abstract conceptions of "right" or "wrong." For if we realize that other cultures and ethics are "equally valid," to use Ruth Benedict's phrase, then we will be jogged into giving up all the more readily our outworn traditions and our illusions of individual autonomy.

"It is not any particular set of values," another anthropologist explains, "but a way of looking at them that is important."

A half-century has gone by and the relativistic, social view of man idea is still gaining. The appetite for cultural anthropology, for example, has been growing at such a rate that Ruth Benedict's *Patterns of Culture,* first published in 1931, has reached, after a phenomenal newsstand sale, the No. 1 best-seller spot in the Mentor paper-book series.

In several essentials, however, the nature of the movement against formalism has changed drastically. What started as a healthy revolt against dogmatism has produced an offshoot that has succeeded in becoming the new dogmatism itself. And since, like all dogmatisms, it promises respite from uncertainty, a society still shell-shocked by the upheavals of the twentieth century hasn't bothered yet to question its effects too closely. To be sure, those of the groupthink leaning customarily speak of themselves as rebels fighting an uphill battle against the enemy ("medievalists," "academicians," "absolutists") but the dog they are kicking is practically dead. They won that battle long ago.

Certainly so in one sector of education. Thanks to a strenuous academic controversy, the momentum of the militantly "progressive" brand was slowed down some time back. Groupthink, however, cannot be contained by a label, and to a formidable body of educators the basic ideal of adjustment to group values is so taken for granted that the only remaining job would appear to be working up better ways of bringing it about. "The American educator," writes one of them, Professor Stewart Cole, "[must] treat pupils as persons-in-groups-in-American-culture at every stage of their social learning." To do this the teacher should borrow from such disciplines as anthropology, the social sciences, psychology, and group dynamics. "The social interactions" of teachers and pupils should be "the primary channel of learning the good life for America."[1]

In this free, permissive atmosphere, the idea that the individual should be regarded as personally accountable for the way he behaves is, of course, old hat. And in the popular view as well. "If your young son sticks his tongue out at you and calls you a nasty old stinkpot," an article in *American Magazine* good-humoredly, but approvingly, counsels, "just ignore the insult and rejoice secretly that you have such a fine normal child. He is simply channeling his aggressive, aggrieved feelings harmlessly by verbal projection."

Where "social interaction" is the watchword, the attitude conditioning is left in large part, to the child's peers. Even more than their elders, they are quick to reward deviance with hefty interaction; and thus in the natural

[1]Educators of this bent cannot be accused of swimming against the current. As a recent Elmo Roper poll indicates, most Americans now feel the second most important reason for sending children to high school is "to teach them to get along better with other people." (No. 1: to get them ready for a job.)

distaste of the crowd for the individualist we now have a social tool. And this, the child learns from the books written for him, is as it should be. In these tales of fire engines and trains as David Riesman has documented in his disturbing study, *The Lonely Crowd,* the neophyte groupthinker is taught that one wins by being directed by others—and that the most important thing in the world is to be a team player.

To further ensure that the child need never be a person-not-in-groups, the necessity for little groupthinkers to think as individuals *all by themselves* may soon be obviated altogether. Individual homework is now to be eliminated. Writes Amy Selwyn in the *Reader's Digest,* "Now authorities generally agree that children learn best if they do their learning in groups and talk out loud about lessons as they work. 'No homework' spokesmen also say if children were not required to spend their leisure studying they would not develop the resentment against study which often kills all incentive to learn anything . . ."

Lest the layman presume to question the drift, groupthinkers explain that their work is rooted in the Scientific Method, and that now being a holy phrase, it is made plain that the debate is closed to outsiders—if indeed any grounds for debate exist at all.[2] "Because this new 'doctrine' has for its base objective findings in anthropology, social psychology, mental hygiene, and scientific child study," Professor Alain Locke of Howard University says, "there is an authoritative consensus back of these newer educational procedures that few would care to challenge."

On the Brink of Nonsense

He is right. Many educators have seriously questioned the excesses of educational groupthink, but a large proportion of them are curiously loath to do it out loud right now. Criticism of the misapplications of science, they know, will be quickly seized as an attack on science itself. To muddy matters even more, those of the extremist fringe (notably Allen Zoll) have succeeded in putting something of the kiss of death on public discussion by their attacks on "progressive" education. They are really attacking something else, of course; their reasoning is erroneous and their motives suspect. Nevertheless, many people who have a respectable argument to make hesitate for fear they will lose their standing as liberals. The debate, however, cannot long be deferred—certainly so when it can be said, with some justification, that the best friend progressive education has today is Allen Zoll.

There are some signs that the wider implications of the groupthink movement may at last provoke a counterrevolution. Significantly, some of the most astringent critiques of groupthink are coming from the ranks of the sociologists (cf. "The Image of Man in the Social Sciences"—Reinhard Bendix in *Com-*

[2]"I should like to see teachers and professors as sure of themselves, as confident in their training and experience, as surgeons are, and as impatient of lay advice"—Margaret B. Pickel, Dean of Women, Columbia University: New York *Times Magazine,* June 3, 1951.

mentary, February, 1951). In its application to the law, Roscoe Pound himself has been led to protest the degree to which the social-utility concept has supplanted firm values. Similarly, in England—which suffers groupthink too—educator Sir Walter Moberly has been stirring the universities to a re-examination of the British variant.

But the best hope may well lie in the ambitions of the groupthinkers themselves. They stand poised, finally, on the threshold of pure nonsense. For a long time they have been growing uncomfortable over their apparent denial of ethical relevance. As the anthropologists themselves point out, man does need a firm sense of right and wrong, and an excessively relative view destroys the old firmness.

This does not mean, however, that the groupthinkers are chastened. Quite the contrary. They now propose to cure this pitfall of scientism with more scientism. Ethics are to be made "a matter of scientific investigation." To some, this merely means an objective study of ethics—certainly a proper enough task. To the groupthinker, however, it means nothing less than a theoretical apparatus for the scientific determination of what is "good" or "bad." And thus "to the innermost citadel of dogmatic thinking, the realm of values," they hopefully turn. "The conquest of the field of values," as one sounds the call, "would be almost the concluding triumph." He couldn't be more correct.

Ethics without Tears

Why should so despairing an ideology be so popularly contagious? In a society where the old family and community ties that so long cemented it have broken down, the impulse for association is an instinctive and healthy response. But a sense of "belonging," a sense of meaningful association with others, has never required that one sacrifice his individuality as part of the bargain. Why, then, do so many rush to embrace a philosophy that tells them it *is* necessary? Why, like the moth, do we fly to the one thing that will consume us? Why, in a country with the sort of healthy political and economic base that has historically nourished individualism, are we so pathetically eager to join up in flatulent brotherhood?

To explain this impulse is to explain our blind faith in scientism as well. For their appeal is common, and many as the variations may be, they come back, eventually, to one simple, compelling theme.

They offer us freedom from moral choice.

Through the deification of group harmony, buck-passing a moral decision becomes itself a moral act; the system—as *The Caine Mutiny* advocates—attends to these things so much better than the individual, and he might just as well relax and enjoy it.

And there is freedom in another sense as well. Moral dilemmas exist because there is uncertainty. If we can now abstract a few parts from the whole of human nature and by analysis predict objectively what will make for group harmony, the intangibles that make individual decisions so poignant may be obviated altogether. Like a general who is blessed with perfect intelligence of the enemy, we will have only one valid course of action before us. We will have finally latched on to certainty.

Why Participate?

Once this denial of moral relevance is made, folly must be the consequence. For groupthinkers go on to assure themselves that in groupthink itself one finds moral fulfillment. It is not put this crudely, of course; by what has now become a ritualistic explanation, our eyes are directed upward to the goal of harmony, group integration, dynamic equilibrium; upward to a golden mean in which everyone will finally attain the blessed state of—grace? No, the state of "participation."

But participation for what? As a fundamental of the democratic process, as a means of self-expression and development, participation is abundantly desirable. In this sense, *Fortune* has argued strongly for participation; it has reported its application to the problems of management and will continue to. But the word, like its blood brothers "communication" and "adjust," is assuming a sort of end-all quality. So let us put the question: *Why* participate?

In the litany of groupthink the answers describe a complete circle. One participates for the end of "social integration," for "community-centered cohesion," for better "interpersonal relations," for "group harmony," for the reduction of "social tensions," for adjustment to the environment. One participates, in other words, that he may participate. And so the end is really only a means after all. Good means, yes—but as an encompassing philosophy, somewhat less than complete.

Even as a means, participation can be a tricky concept. It is easily confused with getting a number of people to do what one did before. And in this aspect, unfortunately, it provides the resolutely pedestrian with a way of cutting down to size their up-and-coming brethren. Similarly it offers the faint of heart an alibi for ducking responsibility—if a broth is to be spoiled, it's convenient to have too many cooks participate.

Perhaps the most extraordinary aspect of groupthink is the success with which its double-talk has used the old concepts of individualism to justify their opposite. By letting others decide, one decides. By submitting oneself to the group, one becomes an individual. "It is precisely this gradual change in our mental horizon—new assumptions and hypotheses taken as factual description—that is sinister," says Lincoln Reis, professor of philosophy at Bard College. "So that while we are presented with a logical horror, we find it established and accepted widely as a fact. Nowhere vulnerable to intelligence, it is as impervious as a nightmare."

It is impervious because the ideal of unity it holds out obscures for us some disagreeable facts of life—and the necessity for facing them on moral grounds. "Communication" is a term in point. As used in its cult sense, it implies the facile premise that the conflicts that plague us are due simply to "blocks" in the communication flow, and that if we get the technical hang of it, all will be well. Up to a point this is true. But people do not always argue because they misunderstand one another; they argue because they hold different goals. These will always be a matter of debate, and attempts to evade it through "nonpartisan" communication or "education" programs simply beg the question.

Unity—or Monotony?

"Unity" is a double-edged sword. As our young corporation wife is witness, group harmony is not an unmixed blessing; conversely, neither are frustrations and tensions necessarily bad. They can be fruitful; indeed, progress is often dependent on producing rather than mitigating them. In large part, also, they stem from the scores of conflicting loyalties and allegiances we enjoy in a fluid society. Unless we forswear these in complete fealty to one embracing organization, there is no easy way to escape the moral decisions they force upon us. *Nor should there be.* The danger, as Clark Kerr points out, "is not that loyalties are divided today, but that they may become undivided tomorrow."

It is precisely this smothering of the individual that the drift to groupthink seems to be making more and more imminent. Few groupthinkers, to be sure, believe themselves against the individual. But in looking so intently at man as a member of the group, they have made man seem important in this role only. There is the frequent explanation, of course, that only by group participation is the individual's potential realized. But this is only a half-truth. Individual excellence must involve something more than a respect for the group and a skill in working with it. "The sphere of individual action," writes Bertrand Russell, "is not to be regarded as ethically inferior to that of social duty. On the contrary, some of the best of human activities are, at least in feeling, rather personal than social. . . . Prophets, mystics, poets, scientific discoverers, are men whose lives are dominated by a vision. . . . It . . . is such men who put into the world the things that we most value."

Few of us are potential geniuses, but the constant admonition to harmonize and integrate affects us nonetheless. Each day we are faced with a multitude of decisions. Should we trust our own judgment? Or does the group's view have an inherent rightness we cannot match?

The new values would incline us to the easy harmony of the group view, for they would have us suppose that the whole is greater than the sum of the parts; that the system has a wisdom beyond the reach of ordinary mortals. But this is not necessarily so. Man can be greater than the group, and his lone imagination worth a thousand graphs.

He is not often a creator, but even as spectator, as "the common man," he can rise in ways his past performance would not predict. To aim at his common denominators in the name of ultimate democracy is to despise him, to perpetuate his mediocrities, and to conceive him incapable of responding to anything better than the echo of his prejudices. The "equilibrium" that is the compact to be made with this boor is inevitably static, and the trouble is not solved by sticking the adjective dynamic in front of it.

Has the individual reached a low enough estate for us to become concerned? When the nation's best-selling novel advocates his abject submission without raising eyebrows; when some corporations make it policy not to hire honor graduates for fear they might not be good mixers; when it is seriously stated that "natural leaders" can be made obsolete, the time has come at least to think about the matter. For if the drift continues, man may soon cease to fret over such things at all. He will finally have engineered for himself that equilibrious society. Gelded into harmonious integration, he will be free from tensions and frustrations, content in the certainties of his special function, no longer tantalized by the sense of infinity. He will at last have become a complete bore.

The answer is not a return to a "rugged individualism" that never was. Nor is it a slackened interest in social science and "human relations." We need, certainly, to find ways of making this bewildering society of ours run more smoothly and we need all the illumination science can give us to do it. But we need something more. Lest man become an ethical eunuch, his autonomy sacrificed for the harmony of the group, a new respect for the individual must be kindled. A revival of the humanities, perhaps, a conscious, deliberate effort by the corporation not only to accommodate dissent but to encourage it—possible approaches to a problem so fundamental cannot easily be spelled out.

Only individuals can do it.

WILLIAM H. WHYTE, JR.

The Outgoing Life

Americans have a curious blind spot. There are few things from which they get such invidious satisfaction as shaking their heads over the collectivization of society that is going on almost everywhere except, presumably, in the U.S. But they really don't have to look quite so far as Europe; indeed, no farther than the outskirts of almost every one of our great cities. For the great self-contained villages that are rising there are not merely a housing phenomenon; within them is developing what is in many respects a new way of life, and it is a way of life that is unmistakably communal.

The residents in these communities are very much aware that they are part of a new social institution and they discuss it with such sophistication that at times it almost seems as if every man were his own resident sociologist. In bull sessions, words like "permissive" and "socio-cultural groups" are frequently tossed about. One particular adjective has become so habitual that even in the most casual conversation you are likely to hear someone described as "outgoing." (Thus: "They are a wonderful outgoing couple.")

The comparisons the new suburbanites draw are many—army-post life is one favorite—but when they speak of being in a fraternity or sorority house, "only with kids," they come nearest the mark. For it may be that their way of life is not so much novel as a projection into the middle years of dormitory life. Not so very long ago graduation from college was considered an entry into the cold, cold world; now, thanks in great part to these new communities, the transition is so smooth that it is becoming more and more difficult to tell just where adolescence stops and middle age begins.

What has brought this about, as *Fortune* pointed out in "The Transients" (May), is in great part the emergence of the large institution, in particular the corporation. For these new communities are not, as many presume, simply the fixed homes of white-collar workers; they have become a series of way stations for the growing number of young managerial people who are incessantly being transferred from one spot to another.

In "The Future, c/o Park Forest" (June) *Fortune* began an account of one particular community, five-year-old Park Forest, Illinois, as an example of the way the young transients are meeting the problems their way of life poses. How they have tackled local government, education, and church building shows that to a remarkable degree they have compensated for their apparent lack of roots through involvement in civic activity. In this article we turn to their more personal, social life, for here, as well as in civic activity, we may discern the values that will later shape their decisions when they and their contemporaries have matured into positions of leadership.

Inconspicuous Consumption

At the center of Park Forest there is a theatre, a large supermarket, and rows of stores joined together by covered walks (from which loudspeakers circulate music). Stretching out toward the horizon from the shopping center are the "courts"—a vast complex of pleasant two-story garden-apartment buildings arranged in a series of squares and rectangles around central parking bays—105 courts in all, separated from each other by generous stretches of lawn and play areas. To the south and west, out beyond the rental area, lie the homes for sale, some 2,000 ranch-type houses (average price $13,000), spotted every sixty feet along undulating "superblocks."

How, the stranger wonders, does one tell rank in a place like Park Forest—or, for that matter, pull it? The usual criteria of status are almost entirely absent. The higher-rent two-apartment buildings, which are sited individually on roads, rather than court fashion, rent for $117, versus $92 to $104 for court apartments, and constitute something of a local gold coast. But aside from these, the houses and apartments differ little in cost and physically are distinguished from each other largely by changes in façade. One's location in the courts, furthermore, is determined largely by chance rather than by personal selection.

Cars aren't much help either. Of the thousands that lie in the parking bays, few are more expensive than the Buick Special, and white-walled tires and other rakish touches are not too frequent. Only in nearby industrial towns do people show exuberance in the captainship of the American car: foxtails and triumphant pennants, like Cyrano's white plume, fly defiantly on cars there, and occasionally from the radiator a devil thumbs his nose at the passing mob. Not at Park Forest; whatever else it has, it has no panache.

To the practiced eye, of course, there is more diversity in the scene than might appear, for the more acclimated to the homogeneity, the more sensitized one becomes to the small differences. At Levittown, Pennsylvania, for example, residents are very much aware of who has what "modification" of the basic ranch-house design, and one house on which the owner has mounted a small gargoyle has become so famous a "sight" that many residents drive out of their way to show it to visitors. Similarly, people have a sharp eye for the smaller variations from the norm of home furnishings, and the acquisition of a new automatic dryer, or an unusually good television set, is always cause for notice.

Lack of such amenities, conversely, is also noted. In one suburb, to cite a rather extreme example, a couple were so sensitive about the bareness of their living room that they smeared their windows up with Bon Ami—and kept them that way until a dinette set arrived.

On the whole, however, there is remarkably little to notice. The fact that the transients don't have much money is, of course, part of the story—but only part of it. "There is no keeping up with the Joneses here" is an observation so chronically and so emphatically voiced as to indicate that inconspicuous consumption is as much an ideology as a necessity. Openly articulated, the reasoning would go something like this: "Most of us are at a pretty critical stage in our careers; it is just about now that we will realize that some of us are really going to go ahead, and some of us aren't. If you find you are going ahead, it is rubbing it in unfairly to make it obvious." You have broken the truce.

The job, then, is not so much to keep up with the Joneses; it is to keep *down* with them. When a resident sees his neighbor vaunting worldly goods, he sees this as an offense not simply to him but to the community as well. Interestingly, when people comment about display they usually make the point that they themselves see nothing wrong with it, *but that other people might,* and that therefore the purchase is ill advised. A used Lincoln one resident got as a bargain is a case in point. "What the hell, Tom could drive a Rolls-Royce for all I care," says one neighbor. "Still, it was bad timing on his part—you know the way some people are around here. I'm beginning to wonder now about his judgment."

The new suburbs not only look classless, residents say, they are classless. That is, Park Foresters would add on second thought, there are no extremes and if the place isn't exactly classless, it is at least *one* class—usually identified as middle or upper middle, according to the inclination of the resident. "We are all," they say, "in the same boat."

The Melting Pot

Actually, they are not. People may come out of the new suburbs middle class; not all those who enter, however, are. Middle-class college-educated transients give the communities their dominant tone, but there are other residents for whom arrival in Park Forest is, psychologically at least, a crossing of the tracks. This expansion of white-collardom is happening in towns and cities as well, yet it is so pronounced in the new suburbs that at times it almost seems as if they were made for that function.

They have become the second great melting pot. Almost because they are a haven for the basically middle-class organization man, they provide a forced-draft education in new values for many others. For one thing, these communities speed up potential switches in religious affiliations, and the couple from, say, a small Ozark town are likely to leave a Fundamentalist allegiance to become Methodists or Presbyterians. People from big-city Democratic wards tend to become Republicans and, if anything, more conservative than the people whose outlook they are unconsciously adopting. Personal tastes change more slowly, though the wives are rather quick to pick up the right cues, and their clothes, be they slacks or cardigan and pearls, show it.

But the pot melts just so far and this shows poignantly in some residents' attitude toward the community. The usual transient affects an attitude of fond detachment—swell place, lots of kicks, but, after all, the sort of place you graduate from. For some, however, the place is less a way station than the end of the road; the permanence of the community, not its impermanence, is what they want to see, and for them the moving van can be an unsettling reminder of a transiency they are not going to share. Then, for others, the new suburb is too much of a personal achievement to take with anything but deadly seriousness, and they are extraordinarily sensitive to any references that might be invidious. "Those pictures are absolutely disgraceful," one resident recently said of some published pictures of her area. "The way they angled them, it makes it look as though this was a *development!*"

The intensity of feeling that many people in this situation develop is no joking matter. Their social enfranchisement is a great achievement of our expanding society, but the process, it is important to remember, is psychologically nonreversible. Of all the groups in America, none is so ill equipped emotionally as the new white-collar group to adjust to a severe economic downturn, and if our society has an Achilles' heel, this might be it. Not without a fight, and one that could become collectively ugly, would they be pushed back across the tracks.

But Park Forest is a melting pot in other respects also. The intellectuals likewise receive an education. "When I first came here I was pretty rarefied," a self-styled "egghead" explained to a recent visitor. "I remember how shocked I was one day when I told the girls in the court how much I had enjoyed listening to *The Magic Flute* the night before. They didn't know what I was talking about. I began to learn that diaper talk is a lot more important to them. I still listen to *The Magic Flute* but now I realize that for most people other things in life seem as important."

In similar fashion, farm-bred Republicans learn to appreciate that all urban Democrats are not Communists. "The people who lived in the other half of our duplex," recalls one Republican, "were as different as could be from us. They were the kind who worshipped F.D.R.'s name. But we got to like them just the same. We just didn't talk politics. We used to go bowling together and that sort of thing. I didn't make him a Republican, but I think he appreciates my views a lot more than he did before."

Yes, Virginia, There Is a Democracy

On balance, however, the similarities among Park Foresters are more significant than the differences. At times Park Foresters tend to get a bit windy when talking about their egalitarianism, but, as with all Americans, their unwillingness to concede class differences is itself a powerful factor in keeping these from crystallizing. Their wish, to put it another way, has been father to the reality.

There is no discernible class structure. Occupation and family background do provide a certain kind of status for individuals, but the individuals have not jelled into groups on this basis. So with civic activity; the most active could make up an elite of sorts, but they do not act in concert and, more to the point, others do not conceive of them as an elite. Similarly, while many people get together according to common interests—interest in world politics, for example, or in gardening—these are only part-time associations and they are so fluid that they carry few overtones of social status. The same is true of religion: vigorous as church activity is, religious allegiances have far less of the clan effect than they have elsewhere. Not so incidentally, many "mixed-marriage" couples have come to Park Forest, for here, they have correctly sensed, is a refuge from the conflicting loyalties that would beset them elsewhere.

But there is one distinction we can draw and it is one of considerable significance for management. *Fortune* came upon it this way. In the course of this survey a special effort was made to find clues that would distinguish the young executive who was going places from his less successful contemporaries. With the help of some corporations that had people at Park Forest, a number of young men who seemed headed for top management were finally spotted.

The sample is too small for firm conclusions; but one denominator turned up so often as to suggest a pretty good working hypothesis. In most cases, the successful junior executive was measurably more inclined than his contemporaries toward what is usually called "culture." He had more and better books on his bookshelves, more and better magazines, and usually a good record collection. His tastes were by no means so highbrow as those of the more culturally intense academic and professional people—Strauss and concertos, you might say, rather than Schönberg and quartets were the rule. Between the successful and the run-of-the-mill junior executive, however, the difference was so great that it is fair to conclude that the "impractical" is more closely related to the attributes of leadership than many businessmen suspect.

But now let us move into the "court" itself, for here is the "family" most inhabitants know. Here, more than many suspect, is where their behavior is altered; and that moment in the rental office when the newly arrived couple is assigned to Court B–14 or Court K–3 is a turning point that is likely to affect them long after they have left Park Forest. For no two courts are exactly alike; each in its own way produces a different pattern of behavior. Will the newcomers turn out to be civic leaders? Will they be churchgoers? The court will have a lot to do with it.

The Incubators

As an illustration of this impact, let us take the current roster of Park Forest's civic organizations and plot the addresses of the leaders on a map of the community. Theoretically, since one's location is determined largely by chance and since turnover is constantly reshuffling each court, the leaders should be distributed fairly evenly throughout the community. Instead of a random distribution, however, there are clusters of leaders here and there in particular courts. So with churchgoing. A plot of the active members of the United Protestant Church also reveals a somewhat geographic pattern, and the overlap between this pattern and that of civic activity is considerable.

The most interesting aspect of these patterns, however, is their durability. Locate the civic leaders as of two years ago and compare that pattern with the current plot, and you will find, court by court, the same concentrations appearing. Similarly, you will also find that despite the growth in the population of the homes area (now accounting for roughly 8,000 of Park Forest's 20,000 people), the rental courts continue to provide community-wide leadership out of all proportion to their numbers.

Reverse indexes illustrate the same phenomenon. Much in the way one college dorm, year in and year out, is notorious as a "hell's entry," some courts consistently produce an above-average number of complaints about litter, parking-space encroachments, ambulance and police calls; those are also the courts most sparsely represented in any plot of community leadership.

Court residents themselves sense the differences. "I can't put my finger on it," says one old resident. "But as long as I have been here this court has had an inferiority complex. We never seem to get together and have the weenie roasts and anniversary parties they have in B–18." Community leaders have an even better working knowledge; and in, say, a fund-raising campaign, they know in advance which areas will probably produce the most money per foot-pound of energy expended on them, and which the least.

Why the differences? It is much the same question as why one city has a "soul" while another, equally blessed economically, does not. In most communities the causes lie so far back that we have trouble discerning them; but at Park Forest, almost as if we were watching stop-action photography, we can see compressed in time what would be spread out over several generations elsewhere.

Of crucial importance, it would appear, is the character of the original settlers. In the early phase the interaction of court people on each other is necessarily intensified; the roads separating one court from another are less avenues than moats, and the court's inhabitants must function as a unit to conquer such now legendary problems as the "mud" of Park Forest, the "rocks and rats" of Drexelbrook, and the like. But though the level of communal sharing and brotherhood is high, even in this period there are important differences; two or three natural leaders concentrated in one court may so catalyze the neighborly qualities in the other people in the court that the one-big-happy-family becomes a tradition. Conversely, only one or two troublemakers can so fragment a court into a series of cliques that the animus will live long after them.

Inevitably, the intensity of activity weakens; as the volunteer policemen are replaced by a regular force, as the mud turns to grass, the old *esprit de corps* subsides into relative normalcy. Pioneers (i.e., those who have been there four and a half years now) complain that Park Forest is in a dead calm. "We used to become so *enraged,*" one nostalgically recalls. "Now it's just like any other place."

Not really. In comparison with the usual community, the court is still a hothouse and its traditions continue to shape newcomers' conduct. Occasionally a once "warm" court may be turned into a cool one through the collision of some unduly forceful personalities. Most courts, however, keep their essential characters. One by one the newcomers are assimilated into the court pattern and as the old leaders depart there is usually someone to whom they can pass on the baton.

The rules of the game that are passed on are more tacit than open, yet in every court there are enough to provide an almost formal ritual. "We live as we please," residents will tell the newcoming couple, who then proceed to learn about the tot yard, about the communal baby-sitting service, about the history of the court, including The Incident, how the round-robin bridge group alternates and how, frankly, you're lucky you didn't get assigned to the next court —oh brother, what a weird crew they are.

The more subtle aspects of court behavior are communicated through what might be called a process of contagion. With surprising frequency certain adjectives and phrases crop up in particular courts, and the newcomers' vocabularies soon reflect this. So with their leisure-time habits. "Charley used to make fun of us for spending so much time planting and mowing and weeding," one resident says of a neighbor. "Well, only the other day he came to ask me—oh, so casually—about what kind of grass seed is best. I didn't kid him—that might have stopped him in his tracks. You ought to see him now—he's got sprays and everything."

The Family

The cumulative effect of all this can be summed up in a word. One is made *outgoing.* "You can really help make a lot of people happy here," says one social activist. "I've brought out two couples myself; I saw potentialities in them they didn't realize they had. Whenever we see someone who is shy and withdrawn, we make a special effort with them."

The education takes, and even those who describe themselves as comparatively withdrawn would, on the outside, be considered something less than bashful. "I've changed tremendously," says one typical transient. "My husband was always the friend maker in the family—everybody always loves Joe, he's so likable. But here I began to make some friends on my own; I was so tickled when I realized it. One night when the gang came to our house I suddenly realized *I* made these friends."

More than ever before, the newcomers get in the habit of doing things with other people. Civic activity, as noted in the previous article in this series, is rife, but this is a fraction of the energies expended in group activity. Court social life throbs with bridge and canasta, bring-your-own-bottle parties, and teas; and when spring brings everyone outdoors, the tempo of activity becomes practically nonstop. "Any excuse for a party," one resident says, happily. "During last week you'd die! You just so much as say party and pretty soon the gang would be setting up a beer keg."

Through the Picture Window

In this participation newcomers learn to shed some former inhibitions. "It's wonderful," says one young wife. "You find yourself discussing all your personal problems with your neighbors—things that back in South Dakota we would have kept to ourselves." As time goes on, this capacity for self-revelation grows; and on the most intimate details of family life, court people become amazingly frank with each other. No one, they point out, ever need face a problem alone.

In the battle against loneliness even the architecture becomes functional. Just as doors inside houses—which are sometimes said to have marked the birth of the middle class—are disappearing, so are the barriers against neighbors. The picture in the picture window, for example, is what is going on *inside*—or, what is going on inside other people's picture windows.

The walls in these new apartments are also dual purpose. Their thinness is occasionally a disadvantage; one court scandal, as a matter of fact, was provoked by a woman who chronically inverted a tumbler against the wall to eavesdrop. But there is more good than bad, many transients say, to the thinness. "I never feel lonely, even when Jim's away," goes a typical comment. "You know friends are nearby, because at night you hear the neighbors through the walls."

The Junior Participators

The children, no less outgoing, are a key factor in determining court behavior. "The kids are the only ones who are really organized here," says the resident of a patio court at Parkmerced in San Francisco, "and we older people sort of tag along after them." Suburbanites elsewhere agree. "We are not really 'kid-centered' here as some people say," one Park Forester observes, "but our friendships are often made on the kids' standards and they are purer standards than ours. When your kids are playing with the other kids, they force you to keep on good terms with everybody."

That they do. With their remarkable sensitivity to social nuance the children are a highly effective communication net, and parents sometimes use them to transmit what custom dictates elders cannot say face to face. "One newcomer gave us quite a problem in our court," says a resident in an eastern development. "He was a Ph.D., and he started to pull rank on some of the rest of us. I told my kid he could tell his kid that the other fathers around here had plenty on the ball. I guess all we fathers did the same thing; pretty soon the news trickled upward to this guy. He isn't a bad sort; he got the hint—and there was no open break of any kind."

So pervasive are the concerns of parenthood that adjustment to court life is almost impossible for childless couples. Unless the wife patently loves children—unless she is the kind, for example, who keeps a cooky jar for the neighbors' kids—her daily routine is painfully out of kilter with the others'. Understandably, the recourse of adopting a child is sought very frequently; equally understandably, adoption agencies look on Park Forest couples as particularly good bets to furnish a stable home.

Not only are transients better parents, older observers believe, they are better mates as well. "The kind of social situation you find here discourages divorce," says United Protestant Church minister Dr. Gerson Engelmann. "Few people, as a rule, get divorces until they break with their groups. I think the fact that it is so hard to break with a group here has had a lot to do with keeping some marriages from going on the rocks."

We Have Each Other

Personal morals? Places like Park Forest are the greatest invention since the chastity belt. There have been, to be sure, some unpleasant occurrences; in one court there was talk of wife-trading several years ago, and there have been affairs here and there since. The evidence is strong, however, that there is less philandering among Park Foresters than among their contemporaries in more traditional communities.

For one thing, it's almost impossible to philander without everyone's knowing about it. One's callers are observed, and if neighbors feel there is anything untoward, Park Forest's phenomenal grapevine will speed the news. This is not mere venom; in a web of relationships as delicate as that of the court an affair can harm not only two marriages—it can upset the whole court applecart. And everyone is aware of the fact.

More important, the neighborliness of court life fills a void in the life of the young wife that is not always filled elsewhere—and this is particularly important for the wife whose husband travels. "You don't find as many frustrated women in a place like this," says one wife. "We gals have each other. A young girl who would get to brooding if she was in an apartment all by herself on the outside can talk things over with us. She's just too busy to get neurotic. Kitty, for example; she's married to a real creep—pardon me, but that's what he is—but when she's disturbed she comes over here for coffee and a little chat, and we have a fine old time yakking away. It helps, for people like her."

The Seeing Eye

So far we have dwelt on the beneficent effects of court living. The emphasis, we believe, is in order; for all the exceptions that we are going to note, the fact that people do get along so well in such propinquity bespeaks a pretty high quotient of kindliness and fundamental decency. But it also bespeaks, unfortunately, something else, too.

To appreciate what this is, let's take a closer look at the question of privacy—and Park Foresters' attitude toward it. Fact One, of course, is that there isn't much. In most small towns there is at least enough space to soften the shock of intimate contact, and besides, there is usually some redoubt to which the individual can withdraw. In Park Forest not even the apartment is a redoubt; people don't bother to knock and they come and go furiously—even when the traffic subsides momentarily the thin walls transmit the knowledge that the court, the group, is omnipresent. The lack of privacy, furthermore, is retroactive; as one resident puts it, "They ask you all sorts of questions about what you *were* doing. Who was that that stopped in last night? Who were those people from Chicago last week? You're never alone, even when you think you are."

With communication so intensive, the slightest misunderstanding can generate a whole series of consequences. If Charley ducks his turn at the lawn mower, if little Johnny sasses Mrs. Erdlick just once more, if Gladys forgets to return the pound of coffee she borrowed, the frictions become a concern of the group and not just of the principals.

For individual spats or feuds threaten the equilibrium of the whole court, and the court, like all informal groups, reacts to discipline the errant. The sanctions are not obvious, indeed people are often unconscious of wielding them, but the look in the eye, the absence of a smile, the inflection of a hello can be exquisite punishment, and they have brought more than one to a nervous breakdown.

The tensions are particularly acute for the wife. In a previous article ("The Wives of Management," October, 1951) *Fortune* noted that husbands got from their wives very little understanding of the social problems of their daytime life; let us now redress the balance by noting that the reverse, in the new suburbs at least, is also true. From eight until six the court is a woman's world, and its social problems are of critical importance to her life. But the husband doesn't see it this way, and neither, curiously, does she, for while men have the faculty of seeing their daytime squabbles in terms of the Principle of the Thing, wives are less likely to. "I don't like to bother Henry about these things," says one wife, currently involved in an unpleasant court conflict. "He just hates gossip. He's right, I guess. We women get so petty."

The Ingoing

From the eye of the court there is no escape. Theoretically, one could keep entirely to himself, and some people do. It is not, however, a happy alternative. Like the double bed, the court enforces intimacy, and self-imposed isolation becomes psychologically untenable. People so ingoing that they have been proof against "bringing out" usually seem less happy than the others, and though the causes of their unhappiness may antedate their entry into the court, some leave at the first opportunity. The court checks off another failure. "At the very end the Smithers were beginning to come out of their shell," one outgoing resident recalls. "But it was too late; they'd already given up their lease. The night they left, you could tell by their faces, the way they tried to get friendly, they wished they weren't leaving. It was so pathetic."

Is there a middle course? The ability to steer it is vouchsafed to very few, and if one had to sum up the characteristic that most marks those likely to rise to leadership this might well be it. The transients' defense against rootlessness, as we have noted, is to get involved in meaningful activity; at the same time, however, like the seasoned shipboard traveler, the wisest transients don't get *too* close. Keeping this delicate balance requires a very highly developed social skill, and also a good bit of experience. "It takes time," explains one transient. "I had to go through fraternity life, then the services, and a stretch at Parkmere before I realized you just get into trouble if you get personally involved with neighbors."

More basically, what is required is a rather keen consciousness of self—and the sophistication to realize that while individualistic tastes may raise eyebrows, exercising those tastes won't bring the world crashing down about you. "One day one of the girls busted in," one upper-middlebrow cheerfully recounts. "She saw I was reading. 'What you got there, hon?' she asked me. You might have known it would be Plato that day. She almost fell over from surprise. Now all of them are sure I'm strange." Actually, they don't think she's overly odd, for her deviance is accompanied by enough tact, enough observance of the little customs that oil court life, so that equilibrium is maintained.

The Signals

For most people the problem of deviance hardly comes up at all. Even the most outgoing, of course, confess that the pace of court life occasionally wears them down, and once in a while they reach such a point of rebellion they don't answer the phone. But, they say, there is no real problem. "You have all this companionship," one resident puts it, "and yet you can have all the privacy you want."

The term needs qualification. With court behavior so participative that doors don't need knocking on, such a purely negative response as not answering the phone is not enough. To gain privacy one has to *do* something. One court resident, for example, moves his chair to the front rather than the court side of his apartment to show he doesn't want to be disturbed. Often a whole court or a wing of it will develop such a signal; a group in one Drexelbrook court has decided that whenever one of them feels he or she has finally had it, the venetian blinds should be drawn all the way down to the bottom of the picture window. Since this position is an unusual one, the rest spot it as a plea to be left alone.

But there is an important corollary of such efforts at privacy—*people feel a little guilty about making them.* Except very occasionally, to shut oneself off from others like this is regarded as either a childish prank or, more likely, an indication of some inner neurosis. The individual, not the group, has erred. So, at any rate, many errants seem to feel, and they are often penitent about what elsewhere would be regarded as one's own business, and rather normal business at that. "I've promised myself to make it up to them," one court resident recently told a confidant. "I was feeling bad and just plain didn't make the effort to ask the others in later. I don't blame them, really, for reacting the way they did. I'll make it up to them somehow."

Privacy has become clandestine. Not in solitary and selfish contemplation but in doing things with other people does one fulfill oneself. Nor is it a matter of overriding importance just what it is that one does with other people: even watching television together—for which purpose, incidentally, several groups have been organized—helps make one more of a real person. The important thing, to borrow a phrase, is the *togetherness.*

Where To?

What does this all add up to? A good many observers have fastened their eyes on the physical homogeneity of the new suburbia and seen it as the avenue to *1984.* But this physical homogeneity is not the real issue. The external similarities in the way of life revealed by the new suburbia are dictated by economic necessity, and it is intellectually irresponsible to bemoan them without facing up to the lack of a reasonable alternative. Rows and rows of identical houses are not in themselves a force for conformity—any more than, say, rows of identical Park Avenue apartments or rows of city houses built at the turn of the century, or, for that matter, some of the identical brick fronts of eighteenth-century America.

It is not in the physical similarities that so preoccupy some observers that the problem lies; nor is it even in the similarities of behavior that mark the young transients. The problem lies in the transients' attitude toward these similarities.

The potential leaders differ, as we have noted, from most of their neighbors. But how much do they differ? They are more the individualist than the rest of their contemporaries, but this is only a relative comparison, for their values also indicate how very far the balance between the group and the individual has shifted. In a more muted fashion many of the potential leaders hold the same basic view of man as a social animal, and though they say it much more intelligently—and know that they are saying it—they, too, tend to equate the lone individual with psychic disorder. "We have learned not to be so introverted," one junior executive, and a very thoughtful and successful one, describes the lesson. "Before we came here we used to live pretty much to ourselves. On Sundays, for instance, we used to stay in bed until around maybe two o'clock reading the paper and listening to the symphony on the radio. Now we stop around and visit with people, or they visit with us. I really think Park Forest has broadened us."

The Pragmatists

A passing phase? The transients' emphasis on the group, it could be argued, is simply a temporary accommodation to the necessities of the dormitory life and will conveniently evaporate as the generation matures. If this hopeful explanation were correct, one proof would be found in the schools; would not the transients have the schools encourage the child's sense of autonomy? Like their parents, the children have developed such high social skill that it would seem redundant to intensify this already pronounced characteristic.

But this is not the way the parents see it. In their more hopeful moments they can view their schools as almost a culmination of contemporary American educational philosophy—and they are probably right. As *Fortune* documented in its June issue, the Park Forest school curriculum seems based on the proposition that learning to get along with people—or "citizenship"—is what the schools need to teach most of all. The value of solitary thought, the fact that conflict is sometimes necessary, and other such disturbing thoughts rarely intrude.

Not merely as an instinctive wish, but as an articulate set of values to be passed on to one's children, the next generation of leaders are coming to deify social utility. *Does it work,* not why, has become the key question. With society having become so complex, the individual can have meaning only as he contributes to the harmony of the group, transients explain—and for them, constantly on the move, ever exposed to new groups, the adapting to groups has become particularly necessary. They are all, as they themselves so often put it, in the same boat.

But where is the boat going? No one seems to have the faintest idea; nor, for that matter, do they see much point in even raising the question. Once people liked to think, at least, that they were in control of their destinies, but few of Park Forest's young executives cherish such notions; most see themselves as objects, more acted upon than acting—and their future, therefore, determined as much by the system as by themselves.

The feeling is understandable enough. For most of the transients, life has been a succession of fairly beneficent environments—college, the paternalistic, if not always pleasant, military life, then, perhaps, graduate work through the G.I. Bill of Rights, a corporation apprenticeship during a period of industrial expansion and high prosperity, and, equally important, the camaraderie of communities like Park Forest. The system, they instinctively conclude, is essentially benevolent.

In one respect, at least, the young transients have been well conditioned: no generation of junior executives has been so well equipped, psychologically as well as technically, to cope with the intricacies of vast organizations; few generations will be so well equipped to lead a meaningful community life; and probably none will be so adaptable to the constant shifts in environment that corporation life is making increasingly necessary.

They will, in short, make excellent technicians. Will they make bold leaders as well? "One thing that has always struck me about the top executives," says a consultant who has intimately studied a great many of them, "is that they are sort of sore at the system. They realize that they are pretty subject to it; but they don't altogether like it; somehow, they're always trying to wrench back the control into their own hands. But these junior executives are a different breed, and I'm not sure it's just that they're young."

To be fair, we must note that the young transients' adaptability is not, as some observers assume, a reversal of our national character. The American genius has always lain, in good part, in our adaptability, in our distrust of dogma, in our regard for the opinion of others and in this respect the transients are true products of the American past. "The more equal social conditions become," de Tocqueville, no friend of conformity, presciently observed over a century ago, "the more men display this reciprocal disposition to oblige each other."

We cannot have it both ways, certainly; we cannot enjoy the advantages of our talent for adjustment without paying some price. We can wonder, however, if we have not finally come to worship what we once took for granted, and in the process come to caricature our virtues into defects. We may have to endure conformity, but we do not have to love ourselves for doing it.

Given the fact of organization society, what is in order is not the impossible cliché of rugged individualism. But it is very much in order that we recognize that we are moving toward the other extreme, that we recognize we cannot go too far in accommodation without making a sacrifice; that in its warmth, the group can be a tyrant as well as a friend. That, in short, there is a time to pull the blind down.

SEYMOUR MARTIN LIPSET

A Changing American Character?

From the time of Tocqueville and John Stuart Mill, Western intellectuals have questioned the fate of human individuality in a mass society. As political and social rights have been extended to ever larger proportions of national populations, many have seen an accompanying trend toward the reduction of personal freedom and individuality. The rule by the mob, or the tyranny by the majority, have been the threatening images in the minds of theorists writing in this intellectual tradition. Recently, these images have been supplemented by a perception of widespread anxiety and restlessness in modern life, attributed to the loss of clearly specified goals and values which once existed in more close-knit social structures.

To this continuing tradition of social criticism David Riesman has been an outstanding recent contributor. In *The Lonely Crowd,* especially, he has tried to describe systematically the impact of industrialization and urbanization on the everyday relations of men. In doing so, his approach is strikingly similar to those of Karl Marx and Thorstein Veblen, to take two key figures who linked technology and social change. Marx and Veblen related technological developments to class relationships, and subsequently to the social organization of whole societies. Riesman has written a book-length interpretation of Veblen and explicitly acknowledges his debt to Erich Fromm and C. Wright Mills, two social scientists who have elaborated many of Marx's insights on the consequences of industrialization. Although Riesman's theory seems applicable to much of world history, he concentrates his analysis on, and draws his evidence from, the differences between nineteenth-century and twentieth-century capitalist society in America. The main consequence of technological change in this period is said to be a transformation of the modal American character from inner-direction to other-direction. Much of this essay will be devoted to discussing the historical adequacy of this interpretation. Before presenting some of the historical evidence, I shall briefly sketch the major connections Riesman perceives between changes in technology and changes in social character.

Capitalism and Other-Direction

Riesman considers the economic order, as it affects social character, under three aspects: production (or the technological problem of physical objects), customers (marketing), and colleagues (intra-firm relations). In the early period of industrialism the emphasis was on production; this was followed by an increasing concern with customers; and today the crucial problem is that of relations between colleagues. Riesman agrees with Marx about the consequences for the worker of the early period, during which the stress is on production:

> It seems possible that the open class struggle is characteristic of societies in the stage of transitional growth [i.e., of production primacy]—this is the period that Marx lived in and observed in western Europe—while in these same societies in the stage of incipient decline the social struggle goes on primarily among people of nominally identical class and status positions, that is, among the vastly increased and differentiated middle classes. [34n][1]

In effect, Riesman argues that during the period of industrial expansion those involved in the market faced problems about things rather than about people, whether as customers or as colleagues. Scarcity of goods and relatively inefficient means of handling the technological problems of extraction, transportation, and manufacturing overshadowed the concern with marketing and personal relations.

> Thus for the inner-directed man production is seen and experienced in terms of technological and intellectual processes rather than in terms of human cooperation. Human relations in industry, as well as relations among industries and between industry and society as a whole, seem to the inner-directed man to be managed by the anonymous cooperation brought about through the "invisible hand." [115]

According to Riesman, propitiating the customer was unnecessary because the customer had nowhere else to go, and the general scarcity of goods admitted no likelihood of overproduction.

The increase in available goods and the problem of overproduction bring about a change in the policies and character of the entrepreneur. He becomes an "other-directed person [who] gives up the one-face policy of the inner-directed man for a multiface policy that he sets in secrecy and varies with each set of encounters." [147] This he does not only in his relations with customers, but also in his relations with colleagues:

> We can contrast the small grocer who must please his individual patrons, perhaps by a "counter-side manner," with the chain-store employee who must please both the patrons and his co-workers in the shop; indeed, in pleasing the patrons he cannot an-

---

[1] [The bracketed page references, here and subsequently, are to the original edition of *The Lonely Crowd* (New Haven: Yale University Press, 1950)—Ed.]

tagonize the co-workers. . . . The colleague, like the peer-grouper, is the very person with whom one engages in competition for the *scarce commodity of approval* and the very person to whom one looks for guidance as to what is desirable [140; emphasis mine, SML]

The eclipse of production problems by marketing or customer relations, and by the new problem of propitiating colleagues and workers, is both favored by, and fosters, other-direction as the ascendant social character. Success in a bureaucracy, and in the proliferating service occupations of modern society, depends primarily on the ability to get along well with others. A premium is therefore set on skill in the manipulation of people.

Riesman does not view the relationship between economic change and social character as a one-way relationship. While the technological changes which accompany advanced industrialization facilitate the emergence of other-direction, the spread of this new character-type itself reduces pressures to achieve. Ambition diminishes, and personality-oriented behavior supplants the older work-orientation:

"Ambition" I define as an indoctrination of goals in the period of inner-direction; it is a striving for fame or for goodness but always for clear goals: to get the job, to win the battle, to build the bridge. Competition in the era depending on inner-direction is frequently ruthless, but at the same time people are in no doubt as to their place in the race—and that there is a race. If they feel guilt it is when they fail, not when they succeed. By contrast, "antagonistic cooperation" may be defined as an inculcated striving among the groups affected by other-direction. Here the important thing is not the goal but the relationship to the "others"; not one's own victory but the others' failure. In this new-style competition people are often in doubt whether there is a race at all, and if so, what its goals are. Since they are supposed to be cooperative rather than rivalrous, they may well feel guilt about success. [104–105]

In making this distinction, Riesman argues that specialization in large corporations and public bureaucracies, with its increased emphasis on the successful handling of others, rather than on coping with things, causes a loss of productive skills akin to the loss of individuality. "If one is successful in one's craft, one is forced to leave it." [133] Demonstration of skill qualifies one for promotion to the better paid ranks of the personality specialists. The best workers become foremen, the competent engineers are made managers, the leading scholars in universities become administrators. This is a distinctive twentieth-century phenomenon, for in the smaller enterprises of the last century there was no need for this kind of specialization.

To be sure, business was always work with people. But when the size of enterprises was small, the head could remain a colleague among other colleagues; he did not cut connections entirely and enter a new milieu. William Allen White's *Autobiography* shows that he was able to maintain all his life the amiable fiction that he was only a working man. [133–134]

These changes in economic life, together with increasing urbanization, have "necessitated" a change in social character and values by altering the processes of socialization. Adults have learned that success depends more and more on winning the good opinion of others, of both clients and colleagues. Gradually they come to feel the importance of teaching their children to succeed by courting popularity. But the family itself has also become less important as an agency of socialization. The near monopoly in this task once held by the farm and small-town family has been invaded by the competing agencies of the urban peer group, the teacher, and the mass media. The child must respond to a wide range of people and situations, which radically complicates the socialization problem. Thus a qualitative change occurs in social character, from inner-direction (responding to a fixed, internal code of morality) to other-direction (responding to demands of others in complex situations). Characterological change hastens a shift in social values, notably a decline in individualism and a subversion of the desire to achieve. Rate-busting, or any outstanding performance, is strongly discouraged by one's peers. Aggressive individualism and competition are modified by the diffuse imperative of antagonistic cooperation. The impact of the changing occupational structure and of increased bureaucratization is portrayed by Riesman as the collapse of individualism before the "change in paths to success and the requirement of more 'socialized' behavior both for success and for marital and personal adaptation." [22] The resulting other-directed man is characterized by (1) orientation toward situational rather than internalized goals, (2) extreme sensitivity to the opinions of others, (3) excessive need for approval, (4) conformity on internal experience as well as on externals, (5) loss of achievement-orientation, and (6) loss of individualism.

This, then, is the sequence of characterological changes posited by Riesman. In the following sections, I will present evidence that the personality traits of the other-directed man have to a considerable extent always existed in the American character and that the values of achievement and individualism persist in American society.

The Materialistic Interpretation of Value Change

The analysis of change in social character and values set forth in *The Lonely Crowd* emphasizes "materialistic" factors. It assumes that a certain type of social character is necessary for each type of economic organization, e.g., large-scale bureaucracies; and that, when a particular set of values or a specific social character is needed, social conditions sooner or later create such values and such character. But while these assumptions are probably valid, the analytic model is oversimplified. Like other materialistic interpretations of history, this scheme tends to ignore the possibility that values may themselves induce change: in particular, that values may be decisive factors in changing social character. In *The Lonely Crowd,* values are treated as dependent variables, changing in response to shifts in technological development and economic organization. This view of change in values as primarily a by-product of other social processes leads to a misinterpretation of the work of Max Weber, who so often stressed the possibility of values acting as an independent source of change. Weber's thesis concerning the role of the Protestant ethic in the genesis of capitalism is turned on its head:

Indeed, just as the rapid accumulation of productive capitalism *requires* that people be imbued with the "Protestant Ethic" (as Max Weber characterized one manifestation of what is here termed inner-direction), so also the decreased number of progeny [in the contemporary American family] *requires* a profound change in *values*—a change so deep that, in all probability, it has to be rooted in character structure. [18; my emphasis]

Weber's thesis in *The Protestant Ethic* does not, however, support this point made in *The Lonely Crowd*. The two arguments are not logically parallel, but opposed to each other, as an examination of the different uses of the word "requires" shows. Weber argued that a value-system compatible with the attitudes and behavior necessary to institutionalize capitalist economic practices is a *prerequisite* for the development of this type of economic organization. Riesman's argument is not that a value-system compatible with the stabilization of the small nuclear family is a prerequisite to a reduction in family size; rather he argues that one of the necessary *consequences* of the emergence of the small family pattern is a change in values. Values do not change or determine anything important, but merely submit to the demands of the material situation.

This methodological commitment to a "superstructural" view of values makes Riesman neglect the possibility that the "other-directedness" of American society might be as much an outgrowth and elaboration of persistent traits in the American value-system, as a result of changes in technology. For whereas Riesman emphasizes the rise of a *new* value-system as the product of a changing technology, it is possible to argue, as did Weber in the case of the genesis of capitalism, that the prevalence of certain values is a prerequisite to other-directedness, and that it is the interplay of these values with the material conditions that leads to the apparent increase in other-directedness.

The Unchanging American Character

The evidence that points in this direction was not unknown to the authors of *The Lonely Crowd*. Early in the book they remarked that some of the defining traits of other-directedness (specifically, extreme sensitivity to others and internal conformity) were also noted by many of the celebrated nineteenth-century foreign travelers:

Yet in some respects this type [the other-directed man] is strikingly similar to *the* American, whom Tocqueville and other curious and astonished visitors from Europe, even before the Revolution, thought to be a new kind of man. Indeed, travelers' reports on America impress us with their unanimity. The American is said to be shallower, freer with his money, friendlier, more uncertain of himself and his values, more demanding of approval than the European. It all adds up to a pattern which, without stretching matters too far, resembles the kind of character that a number of social scientists have seen as developing in contemporary, highly industrialized, and bureaucratic America: Fromm's "marketeer," Mills "fixer," Arnold Green's "middle-class male child." [19–20]

But in making this statement Riesman is far from admitting the prevalence of other-direction in colonial days, or even in the early nineteenth century. He mentions these reports, which seem to contradict his thesis, only to warn us against concluding from the similarities of behavior between the nineteenth-century American of Tocqueville's *Democracy in America* and the contemporary, urban, middle-class American of *The Lonely Crowd,* that other-direction has always been characteristic of America. His way of discounting the travelers' reports is to claim that they *foresaw* rather than *saw* America. Also, so Riesman argues, Tocqueville and most of the other travelers were well-to-do or aristocrats, and drew their information from snobbish, *arriviste* Americans who described their own countrymen in the language used by the anti-American, European upper class. The travelers failed to depict the *inner*-directed men around them, because their interests and backgrounds led them to describe Americans by what differentiated them from Europeans. Presumably, though Riesman does not make this explicit, Americans of the eighteenth and nineteenth centuries, though inner-directed when compared with the contemporary American, were more other-directed than the Europeans of their day.

I shall try to demonstrate below that the foreign travelers' accounts of American life, manners, and character traits seriously challenge the thesis that American character has been transformed during the past century and a half. It is thus unfortunate that the authors of *The Lonely Crowd* cite so few historical references to illustrate the American character in the earlier period. They excuse this dearth by commenting that "On the general problem of whether there is an American character, and if so what are its sources, and how such questions *might be* investigated . . ." they found the works of Oscar Handlin, and the classic sociological investigation, *The Polish Peasant,* more fruitful than the writings of Tocqueville and other foreign travelers. [20]

Since the exact nature of the observations of the nineteenth-cenury American by the foreign travelers is so important for the main argument, it is worth listening to some of these visitors to the America of yesteryear who saw, or "foresaw," the other-directed man of today. Harriet Martineau, in particular, at times might be paraphrasing from *The Lonely Crowd* in her description of the American of 1830.

> [Americans] may travel over the world, and find no society but their own which will submit to the restraint of perpetual caution, and reference to the opinions of others. They may travel over the whole world, and find no country but their own where the very children beware of getting into scrapes, and talk of the effect of actions upon people's minds; where the youth of society determine in silence what opinions they shall bring forward, and what avow only in the family circle; where women write miserable letters, almost universally, because it is a settled matter that it is unsafe to commit oneself on paper; and where elderly people seem to lack almost universally

that faith in principles which inspires a free expression of them at any time, and under all circumstances. . . .

There is fear of vulgarity, fear of responsibility; and above all, fear of singularity. . . . There is something little short of disgusting to the stranger who has been unused to witness such want of social confidence, in the caution which presents probably the strongest aspect of selfishness that he has ever seen. The Americans of the northern states are, from education and habit, so accustomed to the caution of which I speak, as to be unaware of its extent and singularity. . . .

Few persons [Americans] really doubt this when the plain case is set down before them. They agree to it in church on Sundays, and in conversation by the fireside: and the reason why they are so backward as they are to act upon it in the world, is that *habit and education are too strong for them.* They have worn their chains so long that they feel them less than might be supposed.[2]

Harriet Martineau is only one observer of early American life, and not necessarily more reliable than others. But it is significant that her comments on American "other-directedness" and conformism do not flow, as do those of many other nineteenth-century visitors who made comparable observations, from fear or dislike of democracy. Many upper-class visitors, such as Tocqueville or Ostrogorski, saw a threat to genuine individuality and creativity in political and intellectual life, in the fact that democracy and equalitarianism give the masses access to elites, and that the latter must therefore be slaves to public opinion in order to survive. Harriet Martineau, as a left-wing English liberal, did not come to America with such fears or beliefs. She remained an ardent admirer of American democracy, even though she ultimately decided that "the worship of Opinion is, at this day, the established religion of the United States."[3]

The most celebrated post-Civil War nineteenth-century English visitor to America, James Bryce, saw inherent in American society "self-distrust, a despondency, a disposition to fall into line, to acquiesce in the dominant opinion. . . ." This "tendency to acquiescence and submission" is not to be "confounded with the tyranny of the majority . . . [it] does not imply any compulsion exerted by the majority," in the sense discussed by Tocqueville. Rather Bryce, like Harriet Martineau fifty years earlier, described what he felt to be a basic psychological trait of Americans, their "fatalism," which involved a "loss of resisting power, a diminished sense of personal responsibility, and of the duty to battle for one's own opinions. . . ."[4]

Although Harriet Martineau and James Bryce stand out among nineteenth-century visitors in specifying that these other-directed traits were deeply rooted in the *personalities* of many Americans, the general *behavioral* manifestations that they and Tocqueville reported were mentioned by many other foreign travelers. For example, a summary of the writings of English travelers from 1785–1835 states that one important characteristic mentioned in a number of

[2]Harriet Martineau, *Society in America* (New York: Saunders & Otlay, 1837), III, 14–15, 17. (Emphasis mine.)

[3]*Ibid.,* p. 7.

[4]James Bryce, *The American Commonwealth* (New York: Macmillan Co., 1912), II, 351–52.

books "was the acute sensitiveness to opinion that the average American revealed."[5] A German aristocrat, who became a devotee of American democracy and a citizen of the country, stated in the 1830's that, "Nothing can excite the contempt of an educated European more than the continual fears and apprehensions in which even the 'most enlightened citizens' of the United States seem to live with regard to their next neighbors, lest their actions, principles, opinions and beliefs should be condemned by their fellow creatures."[6] An interpreter of nineteenth-century foreign opinion, John Graham Brooks, mentions various other writers who noted the unwillingness of Americans to be critical of each other. He quotes James Muirhead, the English editor of the *Baedeker* guide to the United States, as saying: "Americans invented the slang word 'kicker,' but so far as I could see, their vocabulary is here miles ahead of their practice; they dream noble deeds, but do not do them; Englishmen 'kick' much better without having a name for it." Brooks suggested that it was the American "hesitation to face unpleasant facts rather than be disagreeable and pugnacious about them, after the genius of our English cousins, that calls out the criticism."[7]

The observation that the early Americans were cautious and sensitive has been made not only by foreign visitors but also, at different times, by Americans—as in fact many of the foreign authors report. In 1898, the American writer John Jay Chapman echoed Tocqueville's dictum of seventy years before, that he knew "of no country in which there is so little independence of mind and real freedom of discussion as in America." Chapman saw the general caution and desire to please as the source of many of the ills of his day.

"Live and let live," says our genial prudence. Well enough, but mark the event. No one ever lost his social standing merely because of his offenses, but because of the talk about them. As free speech goes out the rascals come in.

Speech is a great part of social life, but not the whole of it. Dress, bearing, expression, betray a man, customs show character, all these various utterances mingle and merge into the general tone which is the voice of a national temperament; private motive is lost in it.

This tone penetrates and envelopes everything in America. It is impossible to condemn it altogether. This desire to please, which has so much of the shopman's smile in it, graduates at one end of the scale into a general kindliness, into public benefactions, hospitals, and college foundations; at the other end it is seen melting into a desire to efface one's self rather than give offense, to hide rather than be noticed.

In Europe, the men in the pit at the theatre stand up between the acts, face the house, and examine the audience at leisure. The American dares not do this. He cannot stand the isolation, nor the publicity. The American in a horse car can give his seat to a lady, but dares not raise his voice while the conductor tramps over his toes.[8]

---

[5]Jane L. Mesick, *The English Traveller in America, 1785–1835* (New York: Columbia University Press, 1922), p. 301.

[6]Francis J. Grund, *Aristocracy in America* (New York: Harper Torchbooks, 1959), p. 162; see also pp. 52 and 157 for further comments.

[7]J. G. Brooks, *As Others See Us* (New York: Macmillan Co., 1908), p. 95.

[8]*The Selected Writings of John Jay Chapman* (New York: Doubleday Anchor, 1959), p. 278.

Although these accounts by travelers and American essayists cannot be taken as conclusive proof of an unchanging American character, they do suggest that Riesman's thesis of a changing American character may be incorrect.

The Unchanging American Values and Their Connection with American Character

Fully as much as by the other-directedness of Americans, the foreign travelers were also impressed by two basic value orientations—the American insistence on equality in social relations, and on achievement in one's career. Indeed, many perceived an intimate connection between the other-directed behavior they witnessed and the prevalence of these values, such that the behavior could not be understood without reference to them. An analysis of the writings of hundreds of British travelers in America before the Civil War reports: "Most prominent of the many impressions that Britons took back with them [between 1836 and 1860] was the aggressive egalitarianism of the people."[9] If one studies the writings of such celebrated European visitors as Harriet Martineau, the Trollopes (both mother and son), Tocqueville, or James Bryce, it is easy to find many observations documenting this point.

Baedeker's advice to any European planning to visit the United States in the late nineteenth or early twentieth century was that he "should, from the outset, reconcile himself to the absence of deference, or servility, on the part of those he considers his social inferiors."[10] A detailed examination of the comments of European visitors from 1890 to 1910 reports general agreement concerning the depth and character of American equalitarianism.

> Whether they liked what they saw or not, most foreign observers did not doubt that America was a democratic society. . . . Different occupations, of course, brought differences in prestige, but neither the occupation nor the prestige implied any fundamental difference in the value of individuals. . . . The similarity of conclusions based on diverse observations was simply another indication of the absence of sharp class differences. Even hostile visitors confirmed this judgment. . . . Some foreign observers found the arrogance of American workers intolerable.[11]

Even today this contrast between Europe and America with respect to patterns of equality in interpersonal relations among men of different social positions is striking. A comparison of writings of European visitors at the turn of this century with those made by British groups visiting here to study American industrial methods since World War II states that "the foreign descriptions of . . . America in 1890 and 1950 are remarkably similar. . . . The British teams [in the 1950's reported] . . . the same values . . . which impressed visitors a half century ago. Like them they found the American worker is more nearly the

---

[9]Max Berger, *The British Traveller in America, 1836–1860* (New York: Columbia University Press, 1943), pp. 54–55.

[10]Quoted by Philip Burne-Jones, *Dollars and Democracy* (London: Sidney Appleton, 1904), p. 69.

[11]Robert W. Smuts, *European Impressions of the American Worker* (New York: King's Crown Press, 1953), pp. 3–7.

equal of other members of society than the European, with respect not only to his material prosperity, but also to . . . the attitudes of others toward him."[12] And this attitude is apparent at other levels of American society as well. As one commentator put it, when describing the high-status Europeans who have come to America in recent years as political refugees from Nazism and Communism:

> With his deep sense of class and status, integration in American society is not easy for the émigré. The skilled engineer or physician who . . . finally establishes himself in his profession, discovers that he does not enjoy the same exalted status that he would have had in the old country. I met several young Croatian doctors in the Los Angeles area who were earning $25,000 to $35,000 a year, but still felt declassed.[13]

American emphasis on equalitarianism as a dominant value, which has persisted from our early national history down to the present, is significant in determining what to many of the Europeans were three closely related processes: competition, status uncertainty, and conformity. Tocqueville, for example, argued that equalitarianism maximizes competition among the members of a society. In his description of democracy's destruction of aristocracy he says, "They have swept away the privileges of some of their fellow creatures which stood in their way, but they have opened the door to universal competition."[14] And Smuts' study, cited above, draws on a number of comments to conclude that "social and economic democracy in America, far from mitigating competition for social status, intensified it."[15]

But if equalitarianism fosters competition for status, the combination of the two values of equality and achievement results, according to many of the travelers, in an amorphous social structure in which individuals are uncertain about their social position. In fact, those travelers who were so impressed with the pervasive equalitarianism of American society also suggested that, *precisely as a result of the emphasis on equality and opportunity,* Americans were *more* status-conscious than those who lived in the more aristocratic societies of Europe. They believed, for example, that it was easier for the *nouveaux riches* to be accepted in European high society than in American. British travelers *before the Civil War* noted that Americans seemed to love titles more than Englishmen. European observers, from Harriet Martineau and Frances Trollope in the 1830's to James Bryce in the 1880's, and Denis Brogan in recent years, have pointed out that the actual strength of equality as a dominant American value, with the consequent lack of any well-defined deference structure linked to a legitimate aristocratic tradition where the propriety of social rankings is unquestioned, forces Americans to *emphasize* status background and symbolism.[16]

[12] *Ibid.,* p. 54.

[13] Bogden Radista, "Clash of Two Immigrant Generations," *Commentary,* XXV (1958), p. 12.

[14] Alexis de Tocqueville, *Democracy in America* (New York: Vintage Books, 1959), II, 146.

[15] Smuts, *op. cit.,* p. 13.

[16] D. W. Brogan, *U.S.A.: An Outline of the Country, Its People and Institutions* (London: Oxford University Press, 1941), pp. 116–17.

As the latter has remarked, the American value-system has formed "a society which, despite all efforts of school, advertising, clubs and the rest, makes the creation of effective social barriers difficult and their maintenance a perpetually repeated task. American social fences have to be continually repaired; in England they are like wild hedges, they grow if left alone."[17]

Status-striving and the resultant conformism has not been limited solely, or even primarily, to the more well-to-do classes in American society. Many of the early nineteenth-century travelers commented on the extent to which workers attempted to imitate middle-class styles of life in their consumption. Smuts notes that visitors at the turn of this century were struck by "what they regarded as the spendthrift pattern of the American worker's life;" Paul Bourget, a French observer, interpreted this behavior as reflecting "the profound feeling of equality [in America which] urges them to make a show." As Werner Sombart, the German sociologist and economist, put it, "since all are seeking success . . . everyone is forced into a struggle to beat every other individual; and a steeplechase begins . . . that differs from all other races in that the goal is not fixed but constantly moves even further away from the runners." And in an equalitarian democracy "the universal striving for success [becomes a major cause of] . . . the worker's extravagance, for, as Münsterberg [a German psychologist] pointed out, the ability to spend was the only public sign of success at earning.[18] And lest it be thought that such concerns with conspicuous consumption emerged only in the Gilded Age of the 1890's analyzed by Veblen, sixty years earlier a medical study of the "Influence of Trades, Professions, and Occupations, in the United States, in the Production of Disease," described and analyzed behavior in much the same terms:

> The population of the United States is beyond that of other countries an anxious one. All classes are either striving after wealth, or *endeavoring to keep up its appearance.* From the principle of imitation which is implanted in all of us, sharpened perhaps by the existing equality of conditions, the poor follow as closely as they are able the habits and manner of living of the rich. . . . From these causes, and perhaps from the nature of our political institutions, and the effects arising from them, we are an anxious, care-worn people.[19]

While some Europeans explained American behavior that they found strange —the sensitivity, kindliness, concern for others' feelings, and moral meekness— by reference to the nature of political democracy or the overbearing desire to make money, others saw these traits as consequences of the extreme emphasis on equality of opportunity, the basic American value which they properly regarded as unique. Many argued that this very emphasis on equality, and the constant challenging of any pretensions to permanent high status, has made Americans in all social positions extremely sensitive to the opinions of others,

---

[17]D. W. Brogan, *The English People* (London: Hamish Hamilton, 1943), p. 99.

[18]Smuts, *op. cit.*, p. 13.

[19]Benjamin McCready, "On the Influence of Trades, Professions, and Occupations in the United States, in the Production of Disease," *Transactions of the Medical Society of the State of New York,* III (1836–1837), pp. 146–47. (My emphasis.)

and causes status aspirants greater anxiety about the behavior and characteristics indicative of rank than their counterparts in more aristocratic societies. Discussing the writings of various travelers, John Graham Brooks states:

One deeper reason why the English are blunt and abrupt about their rights . . . is because class lines are more sharply drawn there. Within these limits, one is likely to develop the habit of demanding his dues. He insists on his prerogatives all the more because they are narrowly defined. When an English writer (Jowett) says, "We are not nearly so much afraid of one another as you are in the States," he expressed this truth. In a democracy every one at least hopes to get on and up. This ascent depends not upon the favor of a class, but upon the good-will of the whole. This social whole has to be conciliated. It must be conciliated in both directions—at the top and at the bottom. To make one's self conspicuous and disagreeable, is to arouse enmities that block one's way.[20]

One may find an elaboration of this casual analysis among many writers at different periods. Thus Max Weber, after a visit to America in the early 1900's, noted the high degree of "submission to fashion in America, to a degree unknown in Germany" and explained it in terms of the lack of inherited class status.[21] Seven decades earlier another German, Francis Grund, who saw in American equality and democracy the hope of the world, nevertheless also believed that the ambiguous class structure made status-striving tantamount to conformity. He presents both sides of the picture in the following items:

Society in America . . . is characterized by a spirit of exclusiveness and persecution unknown in any other country. *Its gradations not being regulated according to rank and title, selfishness and conceit are its principal elements.* . . . What man is there in this city [New York] that dares to be independent, at the risk of being considered bad company? And who can venture to infringe upon a single rule of society? . . .

This habit of conforming to each other's opinions, and the penalty set upon every transgression of that kind, are sufficient to prevent a man from wearing a coat cut in a different fashion, or a shirt collar no longer *a la mode,* or, in fact, to do, say, or appear anything which could render him unpopular among a certain set. In no other place, I believe, is there such a stress laid upon "saving appearances."[22]

James Bryce, a half century later, also linked conformity to the ambiguity of the status system, particularly as it affected the wealthy classes. He pointed out that it was precisely the emphasis on equality, and the absence of well-defined rules of deference, which made Americans so concerned with the behavior of others and seemingly more, rather than less, snobbish toward each other than were comparably placed Englishmen.

It may seem a paradox to observe that a millionaire has a better and easier social career open to him in England, than in America. . . . In America, if his private character be bad, if he be mean or openly immoral, or personally vulgar, or dishonest, the best society may keep its doors closed against him. In England great wealth, skillfully

[20] Brooks, *op. cit.,* p. 97.

[21] H. H. Gerth and C. Wright Mills (eds.), *From Max Weber: Essays in Sociology* (New York: Oxford University Press, 1946), p. 188.

[22] Grund, *op. cit.,* pp. 52, 157. (Emphasis mine.)

employed, will more readily force these doors to open. . . . The existence of a system of artificial rank enables a stamp to be given to base metal in Europe which cannot be given in a thoroughly republican country.[23]

In comparing the reactions of Englishmen and Americans to criticism, James Muirhead (the editor of the American *Baedeker*) stated that "the Briton's indifference to criticism" is linked to the fact that "England is still the stronghold of the obsolescent institution of caste, that it frankly and even brutally asserts the essential inequality of man. . . . Social adaptability is not his [the Briton's] foible. He accepts the conventionality of his class and wears it as an impenetrable armor."[24]

A number of the foreign travelers, particularly those who visited America after the 1880's, were startled to find overt signs of anti-Semitism, such as placards barring Jews from hotels in upper-class resorts and social clubs which denied them membership.[25] But this, too, could be perceived as a consequence of the fact that "the very absence of titular distinction often causes the lines to be more clearly drawn; as Mr. Charles Dudley Warner says: 'Popular commingling in pleasure resorts is safe enough in aristocratic countries, but it will not answer in a republic.' "[26] The most recent effort by a sociologist, Howard Brotz, to account for the greater concern about close contract with Jews in America than in England, also suggests:

In a democracy snobbishness can be far more vicious than in an aristocracy. Lacking that natural confirmation of superiority which political authority alone can give, the rich and particularly the new rich, feel threatened by mere contact with their inferiors. . . . Nothing could be more fantastic than this to an English lord living in the country in the midst, not of other peers, but of his tenants. His position is such that he is at ease in the presence of members of the lower classes and in associating with them in recreation. . . . It is this "democratic" attitude which, in the first instance, makes for an openness to social relations with Jews. One cannot be declassed, so to speak, by play activities.[27]

The intimate connection between other-directedness and equalitarian values perceived by these observers recalls the same connection perceived by Plato in his theoretical analysis of democracy. In Plato's *Republic* we find these words:

[In a democracy, the father] accustoms himself to become like his child and to fear his sons. . . . Metic [resident alien] is like citizen and citizen like metic, and stranger like both. . . . The schoolmaster fears and flatters his pupils. . . . The young act like their seniors, and compete with them in speech and action, while the old men condescend to the young and become triumphs of versatility and wit, imitating their juniors in order to avoid the appearance of being sour or despotic. . . . And the wonderful equality

[23]Bryce, *op. cit.*, p. 815.

[24]James Fullerton Muirhead, *America, the Land of Contrasts: A Briton's View of His American Kin* (London: Lemson, Wolffe and Co., 1898), p. 91.

[25]Andrew J. Torrielli, *Italian Opinion on America as Revealed by Italian Travelers, 1850–1900* (Cambridge: Harvard University Press, 1941), p. 99.

[26]Muirhead, *op. cit.*, p. 27.

[27]Howard Brotz, "The Position of the Jews in English Society," *Jewish Journal of Sociology*, I (1959), p. 97.

of law and . . . liberty prevails in the mutual relations of men and women . . . the main result of all these things, taken together, is that it makes the souls of the citizens so sensitive that they take offense and will not put up with the faintest suspicion of slavery [strong authority] that anyone may introduce.[28]

Plato's analysis points up the main question to which this paper is addressed: are other-directed traits solely a function of the technology and social structure of a bureaucratic, industrialized, urban society, as Riesman implies, or are they also to some considerable degree an expected consequence of a social system founded upon the values of equality and achievement? It seems that sociological theory, especially that advanced by Max Weber and Talcott Parsons, and much historical and comparative evidence, support the need to include the basic value system as at least a major, if not the pre-eminent, source of these traits.

As Plato "noted," and as the foreign travelers testify, democratic man is deeply imbued with the desire to accommodate to others, which results in kindness and generosity in personal relations, and in a reluctance to offend. All books that are published are "exalted to the skies," teachers "admire their pupils," and flattery is general.[29] The travelers also bear out Plato's remarks about the socialization of children in a democracy. It appears that equalitarian principles were applied to child-rearing early in the history of the republic. Early British opinions of American children have a modern flavor:

The independence and maturity of American children furnished another surprise for the British visitor. Children ripened early. . . . But such precosity, some visitors feared, was too often achieved at the loss of parental control. Combe claimed that discipline was lacking in the home, and children did what they pleased. Marryat corroborated this. . . . Children were not whipped here [as in England], but treated like rational beings.[30]

Harriet Martineau's description of child-rearing in the America of Andrew Jackson sounds like a commentary on the progressive other-directed parent of the mid-twentieth century:

My [parent] friend observed that the only thing to be done [in child-rearing] is to avoid to the utmost the exercise of authority, and to make children friends from the very beginning. . . . They [the parents] do not lay aside their democratic principles in this relation, more than in others. . . . They watch and guard: they remove stumbling-blocks: they manifest approbation and disapprobation: they express wishes, but, at the same time, study the wishes of their little people: they leave as much as possible to natural retribution: they impose no opinions, and quarrel with none: in short, they exercise the tenderest friendship without presuming upon it. . . . the children of America have the advantage of the best possible early discipline; that of activity and self-dependence.[31]

What struck the democratic Miss Martineau as progressive was interpreted quite differently by Anthony Trollope, who visited this country in 1860: "I

---

[28]Plato, *The Republic,* ed. by Ernest Rhys (London: J. M. Dent and Co., 1935), pp. 200–26.

[29]Martineau, *op. cit.,* pp. 63–64.

[30]Berger, *op. cit.,* pp. 83–84.

[31]Martineau, *op. cit.,* pp. 168, 177.

must protest that American babies are an unhappy race. They eat and drink as they please; they are never punished; they are never banished, snubbed, and kept in the background as children are kept with us."[32] And forty years later, another English visitor, typical of the many who described American child-parent relations during a century and a half, tells us that nowhere else, as in America, "is the child so constantly in evidence; nowhere are his wishes so carefully consulted; nowhere is he allowed to make his mark so strongly on society. ... The theory of the equality of man is rampant in the nursery.... You will actually hear an American mother say of a child of two or three years of age: 'I can't *induce* him to do this....' "[33]

If these reports from the middle and late nineteenth century are reminiscent of the contemporary view in *The Lonely Crowd,* it is still more amazing to find, in a systematic summary of English travelers' opinion in the last part of the eighteenth and early years of the nineteenth centuries, that the emphasis on equality and democracy had *already* created the distinctive American child-oriented family which astonished the later visitors:

> A close connection was made by the stranger between the republican form of government and the unlimited liberty which was allowed the younger generation.... They were rarely punished at home, and strict discipline was not tolerated in the schools.... It was feared that respect for elders or for any other form of authority would soon be eliminated from American life.... As he could not be punished in the school, he learned to regard his teacher as an inferior and to disregard all law and order.[34]

Equality was thus perceived by many of the foreign travelers as not only affecting the socialization of the child within the family, but in the school as well. The German psychologist Hugo Münsterberg joins the late-eighteenth-century visitors in complaining, over a century later in 1900, that "The feeling of equality will crop up where nature designed none, as for instance between youth and mature years.... Parents even make it a principle to implore and persuade their children, holding it to be a mistake to compel or punish them; and they believe that the schools should be conducted in the same spirit."[35] Various visitors were struck by the extent to which the schools did carry out this objective. The following description of schools in the New York area in 1833, by an Englishman, sounds particularly modern:

> The pupils are entirely independent of their teacher. No correction, no coercion, no manner of restraint is permitted to be used.... Parents also have as little control over their offspring at home, as the master has at school.... Corporal punishment has almost disappeared from American day-schools; and a teacher, who should now give

[32]Anthony Trollope, *North America* (New York: Alfred A. Knopf, Inc., 1951), p. 142.
[33]Muirhead, *op. cit.*, pp. 67–68. (Emphasis in original.)
[34]Mesick, *op. cit.*, pp. 83–84.
[35]Hugo Münsterberg, *The Americans* (New York: McClure, Phillips and Co., 1904), p. 28.

recourse at such means of enforcing instruction, would meet with reprehension from the parents and perhaps retaliation from his scholars.[36]

Tocqueville also found examples of the American's mistrust of authority "even in the schools," where he marveled that "the children in their games are wont to submit to rules which they have themselves established."[37]

The educational policies which have become linked with the name of John Dewey and labeled "progressive education" actually began in a number of school systems around the country long before Dewey wrote on the subject. Many travelers have commented on this fact. "To name but one example, the lower schools of St. Louis had adopted a system intended to develop spontaneously the inventive and intellectual faculties of the children by the use of games and with no formal teaching of ideas, no matter how practical."[38]

Harriet Martineau also perceived a close connection between childhood socialization practices which stressed love, approbation, and respect for children as equals, and the development of adult personalities impressed with the importance of kindly relations with others:

One reason of the pleasure with which I regarded the freedom of American children was that I took it as a sign that the most tremendous suffering perhaps of human life is probably lessened, if not obviated, there:—the misery which makes the early years of a shy child a fearful purgatory. Yet purgatory is not the word: for this misery purges no sins, while it originates many. I have a strong suspicion that the faults of temper so prevalent where parental authority is strong, and where children are made as insignificant as they can be made, and the excellence of temper in America, are attributable to the different management of childhood in the one article of freedom. There is no doubt that many children are irrecoverably depressed and unnerved for want of being convinced that anybody cares for them. They nourish doubts, they harbour fears and suspicions, and carry within them prejudices and errors, for want of its occurring to them to ask questions; and though they may outgrow these defects and errors, they never recover from them. Unexplained and inexplicable obstacles are thrown in the way of their filial duty,—obstacles which not even the strongest conscientiousness can overcome with grace: the vigor of the spirit is prostrated, or perverted into wilfulness: the calmness of self-respect is forfeited, and so is the repose of a loving faith in others. In short, the temper is ruined, and the life is spoiled; and all from the parents not having made friends of their children from the beginning.[39]

The Adequacy of a Materialistic Interpretation

Many of the observers referred to in the above section explained the other-directedness and status-seeking of Americans by the prevalence of the twin values of equality and achievement, and especially by the former. Character and behavior were thus explained by values. Riesman's explanation differs from this,

[36]Isaac Fidler, *Observations in Professions, Literature, Manners and Emigration, in the United States and Canada, Made During a Residence There in 1832* (New York: J. and J. Harper, 1833), pp. 40–41.

[37]Tocqueville, *op. cit.*, I, 198.

[38]Torrielli, *op. cit.*, p. 115.

[39]Martineau, *op. cit.*, pp. 169–70.

because he explains character *and values* by reference to the supposed demands of a certain type of economy and its unique organization. The economy, in order to be productive, requires certain types of individuals, and requires that they hold certain values. This, in the final analysis, is a purely materialistic interpretation of social phenomena, and is open to the criticisms to which such interpretations are susceptible.

The inadequacy of a materialistic theory as an explanation of changes in values and social character is best demonstrated by comparative analysis. America has no monopoly of entrepreneurs or bureaucrats. British and Swedish society, for example, have for many decades possessed occupational structures similar to that of America. Britain, in fact, reached the stage of an advanced industrial society, thoroughly urbanized, where the majority of the population worked for big business or government, long before any other nation. The occupational profiles of Sweden, Germany, and the United States have been similar for many decades. If the causal connection between technology and social character were as striking as Riesman has implied, then other-direction should have occurred in Great Britain prior to its occurrence in the United States, and should now be found to predominate in other European nations. Yet, presumably Riesman views other-direction as pre-eminently an American trait. The continued strength of deferential norms in European societies, enjoining conformity to class standards of behavior, has weakened their propensity toward an equalitarian society, despite the triumph of the welfare state and mass production.

The criticisms that can be made of the linkage advanced in *The Lonely Crowd* between demographic patterns and social character may further point up the shortcomings of a technological interpretation of social change. Riesman associates population decline with other-direction. He argues that a reduced death rate produces gerontocracy, where social mobility is blocked by the older people's control of the best positions in society. The reduction of opportunities to get ahead, which results from a lengthening life span, prescribes circumspection as a method of competing for the dwindling number of openings, and thus favors other-direction. This trait is also furthered by the concomitant decrease in family size, since Riesman argues that the significance of the peer group as a socializer is greater for those reared in small families as compared with large ones. The syndrome of factors inherent in peer-group socialization—extreme sensitivity to the opinions of others, the norm of antagonistic cooperation, and the fear of being conspicuous—discourages individuality.

A cursory examination of the relationship between changing population rates and the character traits of different nations suggests that Riesman's conclusions regarding the correlates of demographic profiles may be questioned on empirical grounds. As David Potter has pointed out:

> There is a real question whether there are not countries in which the phase of incipient decline is even more clearly established [than in the United States], without any corresponding prevalence of other-directed persons. England is in this phase; so is France, and France has been in it for many decades longer than we. But does the

typical Englishman have a character that is other-directed? Does the typical Frenchman? I do not know how Riesman would answer this question, but most people, I believe, would say "No."[40]

Since the rate of population growth is a major, if not the most important, determinant of social character mentioned in *The Lonely Crowd,* the high American birth rates since World War II also suggest important reservations. The United States, in fact, now has one of the highest rates of population *growth* in the Western world, a trend which presumably should presage a return to inner-direction.[41]

Comparative analysis strongly suggests that the derivation of social character almost exclusively from the traits associated with occupational or population profiles is incorrect. So important an element in a social system as that covered by Riesman's concept of social character must be deeply affected by the dominant value-system. For the value-system is perhaps the most enduring part of what we think of as a society, or a social system. Comparative history shows that nations still present striking differences, even when their technological, demographic, or political patterns are similar. Thus it is necessary to work out the implications of the value-system within a given material setting and, in addition, observe the gradual, cumulative effect that technological change has upon values.

American Patterns and Values: Stable or Changing?

Basic alterations of social character or values are rarely produced by change in population or in the means of production, distribution, and exchange *alone.* Rather, as a society becomes more complex, its institutional arrangements adjust to new conditions within the framework of a dominant value-system. In turn, the new institutional patterns may affect the continuity of the socialization processes which, from infancy up, instill the fundamental traits of personality. Through such a process, value change develops slowly, or not at all. There are constant efforts to fit the "new" technological world into the social patterns of the old, familiar world. Only a profound social revolution, one that destroys the mainstays of the preceding order—habitual social relations, socializing agencies, and ideas of right and wrong—can produce sudden major changes in values and social character.

American nationhood emerged from such a revolutionary break with the ways of the Old World. The historian, J. Franklin Jameson, has argued that the Revolution itself, with the Declaration of Independence as a codification of its values, helped suppress some of the traditional institutions, mores, and values that had been transplanted to the colonies, such as the established church

---

[40]David H. Potter, *People of Plenty: Economic Abundance and the American Character* (Chicago: University of Chicago Press, 1954), p. 61.

[41][Editor's note: In a new preface to *The Lonely Crowd* (New Haven: Yale University Press, 1961), Riesman qualifies his "speculations concerning population": "our use of the population cycle . . . is probably less effective than would have been discussion of economic development, urbanization, and the spread of education" (pp. xxx, xxxi).]

and deferential social relations.[42] The ethic of equality undermined the props of the old status order, both in society at large and within the principal spheres of socialization, the family and the school. It promoted consideration for the rights and feelings of others, and at the same time encouraged all to strive for the universal social esteem that it promised. Since the equalitarian ethic denied claims to respect based solely on inheritance or formal social position, this esteem became the reward for being able to impress others.

The thesis that the same basic American values have continued to shape the society under changing geographical and economic conditions has been advanced by many historians. Thus Henry Nash Smith has sought to show how the rural frontier settlements established in the West on the Great Plains reflected not only the physical environment, but also "the assumptions and aspirations of a whole society."[43] He argued that revisions in the Homestead Act, which would have permitted large farms and a more economical use of arid land, were opposed by the new settlers because they believed in the ideal of the family farm. Walt Rostow suggests there is a "classic American style [which] . . . emerged distinctively toward the end of the seventeenth century as the imperatives and opportunities of a wild but ample land began to assert themselves over various transplanted autocratic attitudes and institutions which proved inappropriate to the colonial scene . . . [and] came fully to life . . . after the War of 1812." And he contends that this style has not changed basically since "the cast of American values and institutions and the tendency to adapt them by cumulative experiment rather than to change them radically has been progressively strengthened by the image of the gathering success of the American adventure."[44] One historian, writing of America in general, has said: "Circumstances change profoundly, but the character of the American people has not changed greatly or the nature of the principles of conduct, public and private, to which they subscribe."[45] Three recent books dealing with American values, by Daniel Boorstin, Louis Hartz, and Ralph Gabriel, have each, in a different way, argued the effective continuity of the fundamental ideals of the society.[46]

The conclusions of these historians are affirmed also in a "lexicographic analysis of alleged American characteristics, ideals, and principles" reported

---

[42]See J. Franklin Jameson, *The American Revolution Considered as a Social Movement* (Boston: Beacon Press, 1956).

[43]Henry Nash Smith, *Virgin Land: The American West as Symbol and Myth* (Cambridge: Harvard University Press, 1950), p. 124.

[44]W. W. Rostow, "The National Style," in Elting E. Morison, *The American Style: Essays in Value and Performance* (New York: Harper & Bros., 1958), pp. 247, 259.

[45]Henry Steele Commager, *Living Ideas in America* (New York: Harper & Bros., 1951), p. xviii.

[46]See Daniel Boorstin, *The Genius of American Politics* (Chicago: University of Chicago Press, 1953), and his *The Lost World of Thomas Jefferson* (New York: Holt, Rinehart & Winston, Inc., 1948) ; Louis M. Hartz, *The Liberal Tradition in America: An Interpretation of American Political Thought since the Revolution* (New York: Harcourt, Brace & Co., 1955) ; and Ralph H. Gabriel, *The Course of American Democratic Thought* (New York: Ronald Press Co., 1956).

in a myriad of books and articles dealing with "the American way." American history was divided for the purposes of the study into four periods, "Pre-Civil War (to 1865), Civil War to World War (1866–1917), World War to Depression (1918–1929), and Depression to present (1930–1940)." For each period a list of traits alleged by observers was recorded, and "when the lists for each of the four time periods were compared, no important difference between the traits mentioned by modern observers and those writing in the earlier periods of American history was discovered." Among the traits mentioned in all four periods were: "Belief in equality of all as a fact and as a right" and "uniformity and conformity."[47]

It is obvious that American society has changed, not only in its technological and ecological aspects, such as industrialization, urbanization, and population growth, but in family structure, education, religion, and "culture" also. But these changes have not altered the social character or the principal values radically. Rather, they have manifested themselves in a constant *conflict* or interplay between the democratic *equalitarianism* proclaimed as a national ideal in the basic documents of the American Revolution, and the strong emphasis on competition, success, and the acquisition of status, the *achievement* orientation which is also deeply embedded in our national value system.

Richard Hofstadter has urged the recurring pattern of value conflict and continuity in commenting on papers presented at a conference on changes in American society:

> Culturally and anthropologically, human societies are cast in a great variety of molds, but once a society has been cast in its mold—Mr. Rostow is right that our mold as a nation was established by the early nineteenth century—the number of ways in which, short of dire calamity, it will alter its pattern are rather limited. I find it helpful also to point to another principle upon which Mr. Rostow has remarked—the frequency with which commentators find societies having certain paradox polarities in them. . . . We may find in this something functional; that is, *societies have a need to find ways of checking their own tendencies. In these polarities there may be something of a clue to social systems. . . .*
>
> Mr. Kluckhohn's report contains some evidence that we have already passed the peak of this shift about which I have been speaking. I find some additional evidence myself in the growing revolt of middle-class parents against those practices in our education that seem to sacrifice individualism and creativity for adjustment and group values. Granted the initial polarities of the success ethic, which is one of the molds in which our society is cast, this ethic must in some way give rise, sooner or later, to a reaction. . . . I do not think that we must be persuaded that our system of values has ceased to operate.[48]

The analyses of American history and culture in the nineteenth and twentieth centuries, by both foreign and native interpreters, often differ according to whether they stress democracy and equality, or capitalism and achievement.

[47]Lee Coleman, "What Is American? A Study of Alleged American Traits," *Social Forces,* XIX (1941), pp. 492–99.

[48]Richard Hofstadter, "Commentary: Have There Been Discernible Shifts in Values During the Past Generation," in E. E. Morison, *op. cit.,* p. 357. (Emphasis mine.)

Generally, conservatives and aristocrats have found fault with the decline of individuality and the pampering of children, and have seen both as manifestations of democracy and equality; while liberals have noted with dismay tendencies toward inequality and aristocracy, and have blamed them upon the growth of big business. These contrary political philosophies have also stamped the interpretation of American culture that predominates at any given period. And Arthur Schlesinger, Sr., has even tried to measure the systematic characteristic duration of the "epochs of radicalism and conservatism [that] have followed each other in alternating order" in American history.[49] A cursory examination of the numerous differences between the conclusions of American social scientists in the 1930's and in the 1950's points up the way in which interpretations of American culture vary with social conditions.

In both the 1930's and the 1950's, commentators have been certain that the country was undergoing major structural changes, changes which in fact had already come to fruition in the period in which they were writing. Writers of the thirties amassed evidence of the decline of equalitarianism and the effect of this on a variety of institutions. Karen Horney in *The Neurotic Personality of Our Time,* for example, named anxiety over chances of economic success as the curse of what she, with many of her contemporaries, regarded as a completely pecuniary, achievement-oriented culture dominated by the giant corporations; more recently, analyses published in the fifties suggest that acquisitiveness and the desire to succeed are much less formidable motives. Analysts of the thirties, like Robert S. Lynd, Harold Laski, and W. L. Warner, all agreed that the *egalitarian emphasis in American democracy was declining sharply* under the growth of the large-scale corporation, monopoly capitalism, and economic competition.[50] They asserted categorically that mobility had decreased, and Warner predicted the development of rigid status lines based on family background. Twenty years later, these interpretations are almost unanimously rejected. Warner himself has implicitly acknowledged his error, for in one of his most recent works he shows that chances of rising into the top echelons of the largest corporations are greater than they were in the 1920's.[51] Typical writers of the fifties, like Riesman and William H. Whyte, contend that the achievement motive and the Protestant ethic of hard work are dying, and think that the new society prefers security, emotional stability, and getting along with others. While Riesman posits a transformation of the American character structure, Whyte considers that values themselves have changed. He argues that the old value-system, the Protestant ethic, which he defines as "the pursuit of individual salva-

---

49Arthur M. Schlesinger, *New Viewpoints in American History* (New York: The Macmillan Co., 1922), p. 123.

50Robert S. Lynd, *Knowledge for What?* (Princeton: Princeton University Press, 1940), p. 75; Harold Laski, *The American Democracy* (New York: Viking Press, 1948); W. L. Warner and Paul S. Lunt, *The Social Life of a Modern Community* (New Haven: Yale University Press, 1941).

51W. L. Warner and J. C. Abegglen, *Occupational Mobility in American Business and Industry* (Minneapolis: University of Minnesota Press, 1953).

tion through hard work, thrift, and competitive struggle," is being replaced by the "social ethic," whose basic tenets are "a belief in the group as the source of creativity, and a belief in the application of science to achieve the belongingness."[52]

In large measure, this difference between writers of the two decades reflects the contrast between the economic circumstances of the times. The depression of the 1930's inclined intellectuals toward an equalitarian radicalism, which condemned capitalism and achievement-orientation as the source of "evils." Even conservatives like Warner were led to emphasize the growth of inequality and the restriction of opportunity. The prosperity of the 1950's, however, renewed the legitimacy of many conservative institutions and values, and discredited some of the innovations of the leftist thirties. The social analyses of the 1950's, even those written by men who still consider themselves liberals or socialists, involve at least a critique of the radical excesses of the former period, if not a critique of equalitarian values themselves. Perhaps the similarity in attitudes between the analysts of the 1950's and many of the foreign travelers of the last century is due to the fact that most of the European visitors have been conservatives, or members of the elite of much more aristocratic societies, while the modern Americans reflect the post-war revival of conservative values.

While Riesman and Whyte would deny that their works contain conservative value preferences, and insist that they are simply analyzing changes, with both good and bad features, it seems fairly evident that, like the more elitist travelers of the nineteenth century, they dislike many of the dominant trends. They point to the spread of progressive education, with its disbelief in rewards for hard work, as illustrating the decay of the Protestant ethic, and they assume, as a result of this, a decline in the opportunity for developing creativity. Whyte points to the shift in scientific research from individual to group projects, which in his opinion are less creative. Neither Riesman nor Whyte explicitly asserts that there is more conformity now than in the past, for the reason that men have always conformed to the values of the day; but both argue that contemporary values and personality traits emphasize accommodation to others, while the declining Protestant ethic and the inner-directed character-structure stressed conformity to a fixed rule of conduct, rather than to the fluctuating actions of others.

This reaction against the apparent decline of the Protestant ethic of achievement and hard work, which has become a dominant theme among the intellectual middle class of the 1950's, should be viewed as the counterpart of the concern with the seeming breakdown of equality which moved comparable groups in the 1930's. The differences in the concerns of the two decades illustrate the important point that although the equalitarian ethos of the American Revolution and the achievement-orientation of the Protestant ethic

---

[52]William H. Whyte, *The Organization Man* (New York: Doubleday Anchor Books, 1956), pp. 5–7.

are mutally supporting, *they also involve normative conflict.* Complete commitment to equality involves rejecting some of the implications of valuing achievement, and the opposite is also true. Thus, when the equalitarianism of left or liberal politics is dominant, there is a reaction against achievement, and when the values of achievement prevail in a conservative political and economic atmosphere, men tend to deprecate some of the consequences of equality, such as the influence of popular taste on culture.

The supremacy of equalitarian values and liberal politics in the thirties was reflected in the school system in the triumph of progressive education, a cause always associated with left-of-center leaders and ideologies; in industry, by the introduction of the human relations approach as an attempt to "keep the worker happy"; and in the society at large, by efforts toward a general redistribution of goods and services. Social scientists and others interested in family structure criticized the supposedly typical middle-class family as too authoritarian and rigid in its treatment of children, suggesting that, as contrasted with the more democratic and affectionate working-class family, it bred "authoritarian" and "neurotic" personalities. Popular psychology saw the "competitive personality" of our time as the source of many personal and social evils. Historians pictured the creators of American industry as "robber barons" and as irresponsible exploiters of American resources.

This equalitarian liberalism was perhaps strongest in the school system, where educators carried the ideal of equal treatment to a point where even intellectual differences were ignored. Special encouragment of the gifted child was regarded as an unfair privilege that inflicted psychic punishment on the less gifted: personality adjustment for *all* became the objective. In New York City, Fiorello La Guardia, the militant progressive mayor, abolished Townsend Harris High School, a special school for gifted boys in which four years of work was completed in three, on the grounds that the very existence of such a school was undemocratic, because it conferred special privileges on a minority. Clearly, the underlying philosophy behind all these analyses and actions of the thirties regarded competition as bad, and favored an ideally equalitarian society.

In the prosperous 1950's, these tendencies were almost completely reversed. Big business and business careers once more became legitimate. The Republicans were in office, and centrists rather than liberals dominated the Democratic Party. Although Keynesian economics remained official government policy, and was still supported by most economists, some leading members of that profession emerged who opposed almost all government intervention. Studies of the social structure of the family have reversed the findings of the thirties, and suggest that the working-class family is more likely to be a source of "authoritarian" personality traits. Vulgarizations of the theses of Riesman and Whyte have been published in many magazines and are cited at P.T.A. meetings all over the country, where outraged middle-class parents demand a return to "old-fashioned" methods of teaching, in which hard work is rewarded and the gifted receive special attention. Many middle-class parents have placed their children in private schools. While the rapid growth of private schools in large part stems from the increasing prosperity of the country, it also reflects the desire of middle-class parents that their children receive an elite education.

The political battle between the thirties and the fifties, between equality and achievement, has been most conspicuously joined today in the debate over schools. As the "progressive educationalists" begin to counterattack, they appeal specifically to the values of equality and democracy. A speech by Professor A. Harry Passow of Columbia University Teachers' College attacked a proposal to create twenty-five elite high schools for gifted children in the following terms:

> It is a perversion of democracy to set aside certain youngsters and give them privileges which automatically set them apart as an elite group of society. It goes against the basic idea of American education, which is to give all children an equal opportunity for the best possible education.[53]

A leading expert who has testified before Congressional committees for the past twenty years or more concerning the need for educational research, once reported that when a committee was discussing research on underprivileged or mentally deficient children, the Democrats on the committee would exhibit great interest; but when the Committee turned to the question of the gifted child, the Republicans peaked up and the Democrats sat back. The two parties did not, of course, oppose each other formally on these questions, since both favored research on all questions; but Republicans were simply more interested in *achievement,* or the problem of the gifted child, while Democrats were more interested in *equality,* or the problem of the underprivileged.

To stress the coincidence of these differing interpretations of American social trends with the political and economic cycle is not to suggest that they are simply ideological reflections of material conditions or of the climate of opinion. Most of them have pointed out genuine aspects of the culture, and in so doing have improved our understanding of the functions of different institutions and values. Both strands, the equalitarian and the achievement-oriented, remain strong, but changing conditions sometimes fortify one at the expense of the other, or alter the internal content of each. Thus opportunity, as measured by the chances of success in building up a major enterprise of one's own, has given way to opportunity measured by advancement in the bureaucratic elites. The politics of liberalism and equality have fostered institutional changes, such as the constant spread of public education and of training facilities within corporations, which have increased opportunities for advancement.

Conclusion

This paper has stressed many of the weaknesses in the historical view of American values and social character presented in *The Lonely Crowd.* Essentially, I have urged that a monistic materialistic interpretation of the cor-

[53]See "Plan of Schools for 'Elite' Scored," *New York Times,* March 25, 1958, p. 25.

relates of American values and behavior sharply underestimates the extent to which basic national values, once institutionalized, affect the consequences of technological and economic change. Clearly, many nations may be described as urbanized, industrialized, and capitalist, but they vary considerably in their status systems, their political institutions, parent-child relations, and so forth. Marxists have frequently joined non-Marxists in citing the absence of a feudal past as one of the major factors determining the failure of American socialism. And the absence of a feudal past, with a concomitant emphasis on equality of manners and of opportunity, has had deep-rooted consequences on those aspects of American behavior which most interest the authors of *The Lonely Crowd*.

The similarities in the descriptive comparisons between America and Europe that have been made for a century and a half in discussing the "other-directedness" of Americans, their child-rearing habits, their propensity for conspicuous consumptions, and their emphasis on equalitarian manners, are sufficient to make it clear that there is something stable in the American character. On the other hand, the consistency of comment does not rule out the possibility of changes in these very areas of behavior. It may be argued that the entire Western world has been moving in the American direction in their patterns of class relationships, family structure, and "other-directedness." The impact of the early democratic values later reinforced by the universalistic norms endemic in urban, industrial civilization has meant that America, which was democratic and equalitarian before industrialization, has led the way in these patterns. Thus, at any given time, the differences between America and much of Europe have remained constant. Foreign visitors have always been struck by the child-centeredness of our family system, by the equalitarianism of our social relations, and by our seeming overconcern for the good opinion of others. But if one compared the America of the 1950's with the America of the 1880's or the 1830's, one would undoubtedly note changes in the direction suggested by Riesman. In this sense he is right that Tocqueville and others "foresaw" the present. That is, the patterns described by them are more highly developed today than they were in the early nineteenth century.

The vast majority of early and mid-nineteenth-century Americans were self-employed and lived on farms or in small towns, while today most people are employees and live in cities. This change alone has many consequences along the lines suggested by *The Lonely Crowd*. An employee has less freedom and motivation to be individualistic than do the self-employed. Farm and small-town dwellers know each other as total human beings rather than as actors in specific relations, and are presumably less motivated to exhibit status-seeking and conformist behavior and to seek the good opinion of those whom they have known all their lives than are those who interact with many "significant others" in a variety of limited contexts. Residents of small communities are judged by their total background and personal history, not by any specific set of acts. As many sociological studies of such communities have revealed, they tend to have a relatively static status system, permitting much less social mobility than that occurring in large cities. Consequently, the resident of the small town tends to be somewhat like the citizens of more rigidly stratified European states. The awareness of the relative permanence of status position reduces the anxiety to win the good opinion of others that exists where status is less stable. It is in the large city, with its more anonymous social relationships and greater economic opportunities to change material status, that men are highly motivated to win prestige through snobbish conformism. These differences between life in small town and large city were explicitly noted in the 1830's by Harriet Martineau when she pointed out that the "other-directed" behavior she so deplored was to be found most commonly in *urban* centers in the middle and upper classes, where people live in a state of "perpetual caution." Nowhere, she stated, does there exist "so much heart-eating care [about others' judgment], so much nervous anxiety, as among the dwellers in the towns of the northern States of America."[54] And Francis Grund also pointed to the concentration of these traits among the Northern urban well-to-do.

There can be little question that Riesman is right also in showing how bureaucratization and urbanization *reinforce* those social mechanisms which breed other-directedness. But it cannot be stressed too often that these mechanisms operate within the context of an historic American value-system and status structure that also generated such traits in a non-bureaucratic and non-urban society. Other-direction, or, to put it less dramatically, sensitivity to the judgments of others, is an epiphenomenon of the American equalitarian ethos, the opportunities for rapid status mobility, *and* the general growth of an urban, bureaucratic society. The increasing complexity introduced by advanced industrialization and urbanization makes adherence to a rigid normative code obsolete, because such a code cannot be used as a guide to the great variety of situations confronting modern, bureaucratic man. This Riesman has well noted, However, the greater flexibility and need to adapt to others that are demanded by urban and bureaucratic life add to an already existing disposition to be concerned with the opinions of others, a disposition caused by equalitarianism and the emphasis on social mobility.

The concern with specifying how various structural changes have weakened the Protestant ethic or inner-directed traits in American life has led Riesman and others similarly oriented to sometimes ignore the beneficial consequences of these changes. Thus, while bureaucratization results in a heightened need to make personality adjustments to win the esteem of colleagues and supervisors, it also sets bounds to arbitrary power. By establishing rules of fair treatment, and by reducing the area of personal discretion in personnel policy, bureaucracy can reduce the fear of the employer or the supervisor. Trade unions, found most commonly under conditions of large industry, accurately reflect their members' desires when their policies involve more, rather than less, bureaucratization. (As an example of this, unions have sought seniority

[54]Martineau, *op. cit.*, p. 18.

rules, in hiring, firing, and promoting, which increase bureaucratization and reduce arbitrary power.) Similarly it may be urged that some of the consequences of bureaucratization reinforce, rather than weaken, strong work and achievement orientations, particularly in the upper echelons of white-collar and executive life.

The shift from the family-owned company to the management-run corporation, as Whyte pointed out, has made group activities and adjustment to group norms seem more important than individual responsibilities within corporate bureaucracies. But whatever else group dynamics in industry may be concerned with, it certainly provides an excellent way of getting men to work hard for the company. Traditionally, it has been a postulate of business management, and an empirical finding of industrial sociology that men do not work as hard as they are able when the rewards of their work seem to be going to others. Holding other factors constant, no one works so hard as the head of an organization, or the self-employed, or the creative professional who is directly rewarded for his labors. By extending the control of work to committees at different levels in the corporation, and by incorporating democratic values into the internal operation of bureaucracy, contemporary American business has found a means of inculcating into a large number of people a sense of responsibility for the whole organization. "Non-owners" now feel responsible, and the number of hard-working "entrepreneurs" who never watch the clock, and who take work home with them, has been enormously enlarged. Thus, while other-direction may have increased, the motivation for competition and hard work remains, because the best are chosen to move up the bureaucratic hierarchy.

It is a peculiar paradox that the same structural processes may account for diverse and even sharply conflicting tendencies. Many analyses of American society have stressed the fact that individualism *and* conformism, creative innovation *and* dominance by low-level mass taste, are outgrowths of identical forces. For example, the pronounced spread of higher education and a high standard of living have caused an unprecedented increase in both the proportion involved in genuinely creative, intellectual activities, and the influence by the populace on the major expressions of art, literature, and drama. Alexis de Tocqueville was fully aware of these dual tendencies when he pointed out that "the same equality that renders him [the American] independent of each of his fellow citizens, taken severally, exposes him alone and unprotected to the influence of the greater number . . . I very clearly discern two tendencies; one leading the mind of every man to untried thoughts, the other prohibiting him from thinking at all."[55] Tocqueville resolved the dilemma by stressing the important role of secondary groupings and formal organizations of all types in countering the pressures on the individual caused by the lack of the protective "vestiges of former aristocratic distinctions." These associations and groupings provide a new basis for group loyalties, and serve the functions of *differentiating* and, at the same time, *binding* society. As Tocqueville said:

[55]Tocqueville, *op. cit.*, I, 12.

The free institutions which the inhabitants of the United States possess, and the political rights of which they make so much use, remind every citizen, and in a thousand ways, that he lives in society. They every instant impress upon his mind the notion that it is the duty as well as the interest of men to make themselves useful to their fellow creatures; and he sees no particular ground of animosity to them, since he is never either their master or their slave, his heart readily leans to the side of kindness.[56]

What Tocqueville (together with many other foreign travelers) saw as characteristic of America was not only conformity and passivity, but also rational individual choice, choice that was developed and protected by the existence of major secondary organizations. Today, too, there are many trends making for an increase in autonomous behavior, in free choice. Various social scientists have recently taken to documenting these countervailing tendencies, a phenomenon that may reflect the ever present cyclical pattern of social analysis. Rowland Berthoff points to the seeming "gradual decline since 1920 of those makeshift communities, the fraternal lodges," which were part of the associational pattern that impressed Tocqueville, and suggests that "the psychic energy that Americans formerly expended on maintaining the jerry-built framework of such 'institutions' as these has in our more assured institutional structure of recent years been freed, at least potentially, for the creation of more valuable kinds of 'culture.' " He also infers that "the recent popular success of books deploring the unworthiness of status striving indicates that Americans are throwing off this obsession and making it, as in other societies, including preindustrial America, merely one concern among many."[57] The political scientist, Robert Wood, suggests in the same vein that "The pattern of inconspicuous consumption, the web of friendship, and the outgoing life that Whyte describes also have something of the flavor of a renaissance. Although 'keeping down with the Joneses' may indicate group tyranny, it is still better than keeping up with them. At least it displays disapproval of overt snobbishness. . . . While Whyte finds pressures for benevolent conformity, he also discovers brotherhood."[58] Daniel Bell has argued that the growth in education, among other factors, has reduced conformity. He comments that "one would be hard put to find today the 'conformity' *Main Street* exacted of Carol Kennicott thirty years ago. With rising educational levels, more individuals are able to indulge a wider variety of interests," such as serious music, good books, high level FM radio, and the like.[59]

It may be fitting to conclude with the paradox presented by Clyde Kluckhohn, who has suggested, "Today's kind of 'conformity' may actually be a step toward more genuine individuality in the United States. 'Conformity' is less of a personal and psychological problem—less tinged with anxiety and guilt. . . . If one accepts outwardly the conventions of one's group, one may have greater

[56] *Ibid.*, p. 112.

[57] Rowland Berthoff, "The American Social Order: A Conservative Hypothesis," *American Historical Review*, LXV (1960), p. 512.

[58] Robert Wood, *Suburbia: Its People and Their Politics* (Boston: Houghton Mifflin Co., 1959), p. 15.

[59] Daniel Bell, "The Theory of Mass Society," *Commentary*, XXII (1956), p. 82.

psychic energy to develop and fulfill one's private potentialities as a unique person. I have encountered no substantial evidence that this 'conformity' is thoroughgoingly 'inward.' "[60] As status-seeking is the by-product of strong equalitarianism, so conformity and other-directedness may permit, or even demand, inner autonomy.

[60]Clyde Kluckhohn, "Have There Been Discernible Shifts in American Values During the Past Generation," in Morison, *op. cit.*, p. 187.

HAROLD ROSENBERG

The Orgamerican Phantasy

America masks its terrors behind patterns of fact. Here the intolerable discloses its presence not in the grimaces of comedy or tragedy but in the bland citations of the scientific report. Since the War, no novel or play has given body to the larger disturbances of the American consciousness. Literature, one hears, is dead, or too enfeebled to risk arduous adventures. Nevertheless, documents keep appearing that touch upon apprehensions equal to any in the history of men: computations of the daily incidence of outlawed sex in America's bedrooms; records of scientific sadism practiced by governments and their programs to transform the will of individuals; estimates by atomic technicians of the flimsiness of the earth and of the natural shape of the human body. When phenomena of this order are explored in a work of the imagination, its author tends to be exiled to the colony of "morbid intellectuals." Given the form of the report or survey, and authorized by the rhetoric of the professions, the most alarming topics overcome the handicap of their profundity and enter into the conversation of solid men of affairs.

Among the grand metaphysical themes of this decade, the one that has proved perhaps most fascinating and persistent has been that of "alienation" —the loss by the individual of personal identity through the operation of social processes. The tone of the post-war imagination was set by Orwell's *1984;* since the appearance of that work, "the dehumanized collective that so haunts our thoughts" (as Mr. William H. Whyte, Jr. calls it in *The Organization Man*) has been a topic for the best-seller lists.

Orwell's melodrama of the pulverized ego was a work of fiction. But Orwell was a Briton; besides, *1984* could be read as a description of life in Stalin's Russia or in a future Labor Party England, rather than of the destiny of America. Of U.S. storytellers who essayed to raise the same spectre, none achieved large public impact. Americans awoke to the menace of robotization when the possibility of it passed from the fiction-writer's yarn to the testimony of the sociologist and cultural anthropologist. Riesman's *The Lonely Crowd,* with its "other-directed" hero-victims of automobile showrooms and P.T.A. meetings, left no doubt that the familiar feeling of being someone else was not a mere after-effect of seeing the wrong movie. Spectorsky's *The Exurbanite,* Whyte's *The Organization Man,* Mills' *White Collar,* Packard's *The Hidden Persuaders* filled in important details of personnel, locale, and method. Like The Man with the Bomb That Can Blow Up the World, The Creature That Lost Himself ceased to be a reflection of the dream-maker's art, or a literary construction of the philosophical moralist, and emerged as a statistical probability from the file-cards of the social scientist.

It goes without saying that the Other-Directed Man, the Exurbanite, the Organization Man, is a *type,* that is to say, the personification of a behavior system, on the order of, say, Sinclair Lewis' Babbitt. In this respect the difference between the sociologist and the novelist reduces itself to the fact that Riesman explains that he is writing about "social characters" and devotes his book to analyzing what they do, while Lewis trots Babbitt out on the stage and has him do it.

The type or character is deficient in individuality *by definition.* Said Strindberg: "The word 'character' . . . became the middle-class expression for the automaton. An individual who had once for all become fixed in his natural disposition, or had adapted himself to some definite role in life—who, in fact, had ceased to grow—was called a character. . . . This middle-class conception of the immobility of the soul was transferred to the stage, where the middle class has always ruled."

Since the immobility or eternal fixedness of the present-day American social type—let us nickname him the Orgman—is presented as something new, in contrast to the dynamism and inwardness of the Inner-Directed Man (Riesman) or the Protestant Ethic Person (Whyte) of the nineteenth century, let us keep in mind Strindberg's point that the image of the person who is identical with his social role has been with us for centuries.

Automata of manners are a feature of traditional literature, as the true automaton, the Golem, Homunculus, Frankenstein, is a familiar figure of mythology and folklore. Most interesting with regard to the type presented by the new American sociology is his relation to the "mechanical man" image conceived by nineteenth-century writers as associated with the effects upon human beings of the new machine culture. Poe, in "The Man Who Was Made Up," imagined a person put together from fabricated parts; while Marx built his political philosophy upon the misery and triumph of that human "product of modern industry," the proletariat.

In the current writings, the type that displaces the human person also originates in the productive and distributive machinery of society. The Orgman is further identified with the older literature of industrial alienation by the part of science in his drama. In Marx, the key force in historical progress is, of course, science; and it is the scientist of revolution who releases the proletariat upon the world; in *1984* the scientist reappears as the personality-crushing interrogator. Says *The Organization Man:* "The first denominator is scientism"; and goes on to demonstrate the presence in all American institutions of the traditional creator of the mannikin, the "mad scientist," now wearing the guise of the personnel expert, the motivational researcher, or some other "soul engineer."

Blood brother to the inhuman "double," the Mr. Hyde, of romantic literature, on the one hand, and to the proletarian of revolutionary socialism, on the other, the Orgman belongs to the latest episode in the saga of the conquest of society by hordes of faceless *directed* men.

Yet the new literature is neither romantic nor revolutionary, and in this lie its most striking characteristics. One no longer hears the metallic lockstep coming closer, like the rising of swarms of beetles or crabs. The enemy of this decade does not come from below. His is neither the face of the ogre over the edge, nor of the ghost behind the window pane. In the muted melodrama of the current sociology, the inhuman does not *invade*. It sits in the living room twisting the TV dial or takes the family for a ride in the two-tone hardtop. It is you.

Recoiling from the outerworld of society's monsters, outcasts, and victims, the analysts of contemporary America center their interest on the majority that benefits from the existing social process. With this shift of attention the spectre has shifted too. The alienated man has left the company town for the suburb; the factory for the office, the drafting room, the lecture hall. The presence within him of the socially constructed Other is, by the testimony of each of our authors, the mark of "the new middle class" man. It is to the absorption of this alter-ego that all his education and training are directed. Says Riesman: "The mass media ask the child to see the world as 'the' child—that is, the other child—sees it." To be inhabited by the abstract social person is what is currently meant by the terms "normal" and "socially adjusted."

The charge that all our social behavior stands as a power over and against us *is a more extreme accusation of existing American society than that of the preceding radicalism.* Implicating *everyone,* without distinction as to social class or function, in a single deepening process of dehumanization, such works as *The Lonely Crowd, The Organization Man, The Hidden Persuaders,* communicate in atmosphere, if not in stated concept, the sinister overtones of a developing totalitarianism from which there is no escape. In this literature with its subdued manners of scientific analysis, Orwell keeps springing up like a red devil. *The Hidden Persuaders* features Big Brother on the jacket and promises the reader "a slightly chilly feeling along the spine"; an effect which the blurb for Whyte's volume has already delivered through billing its hero as the man who "not only works for the Organization: he belongs to it." The smiling credit manager you spoke to this morning is a piece of company apparatus like the filing case from which he extracts the card that is you; his human appearance is a disguise, and his real name isn't Brown but Agent F–362.

With Marx, the conversion of the individual's "living time" into lifeless commodities was restricted to the routine of the wage worker. In the current studies, no one who participates in any capacity in the system of production and distribution can escape the vampire that drains him of himself. Differences in class functions have ceased to matter. Even the division between labor and leisure has lost its meaning; for the psychic mortification of the individual takes place not only in and through his work but by means of his participation in any form, public or private, of social life, from church going, to cocktail parties, to his relations with his wife and children. Whyte and Mills put the major emphasis on the job as the ground of estrangement; Spectorsky gives mode of employment and style of leisure about equal play, seeing one as the extension (laboratory?) of the other; Riesman regards the externally controlled psyche as a phenomenon of "the consumer age"—and is supported by the evidence of *The Hidden Persuaders* concerning supermarket penetration-assaults and the cold war against the customer by means of the new psycho-sales weapons. All our authors are at one in conceiving the flattening of personality in America as a universal effect of our interrelated economic and social practices.

What the Orgman-critics expose is not a flaw in society but the injurious realities of its normal everyday life. These, however, are presented in a perspective that denudes them of radical implications. Here "scientific objectivity" has become the disguise of a philosophy of fatalism. The emergence of the Orgman is conceived in terms far more deterministic than those of the "historical materialists." Neither Riesman's "age of consumption" nor Whyte's "Organization" was brought into being by the choice, nor even the need, of anyone, whether individual, class, or nation. The "other-directed society" of the first is a manifestation of the population-curve; the new corporate "collectivism" of the second, of an immanent process of expansion and stratification. The vocabularies chosen by Riesman and Whyte of themselves exclude human intervention, in the future as in the past: you cannot redirect an other-directed period, any more than you can refill an Orgman with "Protestant Ethic." Even if you could, there would be no point in doing so, since other-direction and the ubiquity of the Organization are necessities of our time.

In any case, the histrionic effect of the new criticism is unmistakable: the bland deadpan of the Objective Observer has definitely replaced the scowl of the radical accuser. For him such words as "capitalist," "class conflict," "profits," "depression" are at once too bulky and needlessly exciting. Since they draw from the same storehouse of material and cultural consumers' goods, all Americans have become "capitalists"; since they are changed into directed beings by their work and social consumption, all have become "proletarianized." On both counts, there is no cause for conflict and a unanimity of interest prevails. All of us, Whyte thinks, will have to revolt. But whatever basis there was for Marx's conception of a metaphysico-political uprising of human machine parts against a minority of opulent personalities has vanished in the universal estrangement.

In the new Organization America there are no fundamental issues, though some old-fashioned people may not yet have gotten rid of the habit of taking sides. To "moralize the flow of words," says Riesman, through which events are apprehended today, is a tendency of "the inner-directed person who remains still extant in this period"—which is a marvellously ironical way of saying that you know what is happening only through what you're told about it in the mass media, and that if you care one way or another you merely define yourself as a relic. The deadpan, apparently, is a requisite not only of the analyst of society but of all of us. If Riesman's irony goes unnoticed, as Whyte complains his has, it is because his language is too consistently detached from his subject matter to admit any sense of contrast: Orgprose, too, is deadpan.

Evoking the sinister concept of man as a tool and as an object, the new sociology does so in an oddly disembodied and unpainful way. Its tone is one of injury but of injury unsuffered. It would seem that among the "groups," particularly the better-paid ones, that have replaced the classes in Orgamerica, the substitution of a corporate identity for one's own is not the unmixed deprivation it might have been for the twelve-hour-a-day factory hand or for the citizen of the slave state. Before the Orgman can feel put upon, it is only fair that he consider the advantages gained. "It is not," explains Whyte, "the evils of the organization that puzzle him, but its very beneficence." Strange literature which, assembling the proof of society's subversion of both the will and the intelligence of its members, cries out, like the man in the joke, "But good. But good."

When the fear of the unreal becomes mixed with an idyllic dependence on it, a kind of mythic euphoria ensues which is related to the essence of the comic. Chinese folklore is full of the pranks of demons who have shed their awfulness and sit on window sills and above doorways minding one's business like so many other-directed neighbors. These every-day fiends may be as spiteful on occasion as one of Whyte's integration-specialists, but their trouble-making only adds gaiety to the way the "system" to which they belong achieves its generous aims. The tale of the Orgman has as much in common with dream farce as with the Orwellian torture phantasy. If its hero suffers it is in the drugged world of *A Midsummer Night's Dream* laden with bodily pleasures and tremors, where, in the words of *The Organization Man,* "the demands for his surrender are constant and powerful, and the more he has come to like the organization the more difficult does he find it to resist these demands, or even to recognize them."

For both radicalism and conservatism, history is a struggle of winners and losers. In the new American scene, everyone has won a fairy-tale luxury and lost himself. The drama of history has been replaced by a pantomime in which, freed of individual or mass conflicts, bewildered, adjusted beings respond as in a narcosis to mysterious signs, whispers, hints, and shocks, which each receives on his Riesman "radar mechanism." The scientific wand-wielder responsible for these psychological pinches and tweaks which inject dream anxieties into their physical serenity is a kind of affable Puck; for even the scientist, since he is necessary, is no longer a real villain; the evil lies rather in his abstract double "scientism." Riesman and Whyte construct their shadow-play in such a way as to leave no point of resistance. As in Whyte's description quoted above, any struggle against surrender on the part of the individual constitutes a wrestle in a dream. Neither Whyte nor Riesman indicates any direction in which the American person can realize himself in the actual world.

Yet disregarding the nature of the type or "character" as automaton, each holds out the hope that the alter-ego he is describing may some day develop into a human individual. This empty happy-ending is excellent as finale in a farce like *The Three Penny Opera;* as a substitute for protest or for tragic pathos in a portrayal of actual life, such sudden optimism arouses the suspicion of an attempt at ingratiation. Whyte looks forward to a time when "men partially liberated might be tantalized into demanding more"—no doubt by means of mass-persuasion techniques. As for Riesman, he can lift his consumer type out of the trap of "belongingness" only by attaching to him the time-fuse of a self-transforming process: "these developments (the mass distribution of art and literature) suggest to me that the process of taste-exchanging holds the promise of transcending itself and becoming something quite different, and of signally contributing to the development of autonomy in other-directed men." As if one could go from the abstract to the concrete, the automaton to the organism. Our sociologists' remedy for alienation is not "scientism"—it is sorcery.

Extremist but neither radical nor conservative, the Organization criticism is inspired not by a passion for social correction but by nostalgia. A sigh over the lost person mars the phantasy of American unanimity which has supplanted the ideological Passion Plays of Marxian condemnation and conflict. Whyte's memoir on his training in the Vicks Vaporub rugged individualist sales force of "the old days" (the late thirties) is the most eloquent and touching passage in this entire literature. The Age of the Giants—alas, gone forever. With Vicks's Richardson extinct, every human degradation may be logically anticipated. Today, the Orgman, the "dominant member of society," still lives among the relics of older types. Tomorrow he will tread the stage alone, in conflict only with himself.

It is the business type of yesterday whom the new social criticism has generalized into its "inner-directed" and "Protestant Ethic" abstraction, and in the name of which it fires its barrages against present-day tendencies. If it takes some daring to bury the boss, it takes less if one also bewails him in public. Especially in a situation where he has much to gain by playing dead. In Whyte's indictment of the human exactions of the Corporation, one hears the voice of the Founder deploring "the drift toward socialization."

Loosed from action, for which it can see no aim, the post-radical criticism often exaggerates its complaints, producing a worse impression of conditions than is warranted by the facts, at the same time that it seeks remedies in the wrong direction. For example, Mills, the most emotionally authentic of these writers, undervalues the personal and social expression of the white-collar worker on the job, with an effect of melancholy that seems unreal when one looks at actual men and women coming out of an office building. On the other hand, the salvation through improvement of taste proposed by Riesman, or through a psychic resistance based on private life (far more impoverished for the clerk than his job) suggested by Whyte, are, as we have seen, equally unreal.

But there is more to the conception of the Orgman than regret for an older social type. As the representative of the new post-war employed intelligentsia, the post-radical critic suffers also a nostalgia for himself as an independent individual. For his former abstract sympathy with a nominal working class, the intellectual of this decade has substituted an examination in the mirror of his own social double as insider of the Organization and the Community. It is what he sees there that has caused him to project a morbid image of society compared with which the old "class struggle" America seems not only naive but as relatively healthy as a war with rifle and cannons.

For in regard to the misery of alienation who is a greater victim of what Whyte calls the split "between the individual as he is and the role he is called upon to play" than the member of the intellectual caste newly enlisted *en masse* in carrying out society's functions? As writer, artist, social scientist, he is one with his talents and his education for creative work; in playing his part in the service of the organization he must eliminate any thought of functioning for himself. Through his personal inventiveness he has in the past fifteen years achieved prosperity and social prestige; yet he is the most dependent of wage earners and the most anxiously conscious of his dependence —*The Exurbanites* chronicles this dependence and anxiety to the last installment dollar. (Applying itself to the narrower spectrum of the commercialized intellectuals, *The Exurbanites* is the most realistic of the works we have been considering.)

The intellectual employee also accepts a more total identification with his role than other workers, in that the editorial director, the designer, the copy writer, etc., sells himself more completely in terms of both psychic energy expended and in number of hours worked. With him the division between work and leisure, discipline and freedom, has truly been erased. If the free artist or the founder of a great enterprise builds his life exclusively out of the substance of his work, today's intellectual unbuilds his life in order to live his job.[1]

[1]The rule quoted by Whyte for corporation executives generally, "You promote the guy who takes his problem home with him," becomes for the intellectual, "You hire the guy who takes his problem to bed with him." His job has a creative side in which his preconscious must also collaborate. Take this into account in computing his average salary, and the difference between the wage-earner of the suburb and of the company town becomes largely a matter of overtime pay. At $2.50 an hour the totally employed intellectual would earn more than $20,000 a year.

Besides being the prime victim and exemplar of self-loss in contemporary society, the "organized" professional cannot escape a conviction of guilt for his part in depriving others of their individuality. He has consented to use his capacities as a tool and to approve in practice the proposition recorded by Whyte that "all the great ideas have already been discovered." His skills tend to relate to human management, e.g., writing, image-making, program-forming; even if his specialty is in engineering or the physical sciences, the results of his work directly augment the force by which society is controlled. The intellectual cannot function as Organization Man without also functioning as Organization-Man moulder; as human object he must also affect others as objects; as manipulated act as manipulator. Thus he cannot help but feel himself to be a betrayer of humanity as of his own mind. Helpless to change anything, he is yet the chief culprit of the alienation drama, the driven "scientist," who directs the undermining of the raw individual, whether as motivational expert, inventor of personnel tests, or as preacher of despairing acceptance.

Self-displacement through one's acts is the innermost problem of life in America as of that in all civilized countries. The Social Type has always been among us, of course, despite Riesman's effort to distinguish today's other-directed man from his nineteenth-century counterpart. Tolstoy's Ivan Ilych, who decorated his house entirely according to his own original ideas only to have it turn out exactly like all other houses of his class, is as good an example of automatic "radared" taste-exchanging (Riesman) as can be found in Fairfield County. Tolstoy explicitly insisted that Ilych was a socially made-up man, an "object" guided by public opinion, an example of "dead" living.

In the United States, nineteenth-century literature, whether in the popular stage comedies of manners or in the symbolism of the romantics, centers on society's human abstractions. We mentioned above Poe's hero who owed to industry his moveable parts. A contemporary of this invention was the ubiquitous Salesman-Preacher, whom Melville, writing in a less unctuous age than ours, named the Confidence Man. Like Whyte, Spectorsky, and Packard, Melville saw in this professional who supplied his countrymen with things, ideas, and feeling, the outstanding specimen of man as social artifice. As his complement, he set up the brooding inner-directed Indian Fighter, paranoiac Ahab of the prairies; while from the silent recesses of the office files, he drew forth the white-collared tomb deity, Bartleby.

What is new in America is not the socially reflexive person but the presence of a self-conscious intellectual caste whose disillusionment has induced its members to volunteer for the part. The predicament in which these individuals find themselves is what casts a bar sinister over their image of America. The fear-augury that the Orgman will become everyone in a quiet, unopposable totalitarianism is not a conclusion based on a social analysis but a projection of the fate they have chosen for themselves. The American landscape has by no means been remade by the "Social Ethic" compression machine into an electrified Eden set out on porcelain grass. Except in the new suburbs, the physical condition of America's cities, towns, and villages is of itself proof enough that decay, shiftlessness, egotism, and other forms of popular expressionism are more than holding their own against other-direction. Granted that the growth of the super-corporation and the absorption and standardization of small business has changed the independent operator into an agent, at the same time that mechanization has been turning the workman into a technician; granted that Whyte's notation that "the collectivization so visible in the corporation has affected almost every field of work" is indisputable; and that today Orgmen reproduce themselves like fruit flies in whatever is organized, whether it be a political party or a museum of advanced art; given this groundwork for the conquest of America by this "type," still the contention that the nation is, or even might be, subordinated to such a master is at least as ludicrous as it is alarming. The increasing concentration of control and the standardization of work present well-known alternatives which we need not discuss here; but for the individual, the last voice in the issue of being or not being himself is still his own.

The inhabitant of the sacred groves has, however, surrendered all choices. Having accepted self-alienation in trade for social place, the post-radical intellectual can see nothing ahead but other-direction and a corporately styled personality. For him the Orgworld has closed for good. Within these limits the deploring of "conformity" is simply an expression of self-pity. The strategy of fighting the organization through secret resistance behind the outer-shaped mask (Whyte) is, by the measure of the ancient intellectual tradition of denunciation or self-exile, only a dreary professional's ruse for holding on to the best of both worlds. That such a proposal should seem relevant is another proof that the Orgman is, with necessary disguises, none other than the new intellectual talking about himself. Certainly the deft management of the corporate Look which solves things for Whyte would be of no help to the farmer or to the workingman, nor would the boss need to make use of it. The "what to do about it" part of the studies of Whyte and Riesman are clearly sermons for their milieu rather than challenges to history in the name of mankind.

The critics of the new America are disheartened by a revolution won—their revolution, which can go no farther than ending the underground life of the American intellectual mass through economic recognition of the services it has to offer. With his own success achieved, the only issue the intellectual can see as remaining for society is "personality." Somehow, this seems unattainable in "the dehumanized collective" that he is taking a leading part in building. The result is depression—and it is by the power of the depression it generates, in contrast to the smugness of the old-time boosting, that the present sociology is a force against a more radical and realistic understanding of American life.

DAVID RIESMAN

The Saving Remnant

In 1794 the Marquis de Condorcet, in hiding from the French Revolutionary Terror, ill and near death, wrote his *Sketch of an Historical View of the Progress of the Human Spirit,* a great monument to faith in human power to shape human destiny. Condorcet refused to be dismayed either by his own experience of human meanness and savagery or by his wide historical reading in the annals of cruelty and error. For he rested his hopes, not only on "observation on what man has heretofore been, and what he is at present," but also on his understanding of the *potentialities* of human nature.

It has proven more difficult than he had perhaps supposed to develop those potentialities. Today we are aware that the raw material of human nature is shaped by what we call culture into the organized force of a particular character structure; that this character structure tends to perpetuate itself from parent to child; that, largely determined by early experience, it determines in turn the adult modes of life and interpretations of new experience. The combination of character structure and social structure in a given culture is therefore relatively intractable to change. Though in America we are near Condorcet's dream of the conquest of poverty, his dream of the conquest of happiness seems ever more remote. It has become fashionable to sneer at him and other philosophers of the Enlightenment for lacking a sense of the human limitations on improvement. The sneer, however, is unimaginative. Condorcet's scientific, empirical method urges us to see precisely how recent changes in character structure, as well as in the conditions that gave rise to them, have helped to deny utopia. His philosophy then invites us to apply human reason and effort to the improvement of the human condition as thus understood.

. . . .

While our helplessness in the world is historically the condition of every advance in our mastery of it, the feeling of helplessness may today be so overpowering that regression, and not advance, ensues. But only when we have understood those forces that make for helplessness can we assay the probable outcome, and see what might be required for the new leap to security and freedom envisaged by Condorcet. One requirement is a type of character

From *Years of the Modern,* edited by John W. Chase. Used by courtesy of David McKay Company.

structure that can tolerate freedom, even thrive on it; I call persons of such type "autonomous," since they are capable of conscious self-direction. The very conditions that produce other-direction on the part of the majority today, who are heteronomous—that is, who are guided by voices other than their own—may also produce a "saving remnant" who are increasingly autonomous, and who find strength in the face of their minority position in the modern world of power.

. . . .

Individual helplessness and collective power play leapfrog with each other throughout history. Today, the helplessness foreseen by a few thinkers, and sensed even in the earlier age of frontiers by many who failed, has become the common attribute of the mass of men. . . .

Today, in the advanced industrial countries, there is only one frontier left—that of consumption—and this calls for very different types of talent and character.

The inner-directed type fitted the conditions of essentially open capitalism, which rewarded ability to envisage new possibilities for production, and zeal to realize those possibilities. To a degree, this is still the case. Nevertheless, we think that, on the whole, contemporary society, especially in America, no longer requires and rewards the old enterprise and the old zeal. This does not mean that the economic system itself is slowing down; total production may continue to rise; but it can be achieved by institutionalizing technological and organizational advance, in research departments, management counsel, and corporate planning staffs. The invention and adoption of new improvements can be routinized, built into the system, so to speak, rather than into the men who run the system. Therefore, the energies of management turn to industrial and public relations, to oiling the frictions not of machines but of men.

Likewise, with the growth of monopolistic competition, the way to get ahead is not so much to make a better mousetrap but rather to "package" an old mousetrap in a new way, and then to sell it by "selling" oneself first. People feel they must be able to adapt themselves to other people, both to manipulate them and to be manipulated by them. This requires the ability to manipulate oneself, to become "a good package," to use a phrase current among personnel men. These pressures are, of course, not confined to business, but operate also in the professions, in government, and in academic life.

As work becomes less meaningful and intense, however, leisure grows and men who are discarded as workers are cultivated in the one role that still matters, that of consumer. This is not an easy role, and people become almost as preoccupied with getting the "best buys" as they once were with finding their proper "calling" in the production economy. They turn, then, to the mass media of communication for advice in how to consume; at the same time, these media help make them anxious lest they fail in the role of consumer. We speak here not merely of "keeping up with the Joneses"—this is part of an older pattern—but rather of the much more unsettling fear of missing those leisure-time experiences, including sex, love, art, friendship, food, travel, which people have been induced to feel they should have.

These changes in the nature of work and leisure have made themselves felt most strongly among the middle classes of the American big cities in the last twenty-five years or so. It is here that we find developing the character type that I call other-directed, a type whose source of direction is externalized. The clear goals and generalized judgments of the inner-directed types are not implanted in the other-directed person in childhood. Rather, he is taught, vaguely, to do the "best possible" in any given situation. As soon as he can play with other children, he is made sensitive to the judgments of this play group, looking to it for approval and direction as to what is best. Parents and other adults come to value the child in terms of his ability to live up to the group's expectations and to wrest popularity from it.

The adult never loses this dependence, but continues to live psychologically oriented to his contemporaries—to what might be called his "peer group." Of course, it matters very much who these others are: whether they are his immediate circle of the moment, or a higher circle he aspires to, or the anonymous circles of whose doings he learns from the mass media of communication.[1] But the great psychological difference from inner-direction is that this modern type needs open approval and guidance from contemporaries. This new need for approval goes well beyond the human and opportunistic reasons that lead people in any age to care very much what others think of them. People in general want and need to be liked, but it is only the other-directed character type that makes others its chief source of direction and its chief area of sensitivity and concern.

These differences in the source looked to for direction lead to different modes of conformity in the two types. The inner-directed person will ordinarily have had an early choice made for him among the several available destinies of the middle-class child. What holds him on course is that he has internalized from his elders certain general aims and drives—the drive to work hard, or to save money, or to strive for rectitude or for fame. His conformity results from the fact that similar drives have been instilled into others of his social class. As against this, the other-directed person grows up in a much more amorphous social system, where alternative destinations cannot be clearly chosen at an early age. The "best possible" in a particular situation must always be learned from the others in that situation. His conformity to the others is thus not one of generalized drives, but of details—the minutiae of taste or speech or emotion which are momentarily "best." Hence he internalizes neither detailed habits nor generalized drives, but instead an awareness of and preoccupation with the *process* of securing direction from others.

We can find exemplars of the other-directed character in leisured urban circles of the past, where the preoccupations were those of consumption, not

[1]These are some of the "anonymous authorities" of whom Erich Fromm has written in *Escape from Freedom* and *Man for Himself.*

production, and where status depended on the opinion of influential others. What is new is the spread of such an outlook over large sectors of a middle class that was once inner-directed. Elements of this outlook, moreover, have now filtered down in America to many members of the lower-middle class.

It is my tentative conclusion that the feeling of helplessness of modern man results from both the vastly enhanced power of the social group and the incorporation of its authority into his very character. And the point at issue is not that the other-directed character is more opportunistic than the inner-directed—if anything, the contrary is true. Rather, the point is that the individual is psychologically dependent on others for clues to the meaning of life. He thus fails to resist authority or fears to exercise freedom of choice even where he might safely do so.

An illustration may clarify my meaning. I have sometimes asked university students why they come to class so regularly day after day, why they do not—as they are technically free to do—take two or three weeks off to do anything they like on their own. The students have answered that they must come to class or otherwise they will flunk, though the fact is that many students get ahead when they finally do break through the routines. It has become apparent that the students cling to such "rational" explanations because, in their feeling of helplessness, freedom is too much of a threat. They fail to see those loopholes of which they could take advantage for their own personal development; they feel safer if they are obeying an authoritative ritual in sympathetic company. Their attendance at class has much the same meaning as the Pueblo Indian's rain-making dance, only the student has less confidence that his "prayer" will be heard. For he has left "home" for good, and all of modern thought teaches him too much for comfort and too little for help.

. . . .

Let us examine several . . . factors that have robbed the middle-class individual of his defenses against the pressure of the group. We shall deal . . . with changes in the nature of private property, of work, and of leisure, all of which at one time functioned as defenses.

In the feudal era, the individual was attached to property, largely land, by feudal and family ties. The breakdown of feudalism meant helplessness for many peasants, who were thrown off the land; but for the middle class the result was a gradual gain in consciousness of strength. A new type of relationship between persons and property developed: the person was no longer attached to property, but attached property to himself by his own energetic actions. Property, including land, became freely alienable; at the same time, it was felt to be an individual, not a family, possession. And property was satisfying, substantial—an extended part of the self. Inside the shell of his possessions, the inner-directed person could resist psychological invasion.

Today, however, property is not much of a defense. Taxes and other state activities, inflation and the panicky desire for liquid assets, have made it factually friable. Moreover, the fears of property-holders outrun the actual dangers. Thus, even powerful groups in America feel more frightened of Communism than its actual power warrants. Property no longer represents the old security for those who hold it, and the fear that it may vanish any day makes it as much a source of anxiety as of strength. The rich no longer dare flaunt wealth, but tread softly, guided by considerations of "public relations." Wealthy students often act as if ashamed of their wealth; I have sometimes been tempted to point out that the rich are a minority and have rights, too.

The change in the meaning of work is even plainer. For the inner-directed person, work seemed self-justifying: the only problem was to find the work to which one felt called. As we have seen, the age of expanding frontiers provided the individual with an inexhaustible list of tasks. Work, like property, moreover, was considered a mode of relating oneself to physical objects, and only indirectly to people. Indeed, the work-hungry inner-directed types of this period sometimes found that they were cut off from family and friends, and often from humanity in general, by their assiduity and diligence. And work, like property, was a defense against psychological invasion, a "do not disturb" sign guarding the industrious man of the middle class.

Today the meaning of work is a very different one, psychologically, though in many professions and industries the older modes still persist. To an increasing degree, the self is no longer defined by its productive accomplishments but by its role in a "Friendship" system. As the "isolate" or "rate-buster" is punished and excluded from the work force in the shop, so the lone wolf is weeded out of management; up-to-date personnel men use deep-probing psychological tests to eliminate applicants, whatever their other gifts, who lack the other-directed personality needed for the job.

To be sure, out of anxiety, a lingering asceticism, and a need for an impressive agenda, the professional and business men and women of the big cities continue to work hard, or more accurately, to spend long hours in the company of their fellow "antagonistic cooperators": "work" is seen as a network of personal relationships that must be constantly watched and oiled. Increasingly, both work and leisure call on the same sort of skills—sociability, sensitivity to others' feelings and wants, and the exercise of taste-preferences freed from direct considerations of economic advantage. Work in this case has a certain unreality for people, since it has almost floated free from any connection with technical crafts. The latter have been built into machines, or can be easily taught; but people must still go to the office and find ways of keeping, or at least looking, busy. Thus in many circles work and leisure are no longer clearly distinguished—as we can see by observing a luncheon or a game of golf among competitors.

The feeling of powerlessness of the other-directed character is, then, the result in part of the lack of genuine commitment to work. His life is not engaged in a direct struggle for mastery over himself and nature; he has no long-term goals since the goals must constantly be changed. At the same time, he is in competition with others for the very values they tell him are worth pursuing; in a circular process, one of these values is the approval of the competing group itself. Hence, he is apt to repress overt competitiveness both out of anxiety to be liked and out of fear of retaliation. In this situation, he is likely to lose interest in the work itself. With loss of interest, he may even find himself little more than a dilettante, not quite sure that he is really able to accomplish anything.

From this it follows that this type of other-directed person is not able to judge the work of others—for one thing, he is no longer sufficiently interested in work as such. He must constantly depend on specialists and experts whom he cannot evaluate with any assurance. That dependence is an inevitable and indeed a valuable fruit of the division of labor in modern society; but the inability even to dare to pass personal judgment is a defect rooted in the character of the other-directed person.

When we turn from the sphere of work to the sphere of leisure, we see again that roles in which the individual could once find refuge from and defense against the group have become stylized roles, played according to the mandates and under the very eyes of the group. The individual in the age of inner-direction had little leisure; often he was so work-driven he could not even use the leisure given him. On occasion, however, he could escape from the pressures and strains of the workaday world into a private hobby or into the resources of culture, either "high-brow" or popular. In either case, the stream of entertainment and communication was intermittent; to come into contact with it required effort. Leisure, therefore, by its very scarcity, provided a change of pace and role. Moreover, beyond these actual leisure roles stood a group of fantasy roles—roles of social ascent, of rebellion against work and inhibition, dreams of world-shaking achievement; the individual was protected against invasion at least of his right to these dreams.

Today, leisure is seldom enjoyed in solitude, nor is it often used for unequivocal escape. Hobbies of the older craft type seem to have declined, and a baseball game is perhaps the only performance where the mass audience can still judge competence. The torrent of words and images from radio, the movies, and the comics begins to pour on the child even before he can toddle; he starts very early to learn his lifelong role of consumer. The quantity of messages impinging on the child becomes increasingly "realistic"; instead of "Just-So Stories" and fairy tales, children are given "here and now" stories of real life, and escape into imaginative fantasy is therefore held at a minimum.

Likewise, movies, fiction, and radio for adults increasingly deal with "here and now" problems: how to handle one's relations with children, with the opposite sex, with office colleagues away from the office. Story writers for the better woman's magazines are instructed to deal with the intimate problems faced by the readers, and soap opera is one long game of Going to Jerusalem: when one problem sits down, another is left standing. Indeed, we might claim, there is no "escape" from leisure. Wherever we turn, in work or in popular culture, we are faced by our peers and the problems they present, including the pressure they put on us to "have fun." A kind of ascetic selflessness rules much of the greatly expanded leisure of the other-directed person: selflessness disguised by the craving for comfort, fun, and effortlessness, but ascetic nonetheless in its tense use of leisure for preparing oneself to meet the expectations of others.

Thus, the newly reached horizons of leisure and consumption made possible by our economic abundance have not been as exhilarating for the individual as the realized horizons of work and production proved to be for many in the age of expanding frontiers. On the frontiers of consumption, limitless in quality and almost equally so in quantity, men stand anxiously, haunted by the fear of missing some consumption-experience which they are supposed to have enjoyed. Young men and women today, for instance, in some urban middle-class circles, often feel they must walk a tightrope in their sex lives: they must have "experiences," yet they must not become involved emotionally on any deep level of human tenderness and intimacy. And the while they are worried lest they are incapable of loving anyone. The word of the "wise" to the young —"don't get involved"—has changed its meaning in a generation. Once it meant: don't get, or get someone, pregnant; don't run afoul of the law; don't get in the newspapers. Today the injunction is more deeply psychological; it seeks to control, not the overt experience, but its emotional interpretation in terms of smooth, unruffled manipulation of the self. This transformation is characteristic of the change from inner-direction, with its clear and generalized mandates, to other-direction, with its emphasis on the process of receiving from others very detailed stage directions in the work-play of life.

To sum up, the inner-directed person had a sense of power as he faced the group because of his relationship to property, to work, and to leisure; and because both he and the group accepted certain specific rights that encouraged any individual to be himself. Such persons often became men of substance and men of the world—they made the world *theirs*. If we look at the portraits of the more eminent men in a centuries-long gallery stretching from Holbein to John Singer Sargent, we can see that they were indeed solid citizens. Today the solid citizen has given way to the "solid sender," the "good Joe," not solid enough to risk offending anyone and afraid of disobeying the subtle and impermeable injunctions of the contemporary "peer group" to whom he looks for approval. He is a sender and receiver of messages in a network of personal ties which, unlike the personal ties of a folk society, neither warm nor protect him.

On the surface, it might appear that the individual today feels powerless because he finds no protection from the hazards of war and depression. He feels weak because he has no control over these vast matters that are decisive for him; to avert war or internal catastrophe he cannot even turn to a ritual. Yet, granting these objective reasons for anxiety and weakness, we must nevertheless ask, why is war so likely, when few people want it? I suggest that one reason—certainly not the only one!—is simply that great numbers of people do not in fact enjoy life enough. They are not passionately attached to their lives, but rather cling to them. The very need for direction that is implied in our phrases of inner-direction and other-direction signifies that one has turned over one's life to others in exchange for an agenda, a program for getting through the day.

To be sure, the abdication is not complete. But the fact remains that the person who is not autonomous loses much of the joy that comes through strength—through the effort to live one's life, not necessarily heroically, but, come what may, in full commitment to it. Modern life, for many people, is full of tense and anxious relationships to people, to production and consumption; therefore, these people are prepared to resign themselves to war which does, after all, promise certain compensations in group companionship and shared meanings.

Thus, we have come full circle from Hobbes' view of man. For him, people risked war because they were selfish individualists, and he reasoned with them that they were better off in the *Leviathan*. Modern man does not want to risk war, but allows it to come with astonishingly little protest because, fundamentally, he is not an individualist. It is tractable men who operate the intractable institutions that now precipitate war, and when it comes, it is they who conduct it.

I do not mean to imply that our society "produces" other-directed people because such people are in demand in an increasingly monopolistic, managerial economy. The relations between character and society are not that simple. Moreover, neither character nor society changes all at once. But it would take us too far afield to trace the many formative agencies in the still far-from-complete shift from inner-direction to other-direction in the middle classes.

Furthermore, I must guard against the implication that I think inner-direction is a way of life preferable to other-direction. Each type has its virtues and its vices: the inner-directed person tends to be rigid and intolerant of others; the other-directed person, in turn, is likely to be flexible and sensitive to others. Neither type is altogether comfortable in the world. But in different ways each finds the discomforts it needs psychologically in order, paradoxically, to feel comfortable. The inner-directed person finds the struggle to master himself and the environment quite appropriate; he feels comfortable climbing uphill. The other-directed person finds equally appropriate the malaise that he shares with many others. Engrossed in the activities that the culture provides, he can remain relatively unconscious of his anxiety and tonelessness. Moreover, the character type must always be judged in context. Many persons who are inner-directed and who, in an earlier age, would have gone through life in relative peace, today find themselves indignant at a big-city world in which they have not felt at home. Other-directed persons also may not feel at home, but home never had the same meaning for them. It would appear to the envious inner-directed observer, that the other-directed manage their lives better in a mass society. Conversely, the other-directed may envy the seeming firmness of the inner-directed, and look longingly back on the security of nineteenth-century society, while failing to see that firmness was often merely stubbornness and security merely ignorance.

What I have said about the loss of the individual's defenses is recognized by many thinkers who, however, feel that through voluntary associations people can attain securities analogous to those which family and clan provided in the era of primary ties, and for which work and property made additional provision in the days of expanding frontiers. They see labor unions as giving a feeling of solidarity to the working class, and even to increasing numbers of white-collar employees; they see racial minorities protected by their defense organizations, and farmers by their cooperatives; they see "group belongingness," in some sort of informal association, available to all but the most depressed. The advocacy of this as the chief remedy for the loneliness of the individual is an admission of his weakness. But it is more than that. It bolsters another set of power-combinations, only slightly democratized by individual participation. And it adds to the pressure on the individual to *join,* to submerge himself in the group—any group—and to lower still further not only his feeling that he can, but that he has a right, to stand on his own.

Conceivably, these associations in the future will succeed in strengthening the individual's feeling of his own powers by providing him with defenses, political, economic, and psychological, and by encouraging him to gain, outside his work, a variety of skills, encounters, and experiences. In the meantime, however, with the balance between helplessness and power tipped in favor of the former, the "voluntary" associations are not voluntary enough to do this job.

I turn now to examine another voluntary association, that between the sexes, whose nature, in our age as in any age, provides a profound clue to the state of subjective feelings of power and helplessness. In this context, the rapid change I discern in the denigration by American women of their own sex seems ominous. Eighty years ago, John Stuart Mill (turning to a theme touched on by Condorcet's *On the Admission of Women to the Rights of Citizenship*) wrote *The Subjection of Women* in order to show how attitudes toward this "minority" poisoned all social life; how both men and women suffered from the power-relations that prevailed between them; and how women's potentialities, even more than those of men were crushed by social pressure. He observed that "the greater part of what women write about women is mere sycophancy to men." But he was gentle with women for he added, "no enslaved class ever asked for complete liberty at once. . . ."

In the intervening period, women did not attain "complete liberty," but they came a long way toward equality with men. In the years after 1890 and until recently, American young women of the middle class insisted on sharing with men the tasks and excitements of civilization. Today there is some evidence that many women of this class have retreated; they have again become enemies of emancipation of their sex; as the weaker power, they judge each other through the eyes of men.

Women today feel under almost as great a pressure to get married as did their pre-emancipation ancestors. In a certain way, they are under greater pressure, since all sorts of psychological aspersions are cast at them if they stay single too long.[2]

Perhaps all this means simply that women have won the battle of emancipation and can relax. I am inclined, however, to think that there is an increasing submissiveness of women to what men want of them, and to the world as men have largely made it. I interpret this, in part, as testimony to the fact that men today are far too anxious, too lacking in psychological defenses against each other, to tolerate critically-minded women. The women they want must be intelligent enough to flatter their vanity but not to challenge their prerogatives as men. Men once complained to their mistresses that their wives did not understand them; now they would complain if they did. For in their own competitive orientation to the world, men would interpret understanding from the side of women as still another, and underhanded, form of competition. This is partly because, since Mill's day, the economic and social power of women has grown; they can no longer be so obviously kept in their places. Hence their gifts, their critical powers, can no longer be patronized by powerful men, but must be subtly destroyed by anxious ones and their willing allies among the women themselves. Men and women, in their weakness, act like those minorities who throughout history have kept each other in subjection in the face of an oppressive power.[3]

In sum, men and women eye each other not as allies, but, at best, as antagonistic cooperators. In their roles as parents, they are uncertain of their children and whether they will be liked by them; in turn, this anxiety is absorbed by the children. In earlier epochs of history, events outside the home were interpreted, often somewhat narrowly, through the perspective of family needs and family morality. Today, the situation is reversed, and the home must be adjusted to the values of the outside. As with the state, "domestic policy" and "foreign policy" are interdependent, and the conflicts and strains of each sphere add to weakness in the other.

[2]Indeed, men, too, feel under pressure to get married early—among other reasons, lest they be thought homosexual.

[3]Something of the same transformation has occurred in the relation between parents and children. Even as men are worried lest they might not pass the test with women, so parents are afraid that their children will not approve of them—a problem that would hardly have troubled the person of inner-directed character. While parents appear to be terribly concerned to give their children approval—as they are told by all the textbooks to do—this disguises the parents' own dependence on being approved of by the children, who stand, as Margaret Mead has noted, for the New, for Youth, for the American Way—or, as I might say, for better other-direction. Moreover, parents assume the role of advisors and managers of their children's competitive struggles. This new family constellation is in fact one of the changes that may partly account for the formation of the other-directed character.

We come, then, to a conclusion that would seem paradoxical: certain groups in society have grown weaker, but others have not gained in strength at their expense; rather, weakness has engendered weakness. And the state, the beneficiary of individual weakness, is ruled by men who are themselves no less weak than the rest. Even the dictators and their henchmen only seem strong under the imagery of modern propaganda. While the savage believes he will gain in potency by drinking the blood or shrinking the head of his enemy, in the modern world no individual gains in strength of character from the weakness of his fellows.

Nevertheless, even under modern conditions, and out of the very matrix of other-directed modes of conformity, some people strive toward an autonomous character. An autonomous person has no compulsive need to follow the other-direction of his culture and milieu—and no compulsive need to flout it, either. We know almost nothing about the factors that make for such positive results; it is easier to understand the sick than to understand why some stay well. It hardly helps to repeat our point that man's helplessness is the condition for his every advance, because this generalization tells us too little about individual cases. However, it seems that the helplessness of modern man in a world of power has been one element in the genesis of some of the extraordinary human achievements of our age. Some of these achievements are the physical and literary productions of men's hands and minds, but other achievements lie in the internal "productions" of men—their characters; it is of these that I speak here.

There were autonomous people of course, in the era of inner-direction, but they were made of sterner stuff; the barriers they encountered were the classic ones: family, religion, poverty. On the other hand, the person who seeks autonomy today in the upper socio-economic levels of the Western democracies is not faced with the barriers that normally restricted him in the past. The coercions against his independence are frequently invisible. An autonomous person of the middle class must work constantly to detach himself from shadowy entanglements with his culture—so difficult to break with because its demands appear so "reasonable," so trivial.

For our study of autonomy, we have drawn freely on Erich Fromm's concept of the "productive orientation" in *Man for Himself*. Fromm shows the orientation of a type of character that can relate itself to people through love, and to objects and the world generally through the creative gift. The struggle for a productive orientation becomes exigent at the very moment in history when solution of the problem of production itself, in the technical sense, is in sight.

All human beings, even the most productive, the most autonomous, are fated, in a sense, to die the death of Ivan Ilyitch, in Tolstoy's "The Death of Ivan Ilyitch," who becomes aware only on his deathbed of his underlived life and his unused potentialities for autonomy. All of us realize only a fraction of our potentialities. Always a matter of degree, always blended with residues of inner-direction or other-direction, autonomy is a process, not an achievement. Indeed, we may distinguish the autonomous by the fact that his character is never a finished product, but always a lifelong growth.

I speak of autonomy as an aspect of character structure, and not in terms of independence of overt behavior. The autonomous person may or may not conform in his behavior to the power-requirements of society; he can choose whether to conform or not. (The Bohemians and rebels are not usually autonomous; on the contrary, they are zealously tuned in to the signals of a defiant group that finds the meaning of life in a compulsive non-conformity to the majority group.) Yet the separation of "freedom in behavior" from "autonomy in character" cannot be complete. Autonomy requires self-awareness about the fact of choice, about possible ways of living. The autonomous person of today exists precisely because we have reached an awareness of the problem of choice that was not required among the Pueblos, or, for the most part, in the Middle Ages, or even in the period after the Reformation, when the concepts of God's will and of duty confined choice for many within fairly narrow bounds.

The very fluidity of modern democratic social systems, that, for the mass of people, results in anxiety and "escape from freedom," forces those who would become autonomous to find their own way. They must "choose themselves," in Sartre's phrase, out of their very alienation from traditional ties and inner-directed defenses which inhibited true choice in the past. However, I think Sartre mistaken in his Kantian notion that men can choose themselves under totalitarian conditions. Likewise, if the choices that matter are made for us by the social system, even if it is in appearance a democratic system, then our sense of freedom also will atrophy: most people need the opportunity for some freedom of behavior if they are to develop and confirm their autonomy of character. Nevertheless, the rare autonomous character we have been describing, the man of high, almost precarious, quality, must arise from that aloneness, that helplessness of modern man, that would overwhelm a lesser person. It is in this quality, and in the mode of life he is groping to achieve, that he has made a contribution to the problem of living in a power-world. Often, in vanity, we judge our own era as the most advanced or the most retrograde, yet the type of perspective on the world and the self that thousands of people have today was probably matched in the past by only a few.

The people I speak of live under urbanized conditions in every land, but they are world citizens in thought and feeling. Sensitive to wide perspectives of time and space, they have largely transcended prejudices of race or time or class. Their guides are diverse, and they feel empathy and solidarity with their colleagues across all national boundaries. There have been cosmopolitans before, but their horizons were limited by want of knowledge, and their view of man was necessarily abstract. There have been internationalists before, but they have been restricted by class and region. The contemporary autonomous person has all the sensitivity to others of the other-directed type: he needs some interpersonal warmth, and close friends mean much to him; but he does not have an irrational craving for indiscriminate approval.

In one relationship, that between the sexes, the men and women who are striving for autonomy are seeking an equality that takes account of differences, an equality of which Mill would have approved. Here women are not the subtle slaves of men, nor do they flatter them as the feminists did by seeking to adopt men's particular privileges and problems. Though we have as yet to attain a new model of marriage, grounded neither in contract nor in sex alone but in mutual growth towards autonomy, we see new sets of roles developed by people who have achieved relationships to which both partners contribute from their productive gifts. It is unlikely, however, that beyond such families, and small groups of friends or colleagues, there exist any sizeable institutions or organizations predominantly composed of autonomous folk. It is hard to imagine an autonomous society coming into being now, even on a small scale, or perhaps especially on a small scale.[4]

The fact is, moreover, that the autonomous group is hardly aware of its own existence. Those who are to some degree autonomous may not always reveal themselves as such, preferring to conform overtly out of conscious choice. As a result, the potentially autonomous often do not discover each other, though they would in that very process strengthen and defend their own autonomy.

Indeed, the potentially autonomous person tends to bewail as a tragedy his isolation from the masses and from power. He passes by the opportunity of his lot—an opportunity to develop his individuality and its fruits in art and character. Hence he wishes he could undergo a metamorphosis and rid himself of the problem of choice, indeed of his very autonomous strivings; he wishes he were like the others—whose adjustment he often overemphasizes—thus revealing his own other-directed components. By these very tendencies to betray himself and his partially achieved autonomy, he becomes weaker and less autonomous.

The autonomous few can do little enough to reduce the strength of atom bombs and of the hands that now hold them, but some can at least defend their own and others' individuality, and pioneer in various ways of living autonomously. They will enjoy this pioneering to a degree, though it will be held against them by the envious and frightened ones who have abandoned the effort toward autonomy.

If these conjectures are accurate, then it follows that, by a process of unconscious polarization which is going on in society, a few people are becoming

[4]Mary McCarthy describes with humor and insight the fate of an imaginary enclave of intellectuals seeking autonomy in her story "The Oasis." (*Horizon,* 19, [1949], 75; see, also, for some of the institutional problems, my article, "Some Observations on Community Plans and Utopia," *Yale Law Journal,* 57, [1947], 173.)

more self-consciously autonomous than before, while many others are losing their social and characterological defenses against the group. The latter, though politically strong, are psychically weak, and the autonomous minority, by its very existence, threatens the whole shaky mode of adaptation of the majority.

Nevertheless, joy in life has its own dynamic. We have said that people today are not sufficiently attached to life. We have traced this to their other-directed character structure, and this in turn to large-scale social changes. Yet character structure is not completely fixed for the individual, so long as life lasts, or for the group. Men have some control over the fate by which their characters are made. By showing how life can be lived with vitality and happiness even in time of trouble, the autonomous people can become a social force, indeed a "saving remnant." By converting present helplessness into a condition of advance, they lay the groundwork for a new society, though, like Condorcet, they may not live to see it.

SIMONE DE BEAUVOIR

Adieu to America

I went to declare the money I had earned during my four months' tour and to pay the required taxes. In France this business would have taken many days, much coming and going. Here the matter was dealt with on a personal level, as always, and settled in half an hour. The official who sat opposite me to check my figures asked for my word of honor, nothing more. He helped me to deduct my expenses: transportation, use of typists, entertaining, hotels, laundry . . . ? It was he who made the suggestions with an enthusiasm that was altogether touching. He then deplored the fact that the total was not bigger and that there was still tax to pay. Two blows with a rubber stamp, and lo! I was free to leave America.

I could leave, I would leave. Evening fell upon New York: my very last evening. And now I was miserable to be leaving this country, which had so often irritated me. I had often been asked during the last few days, "Do you like America?" and I had grown accustomed to answer back: "Half and half" or else: "Fifty-fifty." This simple evaluation, of course, meant little; indeed, it reflected only the fact that I had reservations. Hardly a day had passed without my being stunned by America in some way or without my feeling some disappointment. I did not know if I could live here happily, but I felt sure I would miss it.

Columbus Circle, Broadway, Times Square. Four months had passed. There were the same crowds, taxis, cars and shimmering lights. The drugstores and the skyscrapers had lost none of their peculiar magic. I knew why I liked them. There is a mirage that penetrates right through this civilization of comfort and abundance: that of an existence which would not waste away in attempting to maintain itself and which could give itself wholly to surpassing even what it has achieved. Moving about from one place to another, clothing oneself, eating—all this is done without the slightest effort or waste of time: anything can happen.

The great attraction held for me by America, where the memory of the pioneers is strong, consists of the fact that it appears as a realm still in transcendence; its history is contracted, of course, in time yet stretches splendidly

Reprinted by permission of the publisher from *America day by day* by Simone de Beauvoir. Translated by Patrick Dudley.

across vast spaces; it is the history of the creation of the whole world. For this reason skyscrapers always move me; they proclaim man as a being who does not stagnate but who is, instead, filled with enthusiasm and a desire for expansion and fresh conquest. In the shameless profusion of goods that one finds in the drugstore there is poetry as fantastic as in a baroque church: man has taken raw matter in the toils of his desire and has asserted over it the power of imagination. New York and Chicago reflect the existence of this demi-urge, with its imperial dreams, and that is why they are the most human, the most uplifting cities that I know. There is no room here for any of the dreary caution of the *petit bourgeois* in his carpet slippers, whose only object is to stay at home and wait for death, as the sonnet puts it. To devote one's life to that is living death. Americans in this sense are truly alive; inertia does not appeal to them. A man is judged by his acts: to exist you must do something. The great iron bridges, buildings, Grand Central Station, Park Avenue, the air terminals, the highways and mines, all proclaim this faith.

It would be difficult to tear myself away from these splendid visions of hope; and yet I knew their wiles. In America, life also ebbs away in the effort to survive. "I've been out since 10 A.M.," a taxi driver told me at 10 P.M. "You bet I want to get home!" I remembered how people rushed to the ferryboat that took them across to New Jersey. All my friends had told me how hard the working days were in this city of distances, especially for women who have a job and a home to run at the same time; they are exhausted when night comes: I have often seen them too tired to accept an invitation to go out. I have come to understand that if people drink so much it is not because they have a mania; they need a spur at the end of the afternoon.

That is not all. One has a premonition that anything might happen. But what is actually happening? What do they do with their time and the money they earn? No doubt, I did not get to know the ruling class, those who invent, study and speculate; but they make up only a small minority. Americans, for the most part, are like those with whom I rubbed shoulders; they let their lives go around in circles. They have neither a liking for, nor the sense of, collective life; nor have they any concern for their own personal destinies. This is the source of the sadness that I often felt when with them. This world full of generous promise crushes them; and its splendor soon appears barren, for no one controls it.

Each civilization offers in the "banality of everyday life" a means of escape, but what strikes one here is the point to which this escapism is organized. Neither his education nor the atmosphere in which he develops are designed to shed light on the inner self of the individual. He is aware of himself not only as a human body but also as an organism protected and prolonged by a whole arsenal of devices; he goes from floor to floor by elevator, travels by subway, speaks into the telephone, typewrites, and sweeps the floor with a vacuum cleaner. Between his stomach and the food he eats there is a world of canned food factories, refrigerators, electric cookers. Between his sexual desires and their fulfilment there is the paraphernalia of moral precepts and hygienic practices. He is hemmed in by society from childhood. He searches outside himself, among other people, for his models for conduct; hence what is called American conformism: actually, individuals are just as different and just as isolated one from another in the new world as in the old, but here they find easier means of escape from their individuality and the feeling of "forlornness"; or perhaps they do not find them, but then, at least, they seek them more stubbornly. Like everyone else, they know dissatisfaction, boredom and doubt, but they try to rationalize their own confusion by posing "problems": instead of drawing strength from solitude, or overcoming it by plumbing its depths, they cling to the given facts; they see the source of values and of truth in things, not in themselves.

Their own existences are things of chance to which they attach no importance. That is why they are interested in net results, and not in the spirit that engenders them. In much the same way, they think they can isolate the part from the whole, as witnessed in the call for specialization that one finds in the sciences, technology and education. To use Hegelian terms, one can say that the very negation of the subject leads to the triumph of understanding over the spirit, that is to say, the triumph of abstraction. And that is why in this country, which seems to turn so decidedly toward the concrete world, the word abstraction so often came to my lips; the object set up as an idol loses its human values and becomes abstract, for concrete reality is that which actually envelops object and subject simultaneously. That is the paradox of all positivisms, all pseudo-realisms which forsake humanity to proclaim the importance of things; they are lacking in the object itself, and never attain to anything more than concepts.

I often felt, while listening to American jazz or talking to Americans, that the very time in which they lived was abstract. They respect the past, but only insofar as it is a thing embalmed; the idea of a living past, integrated with the present, is foreign to them. They only want to recognize a present cut by the course of time, and the future they visualize is that which can be deduced mechanically, not one whose ripening, or whose sudden explosion implies unforeseeable risks. They believe in the future of a bridge, for instance, or of an economic plan, but not in the future of an art or of a revolution. Their time is "the physicist's time," an exterior concept which doubles that of space.

Because they refuse to accept the durability of things, they also refuse to recognize their quality; it is not only for economic reasons that "craftsmanship" does not exist in the States. Even in leisured occupations qualitative success is never sought for: food is cooked, just as fruit is ripened, as fast as possible; in every walk of life one must always hurry, lest the result be already outdated by the time it is achieved. Cut off from the past and from the future, the present has no weight. Nothing is more foreign to Americans than the idea of regarding the passing moment as a repetition of time, a mirror of eternity, and of anchoring oneself to it to grasp truths or values that are in themselves timeless. To them, the content of the passing moment is as fragile as the moment itself. Because they will not admit that truths and values *become,* they do not know how to conserve them in the movement that leaves them behind: they just deny them.

History is a great cemetery: men, deeds, ideas die almost as soon as they are born. Each individual existence has a flavor of death; from one minute to the next, the present is merely an honorary past. It must constantly be filled anew to dissemble the curse it carries within itself; that is why Americans like speed, alcohol, horror films and sensational news. The demand for new things and ever newer things, is feverish, since they find no rest in anything. But here, as elsewhere, life repeats itself, day after day, so they amuse themselves with gadgets, and, for lack of projects, they cultivate hobbies; in spite of these crazes they pretend to accept daily life. Sport, the movies and comic strips are distractions. But they end by going back to that from which they tried to escape: the arid basis of American life is boredom. Boredom and solitude.

It has been said a thousand times, and it is true: these people about me are lonely. Because they flee in terror their essential solitude, because they run away from themselves, they have no real self-possession. How are they to extend themselves? How can they receive from others? They are open and friendly, capable of tenderness, passion, sentiment and cordiality; but they rarely know how to create deep love or enduring friendship. They are far from stony-hearted, yet their relations with one another are superficial and cold. They are far from lacking in vitality, enthusiasm or generosity, but they do not know how to devote themselves to the business of their lives, and, to be a Julien Sorel or a Rastignac, one has to take one's self in hand, not run away from one's self. There are very few ambitious people here. They worship heroes, but in a capricious way; few want anything more than to be raised a few rungs on the social ladder; a young man anxious to distinguish himself will wish, at best, to distinguish himself as a citizen rather than as a man; he will not dream of emerging far beyond the set conditions of life, the dream of which is the tree where Julien perches and the hill from which Rastignac proudly looks down over Paris; ambitions of greatness are the source of many disappointments and failures in ways that Americans do not know; they have virtues born of indifference to themselves. They are not embittered, persecuted or ill-willed, envious or egotistical. But they have no inner fire. As a result of losing themselves in pursuit of the object, they find themselves without any object. They experience in another form the "forlornness" that their civilization tries to screen from them. It is the very contrast between their secret fragility and their proud edifices that makes them so pathetic.

I think it is because of the abstract climate in which they live that the importance of money becomes so disproportionate. These people are neither mean nor avaricious—on the contrary, these are faults of which they justly accuse the French; they do not want money in order to amass it; they spend it readily, for other people as well as for themselves; giving comes naturally to them. Nor are they pleasure seekers, for they do not desire money in order to satisfy extravagant appetites. If money is the sole object for so many it is because all other values have been reduced to this one denominator and because it has become the measure of every human accomplishment, whereas it is really only the abstract sign of true riches. It is because they cannot establish or affirm real values that Americans are satisfied with this empty symbol. Actually, they are not satisfied; with the exception of the leading capitalists, they are as self-conscious of their wealth as they are of their leisure.

This is one of the reasons, undoubtedly, why American women have become idols: the dollar is a doleful divinity. Man does not mind justifying his work and his hard-won earnings by dedicating them to a flesh and blood being. Yet their cult of women, like the cult of money, is only a substitute. The existence of the American male would have no meaning if he were unable to give a concrete meaning to that abstract entity, his liberty. This is a vicious circle, for in order to fill this empty liberty, he would have to change the social and political conditions in which he lives and which govern his inertia. Thousands of Americans are daily working to break this circle, and, naturally, there are thousands to whom these remarks do not apply. But insofar as one can generalize, it is the vast majority who are victims of the machine. The escape from solitude and boredom holds them fast to solitude and boredom; through wanting to lose themselves in the world they have lost command of themselves.

One thing which struck me most forcibly was how much they hate to question themselves and existing conditions. They want to believe that Good and Evil can be defined in precise categories, that Good already is, or will be easily, achieved. I felt this from the beginning of my stay, but I have recently had striking confirmation of this. For one thing, I almost incited a riot among the students at Columbia, Yale and Harvard, when I talked to them about the question of conscience in Rousset's book, *The Days Of Our Death:* what criteria should someone employ in making his choice if he found himself in a position to save the lives of two or three people in a camp of deportees? They stubbornly replied, "No one has the right to dispose of human life," or, "What would give him the right to choose?" When I objected that not choosing meant saving no one, and that, in any case, the positive act of saving two lives was worth more than a murderous abstention, they remained silent. I think that they, for their part, would have preferred to let them all die, rather than assume too heavy a responsibility. Or rather, they could not even imagine a situation in which they could have been forced to contribute to an evil. People here refuse to do this, even though it is the only way to fight evil. Even people of goodwill refuse to visualize the actual conflict between justice and liberty, and thus the necessity for inventing a compromise between these concepts; they prefer to deny justice and the lack of freedom. The fact that the complexity of the situation creates problems beyond any virtuous solution is something they will not admit. Evil is a residue which they will eliminate by progressive stages, by applying more rigorously certain institutions which are wholesome in themselves—that is what many idealists think; and if this optimism appears too easy, they will try to create a type of anti-God: the U.S.S.R. That is Evil, and it only needs to be annihilated for the reign of Good to be re-established. This explains why so many of the students, who have such respect for their fellow beings, complacently talked of dropping the atom bomb on the Soviet Union.

If then, in conclusion, I advance so many criticisms, why, in spite of everything, was I so sad to leave? First of all, because one could formulate other criticisms—just as depressing—of our European civilization, and of our French civilization to which I would return. We are unhappy in other ways and false in other ways. That is all. The judgments I made during this journey were not accompanied by any feeling of superiority. I see their faults; I do not forget our own. Embedded in all that I like and all that I loathe in America is something which fascinates me: the tremendous opportunities America offers, the gigantic risks it actually runs today—things in which we all share. All human problems are posed here on a tremendous scale; they will be solved here, but whether we will find these problems, in restrospect, greatly clarified or buried in the darkness of indifference depends largely on the solutions themselves. Yes, I think that is what moved me so strongly as I took my departure. America is one of the world's pivotal points: the future of man is at stake here. To like America, or not to like her: these words are meaningless. Here is a battlefield, and one can only be stirred by the struggle she carries on within herself, a struggle whose stakes are beyond measure.

Selected Writings on American National Character

This bibliography, while not exhaustive, comprises the principal writings of social scientists and historians on culture and personality, national character and American character since 1940. It is limited to published studies in English. Patently impressionistic writings are omitted, without derogation of their value, which is often considerable. It is, however, admittedly difficult and perhaps unwise to distinguish sharply between impressionism and the literature of "social science." If none but rigorously empirical studies were listed here, the bibliography would be very slim indeed. Many are the fringe cases, and this listing aims to survey the literature rather than to prescribe any rigid or invidious principle of exclusion.

An asterisk (*) indicates that the item so marked contains a useful bibliography. Paperbacks and paperback reprints are identified by a dagger (†).

The compiler gratefully acknowledges the assistance of Ernest B. Grundy, Harold W. Holtzclaw, Gerald J. Waldera and Robert D. Willard, present or former graduate students at the University of Denver and co-workers in the vineyard of American Studies.

The bibliography was checked in its formative stages by Reuel Denney, Francis L. K. Hsu, Max Lerner, S. M. Lipset, Walter P. Metzger, David Riesman, Anthony F. C. Wallace and Robin M. Williams, Jr. For their criticisms and suggestions, and for David M. Potter's guidance in the cunning corridors of national character analysis, the compiler is most grateful. Final responsibility is, of course, his own.

The bibliography originally appeared in *American Quarterly*, XV (Summer, 1963, Supplement), 271–88. Brought up to date, it is reprinted here by permission of the *American Quarterly*.

I. CULTURE AND PERSONALITY

Since the 1930s, students of culture and personality, representing the disciplines of psychology, anthropology and sociology, have made vigorous efforts to build bridges which will join conceptually what is felt to be united in experience. The resulting literature is voluminous; it is analytical, descriptive, critical and sometimes polemical. Following is a selective listing of some of the more significant and illuminating writings in the field. In general it may be said that the theoretical underpinnings of the study of national character, as an enterprise of social science, rest on the foundations of culture-and-personality analysis.

* BATESON, GREGORY. "Cultural Determinants of Personality," in J. McV. Hunt, ed., *Personality and the Behavior Disorders* (New York: Ronald Press, 1944), II, ch. 23.

The investigator's task is to identify the cultural regularities in the complex of variant individual behaviors.

EATON, JOSEPH W. "In Defense of Culture-Personality Studies," *Amer. Soc. Rev.*, XVI (Feb. 1951), 98–100.

Because culture and personality studies may often have "broad social significance" they ought not to be abandoned on account of methodological imperfections.

* HALLOWELL, A. IRVING. "Culture, Personality, and Society," in A. L. Kroeber, ed., *Anthropology Today: An Encyclopedic Inventory, infra,* 597–620.

Surveys the field and summarizes the literature to 1952.

HARING, DOUGLAS G., ed. *Personal Character and Cultural Milieu,* 3rd ed. (Syracuse: Syracuse University Press, 1956).

First published in 1949, a valuable compilation. See especially the essays by Bateson, Gorer, Kardiner, C. Kluckhohn and Sapir.

* HONIGMANN, JOHN J. *Culture and Personality* (New York: Harper & Brothers, 1954).

How culture "patterns" the "modal personality."

HSU, FRANCIS L. K. "An Anthropologist's View of the Future of Personality Studies," *Psychiatric Research Reports,* II (Dec. 1955), 155–68.

Analysis of certain unsolved problems of method, with a forceful plea for more cross-cultural studies in depth. "The student of culture and personality must know the way of life of his own society and the values that are prevalent in it; these he will employ in his studies of other ways of life as a comparative basis from which to draw generalizations."

———, ed. *Aspects of Culture and Personality: A Symposium* (New York: Abelard-Schuman, 1954).

Papers and discussions from the Wenner-Gren "Conference on Anthropology and Psychiatry," May 1951. See especially the remarks of Klineberg. Henry and Linton.

———, ed. *Psychological Anthropology: Approaches to Culture and Personality* (Homewood, Ill.: Dorsey Press, 1961).

At once a textbook and a report on "the up-to-date gains in the field of culture-and-personality."

INKELES, ALEX. "Personality and Social Structure," in Robert K. Merton, Leonard Bloom & Leonard S. Cottrell, Jr., eds., *Sociology Today: Problems and Prospects* (New York: Basic Books, 1959), ch. 11.

A theoretically oriented appraisal of the field, arguing that "adequate sociological analysis of many problems is either impossible or severely limited unless we make explicit use of psychological theory and data in conjunction with sociological theory and data," with suggestions as to how this can best be done.

———. "Some Sociological Observations on Culture and Personality Studies," in Clyde Kluckhohn, Henry A. Murray & David M. Schneider, eds. *Personality in Nature, Society, and Culture, infra,* ch. 37.

Charts the "four major foci" in the literature of culture and personality, and urges caution in the attempt to "explain the functioning of specific institutions, and particularly of complex social systems, on the basis of observed group regularities in personality."

KARDINER, ABRAM. "The Concept of Basic Personality Structure as an Operational Tool in the Social Sciences," in Ralph Linton, ed., *The Science of Man in the World Crisis* (New York: Columbia University Press, 1945), 107–22.
Anticipates the fuller statement made in Kardiner's *The Psychological Frontiers of Society, infra.*

———. *The Individual and His Society: The Psychodynamics of Primitive Social Organization* (New York: Columbia University Press, 1939).
"Basic personality structure"—the "constellation of personality characteristics which would appear to be congenial with the total range of institutions comprised within a given culture"—in primitive societies.

——— *et al. The Psychological Frontiers of Society* (New York: Columbia University Press, 1945).
The concept of "basic personality structure," a refinement of the concept of national character, provides "a precise means of delineating the interrelationship of various social practices through their compatibility or incompatibility with certain constant identifiable human needs and desires" in both Alor and "Plainville, U.S.A."

† KLUCKHOHN, CLYDE. "Personality in Culture," in Kluckhohn, *Mirror for Man: The Relation of Anthropology to Modern Life* (New York & Toronto: Whittlesey House, 1949), ch. 8.
Sprightly discussion of the pervasive influence of culture on personality.

——— & O. H. MOWRER. "'Culture and Personality': A Conceptual Scheme," *Amer. Anthropologist,* XLVI (Jan.–Mar. 1944), 1–29. Reprinted in Arthur Weider & David Wechsler, eds., *Contributions Toward Medical Psychology* (New York: Ronald Press, 1953).
An attempt "to delineate a conceptual scheme which would accommodate all of the *determinants* of social stimulus value and which would also systematically order the *components* of 'personality' as thus defined." Updated and substantially revised in the following work.

———, HENRY A. MURRAY & DAVID M. SCHNEIDER, eds. *Personality in Nature, Society, and Culture,* 2nd ed., rev. & enl. (New York: Alfred A. Knopf, 1953).
The basic anthology, first published in 1948. Argues that culture-and-personality investigation is "in the last analysis directly or indirectly oriented to one central type of question: What makes an Englishman an Englishman? an American and American? a Russian a Russian?"

* KROEBER, A. L., ed. *Anthropology Today: An Encyclopedic Inventory* (Chicago: University of Chicago Press, 1953).
See especially the selections by C. Kluckhohn, Hallowell, Mead and Redfield.

* LA BARRE, WESTON. "The Influence of Freud on Anthropology," *Amer. Imago,* XV (Fall 1958), 275–328.
Critique of culture-personality studies from a Freudian standpoint. With distinguished exceptions American anthropologists have been unwarrantedly mistrustful of psychoanalytic method and theory.

LINDESMITH, ALFRED R. & ANSELM L. STRAUSS. "A Critique of Culture-Personality Writings," *Amer. Soc. Rev.,* XV (Oct. 1950), 587–600.
Commentary on unresolved conflicts, especially between the psychoanalytically oriented and those who describe cultural configurations with slight attention to genetic explanations or psychoanalytic concepts.

LINTON, RALPH. *The Cultural Background of Personality* (New York: Appleton-Century-Crofts, 1945).
With Kardiner's books, required reading on the theory of "basic personality."

———. "The Personality of Peoples," *Sc. Amer.*, CLXXXI (Aug. 1949), 11–15.
Raises the "ultimate question": "Is it possible, by extinguishing some of the patterns of a culture and substituting others, to bring about a lasting change in the society's personality norms?"

RIESMAN, DAVID. "Some Problems of a Course in 'Culture and Personality,'" *Jour. of General Education,* V (Jan. 1951), 122–36.
Rewards and risks of interdisciplinary integration in "Social Sciences 2" at the University of Chicago, as seen by both instructors and students.

† SAPIR, EDWARD. *Culture, Language and Personality,* ed. David G. Mandelbaum (Berkeley & Los Angeles: University of California Press, 1961).
A useful introduction to Sapir's pioneer explorations of the field. "To him, more than to any other single person, must be traced the growth of psychiatric thinking in anthropology"—Clyde Kluckhohn.

SARGENT, S. STANSFIELD & MARIAN W. SMITH, eds. *Culture and Personality* (New York: Wenner-Gren Foundation for Anthropological Research, 1949).
An important early collection. See especially the essays by Fromm, Murphy and Bidney.

SPIRO, MELFORD E. "Culture and Personality: The Natural History of a False Dichotomy," *Psychiatry,* XIV (Feb. 1951), 19–46.
The dualistic propensities of western thought have hampered the development of an integrated concept of culture-and-personality.

*——— & Raymond D. Fogelson. "Culture and Personality," in Bernard J. Siegel, ed., *Biennial Review of Anthropology,* 1961 (Stanford: Stanford University Press, 1962).
Descriptive review of trends and literature in the field, 1958–60.

SYKES, RICHARD E. "American Studies and the Concept of Culture: A Theory and Method," *Amer. Quar.,* XV (Summer, 1963, Supplement), 253–70.
Outlines an interdisciplinary approach to American studies based on the concepts of "culture, culture pattern, and culture construct pattern."

*† WALLACE, ANTHONY F. C. "The Cultural Distribution of Personality Characteristics," in Wallace, *Culture and Personality* (New York: Random House, 1961), ch. 3.
Critical review of concepts and approaches to the study of culture and personality, grouping them under the general rubrics of "replication of uniformities" and "organization of diversities." Argues that insufficient attention has been paid to the second, though both are essential to "a progressive science of human behavior."

WHITING, JOHN W. M. & IRVIN L. CHILD. *Child Training and Personality: A Cross-Cultural Study* (New Haven: Yale University Press, 1953).
Analysis of how "culture is integrated through the medium of personality processes" with specific examination of child training practices and customary responses to illness. Especially valuable for attack on methodological problems. Employs data from a careful sample of seventy-five societies, using the methods of the Yale Cross-Cultural Survey.

II. NATIONAL CHARACTER: CONCEPTS AND METHODS

This section focuses on matters of theory and practice, omitting the extensive literature on national stereotypes and the large number of studies of specific nations and peoples. For the most complete listing of such writings see Duijker and Frijda, *National Character and National Stereotypes, infra.*

BEAGLEHOLE, ERNEST. "Character Structure: Its Rôle in the Analysis of Interpersonal Relations," *Psychiatry,* VII (May 1944), 145–62.
"If the study of national character is worthwhile, it can apparently only be fruitfully

studied by the use of better conceptual tools than have been employed in the past" by, e.g., Fromm and Madariaga.

BERGER, MORROE. "'Understanding National Character'—and War," *Commentary,* XI (Apr. 1951), 375–86.

A highly critical review of national character studies.

BIERSTEDT, ROBERT. "The Limitations of Anthropological Methods in Sociology," *Amer. Jour. of Sociology,* LIV (July 1948), 22–30.

Anthropological methods are not adequate to the study of character in large, diverse, literate societies. Specific criticisms of Mead, Gorer *et al.* See Clyde Kluckhohn's "Comment," p. 30.

* DUIJKER, H. C. J. & N. H. FRIJDA. *National Character and National Stereotypes: A Trend Report Prepared for the International Union of Scientific Psychology* (Amsterdam: North-Holland Publishing Co., 1960).

The most extensive treatment of recent and current trends in the study of national character: concepts, methods and prospects. Massive bibliography.

ENDLEMAN, ROBERT. "The New Anthropology and Its Ambitions: The Science of Man in Messianic Dress," *Commentary,* VIII (Sept. 1949), 284–91.

National character studies suffer from an excessive impressionism, an oversimplified and anti-historical holism, an unexamined "American quality" and a naive ambition to reform the world.

FARBER, MAURICE L. "The Problem of National Character: A Methodological Analysis," *Jour. of Psychology,* XXX (1950), 307–16. Reprinted in Howard Brand, comp., *The Study of Personality: A Book of Readings* (New York: John Wiley & Sons, 1954), 387–97.

The cultural heterogeneity and behavioral instability of modern nations, together with certain unsolved methodological "riddles," cast doubt on the validity of national character studies to date.

———. "The Study of National Character: 1955," *Jour. of Soc. Issues,* XI, No. 2 (1955), 52–56.

Brief cautionary comments on the methodology of national character study.

FYFE, HAMILTON. *The Illusion of National Character* (London, 1940).

The idea of national character is an evil fiction employed by a "ruling class" to "deceive people; to make them subservient . . . ; to keep up the delusion that war is natural and necessary." In this work of demolition Fyfe identifies national character with "dangerous and deceptive" national stereotypes.

GINSBERG, MORRIS. "National Character," in Ginsberg, *Reason and Unreason in Society* (Cambridge: Harvard University Press, 1948), ch. 7.

Rescues a "scientific" concept of national character from the strictures of Fyfe, *supra.* National character is best studied by empirical investigation of "the qualities manifested in the collective life of nations, their traditions and public policy."

GORER, GEOFFREY. "The Concept of National Character," *Science News,* No. 18 (1950), 105–22. Reprinted in Kluckhohn, Murray & Schneider, eds., *Personality in Nature, Society, and Culture, supra,* ch. 14.

"The structure, the combination of motives, the national character of a society, is always unique." Psychological tests which emphasize individual differences rather than shared traits should be used with caution.

†———. "National Character: Theory and Practice," in Margaret Mead & Rhoda Métraux, eds., *The Study of Culture at a Distance* (Chicago: University of Chicago Press, 1953), 57–82.

Critique of investigative methods.

HERTZ, FREDERICK. *Nationality in History and Politics: A Study of the Psychology and Sociology of National Sentiment and Character* (New York: Oxford University Press, 1944).

Large-scale generalizations on national character, here defined as "the totality of traditions, interests and ideals which are so widespread and influential in a nation that they mould its image, both in the mind of the nation concerned and in that of others."

* INKELES, ALEX. "National Character and Modern Political Systems," in Francis L. K. Hsu, ed., *Psychological Anthropology, supra,* ch. 6.
Surveys the rather meager number of systematic empirical studies of "the relations between personality patterns . . . and the rise, functioning, and change of political systems," and proposes more effective ways and means of investigation and of delineating, specifically, the "democratic character."

———. "Social Change and Social Character: The Role of Parental Mediation," *Jour. of Soc. Issues,* XI, No. 2 (1955), 12–23.
Discusses the role of the family as transmitter of character traits, drawing on the work of the Harvard Russian Research Center.

——— & DANIEL J. LEVINSON. "National Character: The Study of Modal Personality and Sociocultural Systems," in Gardner Lindzey, ed., *Handbook of Social Psychology* (Cambridge, Mass.: Addison-Wesley Publishing Co., 1954), II, 977–1020.
An exploratory technical essay in methodology to determine "whether national character constitutes a genuine field of study." The most cogent statement of the "modal personality" position: "National character refers to relatively enduring personality characteristics and patterns that are modal among adult members of a society."

KLINEBERG, OTTO. "Recent Studies of National Character," in Sargent & Smith, eds., *Culture and Personality, supra,* 127–42.
Studies by Benedict, La Barre, Gorer *et al.,* leave unresolved the questions of "how basic, how similar, how universal" are character traits said to be national; they take insufficient account of individual variations within and from the cultural norm. Discussion of Klineberg's paper by Benedict, Bateson, Powdermaker.

———. "A Science of National Character," *Jour. of Soc. Psychology,* XIX (Feb. 1944), 147–62.
Appraisal of the literature, stressing method and difficulties to be overcome. "I am reasonably pessimistic about the present status of our 'science,' but I have considerable hope for its future."

LINDESMITH, ALFRED R. & ANSELM L. STRAUSS. "A Critique of Culture-Personality Writings," *supra.*
Studies of national character to date have been boldly impressionistic. "One must view the results and methods with a generous measure of skepticism."

LINTON, RALPH. "The Concept of National Character," in Alfred H. Stanton & Stewart E. Perry, eds., *Personality and Political Crisis* (Glencoe, Ill.: Free Press, 1951), 133–50.
The concept of national character rests on the concept of "basic personality" although the connection has not yet been empirically validated: "the development of objective techniques which might be used for the study of national character has barely begun."

———. "What We Know and What We Don't," in Francis L. K. Hsu, ed., *Aspects of Culture and Personality, A Symposium, supra,* ch. 9.
The methods employed to discover "basic personality" in small, relatively homogeneous groups do not apply to the study of *national* character. Nation-states are so heterogeneous that "one questions whether the common denominator of such diverse groupings would differ very much from the common denominator of human personalities generally." See discussion, pp. 216–18, 271–72, 277–78.

MANDELBAUM, DAVID G. "On the Study of National Character," *Amer. Anthropologist,* LV (Apr.–June 1953), 174–87.
A penetrating critique of Mead's paper published in Kroeber, ed., *Anthropology Today, infra.*

———. "The Study of Complex Civilizations," in William L. Thomas, Jr., ed.,

Current Anthropology: A Supplement of Anthropology Today (Chicago: University of Chicago Press, 1956).
Critical review of the literature, 1946–54. Concludes that the anthropological investigation of complex civilizations has made a vigorous and promising beginning. See also in this volume the remarks of Kroeber, pp. 302–15; Bennett and Wolff, pp. 335–36.

MEAD, MARGARET. "Anthropologist and Historian: Their Common Problems," *Amer. Quar.*, III (Spring 1951), 3–13.
National character studies provide a bridge between the interests and procedures of the cultural anthropologist and the historian.

———. "Effects of Anthropological Field Work Models on Interdisciplinary Communication in the Study of National Character," *Jour. of Soc. Issues,* XI, No. 2 (1955), 3–11.
Comments on the need and nature of interdisciplinary collaboration, with special reference to primitive cultures.

———. "National Character," in A. L. Kroeber, ed., *Anthropology Today, supra,* 642–67.
Discussion of the assumptions on which the study of national character rests, with reply to the critics of the anthropological approach. Present need is for "field studies within accessible complex modern states, involving systematic cooperation with historians and members of other disciplines who work on aspects of modern culture." See commentary on this paper in Sol Tax *et al.*, eds., *An Appraisal of Anthropology Today* (Chicago: University of Chicago Press, 1953), 134–41, especially the remarks of Mandelbaum.

———. "National Character and the Science of Anthropology," in Seymour Martin Lipset & Leo Lowenthal, eds., *Culture and Social Character: The Work of David Riesman Reviewed* (Glencoe, Ill.: Free Press, 1961), ch. 3.
Critique of *The Lonely Crowd* from an anthropological standpoint, emphasizing problems of method and value judgments.

*———. "The Study of National Character," in Daniel Lerner & Harold D. Lasswell, eds., *The Policy Sciences: Recent Developments in Scope and Method* (Stanford: Stanford University Press, 1951), ch. 4.
The combination of "the basic Freudian theories and the methods of cultural anthropology" affords diverse approaches, here reviewed, to the exploration of national character.

METZGER, WALTER P. "Generalizations about National Character: An Analytical Essay," in Louis Gottschalk, ed., *Generalization in the Writing of History: A Report of the Committee on Historical Analysis of the Social Science Research Council* (Chicago: University of Chicago Press, 1963), ch. 6.
An illuminating essay on the problems of character definition and classification. Especially valuable for its discussion of the "dramaturgical model" for the concept and analysis of national character.

PAUKER, GUY J. "'The Study of National Character Away From That Nation's Territory,'" *Studies in International Affairs,* I (June 1951), 81–103.
A student of international affairs, deterred by evidence of subjective "bias" and conceptual confusion in national character research to date, suggests that dominant national values be studied instead. *Studies in International Affairs* was issued by the Committee on International and Regional Studies, Harvard University.

† POTTER, DAVID M. *People of Plenty: Economic Abundance and the American Character* (Chicago: University of Chicago Press, 1954).
An historian explores the possibilities for co-operation with the behavioral sciences in the study of national character.

RIESMAN, DAVID. "Psychological Types and National Character," *Amer. Quar.*, V (Winter 1953), 325–43.
Although "in the present state of our knowledge, the question must remain open

whether each nation has a 'national character,'" the concepts of inner- and other-directedness, despite difficulties, may provide clues to a description of character as "broader than Freud's concept of genitality and narrower than fate."

SHAFER, BOYD. "Men Are More Alike," in Shafer, *Nationalism: Myth and Reality* (New York: Harcourt, Brace & World, 1955), ch. 12.
An historian's homily on the brotherhood of man which strongly questions the validity of the idea of national character but, in fact, succeeds only in demolishing national stereotypes.

SULZBACH, WALTER. *National Consciousness* (Washington, D.C.: American Council on Public Affairs, 1943), ch. 4.
An argument for international amity which criticizes the concept of national character as a simplification which exaggerates the differences between nations and conceals intranational diversities.

WALLACE, ANTHONY F. C. "Individual Differences and Cultural Uniformities," *Amer. Soc. Rev.,* XVII (Dec. 1952), 747–50.
The "infinite variability" of individual experience casts doubt on the concept of homogeneous national character.

III. AMERICAN CHARACTER

AARON, DANIEL, ed. *America in Crisis: Fourteen Crucial Episodes in American History* (New York: Alfred A. Knopf, 1952).
Essays by fourteen scholars, ranging in subject from the Great Awakening to the Nazi-Soviet pact, relating to the ways in which American character and values "have manifested themselves in moments of crisis."

BARRETT, DONALD N., ed. *Values in America* (Notre Dame, Ind.: University of Notre Dame Press, 1961).
Essays on American education, economic life, religion and mass communications.

† BELL, DANIEL. "The Refractions of the American Past: On the Question of National Character," in Bell, *The End of Ideology* (Glencoe, Ill.: Free Press, 1960), ch. 5.
Review of Lerner's *America as a Civilization;* challenges the tendency in American Studies to seek holistic definitions of American character.

*† BOORSTIN, DANIEL J. *The Americans: The Colonial Experience* (New York: Random House, 1958).
A scholarly and provocative re-examination of early American thought and society, developing the main theses of *The Genius of American Politics.*

†———. *The Genius of American Politics* (Chicago: University of Chicago Press, 1953).
These historical observations on the "non-exportable uniqueness" of American political ideas and institutions constitute an important contribution to the analysis of characterological consensus.

*†———. *The Image, or What Happened to the American Dream* (New York: Atheneum, 1962).
A critical look at "the bewitching unrealities" (synthetic images, pseudo-events, contrived illusions) which "clutter our experience and obscure our vision."

BREDEMEIER, HARRY C. & JACKSON TOBY. *Social Problems in America: Costs and Casualties in an Acquisitive Society* (New York & London: John Wiley & Sons, 1960).
Readings and comment on the American pursuit of success conceptualized as materialism, self-reliance, competition and "negotiated exchange."

BROGAN, D. W. *America in the Modern World* (New Brunswick, N. J.: Rutgers University Press, 1960).
Observations by a friendly critic.

†———. *The American Character* (New York: Alfred A. Knopf, 1944).
A once-over-lightly commentary on American values, institutions and behavioral styles "to encourage sympathetic understanding of the Americanism of America."

CAUDILL, WILLIAM & GEORGE DE VOS. "Achievement, Culture and Personality: The Case of the Japanese Americans," *Amer. Anthropologist,* LVIII (1956), 1102–26.
This examination of the hypothesis that there is "a significant compatibility" between Japanese and middle-class American value systems stresses the "need for systematic investigation and interrelation of (a) overt and underlying culture patterns, (b) individual psychodynamic factors, (c) the structure and emotional atmosphere of crucial small group interactive settings. . . ."

COCHRAN, THOMAS C. "The Social Scientists," in Robert E. Spiller & Eric Larrabee, eds., *American Perspectives: The National Self-Image in the Twentieth Century* (Cambridge: Harvard University Press, 1961).
Traces the development of American character analysis since the 1930s.

COLEMAN, LEE. "What Is American? A Study of Alleged American Traits," *Social Forces,* XIX (May 1941), 492–99.
Analysis of most common trait ascriptions emphasizes "the amazing diversity of American life and character" and shows "the hazard involved in asserting that any trait is unqualifiedly American, to the exclusion of all opposing or modifying traits."

† COMMAGER, HENRY STEELE. *The American Mind: An Interpretation of American Thought and Character Since the 1880's* (New Haven: Yale University Press, 1950).
The first and final chapters summarize the salient characteristics of, respectively, the nineteenth- and twentieth-century American.

———. "Portrait of the American," in John W. Chase, ed., *Years of the Modern: An American Appraisal* (New York & Toronto: Longmans, Green & Co., 1949), ch. 1.
An historian's delineation of "some of the more pronounced traits of the American in the mid-twentieth century."

"Conference on the American Character," *Center for the Study of Democratic Institutions Bull.,* Oct. 1961.
Report on the initial conference for the Center's program for the study of American character. See also the Center's current pamphlet series, "Interviews on the American Character."

† CUNLIFFE, MARCUS. "The American Character," in Cunliffe, *The Nation Takes Shape: 1789–1837* (Chicago: University of Chicago Press, 1959), ch. 8.
This portrait of the Jacksonian American by a British historian identifies character traits and polarities of orientation which, in general, "support the assertion that American 'national character' has not altered fundamentally since its early definitions."

CURTI, MERLE. "American Philanthropy and the National Character," *Amer. Quar.,* X (Winter 1958), 420–37.
"American experience in philanthropy has both expressed American character and . . . helped to shape it."

DEGLER, CARL N. "The Sociologist as Historian: Riesman's *The Lonely Crowd,*" *Amer. Quar.,* XV (Winter, 1963), 483–97.
Argues that "other-direction" has been "the dominant element in our national character through most of our history," and that evidence of characterological continuity may render Riesman's major categories "totally inadequate for purposes of historical analysis . . ."

DENNEY, REUEL. "How Americans See Themselves," *Annals of the Amer. Acad. of*

Pol. and Soc. Sc., CCXCV (Sept. 1954), 12–20. Reprinted in Joseph J. Kwiat & Mary C. Turpie, eds., *Studies in American Culture: Dominant Ideas and Images* (Minneapolis: University of Minnesota Press, 1960), 16–26.

Perceptive critical commentary on the approaches to the study of American character and the problems of definition.

DU BOIS, CORA. "The Dominant Value Profile of American Culture," *Amer. Anthropologist,* LVII (Dec. 1955), 1232–39.

Schematic discussion of three major "focal" values—material well-being, conformity, and "effort-optimism"—and of the "strain for consistency in the American value system."

ERIKSON, ERIK H. "Reflections on the American Identity," in Erikson, *Childhood and Society* (New York: W. W. Norton & Co., 1950), ch. 8.

"The functioning American, as the heir of a history of extreme contrast and abrupt changes, bases his final ego identity on some tentative combination of dynamic polarities such as migratory and sedentary, individualistic and standardized, competitive and co-operative, pious and freethinking, responsible and cynical. . . ."

FARBER, MAURICE L. "English and Americans: A Study in National Character," *Jour. of Psychology,* XXXII (1951), 241–49; "English and Americans: Values in the Socialization Process," *ibid.,* XXXVI (Oct. 1953), 243-50.

Comparison by questionnaire of English and American insurance clerks leads to conclusions which are "consonant with existing material" on national character "obtained by other methods."

FROMM, ERICH. *Man for Himself: An Inquiry into the Psychology of Ethics* (New York & Toronto: Rinehart & Co., 1947).

Though this study is not explicitly concerned with national character, Fromm's discussion of the "marketing orientation" as an ideal-type of modern social character anticipates Riesman's "other-directed" personality and Whyte's "organization man."

GILLIN, JOHN. "National and Regional Cultural Values in the United States," *Social Forces,* XXXIV (Dec. 1955), 107–13.

Regional "twists" and special emphases with respect to the national value system, here partially defined.

GOETZMANN, WILLIAM H. "The Mountain Man as Jacksonian Man," *Amer. Quar.,* XV (Fall, 1963), 402–15.

Analysis of the Rocky Mountain fur trade and the careers of 446 trappers reveals the lineaments of the "expectant capitalist" (Hofstadter) and the "venturous conservative" (Meyers).

GORER, GEOFFREY. *The American People: A Study in National Character* (New York: W. W. Norton & Co., 1948).

Perceptions and interpretations, sometimes barbed and often erratic, of a Freudian anthropologist. Revised ed., 1964, with minor modifications and an additional chapter of random observations.

HARTZ, LOUIS, FREDERICK J. HOFFMAN, DAVID M. POTTER, PAUL A. SAMUELSON, and LESLIE A. WHITE. "Individualism in Twentieth-Century America," *Texas Quar.,* VI (Summer, 1963), 97–176.

Papers delivered at a symposium at the University of Texas, December, 1962.

HSU, FRANCIS L. K. *Americans and Chinese: Two Ways of Life* (New York: Henry Schuman, 1953).

An extensive and provocative analysis of cultural contrasts from a "broadly Freudian" angle of vision. No other comparative study, of which we have all too few, approaches it in depth and scope.

———. "American Core Value and National Character," in Hsu, ed., *Psychological Anthropology, supra,* ch. 7.

Difficulties in defining American character, while substantial, are not insurmountable. "What we need to see is that the contradictory American 'values' noted by the sociologists, psychologists, and historians are but manifestations of one core value," namely, "self-reliance."

JOSEPH, FRANZ M., ed. *As Others See Us: The United States through Foreign Eyes* (Princeton: Princeton University Press, 1959).
Twenty versions of the national image by contemporary observers, especially prepared for this volume.

† KLAPP, ORRIN E. *Heroes, Villains, and Fools: The Changing American Character* (Englewood Cliffs, N. J.: Prentice-Hall, 1962).
An impressionistic sociological survey and analysis of "the major social types of American society which serve prominently as its models." Argues that a "deterioration" of the national character is reflected in the presently "dominant role models of Good Joe-smart operator-playboy."

KLINEBERG, OTTO. "American Culture and American Personality: Some Methodological Considerations," *Jour. of Soc. Issues,* VII, No. 4 (1951), 40–44.
Brief resumé of the formidable methodological problems in the study of American character. All conclusions so far are hypothetical.

KLUCKHOHN, CLYDE. "Mid-Century Manners and Morals," in Bruce Bliven, ed., *Twentieth Century Unlimited: From the Vantage Point of the First Fifty Years* (Philadelphia & New York: J. B. Lippincott Co., 1950), ch. 16.
Reflections on the crisis of values in contemporary America.

†———. "An Anthropologist Looks at the United States," in Kluckhohn, *Mirror for Man, supra,* ch. 9.
A "sketch of characteristic thought patterns, values, and assumptions," with a plea for "scientific humanism."

*———. "Have There Been Discernible Shifts in American Values During the Past Generation?" in Elting E. Morison, ed., *The American Style, infra,* 145–217.
A wide-ranging compendium of findings since 1941. Notes, *inter alia,* decline of Protestant Ethic, increase in "other-directedness," explicit valuation of "psychological health," emphasis on "individuality" as against "rugged individualism."

——— & FLORENCE R. KLUCKHOHN. "American Culture: Generalized Orientations and Class Patterns," in Lyman Bryson, Louis Finkelstein & R. M. MacIver, eds., *Conflicts of Power in Modern Culture: Seventh Symposium, Conference on Science, Philosophy and Religion* (New York: Harper & Brothers, 1947), ch. 9.
"It is the purpose of this paper: (1) to analyze out some of the important generalized orientations of our culture; (2) to outline the specific goals of the middle and lower class groups; (3) to point to some of the discrepancies between specific goals and general orientations that seem to be especially productive of tension and aggression."

KLUCKHOHN, FLORENCE R. "American Women and American Values," in Lyman Bryson, ed., *Facing the Future's Risks: Studies Toward Predicting the Unforeseen* (New York: Harper & Brothers, 1953), ch. 8.
The role of the American woman is "badly defined, shot through with contradictions, and in need of major alterations." Such alterations will have to accord with certain dominant values: "Individualism, a future-time orientation, a belief in mastering nature, the conception of human nature as evil but perfectible, and a high evaluation of men in action."

LAMBERT, RICHARD D., ed. "America Through Foreign Eyes," *Annals of the Amer. Acad. of Pol. and Soc. Sc.,* CCXCV (Sept. 1954).
Articles devoted to the contemporary image of America, especially as seen by foreign students in the United States, with occasional reference to traits of national character.

LAPIERE, RICHARD. *The Freudian Ethic* (New York: Duell, Sloan & Pearce, 1959).
An apprehensive account of the replacement of the Protestant Ethic by the "Freudian ethic," here related to "the current American ethos with its liberality toward self-indulgence and irresponsibility." Dustjacket subtitle: "An Analysis of the Subversion of American Character."

LASKI, HAROLD J. *The American Democracy: A Commentary and an Interpretation* (New York: Viking Press, 1948).

Comprehensive interpretation of American culture and character stressing the advance of technology and the system of business power.

LEE, ALFRED MCCLUNG. "Sociological Insights into American Culture and Personality," *Jour. of Soc. Issues,* VII, No. 4 (1951), 7–14.

On criminality and ethnocentrism in American culture.

LEE, EVERETT S. "The Turner Thesis Re-examined," *Amer. Quar.,* XIII (Spring 1961), 77–83.

"The Turner thesis is too simple an explanation for such complexities as American democracy and American character." Argues that it should be regarded as "a special case of an as yet undeveloped migration theory" because "there are few characteristics which are shared by so many Americans as migrant status and spatial movement."

*† LERNER, MAX. *America as a Civilization: Life and Thought in the United States Today* (New York: Simon & Schuster, 1957).

Encyclopedic observations and reflections "on the grand theme of the nature and meaning of the American experience."

LIPSET, SEYMOUR MARTIN. "A Changing American Character?" in Lipset & Lowenthal, eds., *Culture and Social Character: The Work of David Riesman Reviewed, supra,* ch. 7.

"A monistic materialistic interpretation of the correlates of American values and behavior sharply underestimates the extent to which basic national values, once institutionalized, affect the consequences of technological and economic change." Revised for publication in Lipset, *The First New Nation* (New York: Basic Books, Inc., 1963), ch. 3.

†———. "Harriet Martineau's America," in Martineau, *Society in America,* ed. Lipset (Garden City, N. Y.: Anchor Books, Doubleday & Co., Inc., 1962).

The observations of Martineau and other foreign visitors lend support to the argument that "other-direction" in the form of conformity to common opinion was characteristic of Jacksonian America.

MARTIN, WILLIAM E. & CELIA BURNS STENDLER. "The American Character" and "Variations in the American Character," in Martin & Stendler, *Child Development: The Process of Growing Up in Society* (New York: Harcourt, Brace & Co., 1953), 261–82.

Observations, following Fromm, on the themes of conformity, rejection of authority, independence, success, industry, friendliness and puritanism, with a comment on variations of sex, age and social class. See also the discussion of "socialization" in America, chs. 10–16.

MCGRANAHAN, DONALD V. "A Comparison of Social Attitudes among American and German Youth," *Jour. of Abnormal and Soc. Psychology,* XLI (1946), 245–57.

An experimental contribution to the task of locating "international norms in psychology by which to judge the attitudes and traits of character of the people of an entire nation."

——— & IVOR WAYNE. "German and American Traits Reflected in Popular Drama," *Human Relations,* I (Aug. 1948), 429–55. Reprinted as "A Comparative Study of National Characteristics" in James Grier Miller, ed., *Experiments in Social Process: A Symposium on Social Psychology* (New York: McGraw-Hill, 1950), ch. 7.

An experimental comparison of national traits reflected in the 45 "most popular" plays in each country in 1927 and 17 plays in each country in 1909–10.

MEAD, MARGARET. *And Keep Your Powder Dry: An Anthropologist Looks at America* (New York: William Morrow & Co., 1943).

The pioneer anthropological study of American character, evoked by the imperatives of the war and the postwar problem of "reorganizing the world."

† MEYERS, MARVIN. *The Jacksonian Persuasion: Politics and Belief* (Stanford: Stanford University Press, 1957).
The character of Jacksonian America as revealed through political rhetoric, with a valuable discussion of Tocqueville's image of the American democrat as "venturous conservative."

MORISON, ELTING E., ed. *The American Style: Essays in Value and Performance* (New York: Harper & Brothers, 1958).
Papers and discussions of the Dedham Conference, May 1957. Five of the six papers also appear, somewhat shortened, in *Daedalus,* LXXXVII (Spring 1958).

† PARKES, HENRY BAMFORD. *The American Experience: An Interpretation of the History and Civilization of the American People* (New York: Alfred A. Knopf, 1947).
An historian's attempt to "explain the historical forces that molded the American character and to show how that character has been exhibited at different periods both in thought and in behavior."

PARSONS, TALCOTT & WINSTON WHITE. "The Link Between Character and Society," in Lipset & Lowenthal, eds., *Culture and Social Character: The Work of David Riesman Reviewed, supra,* ch. 6.
An alternative interpretation of the institutionalization of the American value system in the social structure.

PERRY, RALPH BARTON. *Characteristically American* (New York: Alfred A. Knopf, 1949).
Philosophical reflections on American values, thought and character with focal emphasis on the spirit of "collective individualism" and on the "characteristic American blend of buoyancy, collective self-confidence, measuring of attainment by competitive success, hope of perpetual and limitless improvement, improvising of method and organization to meet exigencies as they arise."

PIERSON, GEORGE W. "The M-Factor in American History," *Amer. Quar.,* XIV (Summer 1962 Supplement), 275–89.
"What made and kept us different . . . was, first of all, the M-factor: the factor of movement, migration, mobility."

POTTER, DAVID M. "American Women and the American Character," *Stetson University Bull.,* LXII (Jan. 1962), 1–22.
"The historic character of American women is important . . . as a coordinate major part of the . . . study of the American character as a whole."

†———. *People of Plenty, supra.*
The importance of the historical dimension in the study of national character is shown in a perceptive investigation of the influence of economic abundance on American character.

†———. "The Quest for the National Character," in John Higham, ed., *The Reconstruction of American History* (New York: Harper & Brothers, 1962), ch. 11.
The contrasting images of American character—the American as individualist and idealist (Jefferson, Turner) ; the American as conformist and materialist (Tocqueville) —raise questions concerning the validity of generalizations about national character but may perhaps be partially reconciled in terms of a common American equalitarianism.

POWDERMAKER, HORTENSE. *Hollywood, the Dream Factory: An Anthropologist Looks at the Movie-Makers* (Boston: Little, Brown & Co., 1950).
Hollywood is "not a reflection, but a caricature" of certain tendencies in American culture "which, in turn, leave their imprint on the movies."

† RIESMAN, DAVID. *Individualism Reconsidered* (Glencoe, Ill.: The Free Press, 1954).

———. "From Morality to Morale," in Alfred H. Stanton & Stewart E. Perry, eds., *Personality and Political Crisis* (Glencoe, Ill.: Free Press, 1951), 81–120.
Summary statement of the main themes of *The Lonely Crowd.*

———. "The Saving Remnant: An Examination of Character Structure," in John W. Chase, ed., *Years of the Modern, supra,* ch. 5.

Concise statement of the ethical imperative in Riesman's characterology. The "self-consciously autonomous people" are the "saving remnant" in an other-directed society.

———. "Some Observations on the Study of American Character," *Psychiatry,* XV (Aug. 1952), 333–38.

Comments on "some of the perplexities of working with the concept of character in a modern, highly differentiated society," especially with respect to questions of conformity and autonomy.

———. "The Study of National Character: Some Observations on the American Case," *Harvard Library Bull.,* XIII (Winter 1959), 5–24.

Observations on the relations of history and historians to the study of national character, with particular reference to *The Lonely Crowd.*

——— with NATHAN GLAZER. *Faces in the Crowd: Individual Studies in Character and Politics* (New Haven: Yale University Press, 1952).

Twenty-one "portraits," drawn from interviews, which "may indicate the possible usefulness" of Riesman's typology "in the understanding of individual character in its social setting."

†——— with REUEL DENNEY & NATHAN GLAZER. *The Lonely Crowd: A Study of the Changing American Character* (New Haven: Yale University Press, 1950).

SANFORD, CHARLES L. *The Quest for Paradise: Europe and the American Moral Imagination* (Urbana: University of Illinois Press, 1961).

An historical anatomy of the theme of natural innocence in American thought; argues that "The Edenic myth . . . has been the most powerful and comprehensive organizing force in American culture."

SCHLESINGER, ARTHUR M. " 'What Then Is the American, This New Man?' " *Amer. Hist. Rev.,* XLVIII (Jan. 1943), 225–44. Reprinted in Schlesinger, *Paths to the Present* (New York: Macmillan Co., 1949), ch. 1.

An historian's reflective definition of American character and its determinants, with particular emphasis on "the protracted tutelage to the soil."

SIRJAMAKI, JOHN. "A Footnote to the Anthropological Approach to the Study of American Culture," *Social Forces,* XXV (Mar. 1947), 253–63.

Some tentative definitions of psychological and institutional patterns in American culture, with a plea of specific field studies. "The ironical fact is that more is actually understood about the culture of the Trobriand Islanders . . . than of America."

† SMITH, HENRY NASH. *Virgin Land: The American West as Symbol and Myth* (Cambridge: Harvard University Press, 1950).

Examines the 19th-century myths and images of the West and the western hero as keys to American values and character.

SPINDLER, G. DEARBORN. "American Character as Revealed by the Military," *Psychiatry,* XI (Aug. 1948), 275–81. Reprinted in Yehudi A. Cohen, ed., *Social Structure and Personality: A Casebook* (New York: Holt, Rinehart & Winston, 1961), 227–34.

Contrast of American and German values and attitudes in a "control situation" which approximates the heuristic ideal.

STONE, GREGORY P. "American Sports: Play and Dis-Play," *Chicago Rev.,* IX (Fall 1955), 83–100.

An attempt "to demonstrate how certain tensions in American society—between production and consumption, work and play, and between the sexes—and how the tension between play and dis-play [i.e., sport as game and sport as spectacle] contained within sport, itself, cast sport in a uniquely American mold."

STOUFFER, SAMUEL A. *Communism, Conformity, and Civil Liberties: A Cross-section of the Nation Speaks Its Mind* (Garden City, N. Y.: Doubleday & Co., 1955).

An investigation by opinion poll (over 6000 interviews in 1954) of American political tolerance; casts sidelights on the American character in a period of crisis.

STROUT, CUSHING. "A Note on Degler, Riesman and Tocqueville," *Amer. Quar.*, XVI (Spring, 1964), 100–102.
Degler's critique of Riesman (see above) "fails to take seriously enough the difference in method between the historian and the sociologist, and it tends to blur the limiting conditions of the thesis presented in *The Lonely Crowd.*"

† TAYLOR, WILLIAM R. *Cavalier and Yankee: The Old South and American National Character* (New York: George Braziller, 1961).
An examination of the self-images of America in pre-Civil War literature, focusing on the idea of the "divided culture." "The problem for the South was not that it lived by an entirely different set of values and civic ideals but rather that it was forced either to live with the values of the nation at large or, as a desperate solution, to invent others. . . ."

† WARD, JOHN WILLIAM. *Andrew Jackson: Symbol for an Age* (New York: Oxford University Press, 1955).
"Through the age's leading figure were projected the age's leading ideas"—the ideas of nature, providence and will—so that "of Andrew Jackson the people made a mirror for themselves."

† WARNER, W. LLOYD. *American Life: Dream and Reality* (Chicago: University of Chicago Press, 1953).
An effort to place the social behavior and values of Americans "in the scientific framework of social anthropology."

WECTER, DIXON. *The Hero in America: A Chronicle of Hero-Worship* (New York: Charles Scribner's Sons, 1941).
National character is revealed in the choice of national heroes whose selection is "an index to the collective mind and heart."

† WHYTE, WILLIAM H., JR. *The Organization Man* (New York: Simon & Schuster, 1956).
Argues a current shift in America from the Protestant Ethic to the "Social Ethic" among "the dominant members of our society."

WILLIAMS, ROBIN M., JR. "Value Orientations in American Society," in Williams, *American Society: A Sociological Interpretation,* 2nd ed., rev. (New York: Alfred A. Knopf, 1960), ch. 11.
Schematic survey and classification of the patterns of interests, values and general orientations of American culture in relation to its total social structure. Originally published in 1951.

WOLFENSTEIN, MARTHA. "The Emergence of Fun Morality," *Jour. of Soc. Issues,* VII, No. 4 (1951), 15–25. Reprinted with abridgment in Yehudi A. Cohen, ed., *Social Structure and Personality: A Casebook* (New York: Holt, Rinehart & Winston, 1961), 99–106.
A review of changing ideas of child training suggests that "fun, from having been suspect if not taboo" in American culture, "has tended to become obligatory."

——— & NATHAN LEITES. *Movies: A Psychological Study* (Glencoe, Ill.: Free Press, 1950).
Movie themes (e.g., the "good-bad girl") and their emotional bases in relation to the larger patterns of American culture.

IV. THE USES OF NATIONAL CHARACTER STUDIES

* ADORNO, T. W., ELSE FRENKEL-BRUNSWIK, DANIEL J. LEVINSON & R. NEVITT SANFORD. *The Authoritarian Personality* (New York: Harper & Brothers, 1950).

This pioneering study "seeks to develop and promote an understanding of social-psychological factors which have made it possible for the authoritarian type of man to threaten to replace the individualistic and democratic type prevalent in the past century and a half of our civilization, and of the factors by which this threat may be contained." Notable for use of psychoanalytic theory and projective techniques with especial reference to anti-Semitism. While not specifically concerned with "national" character, it draws on predominantly American materials.

† ALMOND, GABRIEL A. "American Character and Foreign Policy," in Almond, *The American People and Foreign Policy* (New York: Harcourt, Brace & Co., 1950), ch. 3.

Ambivalences in the American character make for instability in foreign policy.

BELL, DANIEL. "The National Style and the Radical Right," *Partisan Rev.*, XXIX (Fall 1962), 519–34.

Discussion of the institutional irrelevance of the "classic American style" as "ideologized" by the radical Right.

BRONFENBRENNER, URIE. "Some Possible Effects of National Policy on Character Development in the United States of America and the Soviet Union," in Harold D. Lasswell & Harlan Cleveland, eds., *The Ethic of Power: The Interplay of Religion, Philosophy, and Politics* (New York: Conference on Science, Philosophy and Religion in Their Relation to the Democratic Way of Life, 1962), ch. 17.

Studies of recent changes in family structure and behavior appear to indicate "a change in American character structure in the direction of a milder, less aggressive person more interested in getting along than in getting ahead, perhaps more sensitive to ethical and social issues but less able and less likely to fight for his beliefs." The author finds in this a "threat to our Western civilization" in the cold-war conflict.

CHRISTIE, RICHARD & MARIE JAHODA, eds. *Studies in the Scope and Method of "The Authoritarian Personality": Continuities in Social Research* (Glencoe, Ill.: Free Press, 1954).

Critique and continuation of the earlier work.

INKELES, ALEX. "National Character and Social Structure," *Antioch Rev.*, IX (June 1949), 155–62.

Comment on the conflict between the "political" and "psychological" schools with reference to the question of how national character (specifically German) changes or can be changed.

KLINEBERG, OTTO. *Tensions Affecting International Understanding* (New York: Social Science Research Council, Bull. 62, 1950).

A product of the UNESCO "Tensions Project," this critical survey of techniques and stereotypes argues that the crucial problem is "the development of adequate methods for the scientific study of national differences."

LEITES, NATHAN. "Psycho-Cultural Hypotheses about Political Acts," *World Politics*, I (Oct. 1948), 102–19.

Criticism of impressionism in national character studies, with an appraisal of the utility of psycho-cultural analysis for political science. Concludes with hope that "the advance of psycho-cultural research may furnish more genetic explanations of more complicated dynamically explained syndromes."

MEAD, MARGARET. "The Application of Anthropological Techniques to Cross-National Communication," *New York Acad. of Sciences Trans.*, ser. 2, IX (Feb. 1947), 133–52.

Comparative study of British and American traits of behavior in the interest of "hands across the sea."

PLATT, WASHINGTON. *National Character in Action—Intelligence Factors in Foreign Relations* (New Brunswick, N. J.: Rutgers University Press, 1961).

A "common sense" understanding of national character, instructed by the behavioral sciences but free from their "technical jargon," has utility in intelligence operations.

ROSTOW, W. W. "The National Style," in Elting E. Morison, ed., *The American Style, supra,* 246–313.

"If the study of national character is an effort to establish a collective personality, the examination of national style seeks to define how that collective personality reacts to and acts upon its environment." Examines the "question of how the national style . . . and recent changes in it strengthen or weaken the society's ability to deal with certain major problems it confronts and is likely to confront over the foreseeable future."

SHILS, EDWARD A. *The Torment of Secrecy: The Background and Consequences of American Security Policies* (Glencoe, Ill.: Free Press, 1956).

An illuminating discussion of the nativist component in the American character, with its "traditions" of parochial intolerance, paranoid fear of subversion and conspiracy, and distrust of urbanity and intellectuality, in relation to national security policies.

WILLIAMS, RICHARD HAYS. "American Culture, National Character, and Problems of Mobilization," in Williams, ed., *Human Factors in Military Operations* (Chevy Chase, Md.: Operations Research Office, The Johns Hopkins University, 1954), 91–126.

Though the compression of this study makes for an overgeneralized definition of normative national character traits, the application of findings to the problems of military mobilization is instructive.